Microsoft Azure Development Cookbook

Second Edition

Over 70 advanced recipes for developing scalable services with the Microsoft Azure platform

Roberto Freato

Neil Mackenzie

BIRMINGHAM - MUMBAI

Microsoft Azure Development Cookbook
Second Edition

First published: August 2011

Second edition: September 2014

Production reference: 1180914

Published by Packt Publishing Ltd.
Livery Place
35 Livery Street
Birmingham B3 2PB, UK.

ISBN 978-1-78217-032-7

www.packtpub.com

Cover image by Duraid Fatouhi (duraidfatouhi@yahoo.com)

Credits

Authors

Roberto Freato

Neil Mackenzie

Reviewers

Michael S. Collier

Peter Kirchner

Sarang Kulkarni

Sachin Prakash Sancheti

Aaron Whittaker

Commissioning Editor

Joanne Fitzpatrick

Acquisition Editor

Kevin Colaco

Content Development Editor

Rikshith Shetty

Technical Editors

Indrajit A. Das

Dennis John

Copy Editors

Roshni Banerjee

Karuna Narayanan

Project Coordinator

Kinjal Bari

Proofreaders

Ting Baker

Simran Bhogal

Maria Gould

Sandra Hopper

Indexers

Hemangini Bari

Monica Ajmera Mehta

Tejal Soni

Production Coordinators

Saiprasad Kadam

Conidon Miranda

Alwin Roy

Cover Work

Conidon Miranda

About the Authors

Roberto Freato has been an independent IT consultant since he started working. He worked for several small software firms while he was studying. After completing his MSc in Computer Science and Engineering, where he worked on a thesis on Consumer Cloud Computing, he specialized in cloud and Azure. Today, he works as a freelance consultant for important companies in Italy, helping clients design and kick-off their distributed software solutions. He trains for the developer community in his free time, addressing many conferences. He is a Microsoft MVP since 2010.

Thanks to Simona, Mom, and Dad.

Neil Mackenzie has worked with computers for nearly 3 decades. He started his computer career doing large-scale numerical simulations for scientific research and business planning. Since then, he has primarily been involved in healthcare software and developing electronic medical record systems. He has been using Microsoft Azure since PDC 2008 and has used nearly all parts of the Microsoft Azure platform, including those parts that no longer exist. Neil is very active in the online Microsoft Azure community, contributing to the MSDN Microsoft Azure forums in particular. He is a Microsoft MVP for Microsoft Azure.

I would like to thank all the people from whom I've learned Microsoft Azure. I would also like to thank the staff at Packt Publishing for nursing the project along and Brent Stineman for first suggesting my name to them. I have found the comments from the technical reviewers invaluable, which immeasurably improved the book. Last but not least, I would like to thank my wife, Claire, and my children for suffering through all the late nights and lost weekends that went into the writing of the book.

About the Reviewers

Michael S. Collier serves as a principal cloud architect for Aditi Technologies, a Microsoft NSI partner that focuses on cloud computing. He is a four-time Azure MVP and was the 2012 Azure MVP of the Year for his extraordinary community contributions. Michael has had a successful 12-year career at various consulting and technology firms, where he was instrumental in leading and developing solutions for a wide range of clients. He has many years of experience in helping companies determine the best strategy to adopt cloud computing and providing insight and hands-on experience to ensure that they're successful. He is also a respected technology community leader, and can often be found sharing his Azure insights and experiences at regional and national conferences. You can follow Michael's experiences with Azure on his blog at www.michaelscollier.com and on Twitter at @MichaelCollier.

Peter Kirchner has been working as a technical evangelist at Microsoft, Germany, since 2008. In this role, he addresses conferences and writes articles that focus on cloud computing, with the goal to inspire new technologies and support developers and administrators in developing for and using the Microsoft platform. Before working with Microsoft, Peter gained experience working in the area of SharePoint development and consulting. While studying, he showed interest in network technologies, security, and distributed systems, and graduated with a Diploma in Computer Science.

Sarang Kulkarni lives in Pune, India, with his wife and daughter. He has been coding for food for the last 14 years, and also talking and writing about it for the last 6 years. He has mostly been around the Microsoft stack, with an occasional adventure in SAP ABAP and Amazon AWS. Sarang has been building SaaS products and services on the Azure stack since the "Red Dog" days. He worked with big consulting firms such as Accenture, Avanade, and Cognizant before settling in Zevenseas, a SharePoint company, building and growing its Azure business.

Sarang has previously worked on a collaborative book, *Windows Azure Platform: Articles from the Trenches*, as a co-author.

Thanks to Packt Publishing for approaching me with this interesting opportunity. I would also thank my family and my colleagues at Zevenseas for being supportive of everything I keep on doing.

Sachin Prakash Sancheti hails from a small town in western India called Washim. He has 15 years' experience, much of which was focused on Microsoft-oriented technologies. In the last 4 years, he developed an expertise in cloud computing across both Windows Azure and AWS. An innovative architect with solid technology acumen, Sachin is also an avid blogger and speaker. He calls himself "a whiteboard as well as a keyboard guy." Being proud of his modest origins, Sachin would like to bring recognition in some form to his hometown, Washim.

Currently, Sachin is working with Symphony Teleca, Pune, as a principal architect. Earlier in his career, he was with Infosys and Microsoft, both in India. Immediately prior to Symphony Teleca, he spent a couple of years with a startup called Cumulux, which was acquired by Aditi Technologies for its expertise in Windows Azure.

I would like to thank Packt Publishing for this opportunity to review the book. A special thanks to my wife, Vaidehi, who is my pillar when it comes to clearing the clutter in my mind. Clearly, she is the secret to my ability to focus on the task at hand.

Aaron Whittaker is a Microsoft Virtual Technology Solutions Professional (V-TSP) and a technical account manager. He has spoken at many major technology events, including several Microsoft TechEds. He is a guest author for Microsoft MSDN and TechNet. He proactively learns new technologies and is currently focused on building customer relationships to solve problems.

Aaron has received the vExpert award several times and was the host of a VMWare user group for 5 years. He currently hosts the Brisbane Cloud User Group.

www.PacktPub.com

Support files, eBooks, discount offers, and more

For support files and downloads related to your book, please visit www.PacktPub.com.

Did you know that Packt offers eBook versions of every book published, with PDF and ePub files available? You can upgrade to the eBook version at www.PacktPub.com and as a print book customer, you are entitled to a discount on the eBook copy. Get in touch with us at service@packtpub.com for more details.

At www.PacktPub.com, you can also read a collection of free technical articles, sign up for a range of free newsletters and receive exclusive discounts and offers on Packt books and eBooks.

http://PacktLib.PacktPub.com

Do you need instant solutions to your IT questions? PacktLib is Packt's online digital book library. Here, you can search, access, and read Packt's entire library of books.

Why subscribe?

- ▸ Fully searchable across every book published by Packt
- ▸ Copy and paste, print, and bookmark content
- ▸ On demand and accessible via a web browser

Free access for Packt account holders

If you have an account with Packt at www.PacktPub.com, you can use this to access PacktLib today and view 9 entirely free books. Simply use your login credentials for immediate access.

Instant updates on new Packt books

Get notified! Find out when new books are published by following @PacktEnterprise on Twitter or the *Packt Enterprise* Facebook page.

Table of Contents

Preface

Microsoft Azure is Microsoft's platform for cloud computing. It provides developers with elastic building blocks to build scalable applications. These building blocks are services for web hosting, storage, computation, connectivity, and more. They are usable as standalone services or are mixed together to build advanced scenarios.

This practical cookbook will show you these building blocks, focusing on why we should use one or the other, and when to use them appropriately. Even though reading the entire book will give you an advanced overview of the main blocks of the Azure platform, each chapter is self-contained. So, even an inexperienced reader could jump from one chapter to another without reading the entire book. Each chapter is organized into recipes—standalone units of execution to complete tasks that involve a specific feature/service of the platform. This approach gives readers the capability to focus on the technology for further use in real-world projects.

This book tries to provide a comprehensive overview of the main aspects of the Azure platform from the point of view of a developer. Some building blocks such as virtual machines are deliberately avoided to focus on development tools, development libraries, and development strategies. This is a recipe-based book; expect to dirty your hands with code that is also outside the boundaries of the recipe, as you would do with food in a real recipe.

Finally, Microsoft Azure is an evolving platform. As technical topics have a high decay rate, Azure services are enriched day by day with new features and service models, making the goal of writing a "complete" book almost impossible. However, this book focuses on core concepts, which remain quite stable over time.

What this book covers

Chapter 1, *Developing Cloud Services for Microsoft Azure*, shows you the main compute engine of Azure (also known as web/worker roles). This building block uses a specific service model to run web applications as well as any other custom code on stateless virtual machines. This chapter is also a great introduction to Visual Studio integration for those who are not familiar with it.

Chapter 2, Deploying Quickly with Azure Websites, shows you one of the most advanced Platform as a Service in the market, which lets customers/developers deploy an existing web application in minutes. This building block does not require a specific development skill, as it is a lock-in-free environment that provides advanced integrated features regarding the ALM. This chapter is essential for anyone who wants to start a new project or move an existing project to the cloud.

Chapter 3, Getting Storage with Blobs in Azure, shows you how Azure deals with storage of files (also known as Blobs). This building block is about Blobs' features, management, and administration, with food for thought for advanced scenarios. This chapter will be helpful to those who want to access the storage services programmatically.

Chapter 4, Going Relational with the Azure SQL Database, shows you the RDBMS of Microsoft Azure, enabling existing SQL-Server-based solutions to move into the cloud seamlessly. This building block is about SQL database management, monitoring, and development. This chapter is a good read to identify the correct approach to SQL on Microsoft Cloud.

Chapter 5, Going NoSQL with Azure Tables, shows you how to use the original Table service as a data store for unstructured data. This building block can be used to store entities when there is no strict need of a SQL-based, but scalable, service. This chapter is particularly useful while building a scalable data store of arbitrary entities.

Chapter 6, Messaging and Queues with Storage and Service Bus, shows you how to build scalable systems with message-based, disconnected systems. This building block covers the need for communication between heterogeneous systems, using queues of messages. This chapter also covers the relayed messaging feature and cross-platform communication.

Chapter 7, Managing Azure Resources with the Azure Management Libraries, shows you how to remotely manage a big portion of the Azure services, programmatically, through Management Libraries. The building block is the Management API on which Management Libraries rely. This chapter is suited for automation solutions, custom management tools, or even parts of complex multitenant systems where resources must be created/configured/destroyed dynamically.

Chapter 8, Going In-memory with Azure Cache, shows you how to improve an application's performance with in-memory caching. This building block is of primary importance for situations where there's web traffic and the demand is high, providing good service by storing frequently accessed information. This chapter is about caching, so it is extremely important to read it even if you are not adopting it as part of the implementation.

What you need for this book

This book requires a basic exposure to the main concepts of cloud computing, as well as the C# programming language and the Visual Studio IDE. The software needed to run the samples (and hopefully extend them) are Visual Studio 2012/2013, with the latest Azure SDK, SQL Server Management Studio Express, and a few free tools that are referenced in the book.

Who this book is for

If you are an architect, this book will help you make the correct decisions about which Azure building blocks to use. If you are a developer, this book will help you understand how to use them appropriately, and if you are a .NET developer, this book is a pure delight.

Conventions

In this book, you will find a number of styles of text that distinguish between different kinds of information. Here are some examples of these styles, and an explanation of their meaning.

Code words in text, database table names, folder names, filenames, file extensions, pathnames, dummy URLs, user input, and Twitter handles are shown as follows: "Select **Custom** and specify `Local Folder`."

A block of code is set as follows:

```
<appSettings>
  <add key="DataConnectionString"
value="DefaultEndpointsProtocol=https;AccountName={ACCOUNT_
NAME};AccountKey={ACCOUNT_KEY}"/>
</appSettings>
```

Any command-line input or output is written as follows:

```
C:\Users\Administrator>PowerShell -ExecutionPolicy Unrestricted .\
StartupTask.ps1
```

New terms and **important words** are shown in bold. Words that you see on the screen, in menus or dialog boxes for example, appear in the text like this: "Open Visual Studio, and on the menu bar, navigate to **File | New | Project**."

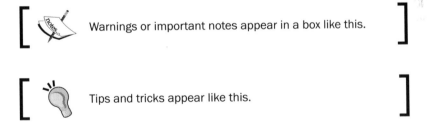

Warnings or important notes appear in a box like this.

Tips and tricks appear like this.

Reader feedback

Feedback from our readers is always welcome. Let us know what you think about this book—what you liked or may have disliked. Reader feedback is important for us to develop titles that you really get the most out of.

To send us general feedback, simply send an e-mail to feedback@packtpub.com, and mention the book title via the subject of your message. If there is a topic that you have expertise in and you are interested in either writing or contributing to a book, see our author guide on www.packtpub.com/authors.

Customer support

Now that you are the proud owner of a Packt book, we have a number of things to help you to get the most from your purchase.

Downloading the example code

You can download the example code files for all Packt books you have purchased from your account at http://www.packtpub.com. If you purchased this book elsewhere, you can visit http://www.packtpub.com/support and register to have the files e-mailed directly to you.

Errata

Although we have taken every care to ensure the accuracy of our content, mistakes do happen. If you find a mistake in one of our books—maybe a mistake in the text or the code—we would be grateful if you would report this to us. By doing so, you can save other readers from frustration and help us improve subsequent versions of this book. If you find any errata, please report them by visiting http://www.packtpub.com/submit-errata, selecting your book, clicking on the **errata submission form** link, and entering the details of your errata. Once your errata are verified, your submission will be accepted and the errata will be uploaded on our website, or added to any list of existing errata, under the Errata section of that title. Any existing errata can be viewed by selecting your title from http://www.packtpub.com/support.

Piracy

Piracy of copyright material on the Internet is an ongoing problem across all media. At Packt, we take the protection of our copyright and licenses very seriously. If you come across any illegal copies of our works, in any form, on the Internet, please provide us with the location address or website name immediately so that we can pursue a remedy.

Please contact us at copyright@packtpub.com with a link to the suspected pirated material.

We appreciate your help in protecting our authors, and our ability to bring you valuable content.

Questions

You can contact us at questions@packtpub.com if you are having a problem with any aspect of the book, and we will do our best to address it.

1

Developing Cloud Services for Microsoft Azure

In this chapter, we will cover the following topics:

- ▸ Setting up solutions and projects to work with Cloud Services
- ▸ Debugging a Cloud Service locally with either Emulator or Emulator Express
- ▸ Publishing a Cloud Service with options from Visual Studio
- ▸ Debugging a Cloud Service remotely with Visual Studio
- ▸ Configuring the service model for a Cloud Service
- ▸ Providing a custom domain name for a Cloud Service
- ▸ Implementing HTTPS in a web role
- ▸ Using local storage in an instance
- ▸ Hosting multiple web sites in a web role
- ▸ Using startup tasks in a Cloud Service role
- ▸ Handling changes to the configuration and topology of a Cloud Service
- ▸ Managing upgrades and changes to a Cloud Service
- ▸ Configuring diagnostics in Cloud Services

Introduction

Cloud Services are classified typically as **Infrastructure-as-a-Service (IaaS)**, **Platform-as-a-Service (PaaS)**, and **Software-as-a-Service (SaaS)**. In the IaaS model, the core service provided is a **Virtual Machine (VM)** with a guest OS. The customer is responsible for everything about the guest OS, including hardening it and adding any required software. In the PaaS model, the core service provided is a VM with a hardened guest OS and an application-hosting environment. The customer is responsible only for the service injected into this environment. In the SaaS model, a service is exposed over the Internet, and the customer merely has to access it.

Microsoft Azure Cloud Services is the paradigm of the **Platform-as-a-Service (PaaS)** model of cloud computing. A Cloud Service can be developed and deployed to any of the desired Microsoft Azure datacenters (regions) located across the world. A service hosted in Microsoft Azure can leverage the high scalability and reduced administrative benefits of the PaaS model.

In later chapters, we do not see how Azure also offers an IaaS alternative, Microsoft Azure Virtual Machines, to let customers get the ability to deploy customized solutions in fully customized environments. Either way, the benefits of using PaaS are strongly evident compared to IaaS. In PaaS, we can reduce the governance of the whole system, focusing only on technology and processes, instead of managing the IT, as we did earlier. PaaS enforces the use of best practices throughout the development process, forcing us to take the right decisions in terms of design patterns and architectural choices.

From an IT architect's perspective, using PaaS is similar to trusting a black-box model. We know that the input is our code, which might be written with some environmental constraints or specific features, and the output is the running application on top of instances, virtual machines, or, generically, something that is managed, in the case of Azure, by Microsoft.

A Cloud Service provides the management and security boundaries for a set of roles. It is a management boundary because a Cloud Service is deployed, started, stopped, and deleted as a unit. A Cloud Service represents a security boundary because roles can expose input endpoints to the public internet, and they can also expose internal endpoints that are visible only to other roles in the service. We will see how roles work in the *Configuring the service model for a Cloud Service* recipe.

Roles are the **scalability unit** for a Cloud Service, as they provide vertical scaling by increasing the instance size and horizontal scaling by increasing the number of instances. Each role is deployed as one or more instances. The number of deployed instances for a role scales independent of other roles, as we will see in the *Handling changes to the configuration and topology of a Cloud Service* recipe. For example, one role could have two instances deployed, while another could have 200 instances. Furthermore, the compute capacity (or size) of each deployed instance is specified at the role level so that all instances of a role are the same size, though instances of different roles might have different sizes.

The application functionality of a role is deployed to individual instances that provide the compute capability for the Cloud Service. Each instance is hosted on its own VM. An instance is stateless because any changes made to later deployment will not survive an instance failure and will be lost. Note that the word *role* is used frequently where the word *instance* should be used.

A central driver of interest in cloud computing has been the realization that horizontal scalability, by adding commodity servers, is significantly more cost effective than vertical scalability achieved through increasing the power of a single server. Just like other cloud platforms, the Microsoft Azure platform emphasizes horizontal scalability rather than vertical scalability. The ability to increase and decrease the number of deployed instances to match the workload is described as elasticity.

Microsoft Azure supports two types of roles: web roles and worker roles. The web and worker roles are central to the PaaS model of Microsoft Azure.

A web role hosts websites using the complete **Internet Information Services** (**IIS**). It can host multiple websites with a single endpoint, using host headers to distinguish them, as we will see in the *Hosting multiple websites in a web role* recipe. However, this deployment strategy is gradually going into disuse due to an emerging powerful PaaS service that is called **Microsoft Azure Web Sites**. An instance of a web role implements two processes: the running code that interacts with the Azure fabric and the process that runs IIS.

A worker role hosts a long-running service and essentially replicates the functionality of a Windows service. Otherwise, the only real difference between a worker role and web role is that a web role hosts IIS, while the worker role does not. Furthermore, a worker role can also be used to host web servers other than IIS; in fact, worker roles are suggested by Microsoft when someone needs to deploy some kind of software that is not designed to run on the default Microsoft web stack. For example, if we want to run a Java application, my worker role should load a process of the JEE Application Server (that is, Glassfish or JBoss) and load the related files needed by the application to run, into it. This deployment model should be helped by some components, often called accelerators, that encapsulate the logic to install, run, and deploy the third-party stack (such as the Java one, for example) in a box, in a stateless fashion.

Visual Studio is a central theme in this chapter as well as for the whole book. In the *Setting up solutions and projects to work with Cloud Services* recipe, we will see the basics of the Visual Studio integration, while in the *Debugging a Cloud Service locally with either Emulator or Emulator Express* and *Debugging a Cloud Service remotely with Visual Studio* recipes, we will see something more advanced.

Setting up solutions and projects to work with Cloud Services

Microsoft Azure Cloud Service is the paradigm for PaaS. As such, Microsoft Azure provides a high-level, application-hosting environment, which is modeled on services, roles, and instances. The specification of the roles in the service is referred to as the service model.

As we mentioned earlier, Microsoft Azure supports two types of roles: web roles and worker roles. We said that a web role is essentially a worker role plus IIS because they comply with the same running model where there is an entry point that interacts with the Azure environment and our custom code, regardless of whether it is a web app or batch process.

Microsoft Azure provides us with a comprehensive set of command-line tools to package our solutions to be deployed on the Cloud, as they should be wrapped into a single deployment unit that is called a package. A package is like a ZIP file with encryption. It contains every project component of the Cloud Service, so it is the self-containing artifact that goes onto the Azure platform to instruct it about setting up machines and code. This package, along with its configuration, represents the whole Cloud Service that Azure Fabric (the big brain of the Azure data center) can deploy wherever it wants. In terms of black-box reasoning, the input of a Cloud Service is package plus configuration, which we can produce using command-line tools or just using Visual Studio, starting from our classic .NET binaries.

The corresponding Visual Studio artifact for the package mentioned earlier is a project template called Microsoft Azure Cloud Service. It is a `.ccproj` project that wraps the .NET projects in order to produce the resulting compressed unit of deployment. Later in the chapter, we call this project wrapper to underline its purpose in the deployment process.

In fact, Visual Studio lets us automatically create the correct environment to deploy web and worker roles, without facing the complexity of the command-line tools, by installing the Microsoft Azure Tools for Visual Studio that, at the time of writing this book, are available in Version 2.3.

In this recipe, we'll learn how to choose the service model for a Cloud Service and create a project environment for it in Visual Studio.

Getting ready

For this recipe, we use Visual Studio 2013 with Microsoft Azure Tools installed. The goal of the recipe is to produce a sample package for the Cloud Service, from new or existing projects.

How to do it...

A Cloud Service is a composition of two scenarios: new or existing projects. We will split our recipe into two branches to support the two scenarios:

1. Open Visual Studio, and in the menu bar, navigate to **File | New | Project**.

2. From the installed templates, choose either the Visual Basic, Visual C#, or Visual F# node, and then, choose the cloud node. You will be prompted later about the actual programming languages you will use in your services.

3. Select Microsoft Azure Cloud Service.

 If you haven't installed the latest SDK, you will probably see something like **Get Microsoft Azure SDK for .NET** or **Enable Microsoft Azure Tools** in the window. This indicates that you have to download the SDK first and then come back to the project creation wizard.

4. In the **Name** text box, enter the name (WAHelloWorld) of your wrapper project. Remember that this name is only used to represent our service container, not a real web project itself.

5. By choosing this project template, VS opens the New Microsoft Azure Cloud Service windows.

6. If you want to create just the wrapper of your existing web/worker project, press **OK** and go ahead to Branch 2. You will add your binaries to the wrapper project later. If you want to create the wrapper and your web/worker projects from scratch, read the *Branch 1* section.

 Branch 1: start from scratch by adding new projects

7. Use the arrow keys to add/remove the projects that will represent your web/worker roles on the right-hand side. You can choose the following two projects:

   - The ASP.NET web role
   - The worker role

8. On the right-hand side pane, there will be the **WebRole1** and **WorkerRole1** entries. Customize the names of the two projects in WebHelloWorld and WorkerHelloWorld, respectively, and go ahead.

9. Customize the project templates you added, with the windows that Visual Studio displays later.

Branch 2: add your existing projects to the wrapper

10. In the **Solution Explorer**, right-click on the solution and choose **Add | Existing Project**.

11. In the browsing window, locate your project and select the **Visual Studio project file**. Now, your existing project is linked to the new solution.

12. In the **Solution Explorer**, right-click on the `Roles` folder in the wrapper project and navigate to **Add | Web Role Project in solution** or **Worker Role Project in solution**.

13. In the **Associate with Role Project** window, choose the project(s) to add and confirm. Now, the project should appear under the `Roles` folder of the wrapper.

 To be a compatible web role project, a project should be a valid web application, regardless of the engine it runs on. On the other hand, every class library could be potentially a worker role project. However, to let Visual Studio add your existing class library, you must edit the project file (`csproj` in C#) as outlined at the end of the recipe.

 Recipe conclusion

14. Right click on the wrapper project and choose **Package**.

15. When prompted with the **Package Microsoft Azure Application** window, leave the default settings and click on **Package**.

 Later in the chapter, we will see how to understand and customize service configuration and deployment options to better understand the **Package Microsoft Azure Application** window.

16. After few seconds of VS operations in the background, you will be prompted with a local filesystem folder with the output of the packaging process.

How it works...

From steps 1 to 5, we created the Microsoft Azure Cloud Service project, the project wrapper that represents the unit of deployment for Azure. As mentioned earlier in the note, be sure to have installed the SDK and the latest VS Tools required to complete the recipe first.

In step 6, we chose between starting from scratch and using existing projects.

In steps 7 and 8, we added two projects, one web role and one worker role, from the choices of the wizard. We could also add another project template such as the following:

- The WCF service web role
- The cache worker role
- The worker role with Service Bus Queue

In step 9, for each .NET project that we added in the step 7, Visual Studio launches the Project Template wizard. In the case of the `WebHelloWorld` one, VS opens the new ASP.NET project window that lets us choose the ASP.NET engine to reference in the project. In the case of `WorkerHelloWorld`, VS simply adds a class library to the solution.

From steps 10 to 13, we showed how to import an existing project into the solution and then into the wrapper project. Finally, in step 15, we built the package using the default settings. Actually, we would choose which service configuration to use to create the configuration file and which build configuration to use to build the assemblies.

There's more

In the note of step 13, we mentioned that every class library could be used in a wrapper project. In fact, the Azure runtime only needs a class library, and it searches in the **Dynamic Link Library DLL** for a class that inherits the `RoleEntryPoint` abstract class as follows:

```
public class WorkerRole:RoleEntryPoint
{
}
```

This requirement is enforced only at runtime. At compile time, however, Visual Studio does not block us if we miss the `RoleEntryPoint` implementation.

However, users who try to add their class library to the wrapper could be shown a grayed option due to the inability of Visual Studio to distinguish a valid worker role from a generic class library.

So, we need to perform a tweak on the project file:

1. Locate the project file (`*.csproj`, for example) of the class library to add it.
2. Open it with Notepad.
3. Before the first `</PropertyGroup>` closing tag, add the following line:

   `<RoleType>Worker</RoleType>`
4. Save the file, and in Visual Studio, reload the project.

See also

Have a look at these MSDN links to get additional information:

> ▸ Information on the latest Azure SDKs with release notes at `http://msdn.microsoft.com/en-us/library/dn627519.aspx`

> ▸ How to upgrade an existing project with the latest version of Azure Tools at `http://msdn.microsoft.com/en-us/library/jj131257.aspx`

Debugging a Cloud Service locally with either Emulator or Emulator Express

As Cloud Services are more like a black-box runtime about which we don't (and shouldn't) need to know anything. However, we should know how they behave different from (or according to) a common IIS installed on a common Windows Server virtual machine.

 The very first versions of Cloud Services had strict restrictions on the interactions with OS, permitted by applications. They had to run in a mode called Microsoft Azure Partial Trust, which isolated an application from the underlying operating system, to prevent the defects and bugs in the code from causing failures in the entire OS. Today, there is no longer an option to isolate an application as a result of developers' continuous requests to let them have control of the VMs under their services.

Despite the capability to access the underlying operating system, it is strongly recommended that you use only the application resources and not rely on false friends such as filesystem, folders structures, and so on. In fact, due to the nature of the PaaS model, the configuration of the operating system as well as the operating system itself could change without any control by the user, but for maintenance or deprecation purposes.

Finally, in the real Azure environment, there are some features available through the Service Runtime API, which is available only when the code is running on Azure or to let developers test their code locally, onto a local emulator shipped with the Microsoft Azure SDK.

The Emulator creates a logical representation of the Azure topology into the machine that runs it. If our service was composed of two web roles and one worker role, for example, the Emulator will start three separate processes in which the application code will behave exactly as it runs on the real platform (with some soft exceptions, which are not discussed in this book). As it needs to open network ports and change some OS settings, the Emulator needs to be started as an administrator. Hence, to start it by simply debugging in Visual Studio, VS itself should be started as an admin. Emulator Express, on its side, runs in a user mode that does not require elevation but has some limitations in terms of emulation coverage.

Getting ready

In this recipe we will explore the debugging options of a Cloud Service using the (full) Emulator and Emulator Express, using the previously created Cloud Service, WAHelloWorld.

How to do it...

In order to explain the differences between the two emulators, we divided it into three parts. Start an elevated Visual Studio window (as an administrator), and proceed as follows:

 Part 1: choosing the emulator to use during debugging

1. In the **Solution Explorer**, right-click on the Azure wrapper project (Cloud Service) and choose **Properties** (or just select the project and press *Alt + Enter*).
2. In the page that just opened, select the **Web** tab.
3. In the **Local Development Server** options group, choose **Use IIS Express**.
4. In the Emulator options group, choose **Use Full Emulator**.

 Part 2: debugging a worker role using the (full) Emulator

5. Locate the Roles folder under the WAHelloWorld wrapper project.
6. Right-click on the WorkerHelloWorld project and go to the properties page.
7. In the **Configuration** tab, locate the **Instance** count box and set the value to 2.
8. Go to the WorkerHelloWorld project, and open the WorkerRole.cs file.
9. Locate the lines with the while (true) block and put a breakpoint on the following code:

   ```
   Trace.TraceInformation("Working", "Information");
   ```
10. Right-click on the Azure wrapper project (WAHelloWorld), and click on **Set as StartUp Project**.
11. Press *F5* or select **Debug**. Start debugging on the main menu.

 At this point, if you run VS in the user mode, you will be prompted with the message, **The Microsoft Azure compute emulator must be run elevated.** If so, close VS and right-click on the VS icon; then, run it as the administrator. Repeat the preceding step.

12. Wait for a few seconds while you are shown the **Starting the Microsoft Azure Debugging Environment** window.

 The first time you run the Emulator, Windows will probably ask you to open some ports on the firewall, because the Emulator needs to run Web Services.

13. After about 10 seconds, VS breaks on the tracing line twice, once per running worker.

 Part 3: understand the compute Emulator interface

14. During debugging, locate the Microsoft Azure Emulator icon in the system tray.

15. Right-click on it and choose **Show Compute Emulator UI**.

16. In the **Microsoft Azure Compute Emulator** (full) window, expand all the items in the tree and click on one of the two green balls.

17. Read the log of the instance, which includes the text sent by our code in the tracing line used earlier.

18. Shut down the deployment by stopping debugging, closing the browser, or clicking on the stop icon in the Emulator UI on the current deployment.

How it works...

In part one, from steps 1 to 4, we chose which Emulator to use in debugging. In the Cloud Service properties, we also find these tabs:

▸ **Application**: This shows the current version of the SDK used by the project

▸ **Build Events**: This lets you customize the pre/post build actions

▸ **Development**: This lets you choose some options related to debugging and emulator

▸ **Web**: This lets you choose which Emulator (Express or Full) to use and which IIS server set to run

In part two, from steps 5 to 7, we customized the number of simultaneous running instances of the WorkerHelloWorld code. On the configuration page, there is a lot of information and a lot of custom points to edit, which we will see later in the chapter.

In step 9, we set a breakpoint on a line of code previously created by the VS wizard process, as shown in the previous recipe. In step 11, VS prepared the project package and started the Emulator.

If you use **Remote Desktop Services** (**RDS**) in conjunction with Visual Studio to develop your Microsoft Azure projects, it is not necessary that only one instance of the Full Emulator will run on a machine at a point of time. Instead, multiple instances of the Emulator Express can run on a machine at the same time, letting you and your team debug on the same machine remotely.

In step 12, Azure Emulator picked the configuration from the wrapper project and set up virtual instances, deploying our custom code to them. The Emulator started a runner for each instance declared: one for the `WebHelloWorld` site and two for the `WorkerHelloWorld` worker.

In step 13, the code stopped twice, as there were two instances deployed to the Emulator. If we deployed 10 instances, the debugger would stop 10 times.

 If you want to perform advanced debugging by temporarily freezing concurrent worker threads, you can use the **Threads** window. You can access this window by navigating to **Debug | Windows | Threads**. Locate the thread ID; then, right-click on it and choose **Freeze**.

In part 3, in steps 14, 15, and 16, we opened the Compute Emulator UI. In the system tray icon context menu, we also noticed the capability to open the Storage Emulator UI and to shut down both the emulators (compute/storage). This feature will be very useful in the upcoming chapters when we talk about storage.

In the final steps, we use the Emulator UI to monitor the parallel workers. In the main windows, we can see the deployment slot with the roles, each one with its own instances. If there are different behaviors between instances, we can monitor the output in the terminal-like window, where it redirects all the tracing output of the worker thread (in both web and worker roles).

There's more...

As the emulator not only emulates the compute engine (web and worker roles) but also the storage engines (which we will see in the upcoming chapters), it is in fact composed of the following:

- Compute Emulator
- Storage Emulator

These two are always referred to as just one, the Azure Emulator. It is also possible to prevent the Storage Emulator from being started during debugging by performing the following steps:

1. Open the **Properties** page of the Azure wrapper project.
2. In the **Development** tab, set the **Start Microsoft Azure storage emulator** option to **False**.

When debugging your code in a (full) Emulator environment with multiple instances running at the same time, be aware that your code will run in the same AppDomain. This is the main difference between the real and Emulator environment (where the code runs on different machines), and this could cause runtime unexpected behaviors. If you use one or more static classes with static fields, this would result in an unavoidable behavior of shared memory between virtual instances. To actually test this sort of scenario, you should write custom code to differentiate virtual instances, relying on something that is related to the instance name (for example, through the Service Runtime API or using the thread references).

See also

Have a look at the following MSDN links to get additional information:

- More information about running the Emulator at `http://msdn.microsoft.com/en-us/library/azure/hh403990.aspx`

- Differences between the "real" Azure and the emulated environment at `http://msdn.microsoft.com/en-us/library/azure/gg432960.aspx`

Publishing a Cloud Service with options from Visual Studio

Microsoft Azure always shipped with an SDK for developers and a complementary toolset for Visual Studio integration. In earlier versions of the official SDK, many features were only available through the online portal at `https://manage.windowsazure.com`. At the time of writing this book, Microsoft released its major SDK update that lets developers quickly manage almost everything of the cloud infrastructure directly from Visual Studio. Hence, it is now simpler to get on Azure and run a Cloud Service compared to the past.

When we publish a Cloud Service into Azure, we should know some foundation concepts in advance, in order to understand the ecosystem better. First, to deploy a Cloud Service, a deployment slot should be created. This could be done through the portal or from Visual Studio, and it consists of creating a DNS name in `[myCS].cloudapp.net` form. This DNS, under the hood, is linked to a load balancer that actually redirects the Internet traffic to the CS, to each instance of our service, choosing it with a round-robin algorithm. This means that regardless of the topology, we are deploying to Azure in this Cloud Service. Every web endpoint that we are publishing stands behind this layer of balancing to provide the system with transparent scaling capabilities.

During the deployment, we also decide the options that CS should be deployed with:

- Production/staging slot
- Remote desktop support
- Diagnostics collection
- Remote debugging
- IntelliTrace support
- Incremental/simultaneous update

After we perform the deployment, our service, comprehensive of all the roles of the package, as defined in the *Setting up solutions and projects to work with Cloud Services* recipe, is running in the cloud and is accessible through the DNS name Azure provided us.

Getting ready

For this recipe, we can create a sample solution on the fly by navigating to **File | New project | Cloud wizard** or using the WAHelloWorld project created earlier.

How to do it...

We are going to see how to deploy a Cloud Service package to the cloud. We can do this by performing the following steps:

1. Right-click on the Azure wrapper project (WAHelloWorld) and select **Publish**.
2. In the **Publish Microsoft Azure Application** window, click on **Sign In to authenticate**.
3. In the browser window, enter the credentials of the Microsoft Account (former Live ID) associated with the Azure account and continue.
4. In the **Choose your subscription** dropdown, choose the subscription that will host your service.
5. If your subscription is empty or it does not contain a Cloud Service, you will be prompted with the **Create Microsoft Azure Services** window.
6. Enter a name into the **Name** box, and choose a location for your service.
7. In the **Cloud Service** dropdown, choose the Cloud Service to which you want your service to be deployed.
8. In the **Environment** dropdown, choose **Production**.
9. In the **Service configuration** dropdown, choose **Cloud**.
10. In the **Build configuration** dropdown, choose the correct build configuration, according to the ones available in your service (in the WAHelloWorld example, choose **Release**).

Configuring the remote desktop is optional.

11. Check on the **Enable Remote Desktop for all roles** checkbox.

12. In the **Remote Desktop Configuration** window, specify a username, a password, and a date for account expiration. Then, click on **OK**.

 Using RDP on Microsoft Azure is not recommended due to the nature of PaaS services. It is recommended that you use it only for dev/test purposes and rely on external or active monitoring to troubleshoot and resolve issues.

 The advanced settings tab is optional.

13. Specify WAHelloWorld Version 1 in the **Deployment** label box.

14. Leave the **Append current date and time** checkbox unchecked.

15. If your subscription is empty or it does not contain a storage account, you will be prompted with the **Create Microsoft Azure Services** window.

16. Enter a name into the **Name** box, and choose a location for your service.

17. In the **Storage account** dropdown, choose the storage account where Visual Studio will upload the package file, letting Azure deploy it from the Blob storage.

18. Uncheck every checkbox except the **Deployment update** one, then click on **Settings**.

19. In the **Deployment** settings window, select **Incremental** update.

20. Check the **If deployment can't be updated, do a full deployment** checkbox and confirm.

 Conclusion.

21. Next, in the **Summary** page of the wizard, check all the information and then save your publish profile file.

22. Click on **Publish**.

23. After few or several minutes (it depends on the size of your deployment), check the **Microsoft Azure Activity Log** tab in VS for completion of the deployment process.

24. At completion, if your service has a role with a valid HTTP endpoint, navigate to it at http://[nameOfCloudService].cloudapp.net.

How it works...

Up to step 3, we link VS with our Microsoft Account (formerly, Live ID). As a Microsoft account could be the administrator and co-administrator of multiple Azure subscriptions at the same time, after the authentication, the dropdown mentioned in step 4 could be a pretty long list of entries.

In step 5, we create a Cloud Service on the Azure platform; this means that we create the deployment slots (one for production, one for staging) to run our service. Every time we create a service in the Azure platform, we must cope with the localization of the service, in terms of the choice of a datacenter. There are actually about 13 datacenters, plus one in China:

- Europe North: Ireland
- Europe West: Netherlands
- US Central: Iowa
- US East: Virginia
- US East 2: Virginia
- US West: California
- US North Central: Illinois
- US South Central: Texas
- Asia Pacific East: Hong Kong
- Asia Pacific Southeast: Singapore
- Japan East: Saitama Prefecture
- Japan West: Osaka Prefecture
- Brazil South: Sao Paulo State

 Two new datacenters in Australia have also been announced, but not yet released to the public.

In steps 7 and 8, we chose which slot to use for deployment and which configuration to publish for it. For each new Cloud Service project, VS creates two service configuration files: a local one and a cloud one.

In step 9, we choose the build configuration. This step is related to the actual build settings of our solution. In the new solution, there are just two configurations (debug/release), but the list could be longer according to real-life projects and complexity.

In steps 10 and 11, we configured the remote desktop. Though this is not recommended, this could let us connect to each instance to troubleshoot any issues and master the OS configuration of an Azure Virtual Machine image. Due to security implications in this process, a self-signed certificate is generated automatically to establish the TLS connection. It is also possible to provide our own valid certificate by clicking on **More Options** in the **Remote Desktop Configuration** window.

We learned that in Azure, we have many instances behind a single load balancer (therefore, a single IP) to RDP the instances we must proceed one-by-one with different combinations of ip:port.

Steps 12 and 13 were straightforward. They indicated the name of the deployment for further administrative tasks.

In steps 14 and 15, we chose a storage account. As we never talked about this feature earlier in the book, just keep in mind that a Cloud Service could be connected to a storage account to provide it with logging and diagnostics data.

From steps 16 to 18, we set up the options for update. As Azure could have a previous online version of our service, we had to decide how to manage the update. By unchecking the **Deployment update** checkbox, we completely bypassed the update process, telling Azure to delete the old deployment because a new one was going to arrive. Otherwise, we can specify how to update the service, gracefully (incremental update) or suddenly (simultaneously update). In the incremental update, Azure updates a service instance by instance, theoretically without service interruption. On the other hand, Azure updates every instance at the same time, causing an interruption of the service. In some cases, a deployment could not be updated. If this is the case, then perform a delete-and-replace operation.

In step 19, we saved the publish settings to use them later, thus avoiding repeating all the steps, by directly clicking on **Publish** from the summary pane. In step 21, we recognized the VS-integrated progress window, refreshed periodically from an Azure service. We can also use it to stop/cancel pending operations, as it reflects the portal operations.

There's more...

If we checked the **Enable Remote Desktop for all roles** checkbox during the publishing process, it is possible to connect to each instance directly from Visual Studio using the following steps:

1. Locate the Microsoft Azure node in the Server Explorer.
2. Locate the Cloud Services subnode and the Cloud Service you want to connect to (in the example, WAHelloWorld).
3. Expand the node, and select the production or staging deployment.
4. Expand the node and the role of interest; it will show a list of the deployed instance.

This list, as for the list of Cloud Services and related roles, could depend on the actual running configuration of your service. Remember that a Cloud Service can contain many roles, and each role can have many instances.

5. Right-click on the selected instance (from instance 0 to instance "N"), and choose **Connect using Remote Desktop....**

6. Confirm the settings in the **Remote Desktop Connection** window and enter the VM. If prompted with a credential set (in most cases, only for the password), type the ones you gave in the publishing process.

7. You are now connected to a real running instance of Azure.

While connected to the real instance of Azure, you can poke around the OS, observing the following:

▶ The filesystem topology (the C: / D: / E)
▶ The virtualized hardware (processor, RAM, and so on)
▶ The network settings (internal IP, gateway, and so on)

We cannot actually rely on the information we gain by browsing the VM, as it is subject to change frequently without control by the user.

See also

Have a look at the following MSDN links to get additional information:

▶ Complete recap of how to publish from Visual Studio at `http://msdn.microsoft.com/en-us/library/ee460772.aspx`

▶ How to constantly maintain the same IP of the CS endpoint at `http://msdn.microsoft.com/en-us/library/jj614593.aspx`

Debugging a Cloud Service remotely with Visual Studio

From the beginning of the Azure era, developers have been asking to be provided with the capability of live debugging solutions in the cloud. As it is not a simple feature, Microsoft figured it out only in 2013. However, now, we do have the strong capability to remotely debug our Cloud Service from Visual Studio to enhance the testing experience and extend it to the live application.

Getting ready

To get ready, we need a ready-to-publish application with at least one valid role. Follow steps 1 to 9 in the previous recipe and proceed with the instructions in the next recipe.

How to do it...

We will configure a Cloud Service to be attached with a remote debugger; then, we will proceed with the debug session, using the following steps:

1. When we follow steps 1 to 9 of the previous recipe, we will see the **Publish Microsoft Azure Application** window.

2. In **Common Settings**, choose **Debug** as the build configuration.

3. Select the **Advanced Settings** tab.

4. Check the **Enable Remote Debugger** option for all roles.

5. Complete the publish process and wait for it to finish.

 Please note that it is strongly recommended that you remote debug only in rare cases and, if needed, possibly for services in an isolated slot. For this purpose, consider to publish the solution into the staging slot of the CS.

 Attach the debugger.

6. Locate a part of your code that is now running in Azure and set a breakpoint.

7. Locate the Microsoft Azure node in the Server Explorer and find the Cloud Service you want to debug.

8. Expand the node and select the deployment slot first; then, right-click on the instance to connect to (that is, **Instance 0** under **Production**).

9. Click on **Attach Debugger**.

10. Perform the appropriate actions on the running code (firing events, for example) to cover the code where the breakpoint is set.

 As this is a fully featured debug session, we can also inspect elements in the heap, add custom watch values, and, of course, use the immediate window against the remote VM instance.

How it works...

From steps 1 to 4, we republished the Cloud Service by enabling the capability to remote debug the running code.

From steps 5 to 10, we executed an **attach to process-like** operation, connecting to a remote Azure instance instead of a local process.

 In step 7, we can also decide to debug the entire service, instead of a single instance. This capability is to be intended as an attach-to-each-role process, with advantages (that is, the first instance that meets the conditions will break the debugger) and disadvantages (that is, if each instance is frozen by the debugger, there will be potentially no thread free to serve the legitimate requests).

There's more...

As remote debugging is not considered a best practice (there is also the Emulator to test our code), there are some constraints you should know about and deal with:

▶ Depending on your Internet connection's quality, debugging will be slower or faster due to the amount of data exchanged between the VMs and the host.

▶ Remember to **softly** use the debugging windows (Immediate, Watch, and Locals) in order to prevent VS from freezing (due to the network transfers).

▶ Attaching the debugger to a single instance is preferable. Attaching it to the whole service (despite there being a limitation of 25 instances per role if remote debugging is enabled) is considered much slower.

▶ To enable remote debugging, the remote VM uses some ports (30400-30424 and 31400-31424 for the time being), so avoid using them in the application as this will result in an error.

 Mostly, the error message is **Allocation failed. Please retry later, try reducing the VM size or number of role instances, or try deploying to a different region**, which is not very user friendly in this context.

Until the Remote Debug feature was available, the only supported method to debug remotely was by collecting the IntelliTrace logs in the live instances and downloading them later in Visual Studio to analyze them. This method is quite complex, and it is not covered in this book.

See also

Have a look at the following MSDN links to get additional information:

▶ How to debug Virtual Machines from VS at `http://msdn.microsoft.com/en-us/library/ff683670.aspx`

▶ How to collect the IntelliTrace data of the remote Cloud Services at `http://msdn.microsoft.com/en-us/library/ff683671.aspx`

Configuring the service model for a Cloud Service

The service model for a Cloud Service in Microsoft Azure is specified in two XML files: the service definition file, `ServiceDefinition.csdef`, and the service configuration file, `ServiceConfiguration.cscfg`. These files are part of the Microsoft Azure project.

The service definition file specifies the roles used in the Cloud Service, up to 25 in a single definition. For each role, the service definition file specifies the following:

▶ The instance size

▶ The available endpoints

▶ The public key certificates

▶ The pluggable modules used in the role

▶ The startup tasks

▶ The local resources

▶ The runtime execution context

▶ The multisite support

▶ The file contents of the role

The following code snippet is an example of the skeleton of the service definition document:

```
<ServiceDefinition name="<service-name>"
  xmlns="http://schemas.microsoft.com/ServiceHosting/2008/
  10/ServiceDefinition" upgradeDomainCount="<number-of-upgrade-
  domains>" schemaVersion="<version>">
  <LoadBalancerProbes>   </LoadBalancerProbes>
  <WebRole …>   </WebRole>
  <WorkerRole …>   </WorkerRole>
  <NetworkTrafficRules>   </NetworkTrafficRules>
</ServiceDefinition>
```

We can mix up to 25 roles from both the web role and worker role types. In the past, there was also a third kind of supported role, the VM Role, which is now deprecated.

All instances of a role have the same size, chosen from standard sizes (A0-A04), memory intensive sizes (A5-A7), and compute intensive sizes (A8-A9). Each role may specify a number of input endpoints, internal endpoints, and instance-input endpoints. Input endpoints are accessible over the Internet and are load balanced, using a round-robin algorithm, across all instances of the role:

```
<InputEndpoint name="PublicWWW" protocol="http" port="80" />
```

Internal endpoints are accessible only by instances of any role in the Cloud Service. They are not load balanced:

```
<InternalEndpoint name="InternalService" protocol="tcp" />
```

Instance-input endpoints define a mapping between a public port and a single instance under the load balancer. An instance-input endpoint is linked to a specific role instance, using a port-forwarding technique on the load balancer. Onto it, we must **open** a range of ports through the `AllocatePublicPortFrom` section:

```
<InstanceInputEndpoint name="InstanceLevelService" protocol="tcp"
  localPort="10100">
  <AllocatePublicPortFrom>
    <FixedPortRange max="10105" min="10101" />
  </AllocatePublicPortFrom>
</InstanceInputEndpoint>
```

An X.509 public key certificate can be uploaded to a Cloud Service either directly on the Microsoft Azure Portal or using the Microsoft Azure Service Management REST API. The service definition file specifies which public key certificates, if any, are to be deployed with the role as well as the certificate store they are put in. A public key certificate can be used to configure an HTTPS endpoint but can also be accessed from code:

```
<Certificate name="CertificateForSSL" storeLocation="LocalMachine"
  storeName="My" />
```

Pluggable modules instruct Azure on how to set up the role. Microsoft Azure tooling for Visual Studio can automatically add/remove modules in order to enable/disable services as follows:

- ▶ Diagnostics to inject Microsoft Azure Diagnostics
- ▶ Remote access to inject remote desktop capability
- ▶ Remote forwarder to inject the forwarding capability used to support remote desktop
- ▶ Caching to inject the In-Role caching capability

Though In-Role caching is not covered in this book, there is a chapter about In-Memory Caching, using the Microsoft Azure Managed Cache service.

The following configuration XML code enables the additional modules:

```
<Imports>
  <Import moduleName="Diagnostics" />
  <Import moduleName="RemoteAccess" />
  <Import moduleName="RemoteForwarder" />
  <Import moduleName="Caching" />
</Imports>
```

Startup tasks are scripts or executables that run each time an instance starts, and they modify the runtime environment of the instance, up to and including the installation of the required software:

```
<Startup>
  <Task commandLine="run.cmd" taskType="foreground"
executionContext="elevated">
    <Environment>
      <Variable name="A" value="B" />
    </Environment>
  </Task>
</Startup>
```

The local resources section specifies how to reserve an isolated storage in the instance, for temporary data, accessible through an API instead of direct access to the filesystem:

```
<LocalResources>
  <LocalStorage name="DiagnosticStore" sizeInMB="20000"
    cleanOnRoleRecycle="false" />
  <LocalStorage name="TempStorage" sizeInMB="10000" />
</LocalResources>
```

The runtime execution context specifies whether the role runs with limited privileges (default) or with elevated privileges that provide full administrative capabilities. Note that in a web role that is running full IIS, the runtime execution context applies only to the web role and does not affect IIS. This runs in a separate process with restricted privileges:

```
<Runtime executionContext="elevated" />
```

In a web role that is running full IIS, the site's element in the service definition file contains the IIS configuration for the role. It specifies the endpoint bindings, virtual applications, virtual directories, and host headers for the various websites hosted by the web role. The *Hosting multiple websites in a web role* recipe contains more information about this configuration. Refer to the following code:

```
<Sites>
  <Site name="Web">
    <Bindings>
      <Binding name="Endpoint1" endpointName="Endpoint1" />
    </Bindings>
  </Site>
</Sites>
```

The contents section specifies whether static contents are copied from an application folder to a destination folder on the Azure virtual machine, relative to the `%ROLEROOT%\Approot` folder:

```
<Contents>
  <Content destination="MyFolder">
    <SourceDirectory path="FolderA"/>
  </Content>
</Contents>
```

The service definition file is uploaded to Microsoft Azure as part of the Microsoft Azure package.

The service configuration file specifies the number of instances of each role. It also specifies the values of any custom configuration settings as well as those for any pluggable modules imported in the service definition file.

Applications developed using the .NET framework typically store application configuration settings in an `app.config` or `web.config` file. However, in Cloud Services, we can mix several applications (roles), so a uniform and central point of configuration is needed. Runtime code can still use these files; however, changes to these files require the redeployment of the entire service package. Microsoft Azure allows custom configuration settings to be specified in the service configuration file where they can be modified without redeploying the application. Any service configuration setting that could be changed while the Cloud Service is running should be stored in the service configuration file. These custom configuration settings must be declared in the service definition file:

```
<ConfigurationSettings>
  <Setting name="MySetting" />
</ConfigurationSettings>
```

The Microsoft Azure SDK provides a `RoleEnvironment.GetConfigurationSetting()` method that can be used to access the values of custom configuration settings. There is also `CloudConfigurationManager.GetSetting()` of the `Microsoft.WindowsAzure.Configuration` assembly that checks in-service configuration first, and if no Azure environment is found, it goes to the local configuration file.

The service configuration file is uploaded separately from the Microsoft Azure package and can be modified independently of it. Changes to the service configuration file can be implemented either directly on the Microsoft Azure Portal or by upgrading the Cloud Service. The service configuration can also be upgraded using the Microsoft Azure Service Management REST API.

The customization of the service configuration file is limited almost to the role instance count, the actual values of the settings, and the certificate thumbprints:

```
<Role name="WorkerHelloWorld">
  <Instances count="2" />
  <ConfigurationSettings>
    <Setting name="MySetting" value="Value" />
  </ConfigurationSettings>
  <Certificates>
    <Certificate name="CertificateForSSL"
       thumbprint="D3E008E45ADCC328CE6BE2AB9AACE2D13F294838"
       thumbprintAlgorithm="sha1" />
  </Certificates>
</Role>
```

The handling of service upgrades is described in the *Managing upgrades and changes to a Cloud Service* and *Handling changes to the configuration and topology of a Cloud Service* recipes.

In this recipe, we'll learn how to configure the service model for a sample application.

Getting ready

To use this recipe, we need to have created a Microsoft Azure Cloud Service and deployed an application to it, as described in the *Publishing a Cloud Service with options from Visual Studio* recipe.

How to do it...

We are going to see how to implement a real service definition file, based on the following scenario, taken from the WAHelloWorld sample. Suppose we have a Cloud Service with two roles (a web role and a worker one). The web role has a medium instance size; it uses the Diagnostics module, has a local storage of 10 GB, has two public endpoints (one at port 80 and another at port 8080), and has a setting value. The worker role is small, and it has an input endpoint to let the various instances communicate together.

For the web role, we proceed as follows:

1. Open the `ServiceDefinition.csdef` file in Visual Studio.

2. Inside the `<ServiceDefinition>` root element, create a `<WebRole>` item:

    ```
    <WebRole name="WebHelloWorld" vmsize="Medium"></WebRole>
    ```

3. Inside the `WebRole` tag just created, add an `<Endpoints>` tag with two `InputEndpoint` tags, one for each public endpoint:

    ```
    <Endpoints>
      <InputEndpoint name="Endpoint1" protocol="http" port="80"
        />
      <InputEndpoint name="Endpoint2" protocol="http"
        port="8080" />
    </Endpoints>
    ```

4. Inside the `WebRole` tag, create a `Sites` element with the correct binding to the web application in the solution:

    ```
    <Sites>
      <Site name="Web">
        <Bindings>
          <Binding name="Endpoint1" endpointName="Endpoint1" />
          <Binding name="Endpoint2" endpointName="Endpoint2" />
        </Bindings>
      </Site>
    </Sites>
    ```

5. Inside the `WebRole` tag, declare the usage of the `Diagnostics` module:

    ```
    <Imports>
      <Import moduleName="Diagnostics" />
    </Imports>
    ```

6. Inside the `WebRole` tag, declare a local storage element of 10 GB:

```
<LocalResources>
  <LocalStorage name="MyStorage" cleanOnRoleRecycle="true"
    sizeInMB="10240" />
</LocalResources>
```

7. Finally, declare the `Settings` section and a setting inside the `WebRole` tag:

```
<ConfigurationSettings>
  <Setting name="MySetting" />
</ConfigurationSettings>
```

Worker role.

8. Create a `WorkerRole` section like the following:

```
<WorkerRole name="WorkerHelloWorld" vmsize="Small"> ...
```

9. Declare `InternalEndpoint` inside a new `Endpoints` section:

```
<Endpoints>
  <InternalEndpoint name="Internal" protocol="tcp" />
</Endpoints>
```

10. In the corresponding `ServiceConfiguration.cscfg` file, configure the instance count as follows:

```
<Role name="WebHelloWorld">
  <Instances count="1" />
</Role>
<Role name="WorkerHelloWorld">
  <Instances count="2" />
</Role>
```

11. Provide a value called `MySetting` for the configuration setting :

```
<ConfigurationSettings>
  <Setting name="MySetting" value="Test"/>
</ConfigurationSettings>
```

12. Save the file, and check the **Visual Studio Error List** window to solve any errors.

How it works...

In step 2, we put an XML tag to declare a `WebRole` tag. The name of the `WebRole` tag must be the name of a valid web application project inside the solution that contains the cloud project itself. In the `WebRole` tag, we also specify the instance size, choosing among the ones in the following table (there are more sizes available actually):

Size	CPU	Memory
ExtraSmall	Shared	768 MB
Small	1	1.75 GB
Medium	2	3.5 GB
Large	4	7 GB
ExtraLarge	8	14 GB
A5	2	14 GB
A6	4	28 GB
A7	8	56 GB

In step 3, we declared two HTTP-based endpoints on ports `80` and `8080`, respectively. Intend this configuration as a load balancer firewall/forward configuration. Saying "There's an endpoint" does not mean there is a real service under the hood, which replies to the request made to the endpoints (except for the default one on port `80`).

In step 4, we bound the WebHelloWorld web application to both the endpoints declared earlier. It is also possible to specify additional configurations regarding virtual directories and virtual applications.

In step 5, we simply told Azure to inject the Diagnostics module into the VM that runs our service. As said earlier, other modules can be injected here.

In step 6, we told Azure to allocate an amount of 10 GB of space on a folder located somewhere on the virtual machine. As this folder will be accessed through an API, it doesn't matter where it's located. What we have to know is the meaning of the `cleanOnRoleRecycle` attribute. If it is true, we agree that isolated storage won't be retained across role recycles; if it is false, we ask it to preserve the data (if possible) instead.

In step 7, we declared the presence of a setting value but not the setting value itself, which is shown instead in the service configuration in step 11.

In step 8, we repeated the process for the worker role, but as it does not run IIS, we don't declare any sites. Instead, due to the initial goal, we declare an internal endpoint. In step 9 in fact, we said that the VM will have an open TCP port. It will be our code's responsibility to actually bind a service to this port.

> In the `InternalEndpoint` tag, we can specify a fixed port number. In the example given earlier, there is no port so that Azure can decide which port to allocate. We can use the `ServiceRuntime` API as the local storage to find out the information at runtime.

Finally, we populate the service configuration with the actual values for the parameters specified in the service definition. One of these is the instance count (for both the roles) and the configuration setting value for the web role.

There's more...

Is there more to the service definition document? First, for example, the capability to influence the update process of our services/roles/instances. Let's introduce the concepts of fault domain and update domain. Microsoft Azure assures that if two or more instances are deployed, it will put them onto an isolated hardware to reduce as much as it can the possibility of a downtime due to a failure. This concept is also known as Fault Domain, as Azure creates instances in separate areas to increase the availability. Therefore, an Update Domain is about how Azure manages the update flow on our instances, taking them offline one by one or group by group to reduce, again, the possibility of a downtime. Think about Upgrade Domain as groups of instances, which have the default value of 5. This means that if five or fewer instances are deployed, they will be updated one by one. If there are more than five instances, the default behavior makes five groups and updates the instances of a group altogether.

> It is not always necessary to update instances one by one, or it is often not feasible to update the system in parts. Despite the occurrence of a downtime, systems often bring online new databases and new logic that modify actual data. Bringing new instances online one by one could lead to the same time coexisting on a different version of data/code that runs on the system. In this case, a simultaneous upgrade as well as the related downtime should be taken into consideration. During development, it is advisable to keep a single instance deployed, to save time during upgrades; however, during testing, it is recommended that you scale out and verify that the application is behaving correctly.

We can suggest a different value for Azure for the Upgrade Domain behavior; we can suggest up to a value of 20. The higher the value, the lower the impact of the upgrade on the entire infrastructure:

```
<ServiceDefinition name="WAHelloWorld" upgradeDomainCount="20"...
```

 Consider letting Azure decide about the Upgrade Domains due to the nature of the PaaS in the event of a breaking change happening to the platform in the future. Designing a workflow based on an Azure constraint is not recommended. Instead, design your update to be resilient without telling Azure anything.

Finally, instances will know about the change that occurred in the topology (upgrades and configuration) that walks the upgrade domains. This means that the instances will know about the change one by one, only when it is their respective turn to change. This is the default behavior.

See also

▶ There is more information on topology changes in the *Handling changes to the configuration and topology of a Cloud Service* recipe

▶ The complete reference to the Service Definition schema at `http://msdn.microsoft.com/en-us/library/ee758711.aspx`

Providing a custom domain name for a Cloud Service

A Cloud Service can expose an input endpoint to the Internet. This endpoint has a load balanced **Virtual IP** (**VIP**) address, which, for the time being, could change at each deployment.

Each VIP has an associated domain of the `[servicednsprefix].cloudapp.net` form. The `servicednsprefix` name is specified when the Cloud Service is created, and it is not changeable following the creation. A Cloud Service might be reached over the Internet at `servicednsprefix.cloudapp.net`. All Cloud Services exist under the `cloudapp.net` domain.

The DNS system supports a CNAME record that maps one domain to another. This allows, for example, `www.servicename.com` to be mapped to `servicednsprefix.cloudapp.net`. The DNS system also supports an A record that maps a domain to a fixed IP address. Unfortunately, reliable use of an A record is not recommended with a Cloud Service, because the IP address can change if the Cloud Service is deleted and redeployed.

It is not possible to acquire a public key certificate for the `cloudapp.net` domain as Microsoft controls it. Consequently, a CNAME is needed to map a custom domain to a `cloudapp.net` domain when HTTPS is used. We will see how to do this in the *Implementing HTTPS in a web role* recipe. In this recipe, we'll learn how to use CNAME to map a custom domain to a Cloud Service domain.

Getting ready

To use this recipe we need to control a custom domain (for example, `customdomain.com`) and must have created a Cloud Service (for example, `theservice.cloudapp.net`).

How to do it...

We are going to see how to use CNAME to map a custom domain to a Cloud Service using the following steps:

1. Go to the dashboard of your DNS provider.
2. On the CNAME management page of your DNS provider, add a new CNAME that maps `www.customdomain.com` to `theservice.cloudapp.net`.
3. If your DNS provider supports the domain-forwarding feature, forward `customdomain.com` to `www.customdomain.com`.
4. Wait for some time as the propagation of the DNS is recorded all around the world.

How it works...

In step 1, we navigated to the dashboard of the DNS service. Each DNS service operates on its own, so the interface might vary a lot from one vendor to another. In step 2, we told the DNS to forward the DNS request to `theservice.cloudapp.net` if the DNS `www.customdomain.com` is requested. In turn, when the Azure DNS is being requested from a remote client with the `theservice.cloudapp.net` record, it returns the actual IP address of the load balancer of the Cloud Service.

Finally, in step 3, we configured (if possible) forwarding so that the `customdomain.com` root/naked name is forwarded automatically to `www.customdomain.com`.

A DNS change could take from a few minutes to a few days, depending on the service provider. Expect the average time to wait until the DNS comes online to be about few hours.

There's more...

Sometimes (we read it as always), it is necessary to test the development environment while calling the production URL into the browser. This is possible by locally mapping (on the development workstation) the domain name to the loopback IP address.

The equivalent of a CNAME mapping in the development environment is a `hosts` file entry that maps `servicename.com` to `127.0.0.1`. The `hosts` file is located in the `%SystemRoot%\system32\drivers\etc` folder. For example, adding the following entry to the `hosts` file maps `servicename.com` to `127.0.0.1`:

```
127.0.0.1  servicename.com
```

Note that we need to remember to remove this entry from the `hosts` file on the development machine after the application is deployed to the Microsoft Azure data center. Otherwise, we will not be able to access the real `servicename.com` domain from the development machine.

We can also map the remote Azure service with this technique as follows:

1. Discover the current IP address of the service by pinging it:

    ping theservice.cloudapp.net

2. Add a line into the `hosts` file that maps the IP just discovered to the domain name.

Implementing HTTPS in a web role

A Microsoft Azure web role can be configured to expose an HTTPS endpoint for a website. This requires an X.509 public key certificate to be uploaded as a service certificate to the Cloud Service and the web role to be configured to use it.

The following steps are used to implement HTTPS for a web role:

▶ Acquire a public key certificate for the custom domain of the web role

▶ Upload the certificate to the Cloud Service

▶ Add the certificate to the web role configuration

▶ Configure the website endpoint to use the certificate

The use of HTTPS requires the website to be configured to use a public key certificate. It is not possible to acquire a public key certificate for the `cloudapp.net` domain as Microsoft owns this domain. Consequently, a custom domain must be used when exposing an HTTPS endpoint. The *Providing a custom domain name for a Cloud Service* recipe shows how to map a custom domain to the `cloudapp.net` domain. For production use, a **Certification Authority (CA)** should issue the certificate to ensure that its root certificate is widely available. For test purposes, a self-signed certificate is sufficient.

The certificate must be uploaded to the Cloud Service using either the Microsoft Azure Portal or the Microsoft Azure Service Management REST API. Note that this upload is to the **Certificates** section for the Cloud Service and not to the **Management Certificates** section for the Microsoft Azure subscription. As a service certificate must contain both public and private keys, it is uploaded as a password-protected PFX file.

The configuration for the certificate is split between the service definition file, `ServiceDefinition.csdef`, and the service configuration file, `ServiceConfiguration.cscfg`. The logical definition and deployment location of the certificate is specified in the service definition file. The thumbprint of the actual certificate is specified in the service configuration file so that the certificate can be renewed or replaced without redeploying the Cloud Service. In both cases, for each web role, there is a hierarchy that comprises a `Certificates` child to the `WebRole` element, which, in turn, includes a set of one or more `Certificate` elements, each referring to a specific certificate.

In this recipe, we'll learn how to implement HTTPS in a web role.

How to do it...

We are going to see how to implement an HTTPS endpoint in a web role only on the `443` port, using a test (self-signed) certificate.

The first stage is creating a test certificate and uploading it to the Cloud Service using the following steps:

1. Use the **Server Certificates** section of IIS 8 to create a self-signed certificate and give it a friendly name of `www.myservice.com`.

> Though IIS is not the purpose of this book, remember to click on the **Create Self-Signed Certificate** link on the right-hand side pane, type the name in the friendly name textbox, and choose the store (**Personal** is the default one).

2. Open the **Microsoft Management** console by typing `mmc` in the **Run** windows of the **Start** menu, and use the certificate snap-in, specifying the local machine level.

3. In the **Personal/Certificates** branch, right-click on the certificate with the friendly name of `www.myservice.com` and navigate to **All Tasks | Export** to open the **Certificate Export Wizard**.

4. Complete the wizard by choosing to export the private key (and otherwise accepting default values) and providing a password and a location for the PFX file.

5. On the Microsoft Azure Portal, select the **Certificates** section for the Cloud Service and click on **Add certificate**.

6. Upload the public key certificate by providing the location for the PFX file and its password.

The next stage is configuring a Cloud Service to use the certificate. We can do this by performing the following steps:

1. Use Visual Studio to create an empty cloud project.

2. Add a web role to the project (accept the default name of **WebRole1**).

3. Right-click on the **WebRole1** item under the `Roles` folder of the cloud project; then go to the **Properties** page and click on the **Certificates** tab.

4. Click on **Add Certificate**, provide a name, select a **Store Location**, and a **Store Name**.

 For certificates at machine level in the personal store, choose `LocalMachine` and `My` for the **Store Location** and **Store Name**, respectively.

5. Click on the **...** icon to browse the store and look for the `www.myservice.com` certificate. Then confirm it.

6. Go to the **Endpoints** tab of the **Properties** page you are on.

7. Modify `Endpoint1` (the default one) to listen on port `443`.

8. Choose **https** as the protocol.

9. Specify the certificate declared at step 4 in the **SSL Certificate Name**.

10. Build the application and deploy it into the Cloud Service.

 The final stage is verifying that we can use HTTPS.

11. Use a browser to access the web role using HTTPS.

12. Choose to ignore the certificate error caused by our use of a test certificate, and view the certificate.

How it works...

From steps 1 to 6, we created and uploaded our test certificate. We need to export the certificate as a password-protected PFX file so that it contains both the public and private keys for the certificate.

In steps 7 and 8, we created a cloud project with a web role.

From steps 9 to 11, we specified the linkage between web role bindings and the certificate. In step 10, we specified the certificate store on each instance into which the Azure fabric deploys the certificate.

In step 13, we modified the default endpoint to listen as an HTTPS endpoint, using the certificate, on port 443. In step 15, we specified the certificate to the endpoint.

In step 16, we built the application and deployed it into the Cloud Service. We verified that we could use HTTPS in steps 17 and 18. We are using a test certificate for which there is no root certificate in the browser. This consequently causes the browser to issue a warning. For demonstration purposes, we ignored the error and looked at the certificate properties to confirm that it was the test certificate.

There's more...

We can use IIS to generate a **Certificate Signing Request** (**CSR**), which we can send to a CA. We do this by opening the **Server Certificates** section of IIS and clicking on **Create Certificate Request**. When generating the request, we specify the fully qualified domain name for the custom domain, for example, www.ourcustomdomain.com, in the **Common Name** field. After the CA issues the certificate, we click on the **Complete Certificate Request in the Server Certificates** section of IIS to import the certificate into the personal certificate store of the local machine level.

From there, we can upload and deploy the CA-issued certificate by starting at step 2 of the recipe.

Using makecert to create a test certificate

We can invoke the makecert command from the Visual Studio command prompt, as follows, to create a test certificate and install it in the personal branch of the local machine level of the certificate store:

```
C:\Users\Administrator>makecert -r -pe -sky exchange
-a sha1 -len 2048 -sr localmachine -ss my
-n "CN=www.ourservice.com"
```

The minimum required bit length for Azure is 2048, and this test certificate has a subject name of www.ourservice.com.

Using local storage in an instance

The Microsoft Azure Fabric Controller deploys an instance of a Microsoft Azure role onto a virtual machine (VM) as three **Virtual Hard Disks** (**VHD**). The guest OS image is deployed to the D drive, the role image is deployed to the E or F drive, while the C drive contains the service configuration and the local storage available to the instance. Only code running with elevated privileges can write anywhere other than the local storage.

> As Azure could change the way it manages the underlying operating system of Cloud Services, the information provided about filesystem topology could change suddenly with no obligation from Microsoft to explain it.

Each instance has read-write access to a reserved space on the C drive. The amount of space available depends on the instance size and ranges from 20 GB for an Extra Small instance to 2,040 GB for an Extra Large instance. This storage space is reserved by being specified in the service definition file, `ServiceDefinition.csdef`, for the service. Note that `RoleEnvironment.GetLocalResource()` should be invoked to retrieve the actual path to local storage.

The `LocalStorage` element for a role in the service definition file requires a name (`Name`) and, optionally, the size in megabytes to be reserved (`sizeInMb`). It also requires an indication of whether the local storage should be preserved when the role is recycled (`cleanOnRoleRecycle`). This indication is only advisory, as the local storage is not copied if an instance is moved to a new VM.

Multiple local storage resources can be specified for a role as long as the total space allocated is less than the maximum amount available.

> In fact, the purpose of the allocated space is just an upper-bound limit, as an exception is thrown only when a write operation actually exceeds the allowed maximum.

This allows different storage resources to be reserved for different purposes. Storage resources are identified by name.

The `RoleEnvironment.GetLocalResource()` method can be invoked to retrieve the root path for a local resource with a specific name. The role instance can invoke arbitrary file and directory-management methods under this path.

In this recipe, we'll learn how to configure and use local storage in an instance.

How to do it...

We are going to access the local storage on an instance and create a file on it. We will write to the file and then read the contents from the file. We will do this using the following steps:

1. Use Visual Studio to create an empty cloud project.

2. Add a worker role to the project (accept the default name of `WorkerRole1`).

3. Right-click on the **WorkerRole1** item under the **Roles** folder of the cloud project. Then, go to the **Properties** page and click on the **Local Storage** tab.

4. Click on **Add Local Storage** and set **Name** as `WorkerStorage`, a size of `10 MB`, and leave the **Clean on role recycle** box unchecked.

5. Add a new class named `LocalStorageExample` to the project:

6. Add the following `using` statements to the top of the class file:

```
using Microsoft.WindowsAzure.ServiceRuntime;
using System.IO;
```

7. Add the following private members to the class:

```
static String storageName = "WorkerStorage";
String fileName;
LocalResource localResource =
    RoleEnvironment.GetLocalResource(storageName);
```

8. Add the following constructor to the class:

```
public LocalStorageExample(String fileName)
{
   this.fileName = fileName;
}
```

9. Add the following method, which writes to the local storage, to the class:

```
public void WriteToLocalStorage()
{
   String path = Path.Combine(
       localResource.RootPath, fileName);

   FileStream writeFileStream = File.Create(path);
   using ( StreamWriter streamWriter =
       new StreamWriter( writeFileStream))
   {
      streamWriter.Write("think but this and all is mended");
   }
}
```

10. Add the following method, which reads the file, to the class:

```
public void ReadFromLocalStorage()
{
    String fileContent = string.Empty;
    String path = Path.Combine(
        localResource.RootPath, fileName);
    FileStream readFileStream = File.Open(path, FileMode.Open);
    using (StreamReader streamReader =
        new StreamReader(readFileStream))
    {
        fileContent = streamReader.ReadToEnd();
    }
}
```

11. Add the following method, using the methods added earlier, to the class:

```
public static void UseLocalStorageExample()
{
    String fileName = "WorkerRoleStorage.txt";

    LocalStorageExample example =
        new LocalStorageExample(fileName);
    example.WriteToLocalStorage();
    example.ReadFromLocalStorage();
}
```

12. Add the following code at the start of the `Run()` method in `WorkerRole.cs`:

```
LocalStorageExample.UseLocalStorageExample();
```

How it works...

In steps 1 and 2, we created a cloud project with a worker role.

In step 3, we used the GUI to locate the local storage section of the project properties. In step 4, we added the definition of the local storage to the service definition file for the Cloud Service. We provided a name by which it can be referenced and a size. We also specified that the content of local storage should be preserved through an instance recycle.

In steps 5 and 6, we set up the `LocalStorageExample` class. In step 7, we added some private members to store the filename and the local storage resource. We initialized the filename in the constructor that we added in step 8.

In step 9, we added a method that created a file and added some text to it. In step 10, we opened the file and read the text.

In step 11, we added a method that invoked the other methods in the class. In step 12, we invoked this method.

See also

Have a look at the following MSDN link to get additional information:

▸ Additional details about local storage behavior and process model at `http://msdn.microsoft.com/en-us/library/azure/ee758708.aspx`

Hosting multiple websites in a web role

Microsoft released Microsoft Azure as a production service in February 2010. A common complaint was that it was too expensive to develop small websites because a web role could support only a single website. The cause of this limitation was that a web role hosted a website using a hosted web core rather than the full IIS.

With the Microsoft Azure SDK v1.3 release, Microsoft Azure added support for full IIS for web roles. This means that a single web role can host multiple websites. However, all of these websites share the same Virtual IP address, and a CNAME record must be used to map the domain name of the website to the `servicename.cloudapp.net` URL for the web role. Each website is then distinguished inside IIS by its distinct host header.

The *Providing a custom domain name for a Cloud Service* recipe shows how to use a CNAME record to map a custom domain to a Cloud Service domain. Note that full IIS is also available on worker roles.

The approach described in this recipe, as it is still valid, is probably not the best you can do with Azure. If you need to host multiple websites in a single role (and in a single unit of scale), the Microsoft Azure Websites could be the best solution to accomplish this. We will talk about Websites in a dedicated chapter, and it is the newest and probably the most advanced PaaS on the market.

The `Sites` element in the `ServiceDefinition.csdef` service definition file is used to configure multiple websites. This element contains one child `Site` element for each website hosted by the web role. Each `Site` element has two attributes: name, which distinguishes the configuration, and `physicalDirectory`, which specifies the physical directory for the website. Note that multiple websites can reference the same physical directory. Each `Site` element has a `Bindings` child element that contains a set of `Binding` child elements, each of which identifies an endpoint used by the website and the host header used to distinguish the website. Each endpoint must correspond to an input endpoint specified in the `EndPoints` declaration for the web role. It is possible to define virtual applications and virtual directories for a website, using the `VirtualApplication` and `VirtualDirectory` elements, respectively. This configuration is a subset of the standard IIS configuration.

The following example shows a fragment of a service definition file for a web role that hosts two websites:

```xml
<WebRole name="MultipleWebsites">
  <Sites>
    <Site name="WebsiteOne" physicalDirectory="..\Web">
      <Bindings>
        <Binding name="HttpIn" endpointName="HttpIn"
              hostHeader="www.websiteone.com" />
      </Bindings>
    </Site>
    <Site name="WebsiteTwo" physicalDirectory="..\Web">
      <VirtualApplication name="Payment"
              physicalDirectory="..\..\Payment">
        <VirtualDirectory name="Scripts"
              physicalDirectory="..\Web\Scripts" />
      </VirtualApplication>
      <Bindings>
        <Binding name="HttpIn" endpointName="HttpIn"
            hostHeader="www.websitetwo.com" />
        <Binding name="HttpsIn" endpointName="HttpsIn"
            hostHeader="www.websitetwo.com" />
      </Bindings>
    </Site>
  </Sites>
  <Endpoints>
    <InputEndpoint name="HttpIn" protocol="http"
        port="80" />
    <InputEndpoint name="HttpsIn" protocol="https"
        port="443" />
  </Endpoints>
  <ConfigurationSettings />
</WebRole>
```

This configuration specifies that the web role hosts two websites: www.websiteone.com and www.websitetwo.com. They share the same physical directory, but www.websitetwo.com also uses a virtual application with its own virtual directory. Both websites are accessible using HTTP, but www.websitetwo.com also exposes an HTTPS endpoint.

In this recipe, we'll learn how to host multiple websites in a single Microsoft Azure web role.

How to do it...

We are going to see how to implement the two websites in a Cloud Service. We do this as follows:

1. Use Visual Studio to create an empty cloud project.

2. Add a web role to the project (accept the default name of `WebRole1`).

The changes from steps 3 to 8 affect the `ServiceDefinition.csdef` service definition file:

1. Set the `name` attribute of the `Site` element to `WebSiteOne`.

2. Add a `physicalDirectory` attribute, with the `"..\..\..\WebRole1"` value, to the `Site` element.

3. Add a `hostHeader` attribute, with the `www.websiteone.com` value, to the `Binding` element for the `Site` element.

4. Copy the entire `Site` element and paste it under itself.

5. Change the `name` attribute of the new `Site` element to `WebsiteTwo`.

6. Change the `hostHeader` attribute of the new `Site` element to `www.websitetwo.com`.

7. Add the following entries to the `hosts` file present in the `%SystemRoot%\system32\drivers\etc` folder:

   ```
   127.0.0.1    www.websiteone.com
   127.0.0.1    www.websitetwo.com
   ```

8. Build and run the Cloud Service.

9. Change the URL in the browser to `www.websiteone.com`, and refresh the browser.

10. Change the URL in the browser to `www.websitetwo.com`, and refresh the browser.

How it works...

On completing the steps, the `WebRole` element in the `ServiceDefinition.csdef` file should be as follows:

```
<WebRole name="WebRole1">
  <Sites>
    <Site name="WebsiteOne" physicalDirectory="..\..\..\WebRole1">
      <Bindings>
        <Binding name="Endpoint1" endpointName="Endpoint1"
            hostHeader="www.websiteone.com"/>
      </Bindings>
```

```
  </Site>
  <Site name="WebsiteTwo" physicalDirectory="..\..\..\WebRole1">
    <Bindings>
      <Binding name="Endpoint1" endpointName="Endpoint1"
            hostHeader="www.websitetwo.com"/>
    </Bindings>
  </Site>
</Sites>
<Endpoints>
  <InputEndpoint name="Endpoint1"
      protocol="http" port="80" />
</Endpoints>
<Imports>
  <Import moduleName="Diagnostics" />
</Imports>
</WebRole>
```

In steps 1 and 2, we created a Cloud project with a web role.

In steps 3 and 4, we configured the `Site` element for the first website. In step 3, we provide a distinct name for the element, and in step 4, we specified the physical directory for the website.

In step 5, we configured the `Binding` element for the `Site` element by specifying the host header we use to distinguish the website.

In step 6, we created the `Site` element for the second website. In steps 7 and 8, we completed the configuration of the second website by providing a name for its configuration and specifying the host header we use to distinguish the website. Note that in this example, we used the same physical directory for both websites.

In step 9, we modified the `hosts` file so that we can use the configured host headers as URLs.

We built and ran the Cloud Service in step 10. We will encounter an error in the browser as there is no default website at `127.0.0.1:81` (or whichever port the Microsoft Azure Compute Emulator has assigned to the Cloud Service). In steps 11 and 12, we confirmed this by replacing `127.0.0.1` in the browser URL with the URLs we configured as host headers for the two websites.

 Note that although we only created two websites in this example, we could have configured additional websites.

There's more...

When we use this Cloud Service, we must use CNAME records to map the two domains to the `ourservice.cloudapp.net` URL of our Cloud Service. Just as we cannot access the Cloud Service locally at `127.0.0.1`, we cannot access the Cloud Service at `ourservice.cloudapp.net`. We will see how to use CNAME to do this mapping in the *Providing a custom domain name for a Cloud Service* recipe.

See also

Have a look at the following MSDN links and blog posts to get additional information:

> ▸ Further information about hosting multiple websites in a web role at `http://msdn.microsoft.com/en-us/library/azure/ee758708.aspx`

> ▸ Blog post about custom build and CSPACK usage for advanced scenarios at `http://michaelcollier.wordpress.com/2013/01/14/multiple-sites-in-a-web-role/`

Using startup tasks in a Microsoft Azure role

Microsoft Azure provides a locked-down environment for websites hosted in IIS (web roles) and application services (worker roles). While this hardening significantly eases administration, it also limits the ability to perform certain tasks such as installing software or writing to the registry. Another problem is that any changes to an instance are lost whenever the instance is reimaged or moved to a different server.

The service definition provides the solution to this problem by allowing the creation of startup tasks, which are script files or executable programs that are invoked each time an instance is started. Startup tasks allow a temporary escape from the restrictions of the locked-down web role and worker role while retaining the benefits of these roles.

A startup task must be robust against errors because a failure could cause the instance to recycle. In particular, the effect of a startup task must be idempotent. As a startup task is invoked each time an instance starts, it must not fail when performed repeatedly. For example, when a startup task is used to install software, any subsequent attempt to reinstall the software must be handled gracefully.

Startup tasks are specified with the `Startup` element in the `ServiceDefinition.csdef` service definition file. This is a child element of the `WebRole` or `WorkerRole` element. The child elements in the `Startup` element comprise a sequence of one or more individual `Task` elements, each specifying a single startup task. The following example shows the definition of a single startup task and includes all the attributes for a `Task` element:

```
<Startup>
  <Task
      commandLine="Startup.cmd"
      executionContext="elevated"
      taskType="simple" />
</Startup>
```

The `commandLine` attribute specifies a script or executable and its location relative to the `%RoleRoot%\AppRoot\bin` folder for the role. The `executionContext` element takes one of two values: `limited`, to indicate the startup task runs with the same privileges as the role, or `elevated`, to indicate the startup task runs with full administrator privileges. It is the capability provided by elevated startup tasks that gives them their power. There are three types of startup tasks, which are as follows:

▶ **Simple**: This indicates that the system cannot invoke additional startup tasks until this one completes.

▶ **Background**: This initiates the startup task in the background. This is useful in the case of a long-running task, the delay in which could cause the instance to appear unresponsive.

▶ **Foreground**: This resembles a background startup task, except that the instance cannot be recycled until the startup task completes. This can cause problems if something goes wrong with the startup task.

Windows PowerShell 2 is installed on Microsoft Azure roles that run guest OS 2.x or higher. This provides a powerful scripting language that is ideal for scripting startup tasks.

The guest OS is the nickname for the version set of Windows Server that runs Azure instances. For the time being, we have four guest OS families:

▶ Guest OS family 4, which is based on Windows Server 2012 R2 and supports the .NET Framework 4.0, 4.5, and 4.5.1.

▶ Guest OS family 3, which is based on Windows Server 2012 and supports the .NET Framework 4.0 and 4.5.

▶ Guest OS family 2, which is based on Windows Server 2008 SP1 and supports the .NET Framework 3.5 and 4.0.

▶ Guest OS family 1 (retired in 2014), which is based on Windows Server 2008 SP2 and supports the .NET Framework 3.5 and 4.0. It does not support Version 4.5 or later.

A PowerShell script named `StartupTask.ps1` is invoked from the startup task command file as follows:

```
C:\Users\Administrator>PowerShell -ExecutionPolicy Unrestricted .\
StartupTask.ps1
```

The `ExecutionPolicy` parameter specifies that `StartupTask.ps1` can be invoked even though it is unsigned.

In startup tasks, we can use `AppCmd` to manage IIS. We can also use the `WebPICmdLine` command-line tool, `WebPICmdLine.exe`, to access the functionality of the Microsoft Web Platform Installer. This allows us to install Microsoft Web Platform components, which includes, for example, PHP.

How to do it...

We are going to use a startup task that uses `AppCmd` to modify the default idle timeout for IIS application pools. We will do this using the following steps:

1. Use Visual Studio to create an empty cloud project.

2. Add a web role to the project (accept the default name of `WebRole1`).

3. Add the `StartupTask.cmd` text file name to the root directory of the web role project.

4. Set its **Copy To Output Directory** property to **Copy always**.

5. Insert the following text in the ASCII-encoded file:

   ```
   %SystemRoot%\system32\inetsrv\appcmd
   set config -section:applicationPools
   -applicationPoolDefaults.processModel.idleTimeout:0.01:00:00
   exit /b 0
   ```

 If the "exit /b 0" clause is not provided, the role will enter a continuous recycle state.

6. Add the following, as a child of the `WebRole` element, to `ServiceDefinition.csdef`:

   ```
   <Startup>
     <Task commandLine="StartupTask.cmd"
         executionContext="elevated" taskType="simple"/>
   </Startup>
   ```

7. Build and deploy the application into the Cloud Service.

8. Open IIS Manager, select **Application Pools**, right-click on any application pool, and select **Advanced Settings...**. Verify that the **Idle Timeout** (minutes) setting is 60 minutes for the application pool.

How it works...

In steps 1 and 2, we created a cloud project with a web role. In steps 3 and 4, we added the command file for the startup task to the project and ensured that the build copied the file to the appropriate location in the Microsoft Azure package. In step 5, we added a command to the file that set the idle timeout to 1 hour for IIS application pools. The exit command ended the batch file with a return code of 0.

In step 6, we added the startup task to the service definition file. We set the execution context of the startup task to elevated so that it had the privilege required to modify IIS settings.

In step 7, we built and deployed the application into a Cloud Service. We verified that the startup task worked in step 8.

There's more...

Note that the web or worker role itself can run with elevated privileges. In a web role, full IIS runs its own process that continues to have limited privileges; only the role-entry code (in WebRole.cs) runs with elevated privileges. This privilege elevation is achieved by adding the following as a child element of the WebRole or WorkerRole element in the ServiceDefinition.csdef service definition file:

```
<Runtime executionContext="elevated"/>
```

The default value for executionContext is limited.

Having done this, we can set the application pool idle timeout in code by invoking the following from the OnStart() method for the web role:

```
private void SetIdleTimeout(TimeSpan timeout)
{
   using (ServerManager serverManager = new ServerManager())
   {
     serverManager.ApplicationPoolDefaults.ProcessModel.IdleTimeout =
timeout;
     serverManager.CommitChanges();
   }
}
```

The ServerManager class is in the Microsoft.Web.Administrator namespace, which is contained in the following assembly: %SystemRoot%\System32\inetsrv\Microsoft.Web.Administration.dll.

Developing startup tasks

When developing startup tasks, it can be useful to log the output of commands to a known location for further analysis. When using the development environment, another trick is to set the startup task script to the following code:

```
start /wait cmd
```

This produces a command window in which we can invoke the desired startup command and see any errors or log them with the DOS redirect (">>"). The /wait switch blocks the caller until the prompt completes.

See also

Have a look at the following MSDN link to get additional information:

▸ Best practices for startup tasks (http://msdn.microsoft.com/en-us/library/jj129545.aspx)

Handling changes to the configuration and topology of a Cloud Service

A Microsoft Azure Cloud Service has to detect and respond to changes to its service configuration. Two types of changes are exposed to the service: changes to the ConfigurationSettings element of the ServiceConfiguration.cscfg service configuration file and changes to the service topology. The latter refers to changes in the number of instances of the various roles that comprise the service.

The RoleEnvironment class exposes six events to which a role can register a callback method to be notified about these changes:

▸ Changing

▸ Changed

▸ SimultaneousChanging

▸ SimultaneousChanged

▸ Stopping

▸ StatusCheck

The Changing event is raised before the change is applied to the role. For configuration setting changes, the RoleEnvironmentChangingEventArgs parameter to the callback method identifies the existing value of any configuration setting being changed. For a service topology change, the argument specifies the names of any roles whose instance count is changing. The RoleEnvironmentChangingEventArgs parameter has a Cancel property that can be set to true to recycle an instance in response to specific configuration setting or topology changes.

The `Changed` event is raised after the change is applied to the role. As for the previous event, for configuration setting changes, the `RoleEnvironmentChangedEventArgs` parameter to the callback method identifies the new value of any changed configuration setting. For a service topology change, the argument specifies the names of any roles whose instance count has changed. Note that the `Changed` event is not raised on any instance recycled in the `Changing` event.

The `SimulteneousChanging` and `SimultaneousChanged` events behave exactly like the `normal` events, but they are called only during a simultaneous update.

> These events fire only if we have the `topologyChangeDiscovery` attribute to `Blast` in service definition file, for example, `<ServiceDefinition name="WAHelloWorld" topologyChangeDiscovery="Blast>` as mentioned in the *Configuring the service model for a Cloud Service* recipe. These events cannot be canceled, and the role will not restart when these events are received. This is to prevent all roles from recycling at the same time.

We will talk about this kind of update in the *Publishing a Cloud Service with options from Visual Studio* recipe.

The `Stopping` event is raised on an instance being stopped. The `OnStop()` method is also invoked. Either of them can be used to implement an orderly shutdown of the instance. However, this must completed within 5 minutes. In a web role, the `Application_End()` method is invoked before the `Stopping` event is raised and the `OnStop()` method is invoked. It can also be used for shutdown code.

> Microsoft Azure takes the instance out of the rotation of the load balancer, and then, it fires the stopping event. This ensures that no shutdown code can execute while legal requests are coming from the Internet.

The `StatusCheck` event is raised every 15 seconds. The `RoleInstanceStatusCheckEventArgs` parameter to the callback method for this event specifies the status of the instance as either `Ready` or `Busy`. The callback method can respond to the `StatusCheck` event by invoking the `SetBusy()` method on the parameter to indicate that the instance should be taken out of the load-balancer rotation temporarily. This is useful if the instance is so busy that it is unable to process additional inbound requests.

In this recipe, we'll learn how to manage service configuration and topology changes to a Cloud Service.

How to do it...

We are going to configure callback methods for four of the six `RoleEnvironment` events. We will do this by performing the following steps:

1. Use Visual Studio to create an empty cloud project.

2. Add a worker role to the project (accept the default name of `WorkerRole1`).

3. Add the following to the `ConfigurationSettings` element of `ServiceDefinition.csdef`:

   ```
   <Setting name="EnvironmentChangeString"/>
   <Setting name="SettingRequiringRecycle"/>
   ```

4. Add the following to the `ConfigurationSettings` element of `ServiceConfiguration.cscfg`:

   ```
   <Setting name="EnvironmentChangeString"
       value="OriginalValue"/>
   <Setting name="SettingRequiringRecycle"
       value="OriginalValue"/>
   ```

 You can perform steps 3 and 4 with the GUI provided by Visual Studio in the **Properties** page of the role, under the **Settings** tab.

5. Add a new class named `EnvironmentChangeExample` to the project.

6. Add the following `using` statements to the top of the class file:

   ```
   using Microsoft.WindowsAzure.ServiceRuntime;
   using System.Collections.ObjectModel;
   using System.Diagnostics;
   ```

 By adding a `WorkerRole` to the cloud project during the wizard phase, VS automatically adds a reference to the most updated `Microsoft.WindowsAzure.ServiceRuntime` library. Only with this reference can the user legally use the `using` clauses of the step 6.

7. Add the following callback method to the class:

   ```
   private static void RoleEnvironmentChanging(object sender,
   RoleEnvironmentChangingEventArgs e)
   {
     Boolean recycle = false;
     foreach (RoleEnvironmentChange change in e.Changes)
     {
   ```

```
RoleEnvironmentTopologyChange topologyChange =
    change as RoleEnvironmentTopologyChange;
if (topologyChange != null)
{
  String roleName = topologyChange.RoleName;
  ReadOnlyCollection<RoleInstance> oldInstances =
      RoleEnvironment.Roles[roleName].Instances;
}
RoleEnvironmentConfigurationSettingChange settingChange
    = change as RoleEnvironmentConfigurationSettingChange;
if (settingChange != null)
{
  String settingName =
      settingChange.ConfigurationSettingName;
  String oldValue =
      RoleEnvironment.GetConfigurationSettingValue(
          settingName);
  recycle |= settingName == "SettingRequiringRecycle";
}
}

// Recycle when e.Cancel = true;
e.Cancel = recycle;
}
```

8. Add the following callback method to the class:

```
private static void RoleEnvironmentChanged(object sender,
  RoleEnvironmentChangedEventArgs e)
{
  foreach (RoleEnvironmentChange change in e.Changes)
  {
    RoleEnvironmentTopologyChange topologyChange =
        change as RoleEnvironmentTopologyChange;
    if (topologyChange != null)
    {
      String roleName = topologyChange.RoleName;
      ReadOnlyCollection<RoleInstance> newInstances =
          RoleEnvironment.Roles[roleName].Instances;
    }
    RoleEnvironmentConfigurationSettingChange settingChange
        = change as RoleEnvironmentConfigurationSettingChange;
    if (settingChange != null)
    {
      String settingName =
          settingChange.ConfigurationSettingName;
```

```
        String newValue =
            RoleEnvironment.GetConfigurationSettingValue(
                settingName);
    }
  }
}
```

9. Add the following callback method to the class:

```
private static void RoleEnvironmentStatusCheck(object sender,
    RoleInstanceStatusCheckEventArgs e)
{
  RoleInstanceStatus status = e.Status;
  // Uncomment next line to take instance out of the
  // load balancer rotation.
  //e.SetBusy();
}
```

10. Add the following callback method to the class:

```
private static void RoleEnvironmentStopping(object sender,
    RoleEnvironmentStoppingEventArgs e)
{
  Trace.TraceInformation("In RoleEnvironmentStopping");
}
```

11. Add the following method, associating the callback methods with the
    `RoleEnvironment` events, to the class:

```
public static void UseEnvironmentChangeExample()
{
  RoleEnvironment.Changing += RoleEnvironmentChanging;
  RoleEnvironment.Changed += RoleEnvironmentChanged;
  RoleEnvironment.StatusCheck += RoleEnvironmentStatusCheck;
  RoleEnvironment.Stopping += RoleEnvironmentStopping;
}
```

12. If the application is deployed to the local Compute Emulator, the
    `ServiceConfiguration.cscfg` file can be modified. It can then be applied
    to the running service using the following command in the Microsoft Azure SDK
    command prompt:

```
csrun /update:{DEPLOYMENT_ID};ServiceConfiguration.cscfg
```

13. If the application is deployed to the cloud, the service configuration can be modified
    directly on the Microsoft Azure Portal.

How it works...

In steps 1 and 2, we created a cloud project with a worker role. In steps 3 and 4, we added two configuration settings to the service definition file and provided initial values for them in the service configuration file.

In steps 5 and 6, we created a class to house our callback methods.

In step 7, we added a callback method for the `RoleEnvironment.Changing` event. This method iterates over the list of changes, looking for any topology or configuration settings changes. In the latter case, we specifically look for changes to the `SettingRequiringRecycle` setting, and on detecting one, we initiate a recycle of the instance.

In step 8, we added a callback method for the `RoleEnvironment.Changed` event. We iterate over the list of changes and look at any topology changes and configuration settings changes.

> In both the previous steps, we respectively get `oldValue` and `newValue` without using them. This is, for example, to get the settings value before and after the changes are made, to eventually use them in a certain situation. However, these events are intended to be used to be notified when particular settings are changed, regardless of which is the actual value before or after the change itself.

In step 9, we added a callback method for the `RoleEnvironment.StatusCheck` event. We look at the current status of the instance and leave the `SetBusy()` call commented out, which would take the instance out of the load balancer rotation.

In step 10, we added a callback method for the `RoleEnvironment.Stopping` event. In this callback, we used `Trace.TraceInformation()` to log the invocation of the method.

In step 11, we added a method that associated the callback methods with the appropriate event.

In step 12, we saw how to modify the service configuration in the development environment. We must replace `{DEPLOYMENT_ID}` with the deployment ID of the current deployment. The deployment ID in the Computer Emulator is a number that is incremented with each deployment. It is displayed on the Compute Emulator UI. In step 13, we saw how to modify the service configuration in a cloud deployment.

There's more...

The `RoleEntryPoint` class also exposes the following virtual methods that allow various changes to be handled:

- `RoleEntryPoint.OnStart()`
- `RoleEntryPoint.OnStop()`
- `RoleEntryPoint.Run()`

These virtual methods are invoked when an instance is started, stopped, or when it reaches a `Ready` state. An instance of a worker role is recycled whenever the `Run()` method exits.

Testing changes with the SDK command line

The `csrun` command in the Microsoft Azure SDK can be used to test configuration changes in the development fabric. The service configuration file can be modified, and `csrun` can be invoked to apply the change. Note that it is not possible to test topology changes that reduce the number of instances. However, when the Cloud Service is started without debugging, it is possible to increase the number of instances by modifying the service configuration file and using `csrun`.

Using LINQ with the RoleEnvironment API

As both `RoleEnvironmentChanging` and `RoleEnvironmentChanged` use the `RoleEnvironment` APIs to check collections, we can also simplify the code in steps 7 and 8 with new LINQ-based implementations as follows:

```
private static void RoleEnvironmentChanging(object sender,
    RoleEnvironmentChangingEventArgs e)
{
    var oldInstances =
        e.Changes.OfType<RoleEnvironmentTopologyChange>()
        .SelectMany(p => RoleEnvironment.Roles[p.RoleName].Instances);
    var oldValues =        e.Changes.OfType<RoleEnvironmentConfigurati
onSettingChange>()
        .ToDictionary(p => p.ConfigurationSettingName,p=>R
oleEnvironment        .GetConfigurationSettingValue(p.
ConfigurationSettingName));
    e.Cancel =oldValues.Any(p=>p.Key=="SettingRequiringRecycle");
}
```

In the code mentioned earlier, we group the old changing instances and the old settings' key-value pairs. In the last line, we recycle the `SettingRequiringRecycle` setting, if there is any.

Step 8 can be modified as mentioned earlier, but by finding new instances and settings' values instead of old ones, while asking the `RoleEnvironment` APIs about them.

Have a look at the following MSDN blog post to get additional information:

▶ Architecture of the Microsoft Azure Role model `http://blogs.msdn.com/b/ kwill/archive/2011/05/05/windows-azure-role-architecture.aspx`

Managing upgrades and changes to a Cloud Service

Microsoft Azure instances and the guest OS they reside in have to be upgraded occasionally. The Cloud Service might need a new software deployment or a configuration change. The guest OS might need a patch or an upgrade to a new version. To ensure that a Cloud Service can remain online 24/7 (an SLA of 99.95%), Microsoft Azure provides an upgrade capability that allows upgrades to be performed without stopping the Cloud Service completely as long as each role in the service has two or more instances.

Microsoft Azure supports two types of upgrade: in-place upgrade and Virtual IP swap. An in-place upgrade applies changes to the configuration and code of existing virtual machines (VM) that host instances of the Cloud Service. A VIP swap modifies the load-balancer configuration so that the VIP address of the production deployment is pointed at the instances that are currently in the staging slot, and the VIP address of the staging deployment is pointed at the instances currently in the production slot.

There are two types of in-place upgrades: configuration change and deployment upgrade. A configuration change can be applied on the Microsoft Azure Portal by editing the existing configuration directly on the portal. A configuration change or a deployment upgrade can be performed on the Microsoft Azure Portal by uploading a replacement service configuration file, `ServiceConfiguration.cscfg`, or by directly modifying the settings in the **Configure** tab of the Cloud Service web page. They can also be performed by invoking the appropriate operations in the Microsoft Azure Service Management REST API. By repeating the *Publishing a Cloud Service with options from Visual Studio* recipe, a deployment upgrade could be initiated directly from Visual Studio. Note that it is possible to do an in-place upgrade of an individual role in an application package.

A configuration change supports only modifications to the service configuration file, which includes changing the guest OS; changing the value of configuration settings such as connection strings, and changing the actual X.509 certificates used by the Cloud Service. Note that a configuration change cannot be used to change the names of configuration settings as they are specified in the service definition file.

A deployment upgrade supports changes to the application package as well as all the changes allowed in a configuration change. Additionally, a deployment upgrade supports some modifications to the `ServiceDefinition.csdef` service definition file. These modifications include changing the following:

- ▸ Role type
- ▸ The local resource definitions
- ▸ The available configuration settings
- ▸ The certificates defined for the Cloud Service

A Cloud Service has an associated set of upgrade domains that control the phasing of upgrades during an in-place upgrade. The instances of a role are distributed evenly among upgrade domains. During an in-place upgrade, all the instances in a single upgrade domain are stopped, reconfigured, and then restarted. This process continues with one upgrade domain at a time until all the upgrade domains have been upgraded. This phasing ensures that the Cloud Service remains available during an in-place upgrade, albeit with roles being served by fewer instances than usual. By default, there are five upgrade domains for a Cloud Service, although this number can be reduced/increased in the service definition file.

The only distinction between the production and staging slots of a Cloud Service is that the load balancer forwards any network traffic that arrives at the service VIP address to the production slot and any network traffic that arrives at the staging VIP address to the staging slot. In a VIP swap, the production and staging slots to which the load balancer forwards network traffic are swapped. This has no effect on the actual VMs running the service; it is entirely a matter of where inbound network traffic is forwarded to. A VIP swap affects the entire service simultaneously and does not use upgrade domains. Nevertheless, as a Cloud Service is a distributed system, there might be a small overlap during a VIP swap, where inbound traffic is forwarded to some instances that run the old version of the service and some instances that run the new version. The only way to guarantee that old and new versions are never simultaneously in production is to stop the Cloud Service while performing the upgrade.

Note that Microsoft occasionally has to upgrade the root OS of a server that hosts an instance. This type of upgrade is always automatic, and Microsoft provides no ability for it to be performed manually.

In this recipe, we'll learn how to upgrade a deployment to a Cloud Service.

Getting ready

We need to deploy an application to the production and staging slots of a Cloud Service. We could use, for example, the Cloud Service we created in the *Using startup tasks in a Microsoft Azure role* recipe.

How to do it...

We are going to use the Microsoft Azure Portal to perform an in-place upgrade, a VIP swap, and a manual guest OS upgrade. In this stage, we will perform an in-place upgrade of the production deployment using the following steps:

1. On the Microsoft Azure Portal, go to the **Dashboard** tab of the Cloud Service in the **Cloud Services** section and then choose the **Production** slot.

2. Click on **Update** and provide a deployment label, a package location, and a configuration location.

3. Choose the roles to update (this is optional) or click on **All** to update the entire service.

 An Azure Cloud Service can comprise many roles in its definition, while it is not necessary to update them all if just one needs updates. This is a very common use case and also an elegant solution for partial updates.

4. Click on either the **Allow the update if role sizes change or if the number of roles change** or **Update the deployment even if one or more roles contain a single instance** boxes and then confirm.

 In this stage, we perform a VIP swap.

5. Repeat steps 1 to 4 in the staging slot.

6. Click on the **Swap** button to perform the VIP swap.

 In this stage, we perform a manual guest OS upgrade of the production deployment.

7. In the **Configure** tab of either the production or staging slot of the Cloud Service, locate the **Operating system** section.

8. Select the desired OS Family and OS Version, and press **Save**.

How it works...

We can perform in-place upgrades of the production and staging slots independently of each other. In step 1, we indicated that we wanted to perform an in-place upgrade of the production slot. In step 2, we specified the details of the upgrade, such as the label and a location for the upgraded application package and service configuration file.

In step 3, we chose which roles have to be upgraded, as it is common to have just a few parts of the entire solution modified by an upgrade. In step 4, we told Azure to continue the upgrade even under those circumstances. Those checkboxes are intended as a double check to avoid unwanted downtime.

We can perform a VIP swap only if there is a Cloud Service deployed to the staging slot, and we ensured this in step 5. We initiated the VIP swap in step 6.

We can perform guest OS upgrades of the production and staging slots independently of each other. In step 7, we located the desired slot to upgrade the guest OS in. We initiated the guest OS upgrade in step 8.

See also

In *Chapter 7, Managing Azure Resources with the Azure Management Libraries,* we will see how to use the Microsoft Azure Management libraries to manage deployments, including performing upgrades.

Have a look at the following MSDN links to get additional information:

- ▸ Advanced scenarios about updating an Azure Cloud Service at `http://msdn.microsoft.com/en-us/library/azure/hh472157.aspx`
- ▸ Swapping deployments using Management REST APIs at `http://msdn.microsoft.com/en-us/library/azure/ee460814.aspx`

Configuring diagnostics in Cloud Services

An Azure Cloud Service might comprise multiple instances of multiple roles. These instances all run in a remote Azure data center, typically 24/7. The ability to monitor these instances nonintrusively is essential both in detecting failure and in capacity planning.

Diagnostic data can be used to identify problems with a Cloud Service. The ability to view the data from several sources and across different instances eases the task of identifying a problem. The process to configure Azure Diagnostics is at the role level, but the diagnostics configuration is performed at the instance level. For each instance, a configuration file is stored in a XML blob in a container named `wad-control-container` located in the storage service account configured for Azure Diagnostics.

A best practice from both security and performance perspectives would be to host application data and diagnostic data in separate storage service accounts. Actually, there is no need for application data and diagnostics data to be located in the same storage service account.

Azure Diagnostics supports the following diagnostic data:

- ▶ **Application logs**: This captures information written to a trace listener
- ▶ **Event logs**: This captures the events from any configured Windows Event Log
- ▶ **Performance counters**: This captures the data of any configured performance counters
- ▶ **Infrastructure logs**: This captures diagnostic data produced by the Diagnostics process itself

Azure Diagnostics also supports file-based data sources. It copies new files of a specified directory to blobs in a specified container in the Azure Blob Service. The data captured by IIS Logs, IIS Failed Request Logs, and Crash Dumps is self-evident. With the custom directories data source, Azure Diagnostics supports the association of any directory on the instance. This allows for the coherent integration of third-party logs.

The Diagnostics Agent service is included as `Active` by default for each new Visual Studio Azure Service project.

The Diagnostics Agent would collect and transfer a user-defined set of logs. The process does not add so much overhead to the `normal` operations, but the more logs collected, the more delays in the running machines.

Then, it is started automatically when a role instance starts, provided the Diagnostics module has been imported into the role. This requires the placement of a file named `diagnostics.wadcfg` in a specific location in the role package. When an instance is started for the first time, the Diagnostic Agent reads the file and initializes the diagnostic configuration for the instance in `wad-control-container` with it. Initial configuration typically occurs in Visual Studio at design time, while further changes could be made either from Visual Studio by the Management API or manually.

In the past, Diagnostic initialization has been made by user code. This is not recommended due to the high volume of hardcoded directives. If needed, the class responsible for this is the `DiagnosticsMonitorConfiguration` class.

Azure Diagnostics supports the use of `Trace` to log messages. Methods of the `System.Diagnostics.Trace` class can be used to write error, warning, and informational messages (the Compute Emulator in the development environment adds an additional trace listener so that trace messages can be displayed in the Compute Emulator UI).

Azure Diagnostics captures diagnostic information for an instance, keeps it in a local buffer, and, periodically, it persists this data to the Azure Storage service. The Azure Diagnostics tables can be queried just like any other table in the Table service. The Diagnostics Agent persists the data mentioned earlier according to the following tables' mapping:

- ▸ Application logs: `WADLogsTable`
- ▸ Event logs: `WADWindowsEventLogsTable`
- ▸ Performance counters: `WADPerformanceCountersTable`
- ▸ Infrastructure logs: `WADDiagnosticInfrastructureLogsTable`

As the only index on a table is on `PartitionKey` and `RowKey`, it is important that `PartitionKey` rather than `Timestamp` or `EventTickCount` be used for time-dependent queries.

In this recipe, we see how to configure and use Diagnostic features in the role environment, collecting every available log data source and tracing info.

Getting ready

This recipe assumes that we have an empty Cloud Service and an empty Storage account. To create the first one, go to the Azure Portal and follow the wizards without deploying anything in it. To create the second one, follow the instructions of the *Managing the Azure Storage Service* recipe in *Chapter 3, Getting Storage with Blobs in Azure*.

We apologize, but as Azure building blocks are interconnected to provide complex services, it is hard to explain a topic atomically. This is the case of Diagnostics for Cloud Services, which requires knowledge of Storage basics.

How to do it...

We are going to create a simple worker role-triggering diagnostics collection using the following steps:

1. In Visual Studio, create a new Azure Cloud Service with a worker role named `Worker`.
2. Right-click on the **Worker** item in the **Roles** folder of the created project and select **Properties**.
3. In the **Configuration** tab, perform the following actions:
   - ❑ Verify that the **Enable Diagnostics** checkbox is checked
   - ❑ Select **Custom plan**

      ❏   In the **Specify the storage account credentials for the Diagnostics results** field, enter the connection string of the Diagnostics storage account (by clicking the **... (more)** button, a wizard could help to build this string)

4. To customize the data collected by the Diagnostic service, click on the **Edit** button of the **Custom plan** option selected earlier.

5. In the **Diagnostics** configuration window, select the logging mix, for example:

      ❏   Application logs: Verbose level, 1-minute transfer, 1024 MB buffer size

      ❏   Event logs: Application + System + Security with verbose level, 1-minute transfer, 1024 MB buffer size

      ❏   Performance counters: 1-minute transfer, 1 MB buffer size, and "% processor time" metric

      ❏   Infrastructure logs: Verbose level, 1-minute transfer, no buffer size

6. Close the window and save the configuration.

7. In the `WorkerRole.cs` file, in the `Run()` method, write this code:

```
while (true)
{
    Thread.Sleep(1000);
    DateTime now = DateTime.Now;
    Trace.TraceInformation("Information: "+now);
    Trace.TraceError("Error: " + now);
    Trace.TraceWarning("Warning: " + now);
}
```

8. Right-click on the **Cloud Service** project and **Publish** it using the following steps:

    1. Select the proper subscription.

    2. In **Common Settings**, select the previously created empty Cloud Service.

    3. In **Advanced Settings**, select the previously created Storage Account.

    4. Confirm, click on **Publish**, and wait for a few minutes.

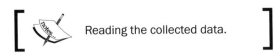
Reading the collected data.

9. In the **Server Explorer** window of Visual Studio, expand the Azure node and locate the proper storage account of the storage subnode.

10. Expand the tables node, and for each table found, right-click on it and select **View Table**.

How it works...

From steps 1 to 3, we prepared the wrapper project to hold the worker role and configure it. By enabling the Diagnostics feature, an `Import` directive was placed into the service definition file. By selecting **Custom plan**, we told Azure to collect user-defined data into the storage account we finally specified.

In steps 4 and 5, we customized the collected data, telling the platform what to log and when to transfer to storage.

Azure instances are stateless, meaning that an instance could be taken down and be replaced by a new one seamlessly. Storing logs in the VM leads to some design issues. What happens if the instance has been recycled? How do you read service-wide logs centrally? This is why a transfer phase is involved in log capturing.

After saving in step 6, we added some tracing code in step 7 and published the Cloud Service as shown in step 8.

A more sophisticated way to trace messages is to use trace sources and trace switches to control the capture of messages. Typically, this control can be configured through the `app.config` file for an application.

In steps 9 and 10, we used the built-in features of the Azure SDK integration for Visual Studio to browse through the storage account elected for the Diagnostics collection.

While each table contains some properties specific to the data being logged, all of them contain the following properties:

- `EventTickCount`
- `DeploymentId`
- `Role`
- `RoleInstance`

The `EventTickCount` property is `Int64`, which represents the time in which the event was generated, to an accuracy of 100 nanoseconds. The `DeploymentId` property identifies the specific deployment, while the `Role` and `RoleInstance` properties specify the role instance that generated the event.

The `WADPerformanceCountersTable` table, for example, contains the following additional properties:

- `CounterName`
- `CounterValue`

> When browsing through the collected data, note that the tables are partitioned by minute. Specifically, when a record is inserted in a table, `PartitionKey` is set to the tick count of the current UTC time with the seconds discarded, with the entire value prepended by a 0. Discarding the seconds has the effect of setting the last eight characters of `PartitionKey` to 0. The `RowKey` property combines the deployment ID, the role name, and the instance ID, along with a key to ensure uniqueness. `Timestamp` represents the time the event was inserted in the table.

There's more...

Once the deployment has been made, the Diagnostics configuration can be edited easily from Visual Studio as follows:

1. In the Cloud Services node of the Azure main node in the Server Explorer windows, select the previously created Cloud Service.

2. Expand the node and select the desired role in the desired slot (staging or production).

3. By selecting **Update Diagnostics Settings** option, we can change the Diagnostics configuration at runtime.

Log directories

As mentioned earlier, we can transfer entire directories into the selected Storage Account, for instance, integrate a third-party tool by logging directly in the filesystem. To do this, we can open the `diagnostics.wadcfg` file and add this code in the `<Directories>` tag:

```
<DataSources>
  <DirectoryConfiguration container="wad-mylog"
directoryQuotaInMB="128">
    <Absolute expandEnvironment="true" path="%SystemRoot%\myTool\logs"
/>
  </DirectoryConfiguration>
</DataSources>
```

Alerts

Azure has an integrated alerting system to notify users with particular events. Despite it is not only related to Cloud Services, the following are some steps to enable it for the previously created one:

▸ In the Azure Portal, go to the Management Services section and click on the **Alter** tab

▸ Add a new rule, specifying the following:

    ❏ The name of the rule

    ❏ Service type: Cloud Service

    ❏ Service name: the one previously created

    ❏ Cloud Service deployment: Production

    ❏ Cloud Service role: Worker

▸ In the second step, choose **CPU Percentage** as the metric to monitor

▸ Set the **greater than** condition to 70% with the remaining default values

This alert will notify the user that creates it and, optionally, the service administrator and co-administrators.

See also

Have a look at the following MSDN links to get additional information:

▸ Best practice about Diagnostics and Cloud Service development at `http://msdn.microsoft.com/en-us/library/azure/hh771389.aspx`

▸ More about Diagnostics collection, blobs, and Q&A at `http://msdn.microsoft.com/library/azure/dn186185.aspx`

2
Deploying Quickly with Azure Websites

In this chapter, we will cover the following topics:

- ▶ Deploying an Azure Website
- ▶ Administering and monitoring a Website
- ▶ Source versioning and continuous integration with Git and TFS
- ▶ Logging abstraction from .NET and PHP
- ▶ Deploying Java with Azure Websites

Introduction

Microsoft Azure is a comprehensive set of building blocks that can used as standalone or mixed services to get complex systems and services. Infrastructure-as-a-Service blocks, as virtual machines and/or virtual networks, in spite of being very common in the IT vendors' scenario, are actually great services. Today, the real value-added service in the cloud computing momentum is PaaS (Platform-as-a-Service).

The Azure Website is an advanced PaaS platform to deploy complex web applications to the cloud, without having a steep learning curve, thus leveraging the existing skill sets. Think about Websites as simple FTP-like endpoints, where we can upload our site's contents (binaries or just plain text/resources) and let them run as they are. In addition, websites offer enterprise-level services, such as scaling, backup, monitoring, logging, and more, around this simple deploy-and-go concept. Last but not least, these Websites provide the capability to deploy applications in several different languages.

At the time of writing this book, Azure Websites support the following:

- .NET applications (with frameworks greater than or equal to Version 2.0)
- PHP applications (up to the Version 5.5 of PHP)
- Java (through the Jetty or Tomcat container)
- Python (both 2.7.3 and 3.4.0 Versions)

> More generally, these Websites support every language and platform that can run on IIS, with FastCGI, plus Python and Java.

The architecture perceived by users of Azure Websites is charming. It is described as follows:

- A user initiates one or more server farms (also known as **Web Hosting Plans**). A *plan* is intended to be a website container tied to a particular pricing scheme.
- In a specific farm/plan, users create one or more websites.
- For each website, users can choose the execution platform just like they did for the monitoring options, run time configuration, and so on.
  - These options, as the running binaries of the Website, are completely isolated from each other, as they were in a sandbox.
- Finally, as users group Websites into farms, they can let specific farms scale up and/or out, resulting in all the Websites running on the initial machine being replicated across all the instances allocated in the farm.

The scenario explained earlier refers to the standard pricing scheme, which is the one we work with along the chapter as the most complete Websites offer of Azure.

At the time of writing this book, the pricing schemes are as follows:

- **Free**: These Websites run in a shared environment. Many options are restricted, no scaling is permitted, and one free web farm is permitted per location.
- **Shared**: These Websites run in a shared environment, but options and scaling are supported.
- **Basic**: On these Websites, some advanced options are restricted.
- **Standard**: These Websites provide a fully featured Azure Websites service.

Therefore, a company can deploy its production services into a single server farm (web-hosting plan), which should considerably scale up and/or out. At the same time, for testing and/or staging environments, the same company can run its services into another smaller web farm (probably, with a smaller machine and no redundancy at all).

What is the drawback of the Websites service? Customization of the runtime environment. In fact, the more abstraction the environment offers, the less control there should be over resources. What could happen if, for example, a single Website (hosted in the same machine/web farm of other N websites) needs an MSI component installed on the underlying operating system? In the case of installation, what guarantees that there will be no conflicts between the existing Websites? Finally, how can we scale out if there is some manually handled configuration of the operating system?

To build complex systems that need to release these constraints, Cloud Services is the right service to choose. In other cases, or better, when we can avoid relying on Cloud Services, Website is probably the leader.

Azure Websites can be simply deployed through FTP or Web Deploy, can have virtual directories and multiple applications, and can also have staging slots. We learn how to deploy an ASP.NET application in the *Deploying a Website* recipe. After deploying, the governance of the Website or the Websites' pool is up to Microsoft; however, advanced configuration, scaling, certificates and SSL, diagnostics, and monitoring is left to the user, as we will see in the *Administering and Monitoring a Website* recipe.

We stated that FTP and Web Deploy are the deployment methods of Websites. The Websites service can also be linked with a source code repository, taking the most recent version of the committed code and integrating it automatically. This method (extended and maintained internally by Microsoft) now supports several third-party providers as the built-in integration with the SaaS version of TFS, Visual Studio Online. In the *Source versioning and continuous integration with Git and TFS* recipe, we will see how to set up the source control integration with Git and **Visual Studio Online** (**VSO**).

In the last two recipes, we dig into the support of alternative software platforms such as PHP and Java. First, in the *Logging abstraction from .NET and PHP* recipe, we will learn how to integrate logging into applications. Later, in the *Deploying Java with Azure Websites* recipe, we will see how to run Java with Tomcat or Jetty.

Deploying a Website

Creating a Website is an administrative task, which is performed in the Azure Portal in the same way we provision every other building block. The Website created is like a "deployment slot", or better, "web space", since the abstraction given to the user is exactly that.

Azure Websites does not require additional knowledge compared to an old-school hosting provider, where FTP was the standard for the deployment process. Actually, FTP is just one of the supported deployment methods in Websites, since Web Deploy is probably the best choice for several scenarios. In the *Source versioning and continuous integration with Git and TFS* recipe, we will learn how to implement continuous integration with Websites, but since this is not always necessary, consider FTP and Web Deploy to be the fastest lane to go live with this service.

Web Deploy is a Microsoft technology used for copying files and provisioning additional content and configuration to integrate the deployment process. Web Deploy runs on HTTP and HTTPS with basic (username and password) authentication. This makes it a good choice in networks where FTP is forbidden or the firewall rules are strict.

Some time ago, Microsoft introduced the concept of **Publish Profile**, an XML file containing all the available deployment endpoints of a particular website that, if given to Visual Studio or Web Matrix, could make the deployment easier. Every Azure Website comes with a publish profile with unique credentials, so one can distribute it to developers without giving them grants on the Azure Subscription.

Web Matrix is a client tool of Microsoft, and it is useful to edit live sites directly from an intuitive GUI. It uses Web Deploy to provide access to the remote filesystem as to perform remote changes.

In the *Hosting multiple websites in a web role* recipe of *Chapter 1, Developing Cloud Services for Microsoft Azure*, we saw that defining multiple websites in a single role is not so easy, even more so if we deal with multiple virtual directories or applications. In Websites, we can host several websites on the same server farm, making administration easier and isolating the environment from the neighborhood. Moreover, virtual directories can be defined from the Azure Portal, enabling complex scenarios or making migrations easier.

In this recipe, we will cope with the deployment process, using FTP and Web Deploy with some variants.

Getting ready

This recipe assumes we have an FTP client installed on the local machine (for example, FileZilla) and, of course, a valid Azure Subscription. We also need Visual Studio 2013 with the latest Azure SDK installed (at the time of writing this, SDK Version 2.3).

How to do it...

We are going to create a new Website, create a new ASP.NET project, deploy it through FTP and Web Deploy, and also use virtual directories. We do this as follows:

1. Create a new Website in the Azure Portal, specifying the following details:

    - The URL prefix (that is, `TestWebSite`) is set to `[prefix]. azurewebsites.net`

□   The Web Hosting Plan (create a new one)

□   The Region/Location (select **West Europe**)

2.   Click on the newly created Website and go to the **Dashboard** tab.

3.   Click on **Download the publish profile** and save it on the local computer.

4.   Open Visual Studio and create a new ASP.NET web application named `TestWebSite`, with an empty template and web forms' references.

5.   Add a sample `Default.aspx` page to the project and paste into it the following HTML:

```
<h1>Root Application</h1>
```

6.   Press *F5* and test whether the web application is displayed correctly.

 Create a local publish target.

7.   Right-click on the project and select **Publish**.

8.   Select **Custom** and specify `Local Folder`.

9.   In the **Publish** method, select **File System** and provide a local folder where Visual Studio will save files. Then click on **Publish** to complete.

 Publish via FTP.

10. Open FileZilla and then open the **Publish** profile (saved in step 3) with a text editor.

11. Locate the FTP endpoint and specify the following:

□   `publishUrl` as the **Host** field

□   `username` as the **Username** field

□   `userPWD` as the **Password** field

12. Delete the `hostingstart.html` file that is already present on the remote space.

 When we create a new Azure Website, there is a single HTML file in the root folder by default, which is served to the clients as the default page. By leaving on in the Website, the file could be served after users' deployments as well if no valid default documents are found.

13. Drag-and-drop all the contents of the local folder with the binaries to the remote folder, then run the website.

Publish via Web Deploy.

14. Right-click on `Project` and select **Publish**.

15. Go to the **Publish Web** wizard start and select **Import**, providing the previously downloaded `Publish Profile` file.

16. When Visual Studio reads the Web Deploy settings, it populates the next window. Click on **Confirm** and **Publish** the web application.

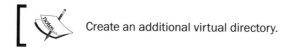

Create an additional virtual directory.

17. Go to the **Configure** tab of the Website on the Azure Portal.

18. At the bottom, in the virtual applications and directories, add the following:

   ❑ `/app01` with the path `site\app01`

   ❑ Mark it as **Application**

19. Open the `Publish Profile` file and duplicate the `<publishProfile>` tag with the method FTP, then edit the following:

   ❑ Add the suffix `App01` to `profileName`

   ❑ Replace `wwwroot` with `app01` in `publishUrl`

20. Create a new ASP.NET web application called `TestWebSiteApp01` and create a new `Default.aspx` page in it with the following code:

   `<h1>App01 Application</h1>`

21. Right-click on the **TestWebSiteApp01** project and **Publish**.

22. Select **Import** and provide the edited `Publish Profile` file.

23. In the first step of the **Publish Web** wizard (go back if necessary), select the **App01** method and select **Publish**.

24. Run the Website's virtual application by appending the `/app01` suffix to the site's URL.

How it works...

In step 1, we created the Website on the Azure Portal, specifying the minimal set of parameters. If the existing web hosting plan is selected, the Website will start in the specified tier. In the recipe, by specifying a new web hosting plan, the Website is created in the free tier with some limitations in configuration.

 The recipe uses the Azure Portal located at `https://manage.windowsazure.com`. However, the new Azure Portal will be at `https://portal.azure.com`. New features will be probably added only in the new Portal.

In steps 2 and 3, we downloaded the `Publish Profile` file, which is an XML containing the various endpoints to publish the Website. At the time of writing this, Web Deploy and FTP are supported by default. In steps 4, 5, and 6, we created a new ASP.NET web application with a sample ASPX page and ran it locally.

In steps 7, 8, and 9, we published the binaries of the Website, without source code files, into a local folder somewhere in the local machine. This **unit of deployment** folder can be sent across the wire via FTP, as we did in steps 10 to 13 using the credentials and the hostname available in the `Publish Profile` file.

In steps 14 to 16, we used the `Publish Profile` file directly from Visual Studio, which recognizes the different methods of deployment and suggests Web Deploy as the default one. If we perform steps 10-13, with steps 14-16 we overwrite the existing deployment.

 Actually, Web Deploy compares the target files with the ones to deploy, making the deployment incremental for those files that have been modified or added. This is extremely useful to avoid unnecessary transfers and save bandwidth.

In steps 17 and 18, we configured a new virtual application, specifying its name and location. We can use an FTP client to browse the root folder of a website endpoint, since there are several folders such as `wwwroot`, `locks`, `diagnostics`, and `deployments`.

In step 19, we manually edited the `Publish Profile` file to support a second FTP endpoint, pointing to the new folder of the Virtual Application. Visual Studio will correctly understand this while parsing the file again in step 22, showing the new deployment option. Finally, we check whether there are two applications: one on the root folder / and one on the /`app01` alias.

There's more...

Suppose we need to edit the website on the fly, editing a CSS of JS file or editing the HTML somewhere. We can do this using Web Matrix, which is available from the Azure Portal itself through a ClickOnce installation:

1. Go to the **Dashboard** tab of the Website and click on **WebMatrix, which is** at the bottom of the page.

2. Follow the instructions to install the software (if not yet installed) and, when it opens, select **Edit live site directly** (the magic is done through the `Publish Profile` file and Web Deploy).

3. In the left-side tree, edit the `Default.aspx` file, and then save and run the Website again.

Azure Websites gallery

Since Azure Websites is a PaaS service, with no lock-in or particular knowledge or framework required to run it, it can host several Open Source CMS in different languages. Azure provides a set of built-in web applications to choose while creating a new website. This is probably not the best choice for production environments; however, for testing or development purposes, it should be a faster option than starting from scratch.

 Wizards have been, for a while, the primary resources for developers to quickly start projects and speed up the process of creating complex environments. However, the Websites gallery creates instances of well-known CMS with predefined configurations. Production environments are manually crafted, customizing each aspect of the installation.

To create a new Website using the gallery, proceed as follows:

1. Create a new Website, specifying from the gallery.

2. Select the web application to deploy and follow the optional configuration steps.

If we create some resources (such as databases) while using the gallery, they will be linked to the site in the **Linked Resources** tab.

See also

Have a look at these MSDN links to get additional information:

▶ Mixed deployment with .NET and PHP at `http://blogs.msdn.com/b/kaushal/archive/2014/04/19/microsoft-azure-web-sites-deploying-wordpress-to-a-virtual-directory-within-the-azure-web-site.aspx`

▶ How to create a Websites from the gallery at `http://azure.microsoft.com/en-us/documentation/articles/web-sites-dotnet-orchard-cms-gallery/`

Administering and monitoring a Website

In the *Deploying a Website* recipe, we saw how to deploy an ASP.NET application into an Azure Website. We saw that there is almost no unique knowledge required (except the skills needed to write the web application), making the deployment process straightforward. However, deploying is just the beginning of the process—leading to tasks such as advanced configuration, monitoring, domain mapping, logging, disaster recovery, and more.

Such activities are performed entirely via the Azure Portal (or through PowerShell), making it the central point of administration of the entire website's infrastructure.

After deployment, we probably focus on the fine-tuning of the runtime environment, making some optimizations to load only the required frameworks, and disabling everything that is not needed by the application. If the deployment will be a production deployment, a custom domain should be mapped to the website and, if we want to avoid confusion in case of errors, the proper logging and diagnostics strategy should take place before making any endpoint publicly accessible.

A good PaaS should also provide tools to avoid repetitive actions. So, how many times have we deployed a web application, forgetting to include directives to perform some sort of instrumentation? What about configuration settings? How many times have you connected remotely to change some settings in the `Web.config` file?

Websites can be the most powerful PaaS service of Microsoft, or even one of the most powerful PaaS services on the market, since many features come day by day, enriching the capabilities while maintaining the environment constraints. One of those features is the capability to define additional deployment slots for a given website. From a technical point of view, this is done with a new website (along with its configuration, web space, publish profile, and so on); however, the additional slots can be swapped with the production one with the help of a few clicks.

In this recipe, we will see some of the customization options of a given Website, preparing it for the production line.

Getting ready

This recipe assumes that we created a Website called `TestWebSite` (or similar), which is empty or has sample content (we can also use the one from the previous recipe). We also need the following:

> ▶ A storage account. Create it in the Azure Portal with default options (to do that, see the *Managing the Azure Storage Service* recipe in *Chapter 3, Getting Storage with Blobs in Azure*).

> ▶ A self-signed SSL certificate. Create it as shown in the *Implementing HTTPS in a web role* recipe of *Chapter 1, Developing Cloud Services for Microsoft Azure*.

> ▶ A custom domain with access to DNS management.

How to do it...

We are going to customize an existing Website with specific options instead of default ones, and we will set up SSL bindings, custom domains, and many other built-in features. We do this as follows, saving each time we perform an action on the Azure Portal:

1. Open the Azure Portal and go to the **Scale** tab of the Website for configuration.
2. If not yet selected, select the **Standard** mode in **Web Hosting Plan** mode and save.

 The Standard mode is a paid mode, so you may be charged. We can disable it at the end of recipe, however.

3. Go to the **Configure** tab, where all options are available now.

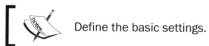 Define the basic settings.

4. Disable the PHP runtime by clicking on **OFF** in the PHP version line.
5. Choose between **Classic** or **Integrated** in the **Managed Pipeline** mode.

What is the difference between Classic and Integrated mode? In previous versions of IIS, the default execution mode was Classic, where ASP. NET runs as an ISAPI extension, exactly as other extensions, in a plugin fashion. With Integrated Managed Pipeline, each request is passed into the ASP.NET stack, giving the capability to write custom modules and intercept everything that happens on the IIS side in the web application.

6. If the running instances are larger in size, select the 64-bit platform.
7. Enable the **Always On** feature.
8. Enable the **Edit in Visual Studio Online** feature.
9. Enable the **Web Server Logging** feature, specifying the **Storage** mode and the **Storage Account** where to save the diagnostics data.
10. Enable **Remote Debugging** with Visual Studio 2013.
11. In the **Monitoring** area, add a new Endpoint:

    ❑ Name: Test

    ❑ URL: This will be auto-populated with the Website URL

    ❑ Test location: Choose up to three remote locations

12. In the **Default Documents** area, remove the unnecessary items, leaving only the `Default.aspx` line.

Custom domain and SSL.

13. Identify the Website URL in the form `[name].azurewebsites.net`. It will be `TestWebSite.azurewebsites.net` in the recipe.

14. Go to the DNS management panel of the custom domain on the domain's registrar company and register a CNAME:

   ❑ From: `azuretest.mydomain.com`

   ❑ To: `testwebsite.azurewebsites.net`

15. In the **Domain Names** section of the **Configure** area of the Website (coming back to the Azure Portal), click on **Manage Domains**.

16. Add the custom third-level domain to the list and confirm.

 While performing the domain mapping, we can take note of the IP address of the load balancer, which is to be used if an A-Record mapping is needed, instead of CNAME.

17. In the **Certificates** section, upload a certificate specifying the self-signed certificate on the local machine with the encrypting password.

18. In **SSL bindings**, choose the previously bound domain name, the previously uploaded certificate, and the SNI SSL method.

Instrumentation and analytics.

19. In the **Developer Analytics** area, select **Add-on**. An empty drop-down window will show up:

   ❑ Click on **View Azure Store** and find **New Relic**

   ❑ Select the free standard version and specify a name (that is, `RelicMonitoring`) and a region (possibly the same as the Website)

20. If needed, come back to the **Configure** tab of the Website, select **RelicMonitoring** as the **Developer Analytics Add-on**, and then save.

21. In the **Add-ons** section of the Azure Portal, select **RelicMonitoring** and click on **Manage** in the bottom menu to go to the third-party website.

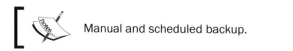

[Manual and scheduled backup.]

22. Go to the **Backups** tab of the Website and, in the **Storage Account** drop-down window, select the storage account provisioned before.

23. To perform a one-time backup, click on **Backup Now** in the bottom menu.

24. To schedule a recurring backup, enable the automated backup feature and specify **Frequency** and **Start date**.

How it works...

In steps 1 and 2, we change the **Pricing/Plan** mode to **Standard**, which means we have full access to the complete feature set of Azure Websites (and we pay too).

In step 4, we disable PHP; since it is not required by our demo, it is useless to keep it enabled. In addition, according the principle *deny all, then allow*, it is recommended to disable everything, enabling only the necessary features.

In step 5, we chose the ASP.NET execution mode, but usually the integrated mode is recommended. Websites can run on 32-bit or 64-bit execution platform, depending on the user need. ASP.NET applications can generally run in both modes, but if the running instance is large-sized, we probably want to address the whole memory surface (7 GB) that we cannot address in 32-bit mode. Conversely, there is no need to run 64-bit mode if the instance is small to medium sized.

In step 7, we tell the instances to warm up application pools after recycles, to make the application always responsive. In steps 8, 9, and 10, we enable an advanced editing feature, the automatic shipping of web server diagnostics data to a storage account, and the capability to remote debug the Website. To remote debug the Website, proceed as follows:

1. In Visual Studio, assuming the latest SDK is installed and the subscription is already linked, locate the Azure node in the **Server Explorer** window.

2. In the **Websites** node, locate the **TestWebSite** Website and select **Attach Debugger** on the **Options** context menu.

In step 11, we instruct Azure to setup a monitoring endpoint, which pings the given URL from remote locations. In the case of loss of availability, this feature acts as a trigger for an alert to be send. In step 12, we customize the `Default Document` section of the `Web.config` file directly from the Azure Portal.

It is interesting how we can customize the `Web.config` settings from the Azure Portal itself. In addition to the `Default Documents` section, we can add/edit the `App Settings` section as for `Connection Strings`. Azure keeps these settings isolated form the actual deployment on the web space. They have precedence over the ones defined in the `Web.config` file.

In steps 13 and 14, we mapped the custom domain with the Website domain name using the CNAME method. In step 15 and 16, we completed the configuration on the Website side, enabling the binding.

CNAME records are like redirect from a given third-level domain to a target domain. However, CNAME cannot start from a naked domain in the form of `mydomain.com`. To bind a naked domain, an A record is needed. A record of type A needs, for a given second-level domain, an IP address to point to.

In steps 17 and 18, we uploaded a self-signed certificate, binding it to the previously bound custom domain. We used the **Server Name Indication** (**SNI**) SSL method because it is cheaper than the standard IP-based SSL. In the IP-based SSL, the host negotiation happens after the SSL handshake, restricting from having multiple SSL certificates for a single IP (so, it is called IP-based). With SNI SSL, the host negotiation happens along with the SSL handshake, allowing multiple certificates to be bound on a single IP.

In step 19, we *purchased* (at no cost, however) an add-on from the Azure Store, a gallery of integrated, third-party add-ons, which are pluggable into Azure applications as building blocks. We buy New Relic, one of the most powerful instrumentation tools on the market and we selected it as an add-on in step 20. Automatically, some settings will appear in the **App Settings** section.

New Relic is a SaaS product (and a software company) used to generate software analytics with not much effort from the developers. When enabled on the Website, it automatically collects valuable information that is useful to identify issues in the code and perform advanced monitoring.

In step 22, we configured the storage account holding the Website backups. In step 23, we started a backup, saving a couple of files into the special, auto-generated `websitebackups` container of the specified storage account. We can also set up a schedule, as shown in step 24.

There's more...

At the beginning of the recipe, we stated that Websites have the capability of being linked to additional deployment slots. They are actually Websites too, but we can swap the content of the main Website with one of the deployment slots without service interruption:

1. In the Website's **Dashboard** section, locate the **Add a new deployment slot** link on the right.

2. Select a name and specify whether to clone its settings from an existing slot or start from scratch.

3. Now, under the main Website, there is an additional/dependent Website with its own public URL, web space, and settings.

Edit in Visual Studio Online

In this the recipe, we enabled the **Edit in Visual Studio Online** features. Now, on the **Dashboard** page, an **Edit in Visual Studio Online** link should appear on the right. By clicking it, we go to `https://[siteName].scm.azurewebsites.net/dev` site, also called project Monaco: a web-based integrated development environment with nice editing features.

Traffic Manager

Traffic Manager (**TM**) is a configurable DNS manager engine that distributes the traffic between URLs, based on a given policy. Typical scenarios for Traffic Manager are as follows:

- **Augment availability**: After providing TM with multiple endpoints of the same application, TM will cycle over them (round-robin) or choose the most responsive one (or nearest one)

- **Avoid downtime between upgrade**: In failover configuration, providing TM with a second endpoint, we can switch it with the primary with no downtime

In real-world scenarios, it is recommended to not expose the DNS name of the Azure Website directly; instead should be mapped to the public DNS name of the Traffic Manager, working under the hood.

See also

Have a look at these MSDN links to get additional information:

- Learn more about DNS and custom domains at `http://azure.microsoft.com/en-us/documentation/articles/web-sites-custom-domain-name/`

- Learn more about Visual Studio Online (Monaco) at `http://blogs.msdn.com/b/monaco/`

Source versioning and continuous integration with Git and TFS

In the *Deploying a Website* recipe, we saw how to deploy a Website directly through FTP or Web Deploy. Those strategies are very fast and effective; however, they are not always suitable in complex scenarios because of the following reasons:

▶ Developers cannot have direct access to the final endpoint or they should not even know what the final endpoint is

▶ Automated builds/tests should be performed after each release and check in, centrally controlled on a specified server

These two scenarios involve new actors while deploying Websites; in addition to the Developer and the Website, now there is also the source repository. In this recipe, we see how to invert the process:

▶ From:

  ❑ Developer upgrades/updates the Website directly

▶ To:

  ❑ Developer saves his or her code somewhere

  ❑ The Website takes that code and deploys it

This inversion of control makes the publishing process an administrative task by establishing a link between the Website and the desired source code repository.

Git is an open source, distributed source control system that is widely used by the developers' community. On the other side, TFS (and its SaaS correspondent Visual Studio Online) is the centrally managed, enterprise-ready software suite to integrate source control, automated builds/tests, and many other features.

In this recipe, we automate the deployment process by establishing proper connections between the Website and the source repositories by using Git and VSO.

Getting ready

This recipe assumes we have Git installed on the local machine. We also use a GUI Git client (TortoiseGit) to operate. To integrate TFS/VSO into the Website, we need a valid Visual Studio Online account. To get it, go to `http://www.visualstudio.com/` and activate a free plan (up to 5 users). After activation, go to the management page and create a team project called `Test01` for further use.

How to do it...

We are going to create a simple Website with static content, deploying it with Git integration. After that, we will create a simple ASP.NET web application, deploying it through TFS/VSO integration. The steps are as follows:

1. In the Azure Portal, create a new Website (that is, `TestWebSite`).

2. Go to the **Dashboard** tab and download the `Publish Profile` file.

Deployment from Git.

3. In the **Dashboard** tab of the created Website, click on the **Set up deployment from source control** link on the right.

4. Choose **Local Git repository** and confirm; a help page will appear.

5. Go to an empty folder with Explorer and right-click on the empty surface.

6. Click on the **Git Init Here** option, or using TortoiseGit, click on the **Git Create repository here** option.

7. Create a new `index.html` file (with Notepad) and paste this code as content:

   ```
   <h1>Hello From Git V1</h1>
   ```

8. Right-click on the file and perform the Git `add` operation, and then perform the Git commit specifying a message (that is, `First version`).

9. Now perform the Git `push` operation, specifying the URL in the form:

   ```
   https://[user]@[site].scm.azurewebsites.net:443/[site].git
   ```

10. Replace [user] with the username attribute found in the `Publish Profile` file (in the form `$siteName`). When Git asks for password, give it the one found in the `Publish Profile` file too.

11. In the **Deployments** tab of the Website page, **Active Deployment** with the name **First version** appears now. Browse the Website.

12. In the local folder, make the following change to the HTML file:

    ```
    <h1>Hello From Git V2</h1>
    ```

13. Repeat steps 8 and 9, specifying **Second version** as the commit message. A new active deployment will appear. Browse the Website.

14. Now click on the **First version** deployment and select **Redeploy** from the bottom menu. Browse the Website.

15. To unlink the Website from the Git repository, click on the **Delete Git repository** link on the right pane of the **Dashboard** tab.

Deployment from TFS/VSO.

16. Open Visual Studio and create a new ASP.NET web application called `DeployFromTFS`, with an empty template and web forms references.

17. Add the `Default.aspx` page and add this line into it:

    ```
    <h1>Hello from TFS V1</h1>
    ```

18. In the **Team Explorer** window, find **Connect to Team Projects** and locate the **Test01** project in the VSO endpoint.

 If this is the first time you are using TFS from Visual Studio, a link must be established before we can select the team project. To do that, in the **Connect to Team Foundation Server** window, click on **Servers** and add a new one in this form, `https://[name].visualstudio.com`, where `[name]` is the VSO account. Use the Microsoft Account with sufficient permission on that account.

19. Right-click on the solution and select **Add Solution to Source Control**.

20. Select a path under the **Test01** team project and confirm.

21. In the **Dashboard** tab of the Website, right-click on **Set up deployment from source control** and select **Visual Studio Online**.

22. Authorize the VSO account and select the team project **Test01**.

23. In Visual Studio, check in all the files of the solution with the **First version** comment.

24. After few seconds/minutes Azure will deploy the Website; browse it.

 Deploying from VSO could be slower than other methods, due to the build process involved.

It may need to remove the old `index.html` file used before in the recipe, or just append `/Default.aspx` to the web path.

25. Make this edit to the `Default.aspx` file from Visual Studio, and have a look at the **Second version** comment:

    ```
    <h1>Hello from TFS V2</h1>
    ```

26. Browse the Website and/or rollback the deployment.

How it works...

In steps 1 and 2, we created a new Website, obtaining its `Publish Profile` file.

In steps 3 and 4, we set up the link between a local Git repository in the Azure Website with the Website's root web space itself. In steps 5 and 6, we initialized a local repository on the local machine, a process that creates a hidden `.git` folder with definitions and settings. In step 7, we created a new HTML file, and we added and commit in step 8. Steps 9 and 10 described how to push/sync the local repository with the remote repository on the Azure side. In step 11, we verified the result.

Instead of using the default credentials shown on the help page of the **Deployment** tab on Azure, we use the credentials specified in the `Publish Profile` file. The first is tied to the administrative user (unique for all Websites), while the one in the `Publish Profile` file is valid for the specific Website, making the approach more secure.

In steps 12 and 13, we made some changes and commit, noticing the automatic replacement of the current deployment, which we rollbacked in step 14. To proceed with the recipe, using the same Website, we unlink Git from it as shown in step 15.

In steps 16 and 17, we created a new ASP.NET project with a sample page. In step 18, we connected to the VSO endpoint. Now the solution can be added to VSO, as shown in steps 19 and 20. Steps 21 and 22 showed you how to bind the Website to a team project in VSO, while in step 23 we checked in the code to trigger the build-and-deploy process.

In step 25, we learned how to trigger a further build just by checking-in an edit.

There's more...

TFS and Visual Studio Online (formerly, TFS) are enterprise-grade software suites with several features and support complex scenarios. The first requirement often needed by many is the capability of a given Website to bind to a specific web application project. In fact, in the recipe, the VSO integration took the first solution (and unique, in that case) it found by alphabetical order, and deployed it.

Let's add a new web application called `DeployWithTFSV2` into the existing solution. How does VSO/Azure know we want that one bound to the Website? If not specified, Azure takes the latest project involved in editing. To control the behavior, perform the following steps:

1. In the **Team Explorer** window of Visual Studio, go to the **build** section.

2. Select the **Build definition** of the desired Website (in the form `[sitename]_CD`).

3. Right-click on it and select **Edit Build Definition**.

4. In the **Process** section, select the **TfvcContinuousDeployment** template.

5. In the **Projects** field, select the specific project of the solution and remove the existing solution.

6. In the **MSBuild Arguments** field, paste this directive:

```
/p:VisualStudioVersion=12.0
```

7. Save and, at the next check-in, Azure will take the specified project.

However, the previous method does not prevent from deploying everything on each check-in, regardless of whether the correct project is involved in the check-in itself. We can simply ignore this or, better, we can change the source control folder of the build definition to the subfolder of the actual project to be built.

See also

Have a look at these MSDN links to get additional information:

- Learn more about the Visual Studio Online service at `http://msdn.microsoft.com/en-us/magazine/dn519923.aspx`
- Behind the scenes of Azure Websites—project Kudu at `https://github.com/projectkudu/kudu/wiki`

Logging abstraction from .NET and PHP

Azure Websites collect diagnostic data from several sources, shipping them on a given storage account or the same virtual filesystem where they reside. We can categorize diagnostic data into the following two groups:

- **Application Diagnostics**: Logs coming from the application code
- **Site Diagnostics**: Logs coming from several infrastructure sources. They are as follows:

  - **Web server logging**: Logs for every arriving HTTP request
  - **Detailed error messages**: HTTP status codes that indicate failures
  - **Failed request tracing**: A complete IIS trace of components involved in processing requests

In this recipe, we focus on the application diagnostics group, collecting application logs in the virtual filesystem, Table Storage, and Blob Storage services.

Getting ready

This recipe assumes we have a valid Azure subscription and Visual Studio 2013 with the latest Azure SDK installed. We also use the Azure command prompt (or the developer command prompt for Visual Studio), an FTP client (FileZilla), and a storage account.

How to do it...

We are going to create a simple website logging some messages in both ASP.NET and PHP. We collect logs in the storage and we stream them with the Azure command-line tools. The steps are as follows:

1. In the Azure Portal, create a new Website named `TestWebSite`.

2. In the **Dashboard** tab, download the `Publish Profile` file.

3. In the **Configure** tab, enable PHP 5.5 and enable application logging:

    ❏ File System (with an error logging level)

    ❏ Table Storage (with an information logging level)

    ❏ Blob Storage (with a verbose logging level)

4. Click on **Manage Table Storage** and select the desired storage account, creating a new table named `logs4testwebsite`.

5. Click on **Manage Blob Storage** and select the desired storage account, creating a new blob container named `logs4testwebsite`.

6. For the **Blob Storage** logs, set a retention of 14 days (default) to prevent excessive space being consumed and then click on **Save**.

ASP.NET Logging.

7. Open Visual Studio and create a new ASP.NET project with an empty template and Web Forms references.

8. Create a `Default.aspx` page with this content:

    ```
    <h1>On load it logs </h1>
    ```

9. Paste this code into the `Page_Load` event of the code:

    ```
    System.Diagnostics.Trace.TraceError("Error from .NET");
    System.Diagnostics.Trace.TraceWarning("Warning from .NET");
    System.Diagnostics.Trace.TraceInformation("Info from
      .NET");
    ```

10. Publish the Website using the `Publish Profile` file and browse the Website.

11. In the Azure node of the **Server Explorer**, find the **TestWebSite** Website, right-click on it, and select **View Streaming Logs**.

12. Wait for the streaming service to connect and trigger some log, refreshing the page on the browser.

13. Open the Blob container and the Table. Then, using the **Server Explorer** functions in the **Storage** node, check whether the different logging levels are correctly set up.

 PHP Logging.

14. Go to the **Dashboard** tab of the **TestWebSite** Website on the Azure Portal and click on **WebMatrix**; then select the **Edit live site directly** option.

15. Create an empty `phpinfo.php` file in the root folder with this content:

```php
<?php
phpinfo();
error_log("Error from PHP",0);
?>
```

16. Trigger the log by browsing the page several times.

17. Open FileZilla and connect to the Website using the credentials in the `Publish Profile` file.

18. Go up in the root Website folder and enter the `LogFiles` folder.

19. Open the `php_errors.log` file.

How it works...

In steps 1 and 2, we created a new website and we downloaded the `Publish Profile` file that contains the endpoint credentials for deployment. In step 3, we configured the Website, enabling the PHP support and the application diagnostics collection. In the production environment, consider just the **Table and Blob** storage methods, since the File System logging has to be intended for testing purposes. In addition, the **File System** logging has a temporary nature of 12 hours from its start; after that, Azure stops writing logs in the File System. In steps 4, 5, and 6, we configured the storage account(s) where to save logs with a retention policy for the Blob storage. File System logging and Blob Storage logging both save information in text files, while in different formats. Refer to the following points:

▶ File System logging, due to its temporary nature, only logs `Timestamp`, `Process ID`, `Level`, and `Message`

▶ Blob storage logging logs `date`, `Level`, `applicationName`, `instanceId`, `eventTickCount`, `eventId`, `pid`, `tid`, `Message`, and `activityId`

▸ Table storage logging logs `Timestamp`, `EventTickCount`, `ApplicationName`, `Level`, `EventId`, `InstanceId`, `Pid`, `Tid`, and `Message`

▸ `PartitionKey` is set to the date and time in the `AAAAMMDDHH` format

In steps 7 and 8, we created an ASP.NET application with a simple `Default.aspx` page with static content. In step 9, we used the `System.Diagnostics.Trace` class to log messages with different levels. After publishing in step 10, we experimented with log streaming in step 11. Since log streaming is available for the File System logging only, we see just the error logs due to the configuration made in step 3. We triggered some log events in step 12, while in step 13 we opened the Table and Blob container where the complete logs (with different log levels) are collected.

In step 14, we browsed the Website content using WebMatrix, adding a simple PHP file with logging code. By default, the PHP logs are collected in `/LogFiles/php_errors.log` relative path.

So, in step 17, we connected to that folder via FTP and we downloaded the logfile.

There's more...

We can stream the logfiles even outside Visual Studio using the command-line tools from the developer command prompt for Visual Studio. To do that, proceed as follows:

1. Open the developer command prompt for Visual Studio (or the Azure command prompt).

2. Download the account setting by typing:

   `azure account download`

3. Import the account settings by typing:

   `azure account import [path_to_file]`

4. Set the desired subscription by typing:

   `azure account set [subscription_name]`

5. Connect to the streaming logs service by typing:

   `azure site log tail [name_of_website]` (i.e. `"TestWebSite"`)

6. Now, browse either the PHP page or the ASP.NET page and enjoy the logs.

Log service can be customized with advanced options by overriding defaults appending new settings in the **App Settings** section of the **Configure** tab of the Website. For File System logs, there is a default limit on the total size of the `Application Logs` folder to 1 MB. To change this, we can append this setting:

`DIAGNOSTICS_TEXTTRACEMAXLOGFOLDERSIZEBYTES`

The desired size is specified in bytes.

See also

Have a look at these MSDN links to get additional information:

- ▶ Read this blog post about logging with Websites at `http://www.hanselman.com/blog/StreamingDiagnosticsTraceLoggingFromTheAzureCommandLinePlusGlimpse.aspx`

- ▶ Read the official documentation about troubleshooting Websites at `http://msdn.microsoft.com/library/azure/dn186185.aspx`

Deploying Java with Azure Websites

Azure Websites also support Java, executed through Tomcat or Jetty (two open source Web servers and Servlet containers). An in-depth discussion of Java language and platform is out of the scope of this book. So, in this recipe, we are going to look at the two supported runtimes.

Tomcat and Jetty's heritage is about 20 years old and they have become the leading platform for web applications written in Java. They are called Servlet container because they implement only the Servlet specification. A Servlet is a Java class that can respond to clients' requests, mostly used to respond to HTTP requests. The Java Servlet specification is part of the Java EE platform. However, both Tomcat and Jetty don't implement the full Java EE stack, as they are only Servlet container.

On the other hand, there are huge projects such as GlassFish or JBoss implementing the full Java EE stack, which includes JSF (Java Server Faces), EJB (Enterprise Java Beans), JTA (Java Transaction API), JPA (Java Persistence API) and more.

As a matter of fact, many web applications only need Servlet and JSPs (web pages with dynamic code) to run, so Tomcat and Jetty are suitable for those projects, also because they are pluggable with third-party components that extend the available features.

 Actually, Apache Software Foundation (the nonprofit group behind Tomcat) developed a JavaEE-compliant version of Tomcat, called TomEE (Tommy).

Tomcat runtime components are as follows:

- ▶ **Catalina**: This is the servlet container; it runs the execution engine of Tomcat.
- ▶ **Coyote**: This is the HTTP connector. It manages the incoming requests, forwarding them to the Tomcat engine.
- ▶ **Jasper**: This is the JSP processor. It compiles a JSP into a servlet to be passed to the Tomcat engine. A **Java Server Page** (**JSP**) is actually a servlet.

Jetty, on the other hand, is often referred to as a fast and small product, embedding some advanced features out of the box. It is developed by Eclipse Foundation and it is used by large clusters of machines for its lightweight runtime.

Getting ready

This recipe uses a sample `Hello World` WAR application file. We can download a sample WAR at `https://tomcat.apache.org/tomcat-7.0-doc/appdev/sample/sample.war`. It also needs an FTP client (FileZilla) to connect to the Website.

How to do it...

We are going to create a new Website with Java support, deploying the sample WAR file in both Tomcat and Jetty. We proceed as follows:

1. In the Azure Portal, create a new Website named `TestWebSite`.
2. In the **Dashboard** tab, download the `Publish Profile` file.
3. In the **Configure** tab, enable Java (click on the most recent Java Version, that is, 1.7.0). Many customization options will now become unavailable.

 Apache Tomcat

4. Select **Tomcat** as the execution environment and click on **Save**.
5. Connect to the Website using the FTP credentials found in the `Publish Profile` file.
6. In the root folder, locate the `webapps` folder and put the WAR file into it.
7. Wait for a few seconds and browse the Website relative path `/sample`.

 Eclipse Jetty

8. After step 3, stop the Website, select Jetty, and start it again. Browse the Website's root to verify.
9. Connect to the Website using FTP credentials found in the `Publish Profile` file.
10. In the `root` folder, locate the `webapps` folder and put the WAR file into it.
11. Wait for a few seconds and browse the Website's relative path `/sample`.

How it works...

In steps 1 and 2, we created a new Website and we downloaded the `Publish Profile` file, which contains the endpoint credentials for deployment. In step 3, we enabled Java, making many other options unavailable. Although .NET and PHP is supported, mixed mode between IIS and Java is not.

In step 4, we selected Tomcat as the servlet container. After saving, Azure creates a `webapps` folder in the root of the Website, where another folder, the `root` one, contains the default `index.jsp` page. This page shows the actual loading of the execution environment.

In steps 5 and 6, we connected to the Website using FTP. Notice the newly created `webapps` folder. In both Tomcat and Jetty, there is a standard deployment process. Every WAR file that we put in the `webapps` folder is automatically deployed in the `/[name]` subfolder. This is why in step 7 we waited for a few seconds and then saw the sample application running.

 This is the default behavior of Tomcat; however, with configuration, many settings are customizable, such as the remapping of the root application.

In step 8, we changed the runtime to Jetty and verified that the runtime was loaded.

 Be sure to see evidence of the desired execution environment at the bottom of the default page, for example (for Jetty), `D:\Program Files (x86)\jetty-distribution-9.1.0.v20131115`.

Steps 9, 10, and 11 were the same as the steps for Tomcat; this is the proof that they are similar in terms of the deployment process.

There's more...

On the Azure Portal (and from gallery), we only have the official supported version of Java and containers (Tomcat and Jetty), and we can also upload and run our version as described in the KB article at `http://azure.microsoft.com/en-us/documentation/articles/web-sites-java-custom-upload/`.

3
Getting Storage with Blobs in Azure

In this chapter, we will cover the following topics:

- ▶ Managing the Azure Storage service
- ▶ Connecting to the Azure Storage service
- ▶ Connecting to the storage emulator
- ▶ Managing access control for containers and blobs
- ▶ Creating a shared access signature for a container or blob
- ▶ Using a container-level access policy
- ▶ Setting properties and metadata for a blob
- ▶ Using blob directories
- ▶ Creating and using a blob snapshot
- ▶ Creating and using the root container for blobs
- ▶ Uploading blocks to a block blob
- ▶ Uploading a VHD into a page blob
- ▶ Downloading a blob asynchronously
- ▶ Using retry policies with blob operations
- ▶ Leasing a blob and implementing distributed locks
- ▶ Using the Azure Content Delivery Network (CDN)

Introduction

The **Azure Storage service** manages the storage of blobs, queues, and tables. It is essential that this data be kept secure so that there is no unauthorized access to it. Each storage account has an account name and two access keys used to authenticate access to the storage service. The management of these access keys is important. The storage service provides two access keys for each storage account so that the access key not being used can be regenerated. We will see how to do this in the *Managing the Azure Storage service* recipe.

The storage service supports **hash-based message authentication** (**HMAC**), in which a storage operation request is hashed with the access key. On receiving the request, the storage service validates it and either accepts or denies it. The Azure Storage library provides several classes that support various ways of creating an HMAC and that hide the complexity of creating and using one. We will see how to use them in the *Connecting to the Azure Storage service* recipe.

 Almost every recipe of the chapter is based on the Storage library. It should be downloaded with NuGet, directly from inside Visual Studio. This guarantees that you are using the latest version available.

The **Azure SDK** provides a compute emulator and a storage emulator. The latter uses a hardcoded account name and access key. We will see the support provided for this in the *Connecting to the storage emulator* recipe.

Blobs are ideal for storing static content, organized in containers and files. A container can be configured either to be private or to allow anonymous access to the blobs (files) in it (blobs in such a container can be downloaded without any authentication at all). We will see how to configure this in the *Managing access control for containers and blobs* recipe.

There is a need to provide an intermediate level of authentication for containers and blobs, a level that lies between full authentication and anonymous access. The Storage service supports the concept of a shared access signature, which is a precalculated authentication token that can be shared in a controlled manner and which allows the bearer to access a specific container or blob for a limited timeframe. We will see how to do this in the *Creating a shared access signature for a container or blob* recipe.

A shared access policy combines access rights with the time for which they are valid. A container-level access policy is a shared access policy that is associated with a container by name. A best practice is to derive a shared access signature from a container-level access policy. Doing this provides greater control over the shared access signature, as it becomes possible to revoke it. We will see how to do this in the *Using a container-level access policy* recipe.

Nearly all the recipes in this chapter use the Storage Client library. Scattered through the recipes are examples of how to use it for basic operations such as creating a container and uploading blobs.

 As it is not covered in this book, it is worthwhile to have some knowledge of the Storage Service REST API, because it is informative to look at the raw REST operations sent over the wire to the storage service when debugging problems with storage operations.

In the *Leasing a blob and implementing distributed locks* recipe, we will see how to use the Lease Blob feature, which is particularly useful while implementing distributed locks.

Later in the chapter, we will see that there are two types of blobs. The first is block blobs, optimized for streaming, and the second is page blobs, optimized for random access. In the *Uploading blocks to a block blob* recipe, we will see how to increase control over the uploading of a block blob by uploading individual blocks and then committing them to create the block blob. In the *Uploading a VHD into a page blob* recipe, we will see how to improve the upload performance by uploading only nonempty pages. The primary use case for page blobs is the storage of **Virtual Hard Disks** (**VHDs**), which can then be attached as OS or data drives in the Azure Virtual Machines.

Blobs can have both properties and metadata associated with them. The properties comprise standard HTTP header fields that provide additional information to the clients who download the blobs. The metadata comprises a sequence of arbitrary name-value pairs. In the *Setting properties and metadata for a blob* recipe, we will see how to use properties and metadata.

The Blob service supports the creation of a blob snapshot to provide a read-only version of the contents of a blob when the snapshot is created. A blob can be rolled back to an earlier state by copying the snapshot over it. The *Creating and using a blob snapshot* recipe will show us blob snapshots in action.

The Blob service stores blobs in a simple two-level hierarchy of containers and blobs. In the *Using blob directories* recipe, we will use the pseudo-directory support provided by the Blob service to simulate a more complex hierarchy that mimics directories in a filesystem. In the *Creating and using the root container for blobs* recipe, we will see how to create a root directory that allows blobs to appear as if they are located at the root of the hierarchy and not inside a container.

The Storage library provides both synchronous and asynchronous versions of almost all the methods that access the Storage service. The asynchronous methods adhere to the Async/Await pattern. In the *Downloading a blob asynchronously* recipe, we will see how easy it is to use the asynchronous methods to download a blob.

A storage operation against the storage service might fail for various reasons. Consequently, the Storage library provides built-in support for retries of failed operations. In the *Using retry policies with blob operations* recipe, we will see how to parameterize the existing retry behavior and implement the custom retry functionality.

In the Blob service, a blob resource is addressed as follows:

```
http://{account}.blob.core.windows.net/{container}/{blob}
```

The {account}, {container}, and {blob} methods represent the name of the storage account, container, and blob, respectively. However, the Azure **Content Delivery Network** (**CDN**) can be used to cache blobs closer to the user. This significantly improves the download performance and latency of blobs. In the *Using the Azure Content Delivery Network (CDN)* recipe, we will see how to use the CDN and configure custom domains for both the Blob service and the CDN.

Managing the Azure Storage service

The data stored by the Azure Storage service must be secured against unauthorized access. To ensure this security, all storage operations against the Table and Queue services must be authenticated. Similarly, other than inquiry requests against public containers and blobs, all operations against the Blob service must also be authenticated. The Blob service supports public containers so that, for example, blobs that contain images can be downloaded directly into a web page anonymously, without any authentication.

Each storage account has a primary access key and secondary access key that can be used to authenticate operations against the storage service. When creating a request against the storage service, one of the keys is used along with various request headers to generate a 256-bit hash-based message authentication code (HMAC). This HMAC is added as an authorization request header to the request. On receiving the request, the Storage service recalculates the HMAC and rejects the request if the received and calculated HMAC values differ. The Azure Storage Library provides methods that manage the creation of the HMAC and attach it to the storage operation request.

There is no distinction between the primary and secondary access keys. The purpose of the secondary access key is to enable continued use of the Storage service while the other access key is being regenerated. While the primary access key is used for authentication against the Storage service, the secondary access key can be regenerated without impacting the service, and vice versa. This can be extremely useful in situations where storage access credentials must be rotated regularly due to the necessity of sharing them with the developers.

As possession of the storage account name and access key is sufficient to provide complete control over the data managed by the storage account, it is essential that the access keys be kept secure (and changed at regular intervals as a security policy). In particular, access keys should never be downloaded to a client such as a smart phone, as this exposes them to potential abuse.

In this recipe, we'll learn how to use the primary and secondary access keys.

How to do it...

We are going to create a storage account, view the access keys, and regenerate the secondary one. We will do this using the following steps:

1. Go to the Azure Portal.

2. In the underlying menu, navigate to **New** | **Data Services** | **Storage** | **Quick Create**.

3. In the URL textbox, specify the name of the endpoint you want the storage account reply from.

Every storage account in the Azure platform is a combination of four services: blobs, tables, queues, and files. As we specify just one account name, Azure appends the `myaccount` suffix to that name to indicate the four different services in the form of respective service endpoints as follows:

- `myaccount.blob.core.windows.net`
- `myaccount.table.core.windows.net`
- `myaccount.queue.core.windows.net`
- `myaccount.file.core.windows.net`

4. In the **Location/Affinity Group** dropdown, select the **Region** that will contain the storage account.

5. Select the **Geo-Replication** type in the dropdown and confirm.

6. After a few minutes, needed by the creation process, go to the **Storage** section of the Azure Portal and click on the newly created account.

7. In the underlying menu, click on the **Manage Access Keys** icon; a popup will appear.

8. In the **Manage Access Keys** popup, locate the secondary access key and click on **Regenerate**.

How it works...

In step 2, we used the general menu of the Azure Portal to create a new resource and a new storage account. In steps 3 and 4, we gave a name to the storage account and chose a location for it.

In step 5, we left the **Geo-Replication** feature of the storage account enabled to ensure that our data is preserved in two distinct regions to prevent data loss in case of a disaster. The Geo-Replication feature, even if it is not required, guarantees a strong level of security for the critical data by maintaining a copy of the entire storage account, for an additional cost.

After waiting for the account to be created in step 6, we opened the **Manage Access Keys** window, where we can choose which access key to regenerate. It is important that we never regenerate the access key that is currently being used, as doing so immediately renders the storage account inaccessible. Consequently, we regenerate only the secondary access key if the primary access key is currently in use, and vice versa.

In the **Manage Access Keys** window, you can copy the account name and the primary and secondary keys to the clipboard.

There's more...

In step 5, we showed how to enable the Geo-Replication feature during the account creation phase. In fact, we could also disable the Geo-Replication feature (which is enabled by default) to reduce the pricing impact by around 25 percent of the total. Indeed, a **Locally Redundant Storage** (**LRS**) account costs less than a **Geo Redundant Storage** (**GRS**) account. Eventually, if you decide to enable the Geo-Replication feature for the second time, be aware of a one-time charge to replicate the existing data to the secondary location.

The third option is **Read Access Geo-Redundant Storage** (**RA-GRS**). This provides read access to a secondary storage replica in case the storage account on the primary location becomes unavailable.

This secondary endpoint is similar to the primary endpoint, except for the `-secondary` suffix. For example, if the primary endpoint is `myccount.<service>.core.windows.net`, the secondary endpoint is `myaccount-secondary.<service>.core.windows.net`.

See also

Have a look at the following MSDN links to get additional information:

- ▶ How to manage storage accounts at `http://azure.microsoft.com/en-en/documentation/articles/storage-manage-storage-account/`
- ▶ Pricing differences between LRS/GRS/RA-GRS at `http://azure.microsoft.com/en-us/pricing/details/storage/`

Connecting to the Azure Storage service

In an Azure cloud service, the storage account name and access key are stored in the service configuration file. By convention, the account name and access key for data access are provided in a setting named `DataConnectionString`. The account name and access key needed for Azure Diagnostics must be provided in a setting named `Microsoft.WindowsAzure.Plugins.Diagnostics.ConnectionString`.

> The `DataConnectionString` setting must be declared in the `ConfigurationSettings` section of the service definition file. However, unlike other settings, the connection string setting for Azure Diagnostics is implicitly defined when the Diagnostics module is specified in the `Imports` section of the service definition file. Consequently, it must not be specified in the `ConfigurationSettings` section.

A best practice is to use different storage accounts for application data and diagnostic data. This reduces the possibility of application data access being throttled by competition for concurrent writes from the diagnostics monitor.

> **What is throttling?**
>
> In shared services, where the same resources are shared between tenants, limiting the concurrent access to them is critical to provide service availability. If a client misuses the service or, better, generates a huge amount of traffic, other tenants pointing to the same shared resource could experience unavailability. **Throttling** (also known as **Traffic Control** plus **Request Cutting**) is one of the most adopted solutions for this issue.

It also provides a security boundary between application data and diagnostics data, as diagnostics data might be accessed by individuals who should have no access to application data.

In the Azure Storage library, access to the Storage service is through one of the `Client` classes. There is one `Client` class for each Blob service, Queue service, and Table service; they are `CloudBlobClient`, `CloudQueueClient`, and `CloudTableClient`, respectively. Instances of these classes store the pertinent endpoint as well as the account name and access key.

The `CloudBlobClient` class provides methods to access containers, list their contents, and get references to containers and blobs. The `CloudQueueClient` class provides methods to list queues and get a reference to the `CloudQueue` instance that is used as an entry point to the Queue service functionality. The `CloudTableClient` class provides methods to manage tables and get the `TableServiceContext` instance that is used to access the **WCF Data Services** functionality while accessing the Table service. Note that the `CloudBlobClient`, `CloudQueueClient`, and `CloudTableClient` instances are not thread safe, so distinct instances should be used when accessing these services concurrently.

The client classes must be initialized with the account name, access key, as well as the appropriate Storage service endpoint. The `Microsoft.WindowsAzure` namespace has several helper classes. The `StorageCredential` class initializes an instance from an account name and access key or from a shared access signature.

In this recipe, we'll learn how to use the `CloudBlobClient`, `CloudQueueClient`, and `CloudTableClient` instances to connect to the Storage service.

Getting ready

This recipe assumes that the application's configuration file contains the following:

```
<appSettings>
  <add key="DataConnectionString"
value="DefaultEndpointsProtocol=https;AccountName={ACCOUNT_
NAME};AccountKey={ACCOUNT_KEY}"/>
    <add key="AccountName" value="{ACCOUNT_NAME}"/>
    <add key="AccountKey" value="{ACCOUNT_KEY}"/>
</appSettings>
```

We must replace {ACCOUNT_NAME} and {ACCOUNT_KEY} with appropriate values for the storage account name and access key, respectively.

We are not working in a Cloud Service but in a simple console application. Storage services, like many other building blocks of Azure, can also be used separately from on-premise environments.

How to do it...

We are going to connect to the Table service, the Blob service, and the Queue service, and perform a simple operation on each. We will do this using the following steps:

1. Add a new class named `ConnectingToStorageExample` to the project.

2. Add the following `using` statements to the top of the class file:

```
using Microsoft.WindowsAzure.Storage;
using Microsoft.WindowsAzure.Storage.Blob;
using Microsoft.WindowsAzure.Storage.Queue;
using Microsoft.WindowsAzure.Storage.Table;
using Microsoft.WindowsAzure.Storage.Auth;
using System.Configuration;
```

 The `System.Configuration` assembly should be added via the **Add Reference** action onto the project, as it is not included in most of the project templates of Visual Studio.

3. Add the following method, connecting the Blob service, to the class:

```
private static void UseCloudStorageAccountExtensions()
{
    CloudStorageAccount cloudStorageAccount =
        CloudStorageAccount.Parse(
        ConfigurationManager.AppSettings[
        "DataConnectionString"]);

    CloudBlobClient cloudBlobClient =
        cloudStorageAccount.CreateCloudBlobClient();
    CloudBlobContainer cloudBlobContainer =
        cloudBlobClient.GetContainerReference(
        "{NAME}");

    cloudBlobContainer.CreateIfNotExists();
}
```

4. Add the following method, connecting the Table service, to the class:

```
private static void UseCredentials()
{
    string accountName = ConfigurationManager.AppSettings[
        "AccountName"];
    string accountKey = ConfigurationManager.AppSettings[
        "AccountKey"];
```

```
    StorageCredentials storageCredentials =
        new StorageCredentials(
        accountName, accountKey);

    CloudStorageAccount cloudStorageAccount =
        new CloudStorageAccount(storageCredentials, true);
    CloudTableClient tableClient =
        new CloudTableClient(
        cloudStorageAccount.TableEndpoint,
        storageCredentials);

    CloudTable table =
        tableClient.GetTableReference("{NAME}");
    table.CreateIfNotExists();
}
```

5. Add the following method, connecting the Queue service, to the class:

```
private static void UseCredentialsWithUri()
{
    string accountName = ConfigurationManager.AppSettings[
        "AccountName"];
    string accountKey = ConfigurationManager.AppSettings[
        "AccountKey"];
    StorageCredentials storageCredentials =
        new StorageCredentials(
        accountName, accountKey);

    StorageUri baseUri =
        new StorageUri(new Uri(string.Format(
            "https://{0}.queue.core.windows.net/",
        accountName)));
    CloudQueueClient cloudQueueClient =
        new CloudQueueClient(baseUri, storageCredentials);
    CloudQueue cloudQueue =
        cloudQueueClient.GetQueueReference("{NAME}");

    cloudQueue.CreateIfNotExists();
}
```

6. Add the following method, using the other methods, to the class:

```
public static void UseConnectionToStorageExample()
{
    UseCloudStorageAccountExtensions();
    UseCredentials();
    UseCredentialsWithUri();
}
```

How it works...

In steps 1 and 2, we set up the class. In step 3, we implemented the standard way to access the storage service using the Storage Client Library. We used the static `CloudStorageAccount.Parse()` method to create a `CloudStorageAccount` instance from the value of the connection string stored in the configuration file. We then used this instance with the `CreateCloudBlobClient()` extension method of the `CloudStorageAccount` class to get the `CloudBlobClient` instance that we used to connect to the Blob service. We can also use this technique with the Table service and the Queue service, using the relevant extension methods, `CreateCloudTableClient()` and `CreateCloudQueueClient()`, respectively, for them. We completed this example using the `CloudBlobClient` instance to get a `CloudBlobContainer` reference to a container and then created it if it does not exist. We need to replace {NAME} with the name for a container.

In step 4, we created a `StorageCredentials` instance directly from the account name and access key. We then used this to construct a `CloudStorageAccount` instance, specifying that any connection should use HTTPS. Using this technique, we need to provide the Table service endpoint explicitly when creating the `CloudTableClient` instance. We then used this to create the table. We need to replace {NAME} with the name of a table. We can use the same technique with the Blob service and Queue service using the relevant `CloudBlobClient` or `CloudQueueClient` constructor.

In step 5, we used a similar technique, except that we avoided the intermediate step of using a `CloudStorageAccount` instance and explicitly provided the endpoint for the Queue service. We used the `CloudQueueClient` instance created in this step to create the queue. We need to replace {NAME} with the name of a queue. Note that we hardcoded the endpoint for the Queue service.

Though this last method is officially supported, it is not a best practice to bind our code to hardcoded strings with endpoint URIs. So, it is preferable to use one of the previous methods that hides the complexity of the URI generation at the library level.

In step 6, we added a method that invokes the methods added in the earlier steps.

There's more...

With the general availability of the .NET Framework Version 4.5, many libraries of the CLR have been added with the support of asynchronous methods with the Async/Await pattern. Latest versions of the Azure Storage Library also have these overloads, which are useful while developing mobile applications, and fast web APIs. They are generally useful when it is needed to combine the task execution model into our applications.

Almost every long-running method of the library has its corresponding `methodAsync()` method to be called as follows:

```
await cloudQueue.CreateIfNotExistsAsync();
```

In the rest of the book, we will continue to use the standard, synchronous pattern.

See also

Have a look at these MSDN links to get additional information:

- Azure Storage scalability targets at `http://msdn.microsoft.com/en-us/library/azure/dn249410.aspx`

- More about Storage connection strings at `http://msdn.microsoft.com/en-us/library/azure/ee758697.aspx`

Connecting to the storage emulator

The Azure SDK provides a **compute emulator** and a **storage emulator** that work in a development environment to provide a local emulation of Azure cloud services and storage services. There are some differences in functionality between storage services and the storage emulator.

 By default, the storage emulator uses `LocalDB`, but it can be configured to use an SQL server. More information on MSDN can be found at `http://msdn.microsoft.com/en-us/library/azure/gg433132.aspx`

An immediate difference is that the storage emulator supports only one account name and access key. The account name is hardcoded as `devstoreaccount1`. The access key is hardcoded to the following code:

```
Eby8vdM02xNOcqFlqUwJPLlmEtlCDXJ1OUzFT50uSRZ6IFsuFq2UVErCz4I6tq/
K1SZFPTOtr/KBHBeksoGMGw==
```

Another difference is that the storage endpoints are constructed differently for the storage emulator. The Storage service uses URL subdomains to distinguish the endpoints for the various types of storage. For example, the endpoint for the Blob service for a storage account named `myaccount` is as follows:

```
myaccount.blob.core.windows.net
```

The endpoints for the other storage types are constructed similarly by replacing the word `blob` with either `table` or `queue`.

This differentiation by the subdomain name is not used in the storage emulator, which is hosted on the local host at `127.0.0.1`. Instead, the storage emulator distinguishes the endpoints for the various types of storage through the use of different ports. Furthermore, the account name, rather than being part of the subdomain, is provided as part of the URL. Consequently, the endpoints used by the storage emulator are as follows:

- `127.0.0.1:10000/devstoreaccount1` Blob
- `127.0.0.1:10001/devstoreaccount1` Queue
- `127.0.0.1:10002/devstoreaccount1` Table

The Azure Storage library hides much of this complexity, but an understanding of it remains important in case something goes wrong. The account name and access key are hardcoded into the Storage library, which also provides simple access to an appropriately constructed `CloudStorageAccount` object.

The Storage Client library also supports a special value for the `DataConnectionString` property in the service configuration file. Instead of specifying the account name and access key, it is sufficient to specify the following:

```
UseDevelopmentStorage=true
```

For example, this is specified as follows for a cloud service in the service configuration file:

```
<Setting name="DataConnectionString" value="UseDevelopm
entStorage=true" />
```

This value can also be used for the `Microsoft.WindowsAzure.Plugins.Diagnostics.ConnectionString` data connection string required for Azure Diagnostics.

The `CloudStorageAccount.Parse()` and `CloudStorageAccount.FromConnectionString()` methods handle this value in a special way to create a `CloudStorageAccount` object that can be used to authenticate against the storage emulator.

In this recipe, we'll learn how to connect to the storage emulator.

How to do it...

We are going to connect to the storage emulator in various ways and perform some operations on blobs. We will do this using the following steps:

1. Add a class named `StorageEmulatorExample` to the project.

2. Add the following `using` statements to the top of the class file:

   ```
   using Microsoft.WindowsAzure.Storage;
   using Microsoft.WindowsAzure.Storage.Blob;
   ```

3. Add the following `private` members to the class:

   ```
   private string containerName;
   private string blobName;
   ```

4. Add the following constructor to the class:

   ```
   StorageEmulatorExample(string containerName, string blobName)
   {
     this.containerName = containerName;
     this.blobName = blobName;
   }
   ```

5. Add the following method, using the `CloudStorageAccount.DevelopmentStorageAccount` property, to the class:

   ```
   private void UseDevelopmentStorageAccount()
   {
       CloudStorageAccount cloudStorageAccount =
           CloudStorageAccount.DevelopmentStorageAccount;

       CloudBlobClient cloudBlobClient =
           cloudStorageAccount.CreateCloudBlobClient();

       CloudBlobContainer cloudBlobContainer =
           cloudBlobClient.GetContainerReference(containerName);
       CloudBlockBlob cloudBlockBlob =
           cloudBlobContainer.GetBlockBlobReference(blobName);

       cloudBlobContainer.CreateIfNotExists();

       cloudBlockBlob.UploadText("Sample text");
       cloudBlockBlob.Metadata.Add("Prop1","Value1");
       cloudBlockBlob.SetMetadata();
   }
   ```

6. Add the following method, using the methods added earlier, to the class:

```
public static void UseStorageEmulatorExample()
{
    StorageEmulatorExample example =
        new StorageEmulatorExample("public", "test.txt");
    example.UseDevelopmentStorageAccount();
}
```

How it works...

In steps 1 and 2, we set up the class. In step 3, we add some `private` members for the container name and blob name, which we initialize in the constructor that we add in step 4.

In step 5, we initialize a `CloudStorageAccount` class from the hardcoded `DevelopmentStorageAccount` property exposed by the class. We then get a reference to a `CloudBlockBlob` class from the specified container (which needs to be created if it does not exist). Then, we upload a text content to the blob and add some metadata.

In step 6, we add a `helper` method that invokes the method we added earlier. We can replace the container and blob names with appropriate names.

There's more...

Fiddler is a program that captures HTTP traffic; this makes it very useful for diagnosing problems when using the Azure Storage service. Its use is completely transparent when cloud storage is being used. However, the data connection string must be modified if you want Fiddler to be able to monitor the traffic to the Development Storage. The data connection string must be changed to the following line of code:

```
UseDevelopmentStorage=true;DevelopmentStorageProxyUri=http://ipv4.
fiddler
```

Fiddler can be downloaded from `http://www.telerik.com/fiddler`.

Protocol versions in Storage Emulator

Sometimes it could happen that Microsoft releases updates to the various libraries (for example, the Storage one) with some misalignment with the Visual Studio SDK. For instance, a further version of a Storage library could not be compatible with the latest version of the Storage Emulator.

This is because in the Storage library, each request is sent over the Internet with a HTTP header that represents the version of the service protocol:

```
x-ms-version: 2013-08-15
```

If the storage emulator implements a different version of the protocol or the operation is not supported in the specified version, it will reply with a **Bad Request** (**400**) error code.

See also

Have a look at the following MSDN links to get additional information:

▸ Storage Emulator Command-Line Tool at http://msdn.microsoft.com/en-us/library/azure/gg433005.aspx

▸ Differences between the Storage Emulator and Azure Storage at http://msdn.microsoft.com/en-us/library/azure/gg433135.aspx

Managing access control for containers and blobs

The Storage service allows the possibility of *unauthenticated access* against the Blob service. The reason is that blobs provide an ideal location to store large static content for a website. For example, the images in a photo-sharing site could be stored as blobs and downloaded directly from the Blob service without being transferred through a web role.

Public access control for the Blob service is managed at the container level. The Blob service supports three types of **access control**: the first type is no public read access, in which all access must be authenticated; the second is public read access, which allows blobs in a container to be readable without authentication; and the third type is full public read access, in which authentication is not required to read the container's data and the blobs contained in it. No public read access is the same access control as for the Queue service and Table service. The other two access control types allow anonymous access to a blob so that, for example, the blob can be downloaded into a browser by providing its complete URL.

In the Azure Storage library, the BlobContainerPublicAccessType enumeration specifies the three types of public access control for a container. The BlobContainerPermissions class exposes two properties: PublicAccess, which specifies a member of the BlobContainerPublicAccessType enumeration, and SharedAccessPolicies, which specifies a set of shared access policies. The SetPermissions() method of the CloudBlobContainer class is used to associate a BlobContainerPermissions instance with the container. The GetPermissions() method retrieves the access permissions for a container.

In this recipe, we'll learn how to specify the level of public access control for containers and blobs managed by the Blob service.

Getting ready

This recipe assumes that the following lines of code are in the application's configuration file:

```
<appSettings>
  <add key="DataConnectionString"value="DefaultEndpointsProtocol=https
;AccountName={ACCOUNT_NAME};AccountKey={ACCOUNT_KEY}"/>
</appSettings>
```

We must replace {ACCOUNT_NAME} and {ACCOUNT_KEY} with the appropriate values for the account name and access key, respectively.

How to do it...

We are going to specify various levels of public access control for a container. We will do this using the following steps:

1. Add a new class named `BlobContainerPublicAccessExample` to the project.

2. Add the following `using` statements to the top of the class file:
   ```
   using Microsoft.WindowsAzure.Storage;
   using Microsoft.WindowsAzure.Storage.Blob;
   using System.Configuration;
   using System.Net;
   ```

3. Add the following method, setting public access control for a container, to the class:
   ```
   public static void CreateContainerAndSetPermission(
   String containerName, String blobName,
   BlobContainerPublicAccessType publicAccessType)
   {
       CloudStorageAccount cloudStorageAccount =
           CloudStorageAccount.Parse(
           ConfigurationManager.AppSettings[
           "DataConnectionString"]);
       CloudBlobClient cloudBlobClient =
           cloudStorageAccount.CreateCloudBlobClient();

       CloudBlobContainer blobContainer =
           cloudBlobClient.GetContainerReference(containerName);
       blobContainer.CreateIfNotExists();

       BlobContainerPermissions blobContainerPermissions =
           new BlobContainerPermissions()
           {
               PublicAccess = publicAccessType
   ```

```
        };
        blobContainer.SetPermissions(blobContainerPermissions);

        CloudBlockBlob blockBlob =
            blobContainer.GetBlockBlobReference(blobName);
        blockBlob.UploadText("Has been changed glorious summer");
    }
```

4. Add the following method, retrieving a blob, to the class:

```
public static void GetBlob(
String containerName, String blobName)
{
    CloudStorageAccount cloudStorageAccount =
        CloudStorageAccount.Parse(
        ConfigurationManager.AppSettings[
        "DataConnectionString"]);
    Uri blobUri = new Uri(cloudStorageAccount.BlobEndpoint +
        containerName + "/" + blobName);

    HttpWebRequest httpWebRequest =
        (HttpWebRequest)HttpWebRequest.Create(blobUri);
    httpWebRequest.Method = "GET";
    using (HttpWebResponse response =
        (HttpWebResponse)httpWebRequest.GetResponse())
    {
        String status = response.StatusDescription;
    }
}
```

5. Add the following method, using the method we just added, to the class:

```
public static void UseBlobContainerPublicAccessExample()
{
    CreateContainerAndSetPermission("container1", "blob1",
        BlobContainerPublicAccessType.Blob);

    CreateContainerAndSetPermission("container2", "blob2",
        BlobContainerPublicAccessType.Container);

    CreateContainerAndSetPermission("container3", "blob3",
        BlobContainerPublicAccessType.Off);

    GetBlob("container1", "blob1");
    //This leads to an exception
    GetBlob("container3", "blob3");
}
```

How it works...

In steps 1 and 2, we set up the class.

In step 3, we added a method that creates a container and blob, and applies a public access policy to the container. We created a `CloudBlobClient` instance from the data connection string in the configuration file. We then created a new container using the `CloudBlobContainer` reference obtained through the `CloudBlobClient` method. Then, we created a `BlobContainerPermissions` instance with the `BlobContainerPublicAccessType` enumeration passed into the method and set the permissions on the container. Note that we must create the container before we set the permissions, as `SetPermissions()` sets the permissions directly on the container. Finally, we created a blob in the container.

> It is also possible to specify the permissions of the container directly into the `Create()` or `CreateIfNotExists()` method. However, as we use the latter method, we do not know in advance if the requested container exists, and consequently, we need to be sure to apply the permission to the existing container.

In step 4, we used an `HttpWebRequest` instance to retrieve the blob without providing any authentication. This request causes a **Not Found** (**404**) error when the request attempts to retrieve a blob that has not been configured for public access. Note that when constructing `blobUri` for the storage emulator, we must add a / into the path after `cloudStorageAccount.BlobEndpoint` because of a difference in the way the Storage Client library constructs the endpoint for the Storage Emulator and the Storage service. For example, we need to use the following code for the Storage Emulator:

```
Uri blobUri = new Uri(cloudStorageAccount.BlobEndpoint + "/" +
    containerName + "/" + blobName);
```

> There are further APIs to list and get blob contents from. This *raw* method has to be used for demonstration purposes only.

In step 5, we added a method that invokes the `CreateContainerAndSetPermission()` method once for each value of the `BlobContainerPublicAccessType` enumeration. We finally invoked the `GetBlob` method for the public container and for the private one. The second call will result in a runtime exception due to the HTTP 404 error, as `container3` has not been configured for unauthenticated public access.

See also

The Blob service provides shared-access signatures, which provide time-limited public access to containers and blobs. We will see how to use them in the *Creating a shared access signature for a container or blob* recipe.

Have a look at the following MSDN link to get additional information:

> ▸ Security options for Azure Storage containers and blobs at `http://msdn.microsoft.com/en-us/library/azure/dd179354.aspx`

Creating a shared access signature for a container or blob

The Azure Blob service supports fully authenticated requests, anonymous requests, and requests authenticated by a temporary access key, referred to as a shared access signature. The latter allows access to containers or blobs to only those in possession of the shared access signature.

A shared access signature is constructed from a combination of the following:

> ▸ Resource (container or blob)
>
> ▸ Access rights (read, write, delete, and list)
>
> ▸ Start time
>
> ▸ Expiration time
>
> ▸ Advanced settings

These are combined into a string from which a 256-bit HMAC is generated. An access key for the storage account is used to seed the HMAC generation. This HMAC is referred to as a shared access signature. The process of generating a shared access signature requires no interaction with the Blob service.

Prior to API Version **2012-02-12**, a shared access signature was valid for up to 1 hour, which limited the allowable values for the start time and expiration time. We must pay attention to those applications that use old APIs, as the behavior could be different from what we expect. In Version **2012-02-12** and newer ones, we must specify the API version while creating a SAS Token.

When using a shared access signature to authenticate a request, it is submitted as one of the query string parameters. The other query parameters comprise information from which the shared access signature was created. This allows the Blob service to create a shared access signature, using the access key for the storage account, and compare it with the shared access signature submitted with the request. A request is denied if it has an invalid shared access signature.

An example of a storage request for a blob named `myBlob` in a container named `test01` is as follows:

```
GET /test01/myBlob.txt
```

An example of the query string parameters is as follows:

```
?sv=2013-08-15&sr=b&sp=r
&st=2013-12-08T15%3A03%3A17Z
&se=2013-12-12T15%3A03%3A17Z
&sig=oPijtM59CPrMvGa4CvfhrumhEWPl6eRhoBF9WCGgY3k%3D
```

The following are the definitions of query string parameters:

- `st`: This parameter is the start time for the validity of the shared access signature.
- `se`: This parameter is the expiration time for the validity of the shared access signature.
- `sr`: This parameter specifies that the shared access signature is for a blob.
- `sp`: This parameter specifies the permissions associated with the shared access signature.
- `sv`: This parameter specifies the API version that is requested.
- `sig`: This parameter is the shared access signature.

 The complete description of these parameters can be found at `http://msdn.microsoft.com/en-us/library/ee395415.aspx`.

Once a shared access signature has been created and transferred to a client, no further verification of the client is required. Hence, it is important for the shared access signature to be created with the minimum period of validity and for its distribution to be restricted as much as possible. It is not possible to revoke a shared access signature created in this manner, except by regenerating the access key of the storage account that is used to generate the SAS Token.

In this recipe, we'll learn how to create and use a shared access signature.

Getting ready

This recipe assumes that the following lines of code are in the application's configuration file:

```
<appSettings>
  <add key="DataConnectionString"
value="DefaultEndpointsProtocol=https;AccountName={ACCOUNT_
NAME};AccountKey={ACCOUNT_KEY}"/>
</appSettings>
```

We must replace {ACCOUNT_NAME} and {ACCOUNT_KEY} with appropriate values for the account name and access key, respectively.

How to do it...

We are going to create and use shared access signatures for a blob. We will do this using the following steps:

1. Add a class named SharedAccessSignaturesExample to the project.

2. Add the following using statements to the top of the class file:

```
using Microsoft.WindowsAzure.Storage;
using Microsoft.WindowsAzure.Storage.Auth;
using Microsoft.WindowsAzure.Storage.Blob;
using System.Configuration;
using System.Security.Cryptography;
```

3. Add the following private members to the class:

```
private String blobEndpoint;
private String accountName;
private String accountKey;
private DateTime utcNow;
```

4. Add the following constructor to the class:

```
SharedAccessSignaturesExample()
{
    CloudStorageAccount cloudStorageAccount =
        CloudStorageAccount.Parse(
        ConfigurationManager.AppSettings[
        "DataConnectionString"]);
    blobEndpoint =
        cloudStorageAccount.BlobEndpoint.AbsoluteUri;
    accountName = cloudStorageAccount.Credentials.AccountName;
    utcNow = DateTime.UtcNow;
```

```
        StorageCredentials accountAndKey =
            cloudStorageAccount.Credentials;
        accountKey =
            accountAndKey.ExportBase64EncodedKey();
}
```

5. Add the following method to the class to obtain a reference to the blob:

```
private static CloudBlockBlob GetBlob
    (String containerName, String blobName)
{
    CloudStorageAccount cloudStorageAccount =
        CloudStorageAccount.Parse(
        ConfigurationManager.AppSettings[
        "DataConnectionString"]);
    CloudBlobClient cloudBlobClient =
        cloudStorageAccount.CreateCloudBlobClient();
    CloudBlobContainer cloudBlobContainer =
        cloudBlobClient.GetContainerReference(containerName);
cloudBlobContainer.CreateIfNotExists();
    CloudBlockBlob cloudBlockBlob =
        cloudBlobContainer.GetBlockBlobReference(blobName);
    return cloudBlockBlob;
}
```

6. Add the following method, creating a container and blob, to the class:

```
private void CreateContainerAndBlob(
    String containerName, String blobName)
{
    CloudBlockBlob cloudBlockBlob =
        GetBlob(containerName, blobName);
    cloudBlockBlob.UploadText("This weak and idle theme.");
}
```

7. Add the following method, creating a shared access signature using the SDK helpers, to the class:

```
private String GetSASWithSDK(
    String containerName, String blobName
    , SharedAccessBlobPermissions permission)
{
    SharedAccessBlobPolicy sharedAccessPolicy =
        new SharedAccessBlobPolicy()
        {
            Permissions = permission,
            SharedAccessStartTime =
```

```
                utcNow.AddDays(-2),
                SharedAccessExpiryTime =
                utcNow.AddDays(2)
        };

    CloudBlockBlob cloudBlockBlob =
        GetBlob(containerName, blobName);

    String sharedAccessSignature =
        cloudBlockBlob.GetSharedAccessSignature(
        sharedAccessPolicy);

    return sharedAccessSignature;
}
```

8. Add the following method, creating a shared access signature manually, to the class:

```
private String GetSASManually(
    String containerName, String blobName
    , String sp)
{
    String iso8601Format = "yyyy-MM-ddTHH:mm:ssZ";
    CultureInfo culture = new CultureInfo("en-US");
    DateTime startTime = utcNow.AddDays(-2);
    DateTime expiryTime = utcNow.AddDays(2);
    String st =
        startTime.ToString(iso8601Format,culture);
    String se =
        expiryTime.ToString(iso8601Format, culture);
    //Latest version at time of writing
    String sv = "2013-08-15";
    String sr = "b";
    String si,rscc,rscd,rsce,rscl,rsct;
    si = rscc = rscd = rsce = rscl = rsct = String.Empty;

    String resource =
        string.Format("/{0}/{1}/{2}",
        accountName, containerName, blobName);

    String stringToSign = sp + "\n" +
                st + "\n" +
                se + "\n" +
                resource + "\n" +
                si + "\n" +
                sv + "\n" +
```

```
                              rscc + "\n" +
                              rscd + "\n" +
                              rsce + "\n" +
                              rscl + "\n" +
                              rsct;

        String sig = String.Empty;
        Byte[] keyBytes = Convert.FromBase64String(accountKey);
        using (HMACSHA256 hmacSha256 = new HMACSHA256(keyBytes))
        {
            Byte[] utf8EncodedStringToSign =
            System.Text.Encoding.UTF8.GetBytes(stringToSign);
            Byte[] signatureBytes =
            hmacSha256.ComputeHash(utf8EncodedStringToSign);
            sig = Convert.ToBase64String(signatureBytes);
        }

        String sharedAccessSignature =
            String.Format("?sv={0}&sr={1}&sig={2}&st={3}&se={4}&
    sp={5}",
            sv, sr, sig, Uri.EscapeDataString(st),
            Uri.EscapeDataString(se), sp);

        return sharedAccessSignature;
    }
```

9. Add the following method, authenticating it with a shared access signature, to the class:

```
private void GetBlobWithSAS(
    String containerName, String blobName,
    String sharedAccessSignature)
{
    StorageCredentials storageCredentials
        = new StorageCredentials(sharedAccessSignature);
    CloudBlobClient cloudBlobClient =
        new CloudBlobClient(new Uri(blobEndpoint),
            storageCredentials);

    CloudBlobContainer cloudBlobContainer =
        cloudBlobClient.GetContainerReference(containerName);
    CloudBlockBlob cloudBlockBlob =
        cloudBlobContainer.GetBlockBlobReference(blobName);
    String blobText = cloudBlockBlob.DownloadText();
}
```

10. Add the following method, using the methods added earlier, to the class:

```
public static void UseSharedAccessSignaturesExample()
{
    String containerName = "test01";
    String blobName = "myBlob.txt";

    SharedAccessSignaturesExample example =
        new SharedAccessSignaturesExample();

    example.CreateContainerAndBlob(containerName, blobName);

    String sharedAccessSignature1 =
        example.GetSASWithSDK(
        containerName, blobName
        , SharedAccessBlobPermissions.Read);
    example.GetBlobWithSAS(
        containerName, blobName, sharedAccessSignature1);

    String sharedAccessSignature2 =
        example.GetSASManually(
        containerName, blobName, "r");
    example.GetBlobWithSAS(
        containerName, blobName, sharedAccessSignature2);
}
```

How it works...

In steps 1 and 2, we set up the class. In step 3, we added some `private` members for the blob endpoint as well as the account name and access key, which we initialize in the constructor we added in step 4.

 We use the `ExportBase64EncodedKey()` method to obtain the original `AccountKey` instance from the `StorageCredentials` instance.

In step 5, we created an internal helper method to get a reference to a specific blob of a specific container. In step 6, we created the container and upload a blob to it.

In step 7, we used the `GetSharedAccessSignature()` method of the `CloudBlockBlob` class to get a shared access signature based on `SharedAccessBlobPolicy` that we passed into it. In this `SharedAccessBlobPolicy`, we specified that we want read access on a blob 2 hours before and after the current time. The fuzzing of the start time is to minimize any risk of the time on the local machine being too far out of sync with the time on the Storage service. This approach is the easiest way to get a shared access signature.

In real scenarios, using the UTC time is always a best practice while dealing with signatures. In the case of SAS, specifications tell that a clock skew of a few seconds might happen. To avoid this, use a generous start time. It would not be a security breach, as the Azure datacenter cannot go in the past!

In step 8, we constructed a shared access signature from first principles. This version does not use the Storage library. We prepared the variables of the string to sign according to the specifications. Dates are formatted in the ISO8601 format. We used Version **2013-08-15**, which introduces new features and new mandatory fields to be used while generating the signature. So, we generated a string to sign from the desired permissions, start time, expiration time, resource to share, and the API version. We initialized an HMACSHA256 instance from the access key and used this to generate an HMAC from the string to sign. We then created the remainder of the query string while ensuring that the data is correctly URL encoded.

In step 9, we used a shared access signature to initialize a StorageCredentials instance, which we use to create a CloudBlobClient instance. We used this to construct the CloudBlobContainer and CloudBlobClient instances that we used to download the content of a blob.

In step 10, we added a helper method that invokes all the methods we added earlier. We tried to get the same blob using the two SAS tokens generated manually and with the SDK. As the tokens are equal, both the HTTP calls are successful.

There's more...

Let's go inside some advanced settings for the SAS generation. As they are completely hidden from the SDK, it is interesting to investigate how they work and how we can perform advanced operations using them.

In step 8, we saw the complete list of the supported fields, even if we did not include them in the query string. We must include these fields in the empty signature.

The sr parameter stands for signedresource and it can have the following values:

- ▶ b: For signing a blob
- ▶ c: For signing a container

The si parameter stands for signedidentifier and represents a reference to a container policy, if used.

The remaining parameters are used to instruct the blob service to append a custom header to the HTTP response, to control the behavior from the client side. The remaining parameters are as follows:

▸ rscc: This represents the cache-control header

▸ rscd: This represents the content-disposition header

▸ rsce: This represents the content-encoding header

▸ rscl: This represents the content-language header

▸ rsct: This represents the content-type header

Finally, the sp parameter (signedpermission) could be r (for read), w (for write), and d (for delete). On a container, it could also be l (for list).

We can get more details about container-level access policies in the *Using a container-level access policy* recipe.

The purpose of shared access signatures is to provide users with access to a fine-grained resource, without giving them access to the entire account. A common scenario is a web application that hosts files (mail attachments and so on) on behalf of the user. When a user, from their own web page, asks for a download of a private resource, this resource should be protected by the service but accessible to the user. Some websites expose private resources through complex URIs (GUID-based), thinking that it could be a good security policy for resources (hoping that no one can guess those complex URIs). However, when a URI is discovered by someone, there is no way to protect it. SASes fill this gap by providing temporary access to private resources via public URIs.

See also

Have a look at the following links to get additional information:

▸ HMAC on Wikipedia at http://en.wikipedia.org/wiki/Hash-based_message_authentication_code

▸ How to use a stored access policy at http://msdn.microsoft.com/en-us/library/azure/ee393341.aspx

Using a container-level access policy

A shared access policy comprises a set of permissions (read, write, delete, and list), combined with start and expiration times for the validity of the policy. There are no restrictions on the start and expiration times for a shared access policy. A **container-level access policy** is a shared access policy associated by name with a container. A maximum of five container-level access policies can be associated simultaneously with a container, but each must have a distinct name.

A container-level access policy improves the management of shared access signatures. There is no way to retract or otherwise disallow a standalone shared access signature once it has been created. However, a shared access signature created from a container-level access policy has validity depending on the container-level access policy. The deletion of a container-level access policy causes the **revocation** of all shared access signatures derived from it, and they can no longer be used to authenticate a storage request.

The container-level access policies for a container are set and retrieved as a `SharedAccessPolicies` collection named as `SharedAccessBlobPolicy` objects. The `SetPermissions()` and `GetPermissions()` methods of the `CloudBlobContainer` class set and retrieve the container-level access policies. A container-level access policy can be removed by retrieving the current `SharedAccessPolicies` objects, removing the specified policy, and then setting the `SharedAccessPolicies` objects on the container again.

A shared access signature is derived from a container-level access policy by invoking the `CloudBlobContainer.GetSharedAccessSignature()` method, passing in the name of the container-level access policy and an empty `SharedAccessBlobPolicy` instance. It is not possible to modify the validity of the shared-access signature using a nonempty `SharedAccessBlobPolicy` class.

In this recipe, we'll learn how to manage container-level access policies and use them to create shared access signatures.

Getting ready

This recipe assumes that the following lines of code are in the application's configuration file:

```
<appSettings>
  <add key="DataConnectionString"
value="DefaultEndpointsProtocol=https;AccountName={ACCOUNT_
NAME};AccountKey={ACCOUNT_KEY}"/>
</appSettings>
```

We must replace {ACCOUNT_NAME} and {ACCOUNT_KEY} with appropriate values for the account name and access key, respectively.

How to do it...

We are going to create, use, modify, revoke, and delete a container-level access policy. We will do this using the following steps:

1. Add a class named `ContainerLevelAccessPolicyExample` to the project.

2. Add the following `using` statements to the top of the class file:

```
using Microsoft.WindowsAzure.Storage;
using Microsoft.WindowsAzure.Storage.Blob;
using System.Configuration;
```

3. Add the following `private` members to the class:

```
private CloudBlobContainer cloudBlobContainer;
```

4. Add the following constructor to the class:

```
ContainerLevelAccessPolicyExample(string containerName)
{
    CloudStorageAccount cloudStorageAccount =
        CloudStorageAccount.Parse(
        ConfigurationManager.AppSettings[
        "DataConnectionString"]);

    CloudBlobClient cloudBlobClient =
        cloudStorageAccount.CreateCloudBlobClient();
    cloudBlobContainer = cloudBlobClient
        .GetContainerReference(containerName);
    cloudBlobContainer.CreateIfNotExists();
}
```

5. Add the following method, creating a container-level access policy, to the class:

```
private void AddContainerLevelAccessPolicy(String policyId)
{
    DateTime startTime = DateTime.UtcNow;
    SharedAccessBlobPolicy sharedAccessPolicy =
        new SharedAccessBlobPolicy()
        {
            Permissions = SharedAccessBlobPermissions.Read |
            SharedAccessBlobPermissions.Write,
            SharedAccessStartTime = startTime,
            SharedAccessExpiryTime = startTime.AddDays(3d)
        };

    BlobContainerPermissions blobContainerPermissions =
        new BlobContainerPermissions();
```

```
blobContainerPermissions.SharedAccessPolicies.Add(
    policyId, sharedAccessPolicy);

cloudBlobContainer.SetPermissions(blobContainerPermissions);
}
```

6. Add the following method, getting a shared access signature using the container-level access policy, to the class:

```
private String GetSharedAccessSignature(String policyId)
{
    SharedAccessBlobPolicy sharedAccessPolicy =
        new SharedAccessBlobPolicy();
    String sharedAccessSignature =
        cloudBlobContainer.GetSharedAccessSignature(
        sharedAccessPolicy, policyId);

    return sharedAccessSignature;
}
```

7. Add the following method, modifying the container-level access policy, to the class:

```
private void ModifyContainerLevelAccessPolicy(String policyId)
{
    BlobContainerPermissions blobContainerPermissions =
        cloudBlobContainer.GetPermissions();

    blobContainerPermissions.SharedAccessPolicies[
        policyId].SharedAccessExpiryTime=
        blobContainerPermissions.SharedAccessPolicies[
        policyId].SharedAccessExpiryTime.Value.AddDays(1);

    cloudBlobContainer.SetPermissions(blobContainerPermissions);
}
```

8. Add the following method, revoking a container-level access policy, to the class:

```
private void RevokeContainerLevelAccessPolicy(String policyId)
{
    BlobContainerPermissions containerPermissions =
        cloudBlobContainer.GetPermissions();

    SharedAccessBlobPolicy sharedAccessPolicy =
        containerPermissions.SharedAccessPolicies[policyId];
    containerPermissions.SharedAccessPolicies.Remove(policyId);
    containerPermissions.SharedAccessPolicies.Add(
```

```
        policyId + "1", sharedAccessPolicy);

    cloudBlobContainer.SetPermissions(containerPermissions);
}
```

9. Add the following method, deleting all container-level access policies, to the class:

```
private void DeleteContainerLevelAccessPolicies()
{
    BlobContainerPermissions blobContainerPermissions =
        new BlobContainerPermissions();

    cloudBlobContainer.SetPermissions(blobContainerPermissions);
}
```

10. Add the following method, using the methods added earlier, to the class:

```
public static void UseContainerLevelAccessPolicyExample()
{
    String containerName = "test01";
    String policyId = "myPolicy";

    ContainerLevelAccessPolicyExample example =
        new ContainerLevelAccessPolicyExample(containerName);

    example.AddContainerLevelAccessPolicy(policyId);
    String sharedAccessSignature1 =
        example.GetSharedAccessSignature(policyId);

    example.ModifyContainerLevelAccessPolicy(policyId);
    String sharedAccessSignature2 =
        example.GetSharedAccessSignature(policyId);

    example.RevokeContainerLevelAccessPolicy(policyId);
    String sharedAccessSignature3 =
        example.GetSharedAccessSignature(policyId + "1");

    example.DeleteContainerLevelAccessPolicies();
}
```

How it works...

In steps 1 and 2, we set up the class. In step 3, we added some `private` members that we initialized in the constructor that we added in step 4. We also created a container in the constructor.

In step 5, we created a `SharedAccessBlobPolicy` instance and added it to the `SharedAccessPolicies` property of a `BlobContainerPermissions` object. Finally, we passed this and also passed a policy name into a `SetPermissions()` method of the `CloudBlobContainer` class to create a container-level access policy name for the container.

In step 6, we got a shared access signature for a container with a specified container-level access policy. Finally, we passed the policy name into the `CloudBlobContainer.GetSharedAccessSignature()` method to get a shared access signature for the container.

In step 7, we invoked `GetPermissions()` on the container to retrieve the shared access policies for it. We then added 1 day to the expiration date for a specified container-level access policy. Finally, we invoked `CloudBlobContainer.SetPermissions()` to update the container-level access policies for the container.

In step 8, we revoked an existing container-level access policy and created a new container-level policy with the same `SharedAccessBlobPolicy` and a new policy name. We again used `GetPermissions()` to retrieve the shared access policies for the container and then invoked the `Remove()` method of the `SharedAccessPolicies` property to perform the revocation. We also added a new policy with a different name. Finally, we invoked `CloudBlobContainer.SetPermissions()` to update the container-level access policies for the container.

In step 9, we deleted all container-level access policies for a container. We created a default `BlobContainerPermissions` instance and passed this into `CloudBlobContainer.SetPermissions()` to remove all the container-level access policies for the container.

In step 10, we added a helper method that invokes all the methods we added earlier.

Setting properties and metadata for a blob

The Azure Blob service allows metadata and properties to be associated with a blob. The metadata comprises a sequence of developer-defined, name-value pairs. The properties comprise HTTP request headers, which include Cache-Control, Content-Encoding, Content-MD5, and Content-Type. The Blob service also supports metadata and properties for blob containers. Requesting a download of the blob attributes, its metadata, and properties is an efficient way of checking blob existence, as only a small amount of data is downloaded.

The Blob service uses the `Content-MD5` property to validate blob upload. When specified, the `Content-MD5` property must be set to the `base64-encoded` value of the MD5 hash's blob data. The Blob service returns an error if this value does not match the value it calculates from the uploaded blob content.

In this recipe, we'll learn how to set and get blob properties and metadata. We will also learn how to calculate the `Content-MD5` property.

Getting ready

This recipe assumes that the following lines of code are in the application's configuration file:

```
<appSettings>
  <add key="DataConnectionString"
value="DefaultEndpointsProtocol=https;AccountName={ACCOUNT_
NAME};AccountKey={ACCOUNT_KEY}"/>
</appSettings>
```

We must replace {ACCOUNT_NAME} and {ACCOUNT_KEY} with appropriate values for the account name and access key, respectively.

How to do it...

We are going to create a blob, and add some metadata and the Content-MD5 property to it. We will then fetch the attributes of the blob to retrieve the property and metadata. We will do this using the following steps:

1. Add a new class named PropertiesMetadataExample to the project.

2. Add the following using statements to the top of the class file:

    ```
    using Microsoft.WindowsAzure.Storage;
    using Microsoft.WindowsAzure.Storage.Blob;
    using System.Configuration;
    using System.Security.Cryptography;
    ```

3. Add the following member to the class:

    ```
    CloudBlobClient cloudBlobClient;
    ```

4. Add the following constructor to the class:

    ```
    public PropertiesMetadataExample()
    {
        CloudStorageAccount cloudStorageAccount =
            CloudStorageAccount.Parse(
            ConfigurationManager.AppSettings[
            "DataConnectionString"]);
        cloudBlobClient =
            cloudStorageAccount.CreateCloudBlobClient();
    }
    ```

5. Add the following method, uploading a blob as a `Byte` array, to the class:

```
private void UploadByteArray(
    String containerName, String blobName)
{
    CloudBlobContainer cloudBlobContainer =
        cloudBlobClient.GetContainerReference(containerName);
    cloudBlobContainer.CreateIfNotExists();

    Byte[] blobData = { 0x41, 0x7A, 0x75, 0x72, 0x65 };
    CloudBlockBlob cloudBlockBlob =
        cloudBlobContainer.GetBlockBlobReference(blobName);
    cloudBlockBlob.Metadata["TodayIs"] = "Wednesday";
    cloudBlockBlob.Properties.ContentMD5 =
        CalculateMD5Hash(blobData);
    cloudBlockBlob.UploadFromByteArray(blobData,0,blobData.
Length);
}
```

6. Add the following method, retrieving `blob` attributes, to the class:

```
private void FetchAttributes(String containerName,
    String blobName)
{
    CloudBlobContainer cloudBlobContainer =
        cloudBlobClient.GetContainerReference(containerName);
    CloudBlockBlob cloudBlockBlob =
        cloudBlobContainer.GetBlockBlobReference(blobName);

    cloudBlockBlob.FetchAttributes();

    BlobProperties blobProperties =
        cloudBlockBlob.Properties;
    IDictionary<string,string> blobMetadata =
        cloudBlockBlob.Metadata;
    foreach (var item in blobMetadata)
    {
        String value = item.Value;
    }
}
```

7. Add a method, calculating the MD5 hash, to the class:

```
private static String CalculateMD5Hash(Byte[] bytes)
{
    MD5 md5 = MD5.Create();
    Byte[] md5Hash = md5.ComputeHash(bytes);
```

```
        String base64EncodedMD5Hash =
            Convert.ToBase64String(md5Hash);

        return base64EncodedMD5Hash;
    }
```

8. Add the following method, using the methods added earlier, to the class:

```
public static void UsePropertiesMetadataExample()
{
    String containerName = "test01";
    String blobName = "myBlob.txt";

    PropertiesMetadataExample example = new
        PropertiesMetadataExample();
    example.UploadByteArray(containerName, blobName);
    example.FetchAttributes(containerName, blobName);
}
```

How it works...

In steps 1 and 2, we set up the class. In step 3, we added a member to hold the `CloudBlobClient` instance that we initialized in the constructor we added in step 4. We initialized the `CloudStorageAccount` instance from the values in the `app.config` file.

In step 5, we added a method that creates a blob out of a `Byte` array, adds the calculated `Content-MD5` property to the blob, and associates some metadata named `TodayIs` with the blob. In step 6, we added a method that retrieves the attributes of a blob and iterates over any metadata associated with it.

In step 7, we added the method that calculates the base64-encoded MD5 hash for a `Byte` array.

In step 8, we added a method that invokes the methods we added to the class.

See also

Have a look at the following MSDN links to get additional information:

▶ Conditional headers for Blob service operations at `http://msdn.microsoft.com/en-us/library/azure/dd179371.aspx`

▶ Properties and metadata for Blob resources at `http://msdn.microsoft.com/en-us/library/azure/dd179404.aspx`

Using blob directories

The Azure Blob service uses a simple organizational structure for containers and blobs. A storage account has zero or more containers, each of which contains zero or more blobs. Containers might contain only blobs and not contain other containers. There is no hierarchy for containers.

The Azure Storage library provides support for a **simulation of a hierarchical directory structure** through an ability to parse blob names that contain a special delimiter character and navigates to the list of blobs while taking the delimiter into account. This delimiter has the forward slash symbol (/). The Azure Storage Client library exposes this feature through the CloudBlobDirectory class.

The CloudBlobDirectory class provides methods that allow blobs to be enumerated in a way that takes into account the directory structure built into the naming convention used. A blob name can include multiple levels of directory.

A CloudBlobDirectory object can be created using either CloudBlobClient. GetDirectoryReference() or CloudBlobContainer.GetDirectoryReference(). The CloudBlobDirectory object refers to a particular level in the directory hierarchy. The blobs and directories in this directory can be retrieved using the synchronous ListBlobs(), the asynchronous BeginListBlobsSegmented(), or the ListBlobsSegmentedAsync() methods. The directory list can be paged through using the ListBlobsSegmented() method.

The various methods to list blobs provide the list as IEnumerable<IListBlobItem>. The IListBlobItem interface is actually the base interface for CloudBlockBlob, CloudPageBlob, and CloudBlobDirectory classes, as well as for the ICloudBlob interface. Consequently, any given item in the list could be from any of these classes, so care must be taken that the item is handled correctly. This is similar to the way in which a file needs to be handled differently from a subdirectory when processing the contents of a directory in a filesystem.

The CloudBlobDirectory class also exposes methods that retrieve strongly typed CloudBlockBlob, CloudPageBlob, or CloudBlobDirectory classes with a specified name that might include multiple levels in the directory hierarchy.

In this recipe, we'll learn how to generate a list of the contents of a directory and traverse a directory hierarchy.

Getting ready

This recipe assumes that the following lines of code are in the application's configuration file:

```
<appSettings>
  <add key="DataConnectionString"
value="DefaultEndpointsProtocol=https;AccountName={ACCOUNT_
NAME};AccountKey={ACCOUNT_KEY}"/>
</appSettings>
```

We must replace {ACCOUNT_NAME} and {ACCOUNT_KEY} with appropriate values for the account name and access key, respectively.

How to do it...

We are going to list the top-level contents of a directory. Then, we will get the top-level directories and list their contents. We will do this using the following steps:

1. Add a new class named BlobDirectoryExample to the project.

2. Add the following using statements to the top of the class file:

```
using Microsoft.WindowsAzure.Storage;
using Microsoft.WindowsAzure.Storage.Blob;
using System.Configuration;
```

3. Add the following member to the class:

```
private CloudBlobContainer cloudBlobContainer;
```

4. Add the following constructor to the class:

```
public BlobDirectoryExample(String containerName)
{
    CloudStorageAccount cloudStorageAccount =
        CloudStorageAccount.Parse(
        ConfigurationManager.AppSettings[
        "DataConnectionString"]);
    CloudBlobClient cloudBlobClient =
        cloudStorageAccount.CreateCloudBlobClient();
    cloudBlobContainer =
        cloudBlobClient.GetContainerReference(containerName);
}
```

5. Add a method, creating a container and adding blobs to it, to the class:

```
private void CreateContainerAndBlobs(String containerName)
{
    cloudBlobContainer.CreateIfNotExists();
    CreateBlob("Yosemite/ElCapitan");
    CreateBlob("Yosemite/ElCapitan/TheNose");
    CreateBlob("Yosemite/ElCapitan/SalatheWall");
    CreateBlob("Yosemite/HalfDome");
    CreateBlob("Yosemite/HalfDome/NorthRidge");
    CreateBlob("Yosemite/HalfDome/NorthWestFace");
    CreateBlob("Yosemite/HalfDome/Trail");
}
```

6. Add a method, uploading a blob, to the class:

```
private void CreateBlob(String blobName)
{
    CloudBlockBlob cloudBlockBlob =
        cloudBlobContainer.GetBlockBlobReference(blobName);
    cloudBlockBlob.UploadText("To be, or not to be");
}
```

7. Add a method, listing the top-level directory items, to the class:

```
private void ListTopLevelItems(String directoryName)
{
    CloudBlobDirectory cloudBlobDirectory =
        cloudBlobContainer.GetDirectoryReference(directoryName);

    IEnumerable<IListBlobItem> blobItems =
        cloudBlobDirectory.ListBlobs();
    foreach (IListBlobItem blobItem in blobItems)
    {
        Uri uri = blobItem.Uri;
    }
}
```

8. Add a method, traversing the directory tree, to the class:

```
private void TraverseDirectoryTree(String directoryName)
{
    CloudBlobDirectory cloudBlobDirectory =
        cloudBlobContainer.GetDirectoryReference(
        directoryName);

    IEnumerable<IListBlobItem> blobItems =
        cloudBlobDirectory.ListBlobs();
```

```
        foreach (CloudBlobDirectory cloudBlobDirectoryItem in
            blobItems.OfType<CloudBlobDirectory>())
        {
            Uri uri = cloudBlobDirectoryItem.Uri;

            IEnumerable<CloudBlockBlob> leafBlobs =
        cloudBlobDirectoryItem.ListBlobs().OfType<CloudBlockBlob>();
            foreach (CloudBlockBlob leafBlockBlob in leafBlobs)
            {
                Uri leafUri = leafBlockBlob.Uri;
            }
        }
    }
```

9. Add the following method, using the methods added earlier, to the class:

```
public static void UseBlobDirectoryExample()
{
    String containerName = "test01";
    String directoryName = "Yosemite";

    BlobDirectoryExample blobDirectoryExample =
        new BlobDirectoryExample(containerName);
    blobDirectoryExample.CreateContainerAndBlobs(
        containerName);
    blobDirectoryExample.ListTopLevelItems(directoryName);
    blobDirectoryExample.TraverseDirectoryTree(directoryName);
}
```

How it works...

In steps 1 and 2, we set up the `BlobDirectoryExample` class. In step 3, we added a member that we initialized in the constructor we add in step 4.

In step 5, we created a container and then invoked `CreateBlob()` multiple times to create the blobs we used in the example. In step 6, we added `CreateBlob()` to upload a blob.

In step 7, we added a `ListTopLevelItems()` method that uses a `CloudBlobContainer` object for the current container to retrieve a `CloudBlobDirectory` object for the specified directory. We then invoked `CloudBlobDirectory.ListBlobs()` to generate a directory-listing query, which we invoke and enumerate. With the example blobs created earlier, this corresponds to the directory listing of Yosemite that retrieves two blobs and two directories.

In step 8, we added a `TraverseDirectoryTree()` method that uses a `CloudBlobContainer` object for the current container to retrieve a `CloudBlobDirectory` object for the specified directory. We then used `CloudBlobDirectory.ListBlobs()` to generate a directory-listing query, which we invoked and enumerated while restricting the enumeration only to `CloudBlobDirectory` objects. We then used these `CloudBlobDirectory` objects as the base of separate `CloudBlobDirectory.ListBlobs()` invocations to retrieve lists of their contents.

In step 9, we added a method to use the methods we added earlier.

Creating and using a blob snapshot

The Azure Blob service supports the creation of read-only snapshots of a blob. A storage account is billed only for those blocks and pages in a snapshot that differ from those in the underlying blob. A blob snapshot is useful in providing a **backup** for a blob, as it can be used to reset the blob to an earlier state. Indeed, multiple snapshots can be made over time, allowing a historic record to be kept of the changes made to a blob.

A blob snapshot is created using the `CloudBlockBlob.CreateSnapshot()` method. Each snapshot of a blob is distinguished by its creation time, which must be provided to operations that are accessing the snapshot. A snapshot created at a particular `datetime` is addressed by appending a `snapshot={datetime}` query string to the URL, thus identifying the underlying blob.

For example, the following is the complete URL for a snapshot taken on `11/25/2010` of a blob named `SnapshotsExample`:

```
http://myaccountname.blob.core.windows.net/ chapter2/
SnapshotsExample?snapshot=2010-11-25T02:02:40.1680568Z
```

The storage account is named `myaccountname`, and the container is named `chapter2`.

In this recipe, we'll learn how to create and use blob snapshots.

Getting ready

This recipe assumes that the following lines of code are in the application's configuration file:

```
<appSettings>
  <add key="DataConnectionString"
value="DefaultEndpointsProtocol=https;AccountName={ACCOUNT_
NAME};AccountKey={ACCOUNT_KEY}"/>
</appSettings>
```

We must replace `{ACCOUNT_NAME}` and `{ACCOUNT_KEY}` with appropriate values for the account name and access key, respectively.

How to do it...

We are going to create a blob and then create a snapshot of it. We are then going to download the snapshot. We will do this using the following steps:

1. Add a new class named `SnapshotsExample` to the project.

2. Add the following `using` statements to the top of the class file:

   ```
   using Microsoft.WindowsAzure.Storage;
   using Microsoft.WindowsAzure.Storage.Blob;
   using System.Configuration;
   using System.IO;
   ```

3. Add the following `private` member to the class:

   ```
   private CloudBlobClient cloudBlobClient;
   ```

4. Add the following constructor to the class:

   ```
   public SnapshotsExample()
   {
     CloudStorageAccount cloudStorageAccount =
        CloudStorageAccount.Parse(
        ConfigurationManager.AppSettings[
        "DataConnectionString"]);
     cloudBlobClient =
        cloudStorageAccount.CreateCloudBlobClient();
   }
   ```

5. Add the following method, creating the container and a blob, to the class:

   ```
   private void CreateContainerAndBlob(
     String containerName, String blobName)
   {
     CloudBlobContainer cloudBlobContainer =
        cloudBlobClient.GetContainerReference(containerName);
     cloudBlobContainer.CreateIfNotExists();

     CloudBlockBlob cloudBlockBlob =
        cloudBlobContainer.GetBlockBlobReference(blobName);
     cloudBlockBlob.UploadText("To be, or not to be");
   }
   ```

6. Add the following method, making a snapshot of the blob, to the class:

```
private DateTime MakeSnapshot(
  String containerName, String blobName)
{
  CloudBlobContainer cloudBlobContainer =
    cloudBlobClient.GetContainerReference(containerName);
  CloudBlockBlob cloudBlockBlob =
    cloudBlobContainer.GetBlockBlobReference(blobName);

  CloudBlockBlob snapshot = cloudBlockBlob.CreateSnapshot();
  return snapshot.SnapshotTime.Value.DateTime;
}
```

7. Add the following method, retrieving the snapshot, to the class:

```
private void RestoreSnapshot(String containerName,
  String blobName)
{

    CloudBlobContainer cloudBlobContainer =
     cloudBlobClient.GetContainerReference(containerName);

    var lastSnapshot = cloudBlobContainer
        .ListBlobs(blobName, true,
        BlobListingDetails.Snapshots)
        .Cast<CloudBlockBlob>()
        .Where(p=>p.IsSnapshot).Last();

    CloudBlockBlob blob = cloudBlobContainer
        .GetBlockBlobReference("restored_"+blobName);
    blob.StartCopyFromBlob(lastSnapshot);
}
```

8. Add the following method, using the methods added earlier, to the class:

```
public static void UseSnapshotsExample()
{
  String containerName = "test01";
  String blobName = "myBlob.txt";

  SnapshotsExample example = new SnapshotsExample();
  example.CreateContainerAndBlob(containerName, blobName);

  DateTime snapshotTime =
      example.MakeSnapshot(containerName, blobName);
```

```
example.RestoreSnapshot(containerName,
        blobName);
}
```

How it works...

In steps 1 and 2, we set up the recipe. In step 3, we added a `private` member that stores a `CloudBlobClient` class that we initialized in the constructor we add in step 4. This constructor retrieves the storage account information from the `app.config` file. In step 5, we created a container and upload the blob to it.

In step 6, we invoked the `CreateSnapshot()` method to make a snapshot of the blob. We returned `SnapshotTime` that, in case, could uniquely identify the snapshot. In step 7, we used the `ListBlobs` method to retrieve all the blobs with the prefix of the original blob, specifying to also list the snapshots that adhere to the rule. With LINQ, we obtained a reference to the last snapshot of the desired blob, and finally, we promoted the snapshot to a new blob with the `StartCopyFromBlob` method.

In step 8, we invoked the methods added earlier to create a blob, make a snapshot, and retrieve it.

See also

Have a look at the following MSDN link to get additional information:

> ▶ More about Snapshot service fees at `http://msdn.microsoft.com/en-us/library/azure/hh768807.aspx`

Creating and using the root container for blobs

The Azure Blob service supports a simple two-level hierarchy for blobs. There is a single level of containers, each of which might contain zero or more blobs. Containers might not contain other containers.

In the Blob service, a blob resource is addressed as follows:

```
http://{account}.blob.core.windows.net/{container}/{blob}
```

The {account}, {container}, and {blob} parts represent the names of the storage account, container, and blob, respectively.

This addressing convention works for most uses of blobs. In certain situations, we need to place content inside the root space. Microsoft added support for a root container named `$root` to the Blob service so that it could host content.

> When using Silverlight, the runtime requires that a cross-domain policy file reside at the root of the domain and not beneath a container as would be the case with the standard addressing for blobs. The cross-domain policy file allows a web client to access data from more than one domain at a time (`http://msdn.microsoft.com/en-us/library/cc197955(VS.95).aspx`). The root container could also be used for this purpose.

There is no need to provide the root container's name when retrieving blobs contained in it. For example, the following is a valid address for a blob named `crossdomain.xml` stored in the root container:

```
http://{account}.blob.core.windows.net/crossdomain.xml
```

Note that the names of root-container blobs must not contain the / symbol to avoid any confusion with blobs being named to simulate a directory tree.

> It is possible to emulate a static website hosting under the root container. By placing the HTML file inside a public `$root` container and subsequently mapping the storage account with a custom DNS name, the resulting URLs are very similar to those of common websites:
>
> ```
> http://www.mydomain.com/index.html
> ```
>
> However, it is not possible to indicate to Azure which is the default document of that website, so it just a good approximation of the original behavior.

In this recipe, we'll learn how to create and use the root container for a storage account.

Getting ready

We need to create a file that we will upload using the recipe. As we do not rely on this file being a cross-domain policy file, we can actually use any file for the recipe.

This recipe assumes that the following lines of code are in the application's configuration file:

```
<appSettings>
  <add key="DataConnectionString"
value="DefaultEndpointsProtocol=https;AccountName={ACCOUNT_
NAME};AccountKey={ACCOUNT_KEY}"/>
</appSettings>
```

We must replace {ACCOUNT_NAME} and {ACCOUNT_KEY} with appropriate values for the account name and access key, respectively.

How to do it...

We are going to create a root container and upload a cross-domain policy file to it. We will do this using the following steps:

1. Add a new class named RootContainerExample to the project.

2. Add the following using statements to the top of the class file:

```
using Microsoft.WindowsAzure.Storage;
using Microsoft.WindowsAzure.Storage.Blob;
using System.Configuration;
```

3. Add the following method, uploading the cross-domain policy file, to the class:

```
private static void UploadCrossDomainPolicyFile(
    String fileName)
{
  String rootContainerName = "$root";
  String crossDomainPolicyName = "crossdomain.xml";
  CloudStorageAccount cloudStorageAccount =
      CloudStorageAccount.Parse(
      ConfigurationManager.AppSettings[
        "DataConnectionString"]);

  CloudBlobClient cloudBlobClient =
      cloudStorageAccount.CreateCloudBlobClient();
  CloudBlobContainer cloudBlobContainer =
      cloudBlobClient.GetContainerReference(
        rootContainerName);
  cloudBlobContainer.CreateIfNotExists();
    cloudBlobContainer.SetPermissions(
        new BlobContainerPermissions()
      {
        PublicAccess=BlobContainerPublicAccessType.Blob
      });

  CloudBlockBlob cloudBlockBlob =
      cloudBlobContainer.GetBlockBlobReference(
        crossDomainPolicyName);
  cloudBlockBlob.UploadFromFile(fileName
      ,System.IO.FileMode.Open);
}
```

4. Add the following method, using `UploadCrossDomainPolicyFile()`, to the class:

```
public static void UseRootContainerExample()
{
    String crossDomainPolicyFilename =
        Path.GetTempFileName();
    UploadCrossDomainPolicyFile(crossDomainPolicyFilename);
}
```

How it works...

In steps 1 and 2, we set up the recipe. In step 3, we created the root container, with the special name `$root`, and then used `UploadFile()` to upload the cross-domain policy file into it. Please note that in this case, the `$root` container must be public, or no clients can correctly locate the contents inside it.

In step 4, we invoked the `UploadCrossDomainPolicyFile()` method we added in step 3, passing a temporary empty file, to test scenarios.

Putting items in the `$root` container makes them available through the root of the Blob service domain such as `http://{account}.blob.core.windows.net/item.txt`. This approach, in conjunction with mapping a custom domain to the storage account, lets us host static content on a generic root domain, using the Blob storage as a host for static websites.

See also

In the *Using blob directories* recipe, we saw how to simulate a directory hierarchy for blobs inside a container.

Have a look at the following MSDN links to get additional information:

▶ Working with the root container at `http://msdn.microsoft.com/en-us/library/azure/hh488356.aspx`

▶ Azure Storage Analytics at `http://msdn.microsoft.com/en-us/library/azure/hh343270.aspx`

Uploading blocks to a block blob

The Azure Blob service supports two types of blobs: block blobs optimized for streaming and page blobs optimized for random access. Block blobs are so named because they comprise blocks (identified by block IDs) and can be updated either by replacing the entire blob or by replacing individual blocks. Page blobs can be updated either by replacing the entire blob or by modifying individual pages.

A block blob can be up to 200 GB in size and comprises blocks that can be up to 4 MB; a block blob cannot exceed 50,000 blocks. Block blobs larger than 64 MB must be uploaded in blocks, and then, a list of uploaded blocks must be committed to create the blob. The various upload methods in the `CloudBlob` class handle this two-phase process automatically. However, there are times when it is worthwhile taking direct control of the block upload and commit process. These include uploading very large blobs, performing parallel uploads of blocks, or updating individual blocks.

At any given time, a block blob can comprise a set of committed blocks and a set of uncommitted blocks. Only the committed blocks are visible when the blob is accessed. The block blob can be updated by committing some mixture of the committed and uncommitted blocks. Any uncommitted blocks are garbage collected 7 days after the last time the blocks were committed to the block blob.

In this recipe, we'll learn how to upload individual blocks and commit them to a block blob.

Getting ready

This recipe assumes that the following lines of code are in the application's configuration file:

```
<appSettings>
  <add key="DataConnectionString"
value="DefaultEndpointsProtocol=https;AccountName={ACCOUNT_
NAME};AccountKey={ACCOUNT_KEY}"/>
</appSettings>
```

We must replace `{ACCOUNT_NAME}` and `{ACCOUNT_KEY}` with appropriate values for the account name and access key, respectively.

How to do it...

We are going to upload some blocks and commit them as a block blob. Then, we are going to upload some more blocks to the same blob and retrieve the block list to confirm that the blob comprises a mixture of committed blocks and uncommitted blocks. Finally, we are going to commit the latest blocks and confirm that all the blocks in the blob have been committed. We will do this using the following steps:

1. Add a new class named `UploadBlockBlobsExample` to the project.

2. Add the following `using` statements to the top of the class file:

   ```
   using Microsoft.WindowsAzure.Storage;
   using Microsoft.WindowsAzure.Storage.Blob;
   using System.IO;
   ```

3. Add the following `private` member to the class:

   ```
   private CloudBlockBlob cloudBlockBlob;
   ```

4. Add the following constructor to the class:

```
public UploadBlockBlobsExample(String containerName,
    String blobName)
{
  CloudStorageAccount cloudStorageAccount =
      CloudStorageAccount.Parse(
      ConfigurationManager.AppSettings[
      "DataConnectionString"]);
  CloudBlobClient cloudBlobClient =
      cloudStorageAccount.CreateCloudBlobClient();

  CloudBlobContainer cloudBlobContainer =
      cloudBlobClient.GetContainerReference(containerName);
   cloudBlobContainer.CreateIfNotExists();
  cloudBlockBlob =
      cloudBlobContainer.GetBlockBlobReference(blobName);
}
```

5. Add the following methods, uploading blobs, to the class:

```
private IEnumerable<String> UploadBlocks(Int32 numberOfBlocks)
{
  String[] base64EncodedBlockIds =
      new String[numberOfBlocks];
  for (Int32 blockId = 0; blockId < numberOfBlocks;
      blockId++)
  {
    base64EncodedBlockIds[blockId] =
        PutBlockFromStream(blockId);
  }

  return base64EncodedBlockIds;
}
```

6. Add the following method, uploading a single block, to the class:

```
private String PutBlockFromStream(Int32 blockId)
{
  String base64EncodedBlockId = Convert.ToBase64String(
      System.BitConverter.GetBytes(blockId));
  String blobText = new String('z', 1000);
  UTF8Encoding utf8Encoding = new UTF8Encoding();
  using (MemoryStream memoryStream = new
      MemoryStream(utf8Encoding.GetBytes(blobText)))
  {
    cloudBlockBlob.PutBlock(base64EncodedBlockId,
```

```
      memoryStream, null);
    }
    return base64EncodedBlockId;
  }
```

7. Add the following methods, handling block lists, to the class:

```
private void PutBlockList(IEnumerable<String> blockList)
{
  cloudBlockBlob.PutBlockList(blockList);
}

private void GetBlockList()
{
  IEnumerable<ListBlockItem> listBlockItems =
      cloudBlockBlob.DownloadBlockList(
          BlockListingFilter.All);
  foreach (ListBlockItem item in listBlockItems)
  {
    Boolean committed = item.Committed;
    String name = item.Name;
    Int64 size = item.Length;
  }
}
```

8. Add the following method, using the methods added earlier, to the class:

```
public static void UseUploadBlockBlobsExample()
{
  String containerName = "test01";
  String blobName = "myBlockBlob.txt";

  UploadBlockBlobsExample example =
      new UploadBlockBlobsExample(containerName, blobName);

  IEnumerable<String> base64EncodedBlockIds =
      example.UploadBlocks(20);
  example.PutBlockList(base64EncodedBlockIds);

  base64EncodedBlockIds = example.UploadBlocks(10);
  example.GetBlockList();
  example.PutBlockList(base64EncodedBlockIds);
  example.GetBlockList();
}
```

How it works...

In steps 1 and 2, we set up the `UploadBlockBlobsExample` class. In step 3, we added a member that stores a `CloudBlockBlob` instance that we initialize in the constructor we added in step 4.

The `UploadBlocks()` method we added in step 5 iterates over the specified number of blocks and invokes the `PutBlockFromStream()` method. The `UploadBlocks()` method passes in the loop counter as a block ID. In step 6, `PutBlockFromStream()` converts the integer into the required Base64 format. For the sake of simplicity, we then created a memory stream based on a simple string and invoke the `CloudBlockBlob.PutBlock()` method to upload the block with the specified Base64 block Id. The `PutBlockFromStream()` method returns the Base64 block ID to `UploadBlocks()`, which in turn returns `IEnumerable<String>`, which contains the sequence of block IDs.

In step 7, we added a `PutBlockList()` method that simply refers to the `CloudBlockBlob.PutBlockList()` method. The `GetBlockList()` method invokes the `CloudBlockBlob.DownloadBlockList()` method to retrieve the list of committed blocks. We then iterated over the list to observe various properties of `GetBlockList()`.

In step 8, we added a method that uses the methods we created earlier. We upload 20 blocks and commit them to a block blob. Then, we uploaded another 10 blocks and invoke the `GetBlockList()` method to verify that we have 20 committed and 10 uncommitted blocks. Finally, we commited the 10 blocks and confirmed with another call to `GetBlockList()` that these blocks have replaced the blob with 20 blocks.

There's more...

The `ListBlobs()` method we saw earlier in another recipe lets us provide an option to the list and also the uncommitted blobs. A blob stands uncommitted if there are blocks uploaded but not yet committed through the `PutBlockList()` method.

The following method lists committed and uncommitted blobs, and then, it takes away the committed ones with LINQ as follows:

```
public IEnumerable<string> ListUncommitted()
{
    return cloudBlockBlob.Container.ListBlobs(null, true,
        BlobListingDetails.UncommittedBlobs)
        .Select(p => p.Uri.ToString())
        .Except(cloudBlockBlob.Container.ListBlobs(null,true)
        .Select(p=>p.Uri.ToString()));
}
```

The Azure Storage library lets us have a fine-grained control over the upload and download of the blocks of files. We can completely rely on methods such as the following:

```
cloudBlockBlob.UploadFromFile("[HUGE FILE]", FileMode.Open);
```

However, sometimes, we may want a higher degree of control around the upload process. The library, by default, splits the file into 4 MB blocks and proceeds with the upload as mentioned in the recipe. Each block is added, one by one, with an HTTP call as follows:

```
hugeBlob?comp=block&blockid=MTAzZTEyMzY3YTI3NGRkYjk3
YmU1MzU5Nzg3YWY5ZDUtMDAwMDAx
```

We can change the size of the block uploaded by the library by modifying the `StreamWriteSizeInBytes` property in the `CloudBlockBlob` instance:

```
hugeBlob.StreamWriteSizeInBytes = 1048576;
```

Finally, we would also go parallel specifying another property:

```
hugeBlob.ServiceClient.ParallelOperationThreadCount = 4;
```

Another strategy is going with the **Task Parallel Library** (**TPL**). The .NET Framework includes libraries that simplifiy the task of parallelizing operations. These provide parallel versions of the traditional `for` and `foreach` statements. The `Parallel.For` and `Parallel.ForEach` methods can be dropped almost as replacements for `for` and `foreach`.

The Blob service has a scalability target (`http://msdn.microsoft.com/en-us/library/windowsazure/dn249410.aspx`) for throughput of about 60 MB per second for an individual blob. This creates a limit for how much performance improvement can be achieved through parallelizing operations on a blob. When contemplating parallelization, it is always worth testing the actual workload to ensure that any expected performance gain is in fact realized.

Uploading a VHD into a page blob

An instance of an Azure role or Azure VM comprises several **virtual disks** (**VHDs**) deployed into a virtual machine. For Windows OS, this VHD must be an NTFS-formatted, fixed-size VHD. The VHD can be created directly as a page blob or uploaded like any other page blob.

The **Disk Management** snap-in for the **Microsoft Management Console** (**MMC**) can be used to create and format a VHD on a local system. Once attached to the local system, files can be copied to or created on the filesystem of the VHD, just as they can be created on any hard drive. The VHD can then be detached from the local system and uploaded as a page blob to the Azure Blob service.

A page blob, which might have a maximum size of 1 TB, comprises a sequence of 512-byte pages. All writes to a page blob must be aligned with a page boundary. There is no charge for an empty page in a page blob. There is no need to upload empty pages in the VHD, which means that bandwidth need not be wasted uploading empty pages. The Blob service identifies these empty pages when a download of one of them is requested, and it merely injects a page full of 0 x 0 bytes into the response stream.

Uploads to block blobs comprise a two-step process: upload the blocks and commit the blocks to the blob. Uploading a page blob is a single-step process: write one or more 512-byte pages to the blob. Once uploaded, these pages immediately form part of the blob. This can cause problems if multiple writers are writing to the page blob simultaneously. The Azure Storage service REST API provides support for a sequence number that can be used to control which writer wins a contest to write to a single page.

In the Storage Client library, the `CloudPageBlob` class provides various methods to support page blob uploads. The `CloudPageBlob` class provides synchronous and asynchronous `WritePages()` methods specifically to upload page blobs. Additionally, there are synchronous and asynchronous forms of the `GetPageRanges()` method that returns `IEnumerable<PageRange>` of the nonempty page ranges in the blob.

In this recipe, we'll learn how to upload a VHD into a page blob.

Getting ready

We use the Disk Management snap-in to create and format a VHD on the local system, which we will upload with the recipe. There is more documentation on the Disk Management snap-in at `http://technet.microsoft.com/en-us/library/dd979539(WS.10).aspx`.

We launch **Disk Management** by clicking on **Start**, typing `diskmgmt.msc` in the **Search** box, and then pressing **Enter**. The **Create VHD** and **Attach VHD** operations are on the **Action** menu.

We use the Disk Management snap-in for the following tasks:

▶ Create a VHD as **fixed** size with a specified size in the specified location (remember that Azure supports page blobs up to 1 TB of size)

▶ A new disk will appear in the Disk Management window; initialize it with a master boot record

▶ Create a new simple volume formatted as NTFS with a specified drive letter

▶ Copy files and directories to the specified drive

▶ Detach the VHD

If the VHD already exists, we use the Disk Management snap-in for the following tasks:

- ► Attach the VHD
- ► Copy files and directories to the specified drive
- ► Detach the VHD

This recipe assumes that the following lines of code are in the application's configuration file:

```
<appSettings>
  <add key="DataConnectionString"
value="DefaultEndpointsProtocol=https;AccountName={ACCOUNT_
NAME};AccountKey={ACCOUNT_KEY}"/>
</appSettings>
```

We must replace {ACCOUNT_NAME} and {ACCOUNT_KEY} with appropriate values for the account name and access key, respectively.

How to do it...

We are going to create a page blob and upload a VHD into it. We will do this using the following steps:

1. Add a new class named UploadVhdExample to the project.

2. Add the following using statements to the top of the class file:

```
using Microsoft.WindowsAzure.Storage;
using Microsoft.WindowsAzure.Storage.Blob;
using System.Configuration;
using System.IO;
```

3. Add the following members to the class:

```
private const Int32 pageSize = 0x200; // 512 bytes
private const Int32 uploadSize = 0x100000; // 1MBytes
private CloudBlobClient cloudBlobClient;
```

4. Add the following constructor to the class:

```
public UploadVhdExample()
{
  CloudStorageAccount cloudStorageAccount =
      CloudStorageAccount.Parse(
      ConfigurationManager.AppSettings[
      "DataConnectionString"]);
  cloudBlobClient =
      cloudStorageAccount.CreateCloudBlobClient();
}
```

5. Add the following method, uploading a VHD, to the class:

```
private void UploadCloudDrive(
  String containerName, String blobName, String vhdPath)
{
  CloudBlobContainer cloudBlobContainer =
     cloudBlobClient.GetContainerReference(containerName);
  cloudBlobContainer.CreateIfNotExists();

  CloudPageBlob cloudPageBlob =
     cloudBlobContainer.GetPageBlobReference(blobName);
  cloudPageBlob.Properties.ContentType =
     "binary/octet-stream";

  using (FileStream fileStream =
    new FileStream(vhdPath, FileMode.Open))
  {
    Int32 blobSize = (Int32)fileStream.Length;
    if ((blobSize % pageSize) != 0)
    {
      throw new ApplicationException(
         "Page blob size must be a multiple of page size");
    }
    cloudPageBlob.Create(blobSize);

    Int32 pageBlobOffset = 0;
    Int32 numberIterations = blobSize / uploadSize;
    for (Int32 i = 0; i < numberIterations; i++)
    {
      pageBlobOffset = UploadPages(
         fileStream, cloudPageBlob, pageBlobOffset);
    }

    pageBlobOffset = UploadFooter(
       fileStream, cloudPageBlob, pageBlobOffset);
  }
}
```

6. Add the following method, uploading pages to a page blob, to the class:

```
private Int32 UploadPages(FileStream fileStream,
  CloudPageBlob cloudPageBlob, Int32 pageBlobOffset)
{
  Byte[] buffer = new Byte[uploadSize];
  Int32 countBytesRead = fileStream.Read(
     buffer, 0, uploadSize);
```

```
        Int32 countBytesUploaded = 0;

        Int32 bufferOffset = 0;
        Int32 rangeStart = 0;
        Int32 rangeSize = 0;
        while (bufferOffset < uploadSize)
        {
          Boolean nextPageIsLast =
              bufferOffset + pageSize >= uploadSize;
          Boolean nextPageHasData =
              NextPageHasData(buffer, bufferOffset);
          if (nextPageHasData)
          {
            if (rangeSize == 0)
            {
              rangeStart = bufferOffset;
            }
            rangeSize += pageSize;
          }

          if ((rangeSize > 0) && (!nextPageHasData ||
              nextPageIsLast))
          {
            using (MemoryStream memoryStream =
                new MemoryStream(buffer, rangeStart, rangeSize))
            {
              cloudPageBlob.WritePages(
                  memoryStream, pageBlobOffset + rangeStart);
              countBytesUploaded += rangeSize;
              rangeSize = 0;
            }
          }
          bufferOffset += pageSize;
        }
      pageBlobOffset += uploadSize;

      return pageBlobOffset;
    }
```

7. Add the following method, uploading the VHD footer, to the class:

```
    private Int32 UploadFooter(FileStream fileStream,
      CloudPageBlob cloudPageBlob, Int32 pageBlobOffset)
    {
      const Int32 numberFooterBytes = 512;
      Byte[] footerBytes = new Byte[numberFooterBytes];
```

```
Int32 countBytesRead = fileStream.Read(
    footerBytes, 0, numberFooterBytes);

using (MemoryStream memoryStream =
    new MemoryStream(footerBytes))
{
    cloudPageBlob.WritePages(memoryStream, pageBlobOffset);
    pageBlobOffset += numberFooterBytes;
}
return pageBlobOffset;
}
```

8. Add the following method, verifying that the page contains data, to the class:

```
private Boolean NextPageHasData(Byte[] buffer,
    Int32 bufferOffset)
{
    for (Int32 i = bufferOffset; i < bufferOffset + pageSize;
        i++)
    {
        if (buffer[i] != 0x0)
        {
            return true;
        }
    }
    return false;
}
```

9. Add the following method, using the methods added earlier, to the class:

```
public static void UseUploadVhdExample()
{
    String containerName = "{CONTAINER_NAME}";
    String blobName = "{BLOB_NAME}";
    String pathName = @"{PATH_TO_THE_VHD}";
    UploadVhdExample example = new UploadVhdExample();
    example.UploadCloudDrive(
        containerName, blobName, pathName);
}
```

How it works...

In steps 1 and 2, we set up the class. In step 3, we defined various constants and the `CloudBlobClient` class that we used to access the Blob service. We initialized this in the constructor we added in step 4.

In step 5, we added the method that controls the upload process. We opened `FileStream` on the VHD and created a page blob of the same size as the VHD. We then iterated over the VHD file in increments of 1 MB, invoking `UploadPages()` to upload the data in each 1 MB window. Finally, we invoked `UploadFooter()` to upload the VHD footer.

In step 6, we added the `UploadPages()` method to upload nonempty pages to the page blob. We read the VHD into a buffer in 1 MB chunks. We then looked for ranges of 512-byte pages that contained some data and uploaded only these ranges. Remember that we do not need to upload empty pages. The tricky part of this process is identifying the end of a range when we come across an empty page or reach the end of the buffer.

In step 7, we added the `UploadFooter()` method to upload the 512-byte VHD footer. We simply loaded the footer into a `Byte[]` buffer and created a `MemoryStream` class on it. We then invoked `WritePages()` to upload this to the page blob.

In step 8, we added a method that returns `false` if every byte of a specified 512-byte page of a buffer is 0 x 0. Otherwise, `NextPageHasData()` returns `true`.

In step 9, we added a method to use the methods added earlier. We must replace `{CONTAINER_NAME}` and `{BLOB_KEY}` with actual values for account name and access key, respectively. We must also replace `{PATH_TO_THE_VHD}` with the actual path to a VHD.

> When uploading an arbitrary file that, unlike the VHD, is not an integral multiple of the upload buffer, we need to correctly handle the final chunk that is smaller than the size of the upload buffer.

There's more...

Uploading a VHD into the Blob storage for further use inside cloud services roles or a virtual machine is a great deal, with one big limitation. Only one instance at a given time can mount the VHD volume in the read/write mode, making filesystem-based shares a hard (or impossible) scenario to set up.

In recent years, developers tried to figure out this limitation by proposing creative solutions, such as the following two, for example:

▶ One instance mounts the VHD in read/write mode; then, it shares it as a network share.

  Additional instances mount the network share using it to read/write data.

▶ Each instance has a local filesystem-based buffer where the application saves the relevant information.

  The local file and folders are sent to the other nodes by peer-to-peer algorithms.

These solutions have some drawbacks, and they are often very hard to implement. The Azure Storage service offers the **Files** feature (at the time of writing this book, in preview), which enables SMB Network Shares between virtual machines and roles inside of Azure environments.

> Azure Files stay at the fourth endpoint of the Azure storage account (`http://[account].file.core.windows.net`), which is enabled by preview; they can be used only for storage accounts that support REST Version 2014-02-14 or newer.

To create a Network Share using Files, proceed as follows:

1. Install the latest Azure PowerShell module (from Web Platform Installer).

2. Download the PowerShell Scripts from `http://go.microsoft.com/fwlink/?LinkID=398183`.

3. Execute this script to import the previously downloaded module:

    ```
    import-module .\AzureStorageFile.psd1
    ```

4. Execute this script to create the Storage Context, replacing `<name>` and `<key>` with actual values:

    ```
    $ctx=New-AzureStorageContext <name> <key>
    ```

5. Execute this script to create the Network Share, replacing `<name>` with the actual value:

    ```
    $s = New-AzureStorageShare <share name> -Context $ctx
    ```

6. Connect to a new or existing Azure Virtual Machine or Cloud Service role (via Remote Desktop); open a command prompt and execute the following script:

    ```
    net use z: \\[account].file.core.windows.net\[share] /u:[account] [key]
    ```

We must replace `[account]` with the Azure Storage account name, `[share]` with the Network Share name created earlier, and `[key]` with the Storage account key obtained from the Management Portal. With this, each Azure instance could read/write data in the same shared location.

See also

Have a look at the following links to get additional information:

▶ VM VHDs in Azure at `http://blogs.msdn.com/b/kdot/archive/2013/06/29/creating-vm-vhds-in-windows-azure.aspx`

▶ The Azure Files (preview) service at `http://blogs.msdn.com/b/windowsazurestorage/archive/2014/05/12/introducing-microsoft-azure-file-service.aspx`

Downloading a blob asynchronously

The Azure Storage library provides synchronous and asynchronous versions of nearly all the methods that access the Azure Storage service.

The asynchronous methods follow the **common language runtime (CLR) Asynchronous Programming Model (APM)**. In this model, asynchronous methods for an action are defined as a pair named `BeginAction` and `EndAction`. The asynchronous operation is initiated through a call to `BeginAction` and is cleaned up by a call to `EndAction`. The `BeginAction` action has a parameter that is a callback delegate, and `EndAction` must be invoked in this delegate.

This apparent complexity can be greatly simplified through the use of a lambda expression to represent the callback delegate. Furthermore, local variables defined in the method that contain the lambda expression are available inside the lambda expression. This removes any difficulty caused by a need to pass variables into the delegate. Using a lambda expression, instead of a callback delegate, makes using the asynchronous methods almost as simple as using the synchronous methods.

In this recipe, we'll learn how to use asynchronous methods to download a blob into a file.

Getting ready

This recipe assumes that the following lines of code are in the application's configuration file:

```
<appSettings>
  <add key="DataConnectionString"
value="DefaultEndpointsProtocol=https;AccountName={ACCOUNT_
NAME};AccountKey={ACCOUNT_KEY}"/>
</appSettings>
```

We must replace `{ACCOUNT_NAME}` and `{ACCOUNT_KEY}` with appropriate values for the account name and access key, respectively.

How to do it...

We are going to download a blob asynchronously. We will do this using the following steps:

1. Add a new class named `DownloadBlobExample` to the project.
2. Add the following `using` statements to the top of the class file:

```
using Microsoft.WindowsAzure.Storage;
using Microsoft.WindowsAzure.Storage.Blob;
using System.Configuration;
using System.Net;
using System.IO;
```

3. Add the following method, creating a container and blob, to the class:

```
private static void CreateContainerAndBlob(
  String containerName, String blobName)
{
  CloudStorageAccount cloudStorageAccount =
    CloudStorageAccount.Parse(
      ConfigurationManager.AppSettings[
      "DataConnectionString"]);
  CloudBlobClient cloudBlobClient =
    cloudStorageAccount.CreateCloudBlobClient();

  CloudBlobContainer cloudBlobContainer =
    cloudBlobClient.GetContainerReference(containerName);
  cloudBlobContainer.CreateIfNotExists();

  CloudBlockBlob cloudBlockBlob =
    cloudBlobContainer.GetBlockBlobReference(blobName);
  cloudBlockBlob.UploadText("To be, or not to be");
}
```

4. Add the following method, downloading a blob, to the class:

```
private static void DownloadBlob(String containerName,
  String blobName, String fileName)
{
  CloudStorageAccount cloudStorageAccount =
    CloudStorageAccount.Parse(
    ConfigurationManager.AppSettings[
    "DataConnectionString"]);
  CloudBlobClient cloudBlobClient =
    cloudStorageAccount.CreateCloudBlobClient();

  CloudBlobContainer cloudBlobContainer =
    cloudBlobClient.GetContainerReference(containerName);
  CloudBlockBlob cloudBlockBlob =
    cloudBlobContainer.GetBlockBlobReference(blobName);

  FileStream fileStream = new FileStream(fileName,
    FileMode.Append);
  IAsyncResult iAsyncResult =
    cloudBlockBlob.BeginDownloadToStream(fileStream,
    (result) =>
    {
      cloudBlockBlob.EndDownloadToStream(result);
      fileStream.Close();
    },
    null);
```

```
        return;
    }
```

5. Add the following method, using the methods added earlier, to the class:

```
public static void UseDownloadBlobExample()
{
    String containerName = "{CONTAINER_NAME}";
    String blobName = "{BLOB_NAME}";
    String fileName = Path.GetTempPath() + @"\{FILE_NAME}";

    CreateContainerAndBlob(containerName, blobName);
     DownloadBlob(containerName, blobName, fileName);
}
```

How it works...

In steps 1 and 2, we set up the class. In step 3, we initialized a `CloudStorageAccount` class from `app.config` file and used it to create a `CloudBlobClient` instance. We used this to create a container and a blob.

In step 4, we followed the same route to get a `CloudBlockBlob` reference to the blob. We used it to invoke the `BeginDownloadToStream()` method. We passed this lambda expression, instead of a callback delegate, and invoked `EndDownloadToStream()` in the lambda expression to clean up the asynchronous call. We used the ability to refer to local objects from inside the lambda expression to close the `FileStream` class used in the download.

 Note that in this example, the main thread ends before the callback is called. To make the sample (given earlier) perform the remote operation, keep in mind to wait for the asynchronous operations to finish.

In step 5, we added a method that sets the parameters for the call to `DownloadBlob()`. We downloaded the blob to a temporary directory. We must replace `{CONTAINER_NAME}` and `{BLOB_NAME}` with the appropriate container and blob names, and `{FILE_NAME}` with the filename.

There's more...

Recently, in the .NET framework, the Async/Await pattern began to take place. This pattern is useful when we work with responsive interfaces (for example, Windows Store/Phone apps) and hides the complexity of the callback mechanism by writing code that *seems* synchronous.

See also

Have a look at the following MSDN links to get additional information:

- ▶ Using cross account blob copy at `http://blogs.msdn.com/b/windowsazurestorage/archive/2013/04/01/azcopy-using-cross-account-copy-blob.aspx`

- ▶ Azure Storage Explorer, an open and free Management Software, at `http://azurestorageexplorer.codeplex.com/`

Using retry policies with blob operations

A storage operation that accesses the Azure Storage service can fail in various ways. For example, there could be an unexpected timeout if the Storage service is moving a partition for performance reasons, so we are dealing with transient errors. It is advisable, therefore, to code defensively in the assumption that failure could occur unexpectedly.

The Azure Storage library supports defensive coding by providing a retry policy for operations to the Storage service. This is done by default, but the retry policy classes support parameterization and customization of the process.

The `CloudBlobClient` class has a `RetryPolicy` property to define it at factory level. In addition, a storage operation on a `blob` object has a retry policy associated with it through the `RetryPolicy` property of its `BlobRequestOptions` parameter. These `RetryPolicy` properties provide access to a `RetryPolicy` instance that implements the `IRetryPolicy` interface and the `ShouldRetry` method, which specifies whether or not a retry should be attempted.

The `Microsoft.WindowsAzure.Storage.RetryPolicies` namespace provides several `RetryPolicy` implementations as follows:

- ▶ The `NoRetry` class does not perform retries

- ▶ The `LinearRetry` delegate performs a number of retries with a fixed interval between them

- ▶ The `ExponentialRetry` delegate performs a number of retries with an exponential back-off time between them (that is, the interval between successive retries roughly doubles)

By default, an `ExponentialRetry` instance is associated with a `CloudBlobClient` class and with any storage operation using it. This default can be overridden for an individual storage operation by associating a `RetryPolicy` property with the storage operation.

The configurability provided by the default retry policies is sufficient for most cases. However, the `IRetryPolicy` interface can be used if more control is needed. For example, none of the default retry policies provided in the `RetryPolicies` namespace uses the exception thrown by a failed operation.

In this recipe, we will see various uses of retry policies. We will see how to have a no-retry policy and a nondefault retry policy, and how to customize the retry process.

Getting ready

This recipe assumes that the following lines of code are in the application's configuration file:

```
<appSettings>
  <add key="DataConnectionString"
value="DefaultEndpointsProtocol=https;AccountName={ACCOUNT_
NAME};AccountKey={ACCOUNT_KEY}"/>
</appSettings>
```

We must replace `{ACCOUNT_NAME}` and `{ACCOUNT_KEY}` with appropriate values for the account name and access key, respectively.

How to do it...

We are going to use various retry policies when uploading a 10 MB blob. We will do this using the following steps:

1. Add a new class named `RetryPoliciesExample` to the project.

2. Add the following `using` statements to the top of the class file:

   ```
   using Microsoft.WindowsAzure.Storage;
   using Microsoft.WindowsAzure.Storage.Blob;
   using Microsoft.WindowsAzure.Storage.RetryPolicies;
   using System.Configuration;
   ```

3. Add the following `private` members to the class:

   ```
   private String blobText = new String('z', 10000000);
   private CloudBlockBlob cloudBlockBlob;
   Add the following constructor to the class:
   public RetryPoliciesExample(String containerName,
       String blobName)
   {
     CloudStorageAccount cloudStorageAccount =
         CloudStorageAccount.Parse(
         ConfigurationManager.AppSettings[
         "DataConnectionString"]);
   ```

```
CloudBlobClient cloudBlobClient =
    cloudStorageAccount.CreateCloudBlobClient();
CloudBlobContainer cloudBlobContainer =
    cloudBlobClient.GetContainerReference(containerName);
cloudBlobContainer.CreateIfNotExists();

cloudBlockBlob =
    cloudBlobContainer.GetBlockBlobReference(blobName);
}
```

4. Add the following method, uploading a blob with a no-retry policy, to the class:

```
private void UploadWithNoRetry()
{
  BlobRequestOptions blobRequestOptions =
      new BlobRequestOptions();
  blobRequestOptions.ServerTimeout= TimeSpan.FromSeconds(2);
  blobRequestOptions.RetryPolicy = new Microsoft
        .WindowsAzure.Storage.RetryPolicies.NoRetry();
    try
    {
        cloudBlockBlob.UploadText(blobText, new UTF8Encoding()
, null, blobRequestOptions);
    }
    catch (Exception)
    {
        //Immediately here, no retry
    }
}
```

5. Add the following method, uploading a blob using an exponential retry policy, to the class:

```
private void UploadWithModifiedRetry()
{
  TimeSpan deltaBackOff = TimeSpan.FromSeconds(2);
  BlobRequestOptions blobRequestOptions =
      new BlobRequestOptions();
  blobRequestOptions.ServerTimeout = TimeSpan.FromSeconds(2);
  blobRequestOptions.RetryPolicy =new Microsoft
        .WindowsAzure.Storage.RetryPolicies
        .ExponentialRetry(deltaBackOff,5);
    try
    {
        cloudBlockBlob.UploadText(blobText, new UTF8Encoding()
, null, blobRequestOptions);
```

```
        }
        catch (Exception)
        {
            //Here after 5 attempts
        }
    }
```

6. Add the following class, implementing a custom retry, in the project:

```
public class MyRetry : IRetryPolicy
{
    public IRetryPolicy CreateInstance()
    {
        return new MyRetry();
    }

    public bool ShouldRetry(int currentRetryCount, int
statusCode, Exception lastException, out TimeSpan retryInterval,
OperationContext operationContext)
    {
        retryInterval = TimeSpan.FromSeconds(1);
        return (DateTime.Today.Day == 15);
    }
}
```

7. Add the following method, uploading a blob with a custom retry policy, to the class:

```
private void UploadWithCustomRetry()
{
  BlobRequestOptions blobRequestOptions =
      new BlobRequestOptions();
  blobRequestOptions.ServerTimeout= TimeSpan.FromSeconds(2);
    blobRequestOptions.RetryPolicy = new MyRetry();

    try
    {
        cloudBlockBlob.UploadText(blobText, new UTF8Encoding()
, null, blobRequestOptions);
    }
    catch (Exception)
    {
        //Never here, if today in the 15th of any month.
        //Else, immediately here
    }
}
```

8. Add the following method, using the methods just added, to the class:

```
public static void UseRetryPoliciesExample()
{
    String containerName = "test01";
    String blobName = "myBlob.txt";

    RetryPoliciesExample retryPoliciesExample =
        new RetryPoliciesExample(containerName, blobName);

    retryPoliciesExample.UploadWithNoRetry();
    retryPoliciesExample.UploadWithModifiedRetry();
    retryPoliciesExample.UploadWithCustomRetry();
}
```

How it works...

In this recipe, we used a short timeout of 2 seconds when uploading a 10 MB blob with the deliberate intent of making the upload operation fail so that we can see various retry policies in action.

 The `ServerTimeout` property is a query string parameter appended to the request with the intent of telling the Storage service to fail if it cannot complete the request in the specified timeout. With this property, we can force a level of service for our applications, stating that the operation should complete in that time or never complete at all.

The blob size can be increased if the upload speed is so fast that the upload succeeds without the retry policy being invoked. This recipe should be used with the Storage service rather than the Storage Emulator to take advantage of the slower connection speeds on the Internet.

In steps 1 and 2, we set up the class. In step 3, we initialized the string that will upload to the blob and defined a `CloudBlockBlob` instance that we initialized in the constructor we added in step 4. We also created a container in the constructor.

In step 5, we uploaded a blob while using the no-retry policy. We do this by creating a `BlobRequestOptions` instance and assigning an instance of the `NoRetry` class to `RetryPolicy` of the `BlobRequestOption` class for the `CloudBlockBlob`. `UploadText()` operation. When this method is invoked, it makes a single call to the Blob service. It throws an exception if the operation times out. With no retries, the code immediately goes into the catch block.

In step 6, we uploaded a blob while using an exponential retry policy. We do this by creating a `BlobRequestOptions` instance and assigning a `ExponentialRetry` instance to `RetryPolicy` of the `BlobRequestOption` class for the `CloudBlockBlob.UploadText()` operation. This retry policy performs five retries of a failed operation with a 2-second back-off interval. The default policy is set to three retries and 4 seconds for the back-off interval.

In step 7, we added a custom implementation of `IRetryPolicy`, which specifies that if the current date lies on the 15th day of any month, a retry should be performed, without taking care of the context. This is a clearly strange behavior, just for example purposes.

In step 8, we uploaded a blob using a custom retry policy. The library will call the `ShouldRetry` method of our class to evaluate whether to perform a retry.

In step 10, we added a method that invokes the three upload methods.

There's more...

The Transient Fault Handling Application Block, part of the Microsoft Enterprise library, adds some infrastructure features that are helpful in handling transient errors due to the nature of network protocols or raised by remote services. After installing **Topaz** (the library) from NuGet, we can use the retry policies provided (along with the related classes) instead of the built-in classes of the Storage library.

If you are wondering why you should use this external library instead of the simple built-in support, note that Topaz is service agnostic and lets us wrap every service of action we want into retry policies by applying the same coding pattern.

In Topaz, a retry policy uses a detection strategy to determine if an error is transient or it is just an application error. This great degree of customization makes Topaz extendable as follows:

```
public class MyDetectionStrategy : ITransientErrorDetectionStrategy
{
    public bool IsTransient(Exception ex)
    {
        var we=ex as WebException;
        if (we!=null)
        {
            var resp=we.Response as HttpWebResponse;
            if (resp != null)
            {
                return resp.StatusCode == HttpStatusCode.
InternalServerError;
            }
        }
```

```
        return false;
    }
}
```

The preceding class treats the exception as transient if it is related to a HTTP error code 500; otherwise, the exception should be given back to the application code. To instantiate a retry policy using an existing implementation, proceed as follows:

```
var retryPolicy = new RetryPolicy<MyDetectionStrategy>(
    new ExponentialBackoff(5, TimeSpan.FromMilliseconds(10),
    TimeSpan.FromMilliseconds(10000), TimeSpan.
FromMilliseconds(200)));
Finally, to use it, do this:
retryPolicy.ExecuteAction(() => { /*Action*/ });
```

See also

Have a look at these links to get additional information:

- ▶ Retry policy recommendations at `http://azure.microsoft.com/blog/2014/05/22/azure-storage-client-library-retry-policy-recommendations/`

- ▶ Transient fault-handling application block at `http://msdn.microsoft.com/en-us/library/hh680934(v=pandp.50).aspx`

Leasing a blob and implementing distributed locks

As the same services of Azure consume the Blob storage as a service, it needed some features to be enabled for complex scenarios. One of these is to allow an Azure virtual machine to **exclusively access** a blob (a VHD, for example), preventing other clients to access it in any way. To provide this feature, Blob Storage has the lease function: a lock-like status in which a blob cannot be written by anybody except the one who owns the lease.

A blob can be leased for 15 seconds up to 60 seconds (or infinite), and it can be renewed as many times as needed (while it is still locked). This is particularly useful with page blobs as they can be updated with random writes. Indeed, the Azure virtual machines use leases to ensure that only one instance at a time can mount a VHD page blob as a disk.

There are five blob-leasing actions:

- ▸ Acquire
- ▸ Renew
- ▸ Change
- ▸ Release
- ▸ Break

The Acquire action is invoked on a blob to acquire a lease on it for a specified amount of time. This lease is identified by a lease ID that must be presented with any operation that modifies the blob. The Renew action renews an existing lease for another timeframe that is equal to the Acquire one. The Change action changes the lease ID from one value to another to permit a graceful transition between two holders without interference from outside. The Release action ends the lease immediately so that the blob can be updated without presenting the lease ID. The Break action ends the lease but does not allow the blob to be updated until the expiration of the current lease period.

The Change operation is probably the most interesting action to be performed on a leased blob. There are, in fact, certain scenarios where the workflow manager should pass the ownership of a resource to a specific process/actor. In this case, a release would be impossible as any process/ actor could subsequently obtain the lease and override the correct workflow. In such situations, the manager transfers the ownership of the lease directly to another process (changing the lease ID), never leaving the blob in an inconsistent state.

Remember that a lease could be acquired for an infinite time span, passing a null value instead of a TimeSpan interval. In the case of infinite leases, the Break operation would break immediately. In this recipe, we will show how to use leases on blobs.

Getting ready

This recipe assumes that the following lines of code are in the application's configuration file:

```
<appSettings>
  <add key="DataConnectionString"
value="DefaultEndpointsProtocol=https;AccountName={ACCOUNT_
NAME};AccountKey={ACCOUNT_KEY}"/>
</appSettings>
```

We must replace {ACCOUNT_NAME} and {ACCOUNT_KEY} with appropriate values for the account name and access key, respectively.

How to do it...

We are going to lease a blob and attempt some operations such as `acquire again,` `change`, `renew`, and `release`. We will do this using the following steps:

1. Add a new class named `LeaseBlobsExample` to the project.

2. Add the following `using` statements to the top of the class file:

    ```
    using Microsoft.WindowsAzure.Storage;
    using Microsoft.WindowsAzure.Storage.Auth;
    using Microsoft.WindowsAzure.Storage.Blob;
    ```

3. Add the following `private` members:

    ```
    private String leaseIdForProcessA;
    private String leaseIdForProcessB;
    private CloudBlockBlob cloudBlockBlob;
    ```

4. Add the following constructor that initializes the blob:

    ```
    public LeaseBlobsExample(String containerName,
        String blobName)
    {
        CloudStorageAccount cloudStorageAccount =
            CloudStorageAccount.Parse(
            ConfigurationManager.AppSettings[
            "DataConnectionString"]);
        CloudBlobClient cloudBlobClient =
            cloudStorageAccount.CreateCloudBlobClient();
        CloudBlobContainer cloudBlobContainer =
            cloudBlobClient.GetContainerReference(containerName);
        cloudBlobContainer.CreateIfNotExists();

        cloudBlockBlob =
            cloudBlobContainer.GetBlockBlobReference(blobName);
        cloudBlockBlob.UploadText("The slings and arrows");
    }
    ```

5. Add the following methods to the class, one for each lease action (except `break`):

    ```
    private void AcquireLease(string leaseId)
    {
        cloudBlockBlob.AcquireLease(TimeSpan.FromSeconds(30),
    leaseId);
    }
    private void RenewLease(string leaseId)
    {
    ```

```
        cloudBlockBlob.RenewLease(
            new AccessCondition() { LeaseId = leaseId });
    }
    private void ReleaseLease(string leaseId)
    {
        cloudBlockBlob.ReleaseLease(new AccessCondition()
        {
            LeaseId = leaseId
        });
    }
    private void ChangeLease(string sourceLeaseId, string
    destinationLeaseId)
    {
        cloudBlockBlob.ChangeLease(destinationLeaseId, new
    AccessCondition()
        {
            LeaseId = sourceLeaseId
        });
    }
```

6. Add the following method to write content to the blob:

```
    private void WriteContent(string content,string leaseId=null)
    {
        cloudBlockBlob.UploadText(content,null,
            leaseId!=null?new AccessCondition()
    {LeaseId=leaseId}:null);
    }
```

7. Add the following method, using the code above, to the class:

```
    public static void UseLeaseBlobsExample()
    {
        String containerName = "test01";
        String blobName = "myBlob.txt";

        LeaseBlobsExample leaseBlobsExample =
            new LeaseBlobsExample(containerName, blobName);

        leaseBlobsExample.leaseIdForProcessA
            = Guid.NewGuid().ToString();
        leaseBlobsExample.leaseIdForProcessB
            = Guid.NewGuid().ToString();

        leaseBlobsExample.AcquireLease(leaseBlobsExample
            .leaseIdForProcessA);
```

```
try
{
    //This call fails
    leaseBlobsExample.AcquireLease(leaseBlobsExample
        .leaseIdForProcessB);
}catch{}

leaseBlobsExample.ChangeLease(leaseBlobsExample
    .leaseIdForProcessA, leaseBlobsExample.
leaseIdForProcessB);
    //Now is permitted
    leaseBlobsExample.AcquireLease(leaseBlobsExample
        .leaseIdForProcessB);

try
{
    //This call fails
    leaseBlobsExample.WriteContent("Sample");
}
catch { }

leaseBlobsExample.WriteContent("Sample"
    , leaseBlobsExample.leaseIdForProcessB);
leaseBlobsExample.RenewLease(leaseBlobsExample
    .leaseIdForProcessB);
leaseBlobsExample.ReleaseLease(leaseBlobsExample
    .leaseIdForProcessB);
leaseBlobsExample.AcquireLease(leaseBlobsExample
    .leaseIdForProcessA);
}
```

How it works...

In steps 1 and 2, we set up the class. We added some members to the class in step 3 and initialized the blob in the constructor we add in step 4.

In step 5, we created one method for each lease operation, except the break one. The AcquireLease operation calls the corresponding operation on the blob using the leaseId parameter passed as an argument and a default 30-second timeframe for the lease. The RenewLease operation does not need a TimeSpan interval (as the release operation reflects the original interval requested while acquiring) but the leaseId to authorize the renewal.

The `ChangeLease` operation requires, in addition to the current `leaseId` parameter, the new `leaseId` parameter to switch to. Keep in mind that some operations would not complete correctly if the conditions are not met (that is, changing a lease with the wrong source `leaseId` parameter or renewing a lease on an expired lease).

In step 6, we added a method that writes sample content to the blob.

In step 7, we generated two lease IDs (emulating a two-actor environment), and we initially acquired a lease from actor A. The second `acquire` call, from actor B, will fail, because A owns the lease and the blob is currently locked. So, with the `ChangeLease` operation, we transferred the ownership from A to B; after that, B can acquire the lease again.

 The difference between the `Acquire` and `Renew` operations performed on a locked blob is that in the former, we can specify a shorter or longer timeframe instead of the original one, while the latter always assumes the same timeframe of the original `Acquire` operation.

We can try to write some content without a `leaseId` parameter (failing, of course), and we immediately retry specifying the `correct` leaseId parameter. Finally, we renewed and released the lease to finally allow process A to acquire the lock.

 To explore the REST API around the lease actions, run this code with the Fiddler listening.

There's more...

There is a Lease Container API designed to control or prevent deletion of containers. The available actions are the same for blobs, except that the behavior is like lock for deletion. It can be used to organize workers who access specific containers and APIs, one by one.

See also

Have a look at the following links to get additional information:

- More information about lease container at `http://msdn.microsoft.com/en-us/library/azure/jj159103.aspx`
- One of the most popular Azure Storage Management Tools at `http://www.cerebrata.com/products/azure-management-studio/introduction`

Using the Azure Content Delivery Network (CDN)

The Azure Blob service is hosted on a small number of Azure datacenters worldwide. The Azure CDN is a service that enhances end user experience by caching blobs in more than 20 strategic locations across the world (a complete listing can be found at `http://msdn. microsoft.com/library/azure/gg680302.aspx`).

After the CDN is enabled for a storage account, a CDN endpoint can be used, instead of the storage-account endpoint, to access a cached version of publicly accessible blobs in the storage account. The CDN endpoint is location aware, and a request to the CDN endpoint is directed automatically to the closest CDN location. If the blob is not currently cached there, the CDN retrieves the blob from the Blob service endpoint and caches it before satisfying the request.

The cache-control property of the blob can be used to specify a time to live in the cache. Otherwise, the CDN uses a heuristic based on how old the blob is and caches the blob for less than 72 hours or 20 percent of the time since the blob was last modified.

A custom domain can be associated with a CDN endpoint. As with a custom domain for a storage account, this provides a convenient alias for the CDN endpoint. When configuring a custom domain for either a CDN or a storage account, it is necessary to validate the custom domain by demonstrating access to the DNS records for the domain.

The endpoints for the Blob service and CDN are as follows:

- `http://{account_name}.blob.core.windows.net`
- `http://{CDN_name}.vo.msecnd.net`

The `{CDN_name}` part is the unique identifier the Azure Portal uses to specify the CDN for the storage account. When the account name and CDN endpoints are associated with custom domains, they can be addressed as follows:

- `http://blobs.{domain}.com`
- `http://cdn.{domain}.com`

In this recipe, we'll learn how to enable a CDN for a Blob service endpoint and associate a custom domain with it.

How to do it...

We are going to enable the CDN and validate it. Then, we will add a custom domain to it. We will do this using the following steps:

1. On the Azure Portal, navigate to **New | App Services | CDN | Quick Create**.

2. In the **Origin Domain** dropdown, choose the storage account you want to enable on **Content Delivery Network** and confirm.

3. In the **CDN** section of the portal, a new item is created with a name similar to azNNNNNN; select it.

4. In the footer menu, enable **HTTPS** and **Query String**.

5. Click on **Manage Domains**. In the pop-up dialog, enter the desired custom domain.

6. Azure will ask for a validation of the domain proposed. This can be done by creating a DNS record just for validation purposes or by creating the real DNS mapping between the custom domain and CDN.

7. After the domain is validated, confirm the settings.

How it works...

In step 2, we use the Azure Portal to enable the CDN for a specific storage account, and in step 3, we navigated to the newly created item.

In step 4, we enabled the HTTPS endpoint (with a valid certificate provided by Microsoft) and the Query String support. The Query String support is useful, as the CDN, which is similar to a web cache, treats two URIs that point to the same resource as two different resources if different query strings are provided.

In steps 5 and 6, we demonstrated our control over the custom domain through a validation process. The Azure Portal provides a specific validation domain that we must use to create a CNAME mapping from the custom domain to Azure custom domain's verification endpoint. We then go back to the Azure Portal and validate the domain.

Having validated the custom domain, we confirm the mapping from our custom domain to the CDN endpoint.

 We add a custom domain for a storage account endpoint in exactly the same way. Remember that custom SSL certificates are not available while accessing CDNs or storage accounts with custom domains.

See also

Have a look at the following link to get additional information:

▸ How to use Azure CDN at `http://azure.microsoft.com/en-en/documentation/articles/cdn-how-to-use/`

4

Going Relational with the Azure SQL Database

In this chapter, we will cover the following topics:

- ▶ Creating a SQL Database server and database
- ▶ Managing SQL Database logins and firewall rules
- ▶ Developing a SQL Database with Visual Studio
- ▶ Connecting to a SQL Database with ADO.NET
- ▶ Connecting to a SQL Database with Entity Framework
- ▶ Connecting to a SQL Database from PHP and Java
- ▶ Migrating a database to a SQL Database
- ▶ Leveraging backup solutions with SQL Database
- ▶ Monitoring SQL Database with the dynamic management views
- ▶ Handling connection failures to a SQL Database

Introduction

An Azure SQL Database provides relational database technology to the Azure platform. It is a specific derived version of the SQL Server. However, Microsoft provides all management of the physical server, leaving the customer responsible for managing individual databases on a logical but not a physical level.

The SQL Database administrator must provision a SQL Database *server*, which is the administrative and security boundary for a collection of SQL Databases This is a logical server, more like a container than a physical server, as the SQL Database customer has no access to the physical servers on which SQL Databases are stored. In the *Creating a SQL Database server and database* recipe, we will see how to create one using the Azure Portal.

The next step after creating a SQL Database server is to create some SQL Databases in it. We can do this using either the Azure Portal or by invoking a Transact SQL operation. This is almost the same as the traditional Microsoft SQL Server, except that there are constraints on database size, edition, and location. Furthermore, any attempt to specify the physical placement of data and logs is forbidden, as the SQL Database administrator has no control over physical placement. Finally, specific firewall rules must be set to grant access rights to any client that wants to connect, as we will see in the *Managing SQL Database logins and firewall rules* recipe.

Having created a SQL Database, we might need to create tables in it and populate it with data from an existing Microsoft SQL Server database. We will see how to use the **SQL Database Migration Wizard** to do this in the *Migrating a database to a SQL Database* recipe.

Maintaining a SQL Database on Azure can be challenging, so we will see a non-Azure technology useful to build even complex databases with a more rational approach. We will see Visual Studio database projects in the *Developing a SQL Database with Visual Studio* recipe.

SQL Database is a shared, multitenant database system in which the databases of many customers might coexist on the same physical hardware. This causes resource constraints on maximum size and operational throughput. Monitoring the usage of these resources is consequently important. In the *Monitoring SQL Database with the dynamic management views* recipe, we will see how to use dynamic management views to look at the current resource consumption.

An important feature of SQL Database is its similarity to Microsoft SQL Server. Often, code that works against the Microsoft SQL Server can be used against SQL Database merely by changing the connection string to point to the SQL Database. We will see how to do this in the *Connecting to a SQL Database with ADO.NET* and *Connecting to a SQL Database with Entity Framework* recipes. This principle is also valid for non-.NET environments, so we will see this in the *Connecting to a SQL Database from PHP and Java* recipe.

Architects should build available systems, implementing the proper policy for disaster recovery and application errors, which could lead up to unavailability. Backup solutions are always one of the most important aspects of a given architecture. With SQL Database, various approaches can be implemented, as we will see in the *Leveraging backup solutions with a SQL Database* recipe.

An increased likelihood of dropped connections is an important consequence of the resource constraints imposed by the shared nature of SQL Database. It is important for an application to have some easy mechanism to handle this. In the *Handling connection failures to a SQL Database* recipe, we will see how to do this using the **Transient Fault Handling Framework**.

Creating a SQL Database server and database

SQL Database is a multitenanted database system in which many distinct databases are hosted on many physical servers managed by Microsoft. SQL Database administrators have no control over the physical provisioning of a database to a particular physical server. Indeed, to maintain high availability, a primary and two secondary copies of each SQL Database are stored on separate physical servers, and users can't have any control over them.

Consequently, SQL Database does not provide a way for the administrator to specify the physical layout of a database and its logs when creating a SQL Database. The administrator merely has to provide a name, maximum size, and service tier for the database.

A SQL Database server is the administrative and security boundary for a collection of SQL Databases hosted in a single Azure region. All connections to a database hosted by the server go through the service endpoint provided by the SQL Database server. At the time of writing this book, an Azure subscription can create up to six SQL Database servers, each of which can host up to 150 databases (including the master database). These are soft limits that can be increased by arrangement with Microsoft Support.

From a billing perspective, only the database unit is counted towards, as the server unit is just a container. However, to avoid a waste of unused resources, an empty server is automatically deleted after 90 days of non-hosting user databases.

The SQL Database server is provisioned on the Azure Portal. The Region as well as the administrator login and password must be specified during the provisioning process. After the SQL Database server has been provisioned, the firewall rules used to restrict access to the databases associated with the SQL Database server can be modified on the Azure Portal, using Transact SQL or the SQL Database Service Management REST API.

The result of the provisioning process is a SQL Database server identified by a fully-qualified DNS name such as SERVER_NAME.database.windows.net, where SERVER_NAME is an automatically generated (random and unique) string that differentiates this SQL Database server from any other. The provisioning process also creates the master database for the SQL Database server and adds a user and associated login for the administrator specified during the provisioning process. This user has the rights to create other databases associated with this SQL Database server as well as any logins needed to access them.

Remember to distinguish between the SQL Database service and the famous SQL Server engine available on the Azure platform, but as a plain installation over VMs. In the latter case, you will continue to own the complete control of the instance that runs the SQL Server, the installation details, and the effort to maintain it during the time. Also, remember that the SQL Server virtual machines have a different pricing from the standard VMs due to their license costs.

An administrator can create a SQL Database either on the Azure Portal or using the CREATE DATABASE Transact SQL statement.

At the time of this writing this book, SQL Database runs in the following two different modes:

- **Version 1.0**: This refers to Web or Business Editions
- **Version 2.0**: This refers to Basic, Standard, or Premium service tiers with performance levels

The first version is deprecating in few months. Web Edition was designed for small databases under 5 GB and Business Edition for databases of 10 GB and larger (up to 150 GB). There is no difference in these editions other than the maximum size and billing increment.

The second version introduced service tiers (the equivalent of Editions) with an additional parameter (performance level) that sets the amount of dedicated resource to a given database. The new service tiers (Basic, Standard, and Premium) introduced a lot of advanced features such as active/passive Geo-replication, point-in-time restore, cross-region copy, and restore. Different performance levels have different limits such as the **Database Throughput Unit** (**DTU**) and the maximum DB size. An updated list of service tiers and performance levels can be found at http://msdn.microsoft.com/en-us/library/dn741336.aspx.

Once a SQL Database has been created, the ALTER DATABASE Transact SQL statement can be used to alter either the edition or the maximum size of the database. The maximum size is important as the database is made read only once it reaches that size (with the **The database has reached its size quota** error message and number 40544).

In this recipe, we'll learn how to create a SQL Database server and a database using the Azure Portal and T-SQL.

Getting ready

To perform the majority of operations of the recipe, just a plain Internet browser is needed. However, to connect directly to the server, we will use the SQL Server Management Studio (also available in the Express version).

How to do it...

First, we are going to create a SQL Database server using the Azure Portal. We will do this using the following steps:

1. On the Azure Portal, go to the **SQL DATABASES** section and then select the **SERVERS** tab.

2. In the bottom menu, select **Add**.

3. In the **CREATE SERVER** window, provide an administrator login and password.

4. Select a **Subscription** and **Region** that will host the server.

> To enable access from the other service in WA to the server, you can check the **Allow Windows Azure Services to access the server** checkbox; this is a special firewall rule that allows the 0.0.0.0 to 0.0.0.0 IP range.

5. Confirm and wait a few seconds to complete the operation.

6. After that, using the Azure Portal, go to the **SQL DATABASES** section and then the **SERVERS** tab.

7. Select the previously created server by clicking on its name.

8. In the server page, go to the **DATABASES** tab.

9. In the bottom menu, click on **Add**; then, after clicking on **NEW SQL DATABASE**, the **CUSTOM CREATE** window will open.

10. Specify a name and select the Web Edition. Set the maximum database size to 5 GB and leave the **COLLATION** dropdown to its default.

> SQL Database fees are charged differently if you are using the Web/Business Edition rather than the Basic/Standard/Premium service tiers. The most updated pricing scheme for SQL Database can be found at http://azure.microsoft.com/en-us/pricing/details/sql-database/

11. Verify the server on which you are creating the database (it is specified correctly in the **SERVER** dropdown) and confirm it.

12. Alternatively, using Transact SQL, launch **Microsoft SQL Server Management Studio** and open the **Connect to Server** window.

13. In the **Server** name field, specify the fully qualified name of the newly created SQL Database server in the following form: serverName.database.windows.net.

14. Choose the **SQL Server Authentication** method.

15. Specify the administrative username and password associated earlier.

16. Click on the **Options** button and specify the **Encrypt** connection checkbox.

> This setting is particularly critical while accessing a remote SQL Database. Without encryption, a malicious user could extract all the information to log in to the database himself, from the network traffic. Specifying the Encrypt connection flag, we are telling the client to connect only if a valid certificate is found on the server side.

17. Optionally check the **Remember password** checkbox and connect to the server.

> To connect remotely to the server, a firewall rule should be created. To do this, follow the instructions in the *Managing SQL Database logins and firewall rules* recipe.

18. In the **Object Explorer** window, locate the server you connected to, navigate to **Databases | System Databases**, and then right-click on the master database and select **New Query**.

19. Copy and execute this query and wait for its completion:.

```
CREATE DATABASE DATABASE_NAME
(
   MAXSIZE = 1 GB
)
```

How it works...

The first part was pretty straightforward. In steps 1 and 2, we went to the SQL Database section of the Azure portal, locating the tab to manage the servers. In step 3, we filled in the online popup with the administrative login details, and in step 4, we selected a Region to place the SQL Database server. As a server (with its database) is located in a Region, it is not possible to automatically migrate it to another Region. This is possible by manually transferring the database contents or using any of the methods explained in the *Migrating a database to a SQL Database* or *Leveraging backup solutions with SQL Database* recipe.

After the creation of the container resource (the server), we created the SQL Database by adding a new database to the newly created server, as stated from steps 6 to 9. In step 10, we could optionally change the default collation of the database and its maximum size.

In the last part, we used the **SQL Server Management Studio** (**SSMS**) (step 12) to connect to the remote SQL Database instance. We noticed that even without a database, there was a default database (the master one) we could connect to. After we set up the parameters in step 13, 14, and 15, we enabled the encryption requirement for the connection. Remember to always set the encryption before connecting or listing the databases of a remote endpoint, as every single operation without encryption consists of plain credentials sent over the network. In step 17, we connected to the server if it granted access to our IP. Finally, in step 18, we opened a contextual query window, and in step 19, we executed the creation query, specifying a maximum size for the database.

Note that the **Database Edition** should be specified in the CREATE DATABASE query as well. By default, the Web Edition is used. To override this, the following query can be used:

```
CREATE DATABASE MyDB ( Edition='Basic' )
```

There's more...

We can also use the web-based **Management Portal** to perform various operations against the SQL Database, such as invoking Transact SQL commands, altering tables, viewing occupancy, and monitoring the performance. We will launch the **Management Portal** using the following steps:

1. Obtain the name of the SQL Database server that contains the SQL Database.

2. Go to https://serverName.database.windows.net.

3. In the **Database** fields, enter the database name (leave it empty to connect to the master database).

4. Fill the **Username** and **Password** fields with the login information and confirm.

Increasing the size of a database

We can use the ALTER DATABASE command to increase the size (or the Edition, with the Edition parameter) of a SQL Database by connecting to the master database and invoking the following Transact SQL command:

```
ALTER DATABASE DATABASE_NAME
MODIFY
(
  MAXSIZE = 5 GB
)
```

We must use one of the allowable database sizes.

See also

Have a look at the following MSDN links to get additional information:

- ▸ Comparison of an SQL Server with a SQL Database at `http://social.technet.microsoft.com/wiki/contents/articles/996.comparison-of-sql-server-with-azure-sql-database.aspx`

- ▸ Managing a SQL Database using SSMS at `http://azure.microsoft.com/en-us/documentation/articles/sql-database-manage-azure-ssms/`

Managing SQL Database logins and firewall rules

The Azure SQL Database is a fully managed service that offers a relational database with capabilities very similar to the Microsoft SQL Server, except for some features, especially related to the actual topology of the installation and server setup. Due to this nature, an SQL Database can be considered as a subset of the on-premises version. This behavior is also found in SSMS, where a connection to a SQL Database offers fewer functionalities than a connection to an on-premises SQL Server instance.

While connecting to n SQL Database, we do not have the same wizards we had for an SQL Server, even if connecting through the SSMS. Some of the high-level settings of SQL Database can be configured in the Azure Portal, as mentioned in the *Creating a SQL Database server and database* recipe. The portal allows us to set up the firewall rules at server level, and the administrative login can be set/reset there.

Instead, the database-level firewall rules, as for the database-level logins, must be set using the T-SQL script while connecting to the database using valid credentials. In this recipe, we dig into the management of firewall rules and credentials.

Getting ready

Before starting the recipe, a SQL Database server is needed. Consider to provision it following the *Creating a SQL Database server and database* recipe. We just need a server name, username, and password to login.

How to do it...

We want to connect to the SQL Database's master database through SSMS, configuring the firewall rules for the entire server, using T-SQL as follows:

1. Go to the Azure Portal; then, open the **SQL DATABASES** window.

2. In the **SERVERS** tab, select the server previously created and go to the **CONFIGURE** tab.

3. In the **allowed id addresses** section, click on the **ADD TO THE ALLOWED IP ADDRESSES** button to allow the specified IPs to connect to the database IP, and then click on **Save**.

4. Launch **Microsoft SQL Server Management Studio** and open the **Connect to Server** window.

5. In the **Server** name field, specify the fully qualified name of the newly created SQL Database server in the following form: `serverName.database.windows.net`.

6. Choose the **SQL Server Authentication** method.

7. Provide administrative credentials associated earlier.

8. Click on the **Options** button and check the **Encrypt connection** checkbox.

9. Optionally, check the **Remember password** checkbox and connect to the server.

10. Launch a **New Query** window on the master database and run the following query to list all the active firewall rules on the server:

```
select * from sys.firewall_rules
```

 In the **Results** pane, a firewall rule named **AllowAllWindowsAzureIps** could be shown, with the starting and ending addresses equal to `0.0.0.0`. This rule is added by Azure Portal when the user chooses to allow Windows Azure Services to access the database (the **Yes/No** toggle in the server's **CONFIGURE** tab).

11. Run this query to grant access to the `0.0.0.80` example IP:

```
exec sp_set_firewall_rule N'ExampleRule','0.0.0.80','0.0.0.80'
```

12. Create a new database as follows:

```
CREATE DATABASE myTest
```

13. Open a **New Query** window on the newly created database.

14. Run this query to grant access to everyone to the newly created database only:

    ```
    exec sp_set_database_firewall_rule N'PermitAllRu
    le','0.0.0.0','255.255.255.255'
    ```

 Consider to avoid opening the firewall to everything due to the natural security consequences while exposing the database surface to external attacks.

15. Run this query to remove the rule created in the previous step:

    ```
    exec sp_delete_database_firewall_rule N'PermitAllRule'
    ```

 The equivalent call to remove a server-level firewall rule is as follows:

    ```
    exec sp_delete_firewall_rule N'RuleName'
    ```

In this second part, we create credentials with the permission to connect to the newly created database only.

16. Open a **New Query** window into the master database, and create a login as follows:

    ```
    CREATE LOGIN myTestLogin WITH password='myComplexPa$$word';
    ```

17. Move to a **New Query** window on the **myTest** database, and create the database user for the login:

    ```
    CREATE USER myTestUser FROM LOGIN myTestLogin;
    ```

18. Assign the db_owner permissions to the newly created database user:

    ```
    EXEC sp_addrolemember 'db_owner', 'myTestUser';
    ```

19. Connect to SSMS using the newly created credentials (use myTestLogin as username), specifying the myTest database instead of the default (master) one.

How it works...

In steps 1 and 2, we connected to the Azure Portal to enable access to the SQL Database server by our development machine. In step 3, we saved the rule by telling Azure to permit traffic from that range of IPs. Note that the Portal suggests the calling IP. Do not make a mistake by adding a LAN IP in the firewall exceptions.

The IP address of your computer might not be a global IP address. Your company and/or ISP will have the globally visible IP, and you would most probably be behind an **Network Address Translation** (**NAT**). You can use a service such as `http://ping.eu` to get the global IP you are NATted behind.

In steps 4 to 9, we connected to the SQL Database server using SSMS, as mentioned in the first recipe of the chapter. We asked SQL the Database for a list of the current firewall rules in step 10, opening a **New Query** on the master database. It is not possible to switch between databases using the `USE` keyword. Instead, we must connect to each database to perform queries. In step 11, we added a server-level rule for the sample IP. This rule grants that IP access to every database contained in the SQL Database server instance. In step 12, we created a new database and we connected to it in step 13, then we added a **permit all** firewall rule on that database in step 14. A database-level firewall rule is valid only for the database which it applies to. If there are no firewall exceptions for the master database but for a single database, only that one can listen to remote endpoints. This is generally considered a good practice, avoiding publicly exposing the master database. Finally, in step 15, we restored the original situation by removing the firewall rule.

In step 16, we opened a query window on the master database to create a valid server-level login. Remember that a server-level login must exist in order to create a database-level valid credential. After the login was created, we created a database-level user mapped to this login in step 17, and in step 18, we assigned the `db_owner` permissions to this user (a **Login** is required to log in to the server, and a **User** is required to access the database). In step 19, we showed that it is now possible to connect to the database using the new credentials.

See also

Have a look at the following MSDN links to get additional information:

- More about the `sys.firewall_rules` procedure at `http://msdn.microsoft.com/en-us/library/ff951627.aspx`
- More about the SQL Database firewall at `http://msdn.microsoft.com/en-us/library/ee621782.aspx`

Developing a SQL Database with Visual Studio

While developing a database as the data tier for our applications, there are many tools to help us in creating tables, views, stored procedures, starting from a design phase and more or less adhering to the ER conceptual modeling.

Developers often delegate DBAs to build a powerful database that meets their application's needs, and in most cases, the **DB Team** is somehow disconnected from the **Dev Team**. From a process-management perspective, as the requirements are part of the same software artifact, a unified toolset is desirable. Why not use the same IDE to develop the application as well? Why not use Visual Studio?

For a while now, Visual Basic has offered to create a database project, a kind of project template that provides developers with the correct environment to deal with database design, which is particularly useful in complex scenarios. Using a database project, we are demanding the following issues from a well-known IDE:

- ▶ **Organize DB objects in a semantic structure**: Whatever be the project scope, it is always better to group the same object types logically together (the tables in the `Tables` folder, as they are represented in the RDBMS itself). This pattern creates a similarity with Management Studio, where objects in the database are grouped by type.

- ▶ **Work focused on a single object without affecting other objects**: It is better to open a file that represents the `Users` table, instead of opening a long all-in-one creation script. It is also useful to group other kinds of objects, such as constraints, schemas, keys, and so on, to focus on the single unit of work.

- ▶ **Check the consistency of the resulting database in a build-like fashion**: A good toolset for SQL development always performs a syntax check before running a script. In addition, it is common to have suggestions to fix errors, but if we make a *grammar* error (for example, a foreign key to a field with a different type) the check is often performed at runtime, while actually executing the script. In the VS environment, the `Build` operation against a database project results in a strong check of the entire database structure; this guarantees consistency before applying changes to the real database.

- ▶ **Deploy the differences to a target database without dealing with a lot of scripts**: As the complexity of the database grows, it is mandatory to implement a structured process to maintain the up/down scripts or rather use these scripts to alter a database object to the next version and to rollback it to the previous one. The database project, instead of keeping a history of the full scripts, maintains a different script of subsequent changes between the sources and the target database. To deploy the *previous* version of a table, we will only need to change the table's definition in the sources and let VS do the rest.

▶ **Version the database with the integrated source control system**: To complete the previous point, as the database project is a VS project, it could be part of a **Source Control** system, with the integrated features of Visual Studio. This permits us to save different versions of a given table and to reverse to that version as we reverse a file of code.

Developing a database with a database project is not only a technical matter, but it is also a best practice to make a complex process as structured as the software development itself should be. In this recipe, we will see how to create a database project (currently called the SQL Server Database Project) that targets a SQL Database by comparing the local version to the remote version and applying differences in Visual Studio with minimal T-SQL knowledge.

Getting ready

To work with the database projects, we will install the SQL Server Data Tools package and create a SQL Database, as mentioned in the *Creating a SQL Database server and database* recipe. We assume that the database has a firewall rule to be accessed from the development machine.

How to do it...

We are creating and deploying a database to a SQL Database server using Visual Studio. The first part is to create a project that will contain the database definition as follows:

1. In Visual Studio, open the **New Project** window.

2. Navigate to **Other Languages | SQL Server**, choose **SQL Server Database Project**, and enter a name for the new project and confirm.

3. In the **Project Settings** tab of the project properties window, change **Target platform** to **Azure SQL Database**.

> The SQL Server database project is designed to work well with many versions of the SQL Server (including the Azure SQL Database), starting from the 2005 version. If a version different from the SQL Database is selected, many customizations are permitted in the **Database Settings** window of project settings. However, as the SQL Database is fully managed, minimal customization is available while targeting Azure.

4. In **Solution Explorer**, right-click on the project; then, navigate to **Add | New Item** and add a table object named **Customers**.

In the **Add New Item** window, VS suggests many types of object to add in the database project. They are all SQL scripts, but to select an object type from the window, a sample implementation is provided; it aids developers with the SQL syntax that they are not always familiar with.

5. Fill the `Customers.sql` file as follows:

```sql
CREATE TABLE [dbo].[Customers](
    [CustomerID] [nchar](5) NOT NULL PRIMARY KEY,
    [CompanyName] [nvarchar](40) NOT NULL,
    [ContactName] [nvarchar](30) NULL,
    [ContactTitle] [nvarchar](30) NULL,
    [Address] [nvarchar](60) NULL,
    [City] [nvarchar](15) NULL,
    [Region] [nvarchar](15) NULL,
    [PostalCode] [nvarchar](10) NULL,
    [Country] [nvarchar](15) NULL,
    [Phone] [nvarchar](24) NULL,
    [Fax] [nvarchar](24) NULL,
)
```

6. Create an `Orders` table and fill it as follows:

```sql
CREATE TABLE [dbo].[Orders](
    [OrderID] [int] IDENTITY(1,1) NOT NULL PRIMARY KEY,
    [CustomerID] [nchar](3) NULL
    FOREIGN KEY REFERENCES [dbo].[Customers]([CustomerID]),
    [EmployeeID] [int] NULL,
    [OrderDate] [datetime] NULL,
    [RequiredDate] [datetime] NULL,
    [ShippedDate] [datetime] NULL,
    [ShipVia] [int] NULL,
    [Freight] [money] NULL,
    [ShipName] [nvarchar](40) NULL,
    [ShipAddress] [nvarchar](60) NULL,
    [ShipCity] [nvarchar](15) NULL,
    [ShipRegion] [nvarchar](15) NULL,
    [ShipPostalCode] [nvarchar](10) NULL,
    [ShipCountry] [nvarchar](15) NULL,
)
```

7. Build the project and notice the error:

   ```
   "SQL71515: The column '[dbo].[Customers].[CustomerID]' is not
   the same data type as the referencing column '[dbo].[Orders].
   [CustomerID]' in the foreign key.
   ```

8. Fix the error by changing [nchar](3) to [nchar](5) in the Orders table and build the project.

9. In the **Project contextual** menu, select **Publish**.

10. In the **Publish Database** window, edit the target connection to point to an existing SQL Database. Remember to use the SQL Server's Authentication and Encrypt connection flags.

11. Confirm the process by clicking on **Publish** and wait for the completion of the publishing process in the **Data Tools Operations** window in VS.

    In the second part, we make changes to the database structure (on the project side) and compare it with the target database.

12. Before editing the database schema, right-click on the project and select the **Snapshot Project** action.

This method is a built-in feature that allows us to make a backup copy of the current database structure in a single DACPAC file. It is strongly recommended that you use a Source Control system in conjunction with the database project to keep track of better fine-grained changes.

13. Add an Employees table to the project, as follows:

```
CREATE TABLE [dbo].[Employees](
    [EmployeeID] [int] IDENTITY(1,1) NOT NULL PRIMARY KEY,
    [LastName] [nvarchar](20) NOT NULL,
    [FirstName] [nvarchar](10) NOT NULL,
    [Title] [nvarchar](30) NULL,
    [TitleOfCourtesy] [nvarchar](25) NULL,
    [BirthDate] [datetime] NULL,
    [HireDate] [datetime] NULL,
    [Address] [nvarchar](60) NULL,
    [City] [nvarchar](15) NULL,
    [Region] [nvarchar](15) NULL,
    [PostalCode] [nvarchar](10) NULL,
    [Country] [nvarchar](15) NULL,
    [HomePhone] [nvarchar](24) NULL,
    [Extension] [nvarchar](4) NULL,
```

```
[Photo]  [image] NULL,
[Notes]  [ntext] NULL,
[PhotoPath]  [nvarchar](255) NULL,
)
```

14. Change the EmployeeID field of the Orders table to point to the Employees table:

    ```
    [EmployeeID]  [int]  NULL
    FOREIGN KEY REFERENCES [dbo].[Employees]([EmployeeID])
    ```

15. Right-click on the project and choose **Schema Compare**; the **SqlSchemaCompare1** tab will appear.

16. In the **Select Target** drop-down menu, select the previously used database and confirm.

17. Click on the **Compare** button and wait for the results page that shows the differences between the source and the target databases.

18. Select only **Add difference**, unchecking the **Change** checkbox.

19. Click on **Update** to invoke the update script to the remote database.

How it works...

In steps 1 and 2, we created a new project using the **SQL Server Database Project** template. In step 3, we made a change to the project properties to target a SQL Database, instead of the default target (the latest version of the SQL Server). If we also need to deploy the database to a local instance of the SQL Server, no change is needed. We could see the SQL Database target as a *subset* of a full SQL Server instance, so the further publishing process will complete successfully as well. However, if you change the target to an on-premise version of SQL Server, a bunch of customization settings will be available in the **Database Settings** window.

In step 4, we added a Table object to the project. As we could notice from the **Add New Item** window, we can drill down to a large amount of object types. The goal of a database project is also to force the developer to realize a well-organized folder structure of database items, to make the development easier with the natural growth of the overall complexity.

In steps 5 and 6, we added the definition to the Customers table and the Orders table, respectively. Note that we introduced an error intentionally to make the build process fail, as shown in step 7. It is very interesting to rank the database correctness as we did for a software application, with a build operation.

In step 8, we finally corrected the error and built the project to publish the resulting script to the real database, as shown in steps 9, 10, and 11. In these last steps, we just filled the database endpoint details, and VS does the rest.

In the **Publish Database** window, there is an **Advanced** button that goes to a settings page for the publishing process. Moreover, these settings for the target database can be saved through the **Save Profile As...** button. Consider this approach to save a profile for each target database of the environment (staging, test, production, and so on).

In the second part, we added some changes to the database's definition. First, in step 12, we created a local backup of the schema definition.

A DACPAC is a self-contained unit with the database definition. It is an abstraction layer between the database engine (DACPACs are available from SQL Server 2005 or later versions) and the developers.

In step 13, we added another table, and in step 14, we changed an *old* table by adding a foreign key that pointed to the new one. In step 15, we added a Schema Compare object to the database, comparing (in step 17) the current online version (the right pane of the compare window) with the current source version (the left pane of the compare window). In step 18, we intentionally deployed just a part of all the changes to the real database, to show that it is possible to select what to apply and what to leave in the sources. However, if we keep the **Add difference to the target database** option off, even the **Change difference** option would be taken off from VS, as it detects the dependencies between changes in the database schema.

In step 19, we finally deployed the differences to the target database.

If the target database has data and the differences to be deployed could cause a data loss, by default, VS interrupts the process to avoid it. An example of this is when we try to remove a field or downgrade a bigint field type to an int one. To customize (and in case override) this and other behaviors, click on the **Schema Compare** options in the **Schema Compare** window. A list of options will appear, which lets you decide what to do or what not to do during the publish process.

There's more...

Database projects are very useful to set a common framework between software development and database development. Unfortunately, we do not always have the capability to start from scratch with a new database, often starting from an existing one of the partial work from someone in the team, using a plain SQL editor.

With a new database project, we can also import an existing definition from both an SQL script (or DACPAC) and from an existing database. To do this, proceed as follows:

1. Right-click on an empty database project and select **Import Script** (*.sql)

2. In the **Import SQL Script File** window, follow the wizard steps and select the SQL script (that is a sample Northwind database).

3. After the wizard's completion, the project will be filled with many files, representing the objects of the database.

Because it is not as accurate as the manual work (that is, the constraints are together with the tables' definitions), it is a good starting point to reduce an existing work to a database project.

See also

Have a look at the following MSDN links to get additional information:

- ▶ Creating database and data-tier applications at http://msdn.microsoft.com/en-us/library/vstudio/dd193245(v=vs.110).aspx

- ▶ Understanding data-tier applications at http://technet.microsoft.com/en-us/library/ee240739(v=sql.105).aspx

Connecting to a SQL Database with ADO.NET

An application communicates with a SQL Database using the same **tabular data stream** (**TDS**) format used in communicating with Microsoft SQL Server. This simplifies the task of migrating from the Microsoft SQL Server to SQL Database, as an application need only change to the appropriate connection string.

Official documentation often talks about the simplicity to migrate an existing SQL Server database to a SQL Database one. However, there are some features that are not supported in Azure, as mentioned in the official documentation. The key point to understand is that if an existing feature relies on some server dependency, topology dependency, or filesystem dependency, it probably would not be supported.

When a SQL Database server is provisioned, it is assigned a fully qualified DNS name of the `SERVER_NAME.database.windows.net` form. A database name must be provided when the SQL Database is created. SQL Database logins are created in precisely the same way they are in Microsoft SQL Server, as you can see in the *Managing SQL Database logins and firewall rules* recipe. It is conventional to specify SQL Database logins in the `LOGIN@SERVER_NAME` form, even if it is not required. All communication with the SQL Database is over an encrypted channel, and it is recommended that the server certificate used with this channel not be trusted. This leads to a connection string as follows:

```
Data Source=SERVER_NAME.database.windows.net;Initial Catalog=DATABASE_
NAME;
User ID=LOGIN@SERVER_NAME;Password=PASSWORD;
Encrypt=True;TrustServerCertificate=False
```

This connection string can be retrieved from the application's configuration, or it can be created using the `SqlConnectionStringBuilder` class. Note that the SQL Database forces the connection to be encrypted, even if the client does not specify encryption. The `TrustServerCertificate` parameter forces the client to validate the server certificate, helping avoid man-in-the-middle attacks.

ADO.NET is a set of classes that abstracts the data access services to the developers. It can be used to connect to different data sources, using an efficient driver model. In recent years, using ADO.NET directly in applications is considered somehow low-level programming, as there are frameworks (on top of ADO.NET) that make the DB access simpler and more productive. However, in this recipe, we will learn how to connect to the SQL Database from the lowest but most efficient level, using ADO.NET.

How to do it...

We are going to connect to the SQL Database using ADO.NET and perform various **data definition language** (**DDL**) and **data manipulation language** (**DML**) operations. We will do this using the following steps:

1. Add a new class named `StandardConnectionExample` to the project.

2. Add the following `using` statements to the top of the class file:

```
using System.Data;
using System.Data.SqlClient;
```

3. Add the following `private` member to the class:

```
String connectionString;
```

4. Add the following constructor to the class:

```
public StandardConnectionExample( String server,
  String database, String login, String password)
{
  SqlConnectionStringBuilder connStringBuilder;
  connStringBuilder = new SqlConnectionStringBuilder();
  connStringBuilder.DataSource =
      String.Format("{0}.database.windows.net", server);
  connStringBuilder.InitialCatalog = database;
  connStringBuilder.Encrypt = true;
  connStringBuilder.TrustServerCertificate = false;
  connStringBuilder.UserID = String.Format("{0}@{1}",
      login, server);
  connStringBuilder.Password = password;
  connectionString = connStringBuilder.ToString();
}
```

5. Add the following method, retrieving the session tracing ID, to the class:

```
public String GetSessionTracingId()
{
  String commandText =
      "SELECT CONVERT(NVARCHAR(36), CONTEXT_INFO())";
  String sessionTracingId;
  using (SqlConnection connection =
      new SqlConnection(connectionString))
  {
    connection.Open();
    using (SqlCommand sqlCommand =
        connection.CreateCommand())
    {
      sqlCommand.CommandText = commandText;
      sessionTracingId =
          sqlCommand.ExecuteScalar() as String;
    }
  }
  return sessionTracingId;
}
```

6. Add the following method, creating the `Writer` table, to the class:

```
public void CreateTable()
{
    String commandText =
     @"CREATE TABLE Writer (
        Id int PRIMARY KEY NOT NULL,
        Name nvarchar(20) NOT NULL,
        CountBooks int NULL)";

    using (SqlConnection connection =
        new SqlConnection(connectionString))
    {
        connection.Open();
        using (SqlCommand sqlCommand =
            connection.CreateCommand())
        {
            sqlCommand.CommandText = commandText;
            sqlCommand.ExecuteNonQuery();
        }
    }
}
```

7. Add the following method, dropping the `Writer` table, to the class:

```
public void DropTable()
{
    String commandText = "DROP TABLE Writer";
    using (SqlConnection connection =
        new SqlConnection(connectionString))
    {
        connection.Open();
        using (SqlCommand sqlCommand =
            connection.CreateCommand())
        {
            sqlCommand.CommandText = commandText;
            sqlCommand.ExecuteNonQuery();
        }
    }
}
```

8. Add the following method, querying the `Writer` table, to the class:

```
public void QueryTable()
{
  String commandText = "SELECT * FROM Writer";
  using (SqlConnection connection =
    new SqlConnection(connectionString))
  {
    connection.Open();
    using (SqlCommand sqlCommand =
        new SqlCommand(commandText, connection))
    {
      using (SqlDataReader reader =
          sqlCommand.ExecuteReader())
      {
        Int32 idColumn = reader.GetOrdinal("Id");
        Int32 nameColumn = reader.GetOrdinal("Name");
        Int32 countBooksColumn =
              reader.GetOrdinal("CountBooks");
        while (reader.Read())
        {
          Int32 id = (Int32)reader[idColumn];
          String name = reader[nameColumn] as String;
          Int32? countBooks =
                reader[countBooksColumn] as Int32?;
        }
      }
    }
  }
}
```

9. Add the following method, inserting rows in the `Writer` table, to the class:

```
public Int32 InsertRows()
{
  String commandText =
    @"INSERT INTO Writer
        (Id, Name, CountBooks)
      VALUES
        (1, N'Cervantes', 2),
        (2, N'Smollett', null),
        (3, 'Beyle', 4)";
```

```
    Int32 rowsAffected;
    using (SqlConnection connection =
        new SqlConnection(connectionString))
    {
      connection.Open();
      using (SqlCommand sqlCommand =
          new SqlCommand(commandText, connection))
      {
        rowsAffected = sqlCommand.ExecuteNonQuery();
      }
    }
    return rowsAffected;
}
```

10. Add the following method, updating a row in the `Writer` table, to the class

```
public Int32 UpdateRow()
{
    String commandText =
      @"UPDATE Writer
        SET Name=@Name
        WHERE Id=3";

    Int32 rowsAffected;
    using (SqlConnection connection =
        new SqlConnection(connectionString))
    {
      connection.Open();
      using (SqlCommand sqlCommand =
          new SqlCommand(commandText, connection))
      {
        SqlParameter sqlParameter = new SqlParameter()
        {
          ParameterName = "@Name",
          Value = "Stendhal",
          SqlDbType = SqlDbType.NVarChar,
          Size = 20
        };
        sqlCommand.Parameters.Add(sqlParameter);
        rowsAffected = sqlCommand.ExecuteNonQuery();
      }
    }
    return rowsAffected;
}
```

11. Add the following method, using the methods added earlier, to the class:

```
public static void UseStandardConnectionExample()
{
    String server = "SERVER_NAME";
    String database = "DATABASE_NAME";
    String login = "LOGIN";
    String password = "PASSWORD";

    StandardConnectionExample example =
        new StandardConnectionExample(
            server, database, login, password);

     example.GetSessionTracingId();
    example.CreateTable();
    example.InsertRows();
    example.QueryTable();
    example.UpdateRow();
    example.QueryTable();
    example.DropTable();
}
```

How it works...

In steps 1 and 2, we set up the class. In step 3, we added a `private` member for the connection string that we initialized in the constructor we added in step 4 using a `SqlConnectionStringBuilder` instance. Configuring a connection string for the SQL Database is precisely the same as for the Microsoft SQL Server, apart from the way in which the DataSource is specified—using the fully qualified DNS name. We turned encryption `on`, as this is required and set `TrustServerCertificate` to `false` so that the server certificate was validated. Instead of building the connection string like this, we could have loaded it from a configuration file.

In step 5, we created and open `SqlConnection`, which we used to create `SqlCommand`. The connection is closed automatically when we exit the `using` block. We used the `SqlCommand` class to retrieve the session tracing ID for the connection. This is a GUID that identifies a particular connection, which can be provided to **SQL Database Support** when its help is sought in debugging a problem.

In step 6, we invoked a `CREATE TABLE` operation on the SQL Database to create a table named `Writer`. The table has three columns: the primary key is the ID column, and the remaining columns store the name of a writer and the number of books they wrote.

In step 7, we invoked a `DROP TABLE` operation on the SQL Database to drop the `Writer` table.

In step 8, we retrieved all rows from the `Writer` table and then iterated over them to examine the content of each column. In step 9, we inserted three rows into the `Writer` table and updated one of the rows in step 10.

In step 11, we added a method that invoked the methods added earlier. We need to provide the server name, database name, login, and password.

> Note that with an appropriately configured connection string, all the code in this recipe can be run against the Microsoft SQL Server with the exception of retrieval of the session-tracing ID in step 5.

There's more...

There is a software package, which is available on the Microsoft Download Center (or through a SQL Server installation), that allows us to connect to a TDS endpoint to perform T-SQL command, `sqlcmd` (part of the command-line utilities for the SQL Server). Once installed, we can connect to a SQL Database instance from the command prompt as follows:

1. Open a command prompt with the path environment pointing to `sqlcmd`

2. Enter the following command to connect to the master database:

    ```
    sqlcmd -U [user]@[server] -P [password] -S [server].database.
    windows.net -d master
    ```

3. Enter the following command to create a new database and exit from the current session (the USE clause is not permitted in WASD):

    ```
    CREATE DATABASE MySqlCmdTest;
    GO
    EXIT
    ```

4. Reconnect to the newly created database:

    ```
    sqlcmd -U [user]@[server] -P [password] -S [server].database.
    windows.net -d MySqlCmdTest
    ```

5. Create a new table using the plain SQL syntax:

    ```
    CREATE TABLE TestTable (ID int primary key, Name varchar(20));
    GO
    ```

6. List all the records of the table with the following command:

    ```
    SELECT * FROM TestTable
    GO
    ```

To make the above scripts work, we must replace the `[user]`, `[server]`, and `[password]` fields with the real values.

Through the Microsoft ODBC Driver for the SQL Server (available for Windows, SUSE Linux, and Red Hat Linux), it is also possible to connect to the SQL Database using the **Open Database Connectivity** (**ODBC**).

See also

Have a look at the following MSDN link to get additional information:

▸ Connect to the Azure SQL Database using the ODBC at `http://msdn.microsoft.com/en-us/library/hh974312.aspx`

Connecting to a SQL Database with Entity Framework

The Azure SQL Database is a SQL Server-like fully managed relation database engine. In many other recipes, we showed you how to connect transparently to the SQL Database, as we did in the SQL Server, as the SQL Database has the same TDS protocol as its on-premise brethren. In the *Connecting to a SQL Database with ADO.NET* recipe, we see how to connect directly with ADO.NET, which is very efficient but requires much work from the developer. In addition, using the *raw* ADO.NET could lead to some of the following issues:

▸ **Hardcoded SQL**: In spite of the fact that a developer should always write good code and make no errors, there is the finite possibility to make mistakes while writing stringified SQL, which will not be verified at design time and might lead to runtime issues. These kinds of errors lead to runtime errors, as everything that stays in the quotation marks compiles. The solution is to reduce every line of code to a command that is compile time safe.

▸ **Type safety**: As ADO.NET components were designed to provide a common layer of abstraction to developers who connect against several different data sources, the interfaces provided are generic for the retrieval of values from the fields of a data row. A developer could make a mistake by casting a field to the wrong data type, and they will realize it only at run time. The solution is to reduce the mapping of table fields to the correct data type at compile time.

▸ **Long repetitive actions**: We can always write our own wrapper to reduce the code replication in the application, but using a high-level library, such as the ORM, can take off most of the repetitive work to open a connection, read data, and so on.

Entity Framework hides the complexity of the data access layer and provides developers with an intermediate abstraction layer to let them operate on a collection of objects instead of rows of tables. The power of the ORM itself is enhanced by the usage of LINQ, a library of extension methods that, in synergy with the language capabilities (anonymous types, expression trees, lambda expressions, and so on), makes the DB access easier and less error prone than in the past.

This recipe is an introduction to Entity Framework, the ORM of Microsoft, in conjunction with the Azure SQL Database.

Getting ready

The database used in this recipe is the **Northwind** sample database of Microsoft. It can be downloaded from CodePlex at `http://northwinddatabase.codeplex.com/`.

How to do it...

We are going to connect to the SQL Database using Entity Framework and perform various operations on data. We will do this using the following steps:

1. Add a new class named `EFConnectionExample` to the project.

2. Add a new ADO.NET Entity Data Model named `Northwind.edmx` to the project; the **Entity Data Model Wizard** window will open.

3. Choose **Generate from database** in the **Choose Model Contents** step.

4. In the **Choose Your Data Connection** step, select the **Northwind** connection from the dropdown or create a new connection if it is not shown.

5. Save the connection settings in the `App.config` file for later use and name the setting `NorthwindEntities`.

> If Visual Studio asks for the version of EF to use, select the most recent one.

6. In the last step, choose the object to include in the model. Select the `Tables`, `Views`, `Stored Procedures`, and `Functions` checkboxes.

7. Add the following method, retrieving every `CompanyName`, to the class:

```
private IEnumerable<string> NamesOfCustomerCompanies()
{
    using (var ctx = new NorthwindEntities())
    {
        return ctx.Customers
            .Select(p => p.CompanyName).ToArray();
    }
}
```

8. Add the following method, updating every customer located in Italy, to the class:

```
private void UpdateItalians()
{
    using (var ctx = new NorthwindEntities())
    {
        ctx.Customers.Where(p => p.Country == "Italy")
            .ToList().ForEach(p => p.City = "Milan");
        ctx.SaveChanges();
    }
}
```

9. Add the following method, inserting a new order for the first Italian company alphabetically, to the class:

```
private int FirstItalianPlaceOrder()
{
    using (var ctx = new NorthwindEntities())
    {
        var order = new Orders()
            {
                EmployeeID = 1,
                OrderDate = DateTime.UtcNow,
                ShipAddress = "My Address",
                ShipCity = "Milan",
                ShipCountry = "Italy",
                ShipName = "Good Ship",
                ShipPostalCode = "20100"
            };
        ctx.Customers.Where(p => p.Country == "Italy")
            .OrderBy(p=>p.CompanyName)
            .First().Orders.Add(order);
        ctx.SaveChanges();
        return order.OrderID;
    }
}
```

10. Add the following method, removing the previously inserted order, to the class:

```
private void RemoveTheFunnyOrder(int orderId)
{
    using (var ctx = new NorthwindEntities())
    {
        var order = ctx.Orders
            .FirstOrDefault(p => p.OrderID == orderId);
        if (order != null) ctx.Orders.Remove(order);
        ctx.SaveChanges();
    }
}
```

11. Add the following method, using the methods added earlier, to the class:

```
public static void UseEFConnectionExample()
{
    var example = new EFConnectionExample();
    var customers=example.NamesOfCustomerCompanies();
    foreach (var customer in customers)
    {
        Console.WriteLine(customer);
    }
    example.UpdateItalians();
    var order=example.FirstItalianPlaceOrder();
    example.RemoveTheFunnyOrder(order);
}
```

How it works...

This recipe uses EF to connect and operate on a SQL Database. In step 1, we created a class that contained the recipe, and in step 2, we opened the wizard for the creation of **Entity Data Model** (**EDMX**). We created the model, starting from an existing database in step 3 (it is also possible to write our own model and then persist it in an empty database), and then, we selected the connection in step 4. In fact, there is no reference in the entire code to the Azure SQL Database. The only reference should be in the App.config settings created in step 5; this can be changed to point to a SQL Server instance, leaving the code untouched. The last step of the EDMX creation consisted of concrete mapping between the relational table and the object model, as shown in step 6.

 This method generates the code classes that map the table schema, using strong types and collections referred to as Navigation properties. It is also possible to start from the code, writing the classes that could represent the database schema. This method is known as Code-First.

In step 7, we asked for every `CompanyName` of the `Customers` table. Every table in EF is represented by `DbSet<Type>`, where `Type` is the class of the entity. In steps 7 and 8, `Customers` was `DbSet<Customers>`, and we used a lambda expression to project (select) a `property` field and another one to create a filter (`where`) based on a `property` value. The `SaveChanges` method in step 8 persisted to the database the changes detected in the disconnected object data model. This magic is one of the purposes of an ORM tool.

In step 9, we used the navigation property (`relationship`) between a `Customers` object and the `Orders` collection (`table`) to add a new order with sample data. We used the `OrderBy` extension method to order the results by the specified property, and finally, we saved the newly created item. Even now, EF automatically keeps track of the newly added item. Additionally, after the `SaveChanges` method, EF populates the `identity` field of `Order` (`OrderID`) with the actual value created by the database engine.

In step 10, we used the previously obtained `OrderID` to remove the corresponding order from the database. We used the `FirstOrDefault()` method to test the existence of the ID, and then, we removed the resulting object like we removed an object from a plain old collection.

In step 11, we used the methods created to run the demo and show the results.

See also

Have a look at the following links to get additional information:

▸ Entity Framework's official page at `http://msdn.microsoft.com/en-us/data/ef.aspx`

▸ EF connection resiliency specifications at `http://entityframework.codeplex.com/wikipage?title=Connection%20Resiliency%20Spec`

Connecting to a SQL Database from PHP and Java

Not every software application in the world is written in .NET and with Microsoft technologies, and of course, Azure could be used from another development environment and language. Azure is a collection of services, so the ability to use them all or a mix between them and other cloud providers is up to the consumer of the service. From a developer's perspective, the SQL Database is a fully managed relation database service, so a .NET client should connect to it like a PHP or Java application could.

It is just a matter of drivers and software components that mediate between the application and the data layer, implementing the product-specific feature of a particular **Relational Database Management System (RDBMS)**.

In this short recipe, we connect to the SQL Database using PHP and Java.

Getting ready

In this recipe, we will use:

- Visual Studio and IIS Express as the PHP environment
- Eclipse (http://www.eclipse.org/) as the Java environment
- PHP 5.4 (http://php.net)
- Latest JRE (http://www.java.com)
- SQL Server Driver 3.0 for PHP (http://sqlsrvphp.codeplex.com/)
- SQL Server JDBC Driver (http://www.microsoft.com/download/details. aspx?id=11774)

In the recipe, we will use a SQL Database version of the Northwind database, available on CodePlex at http://northwinddatabase.codeplex.com/ (consider a brief read at the *Migrating a Database to a SQL Database* recipe to know how to port that DB to Azure).

To register the SQL Server Driver for PHP, extract the content of the downloaded archive into the ext folder of the PHP installation. In the PHP.INI file of the PHP installation, add the following line:

```
Extension=[pathToPHP]/ext/php_sqlsrv_54_ts.dll
```

To enable IIS Express to work with PHP, we must register the engine for the PHP pages that execute the following two commands in the command prompt:

```
"C:\Program Files (x86)\IIS Express\appcmd.exe" set config /
section:system.webServer/fastCGI /+[fullPath='"C:\[locationOfPHP]\php-
cgi.exe"']
```

```
"C:\Program Files (x86)\IIS Express\appcmd.exe" set config /
section:system.webServer/handlers /+[name='PHP_via_FastCGI',path='*.php'
,verb='*',modules='FastCgiModule',scriptProcessor='"C:\[locationOfPHP]\
php-cgi.exe"',resourceType='Unspecified']
```

In both commands, we assume that IIS Express stays in the default installation folder.

How to do it...

In the first part, we create a PHP page that connects to the Northwind database, listing all the rows in the Customers table as follows:

1. Create an empty web application and make sure in that the **Web** tab of the **Properties** page, the debug is targeted to IIS Express.

2. Add a `Reader.php` file to the project and fill it as follows:

```html
<html>
 <head>
  <title>SQL Database Reader</title>
 </head>
 <body>
 <?php echo '<p>PHP Working</p>'; ?>
 </body>
</html>
```

3. Debug the project and point it to `http://localhost:[port]/Reader.php`.

4. Verify that the PHP engine is installed correctly.

5. Before the closing of the body tag, add the following block of HTML/PHP code:

```php
<table>
 <tr><td>Company Name</td><td>Contact Name</td></tr>
 <?php

    $serverName = "tcp:[serverName].database.windows.net,1433";
    $userName = '[user]@[serverName]';
    $userPassword = '[password]';
    $dbName = "Northwind";
    $table = "Customers";

    $connectionInfo = array("Database"=>$dbName,
    "UID"=>$userName, "PWD"=>$userPassword,
    "MultipleActiveResultSets"=>true);

    sqlsrv_configure('WarningsReturnAsErrors', 0);
    $conn = sqlsrv_connect( $serverName, $connectionInfo);
    if($conn != false)
    {
     $tsql = "SELECT * FROM [$table]";
      $stmt = sqlsrv_query($conn, $tsql);

     while($row = sqlsrv_fetch_array($stmt, SQLSRV_FETCH_NUMERIC))
     {
       echo "<tr>";
       echo "<td>".$row[1]."</td>";
       echo "<td>".$row[2]."</td>";
       echo "</tr>";
     }
```

```
        sqlsrv_free_stmt($stmt);
        sqlsrv_close($conn);
    }
?>
</table>
```

6. Debug the page as done in step 3.

 In the second part, we show the same data from a Java application.

7. In Eclipse, navigate to **File | New** and select **Java Project**.

8. In the **Create a Java Project** page of the wizard, give a project name and leave the other options at their default values.

9. In the **Java Settings** wizard page, select the **Libraries** tab, locate the `sqljdbc4.jar` driver that presses the **Add External JARs** button, and click on **Finish**.

10. Right-click on the `src` folder on the project created; click on **New** and then on **Class**.

11. In the **New Java Class** window, give a package and class name and check the **public static void main(String[] args)** checkbox.

12. At the top of the class, add these `import` clauses:
```
import java.sql.Connection;
import java.sql.DriverManager;
import java.sql.ResultSet;
import java.sql.Statement;
```

13. Modify the signature of the `main(...)` method as follows:
```
public static void main(String[] args) throws Exception
```

14. Add the following code, to list the customers, to the main method:
```
// Create the connection string.
String connectionUrl = "jdbc:sqlserver://[database_name].database.
windows.net;"
    + "databaseName=Northwind;user=[user]@[database_
name];password=[password]";

// Declare the JDBC objects.
Connection con = null;
Statement stmt = null;
ResultSet rs = null;

// Load the appropriate driver
Class.forName("com.microsoft.sqlserver.jdbc.SQLServerDriver");
con = DriverManager.getConnection(connectionUrl);
```

```
// Create and execute a SQL statement
String SQL = "SELECT TOP 10 * FROM Customers";
stmt = con.createStatement();
rs = stmt.executeQuery(SQL);

// Print the results.
while (rs.next()) {
  System.out.println(rs.getString(2) + " - " + rs.getString(3));
}
```

15. Debug the `file` class and look at the results.

How it works...

In step 1, we created an empty web application to contain the sample PHP page. The application was formally an ASP.NET web application, so we could add .NET contents as well. The key point is to set up the environment to let IIS Express run the PHP code. In step 2, we added a PHP file with sample content to test whether the prerequisites setup was correct by launching the VS debugger in steps 3 and 4.

In step 5, we added the code to list the contents of the `Northwind` database. In the first few lines, we had to replace the `[serverName]`, `[user]`, and `[password]` fields with the actual values. With `sqlsrv_connect`, we used the settings to connect to the SQL Database, and if the connection was made, we executed a standard SQL statement against the DB, fetching row by row and showed the results as an HTML table.

In the second part, we made the same tool for the Java environment. From steps 7 to 9, we started Eclipse and set up the new project, adding the dependency to the JAR file (the equivalent of a .NEL assembly/dll), which holds the SQL Server JDBC Driver. In steps 10 and 11, we added a class and the main method as the entry point of the application. In step 12, we added the `import` clauses (similar to the `using` statement of C#) to work with JDBC objects, and in step 13, we modified the main method to propagate the exceptions to the operating system. Finally, in step 14, we added the code to load the driver, connect to the SQL Database, and iterate over the results and display them in the console (note that the `ResultSet` object has a `1-based` index convention).

See also

Have a look at the following link to get additional information:

▸ JDBC on Wikipedia at `http://en.wikipedia.org/wiki/Java_Database_ Connectivity`

Migrating a database to a SQL Database

The SQL Database supports many but not all the features of Microsoft SQL Server. For example, all SQL Database tables must have a clustered index, as the SQL Database does not support heap tables. Consequently, although it is not difficult to migrate a Microsoft SQL Server database to the SQL Database, some attention must be paid when doing so. This involves identifying the features that are not supported and modifying the Transact SQL script so that it can run correctly in Azure SQL Database.

The SQL Database Migration Wizard (`http://sqlazuremw.codeplex.com/`) is a CodePlex project that can be used to analyze a Microsoft SQL Server database to identify the features not supported in the SQL Database. It generates a Transact SQL script that can recreate the database and modifies to a valid form any statement not supported by Azure. The SQL Database Migration Wizard can then migrate the database by applying the script to a SQL Database and using `bcp`, a bulk-copy utility, to copy the data from the Microsoft SQL Server database and upload it to the SQL Database.

The default mode of the SQL Database Migration Wizard works well. The method it uses to identify features that are not supported is configurable and can be changed, if necessary. The SQL Database Migration Wizard can also be used to analyze an arbitrary Transact SQL script to ensure that it is valid when used with Azure.

In this recipe, we will learn how to use the SQL Database Migration Wizard to migrate a Microsoft SQL Server database to Azure.

Getting ready

The SQL Database Migration Wizard only uploads data into an existing SQL Database. If necessary, we must create the SQL Database before we invoke the SQL Database Migration Wizard. We will see how to do this in the *Creating a SQL Database server and database* recipe.

How to do it...

We are going to migrate a Microsoft SQL Server database to an SQL Database using the SQL Database Migration Wizard. We will do this using the following steps:

1. Download the SQL Database Migration Wizard from CodePlex at `http://sqlazuremw.codeplex.com/`.
2. Extract the files from the compressed downloaded file.
3. Start the **SQLAZureMW** executable to bring up the **Script Wizard** dialog.
4. In the **Select Process** dialog, select **Database** and press **Next**.

5. In the **Connect** dialog, specify the **Microsoft SQL Server name** source (or leave it as **localhost**) and press **Connect**.

6. On the **Select Source** dialog, select the source database and press **Next**.

7. On the **Choose Object** dialog, press **Next**.

8. On the **Script Database Summary** dialog, press **Next**.

9. On the **Generate Script** popup, press **Yes**.

10. In the **Result Summary** dialog, press **Next** to continue with the migration.

11. On the **Connect** popup, select **Use a specific user ID and password**.

12. Specify a user name

13. Specify a password

14. Select the **Specify** database

15. Specify a database name

16. Press **Next**.

17. On the **Execute Script** popup dialog, press **Yes**.

18. In the **Target Server Response** dialog, we can view the summary of the database migration and verify its success.

How it works...

In step 1, we downloaded the latest version of the SQL Database Migration Wizard from CodePlex. In step 2, we extracted it to a suitable location.

In step 3, we launched the SQL Database Migration Wizard. This progressed in two phases, analysis and migration, through the remaining steps in the recipe. In the analysis phase, we specified the **Microsoft SQL Server database** source. The SQL Database Migration Wizard analyzed it and generated scripts that could recreate the database tables on the SQL Database and use bcp to extract the data. In the migration phase, we specified the SQL Database to which we were going to migrate the database, and then, the SQL Database Migration Wizard extracted the data and uploaded it to the newly created tables in the destination SQL Database.

In step 4, we specified that we wanted to analyze and migrate a Microsoft SQL Server database to Azure. We had other choices here, including specifying that we only wanted to perform the analysis. In steps 5 through 9, we specified the source Microsoft SQL Server instance and the source database, and started the analysis process.

On completion of the analysis phase, we could see both the Transact SQL script required to regenerate the tables in a SQL Database and a summary that showed the modifications required to handle the limitations of Azure SQL Database. We then specified that we wanted to continue with the migration process.

In step 11, we provided the information required to connect to the destination SQL Database. In steps 12 and 13, we completed the configuration and started the migration process.

We viewed the result of the migration phase in step 14.

There's more...

In **SQL Server Management Studio** (**SSMS**) 2012 or newer, there is a nice feature to deploy a local database to the SQL Database with minimal effort. Unfortunately, this method tries to deploy the database as is, resulting often in a failure due to the T-SQL limitations of Azure. However, if we are dealing with local databases that are already fixed for the deployment of the SQL Database (or they are created with SQL standard tools), the following method will save us much time.

1. Open SSMS and connect to the local database

2. Right-click on the local database and select **Tasks** and then **Deploy Database to SQL Azure**.

3. Click on the **Connect** button to populate the **Server connection** field.

4. Specify a new database name (Azure will create it) and the corresponding **Edition** and **Maximum** size.

5. Go ahead with the wizard and complete it.

See also

Have a look at the following MSDN links to get additional information:

▶ Migrating Databases to the Azure SQL Database at `http://msdn.microsoft.com/en-us/library/ee730904.aspx`

▶ How to import/export a SQL Database at `http://msdn.microsoft.com/en-us/library/hh335292.aspx`

Leveraging backup solutions with SQL Database

Microsoft completely manages its services in Azure from the disaster-recovery point of view. This means that in case of hardware failure or in case of events not dependent on the application surface, Microsoft takes care of the process of recovering data. All these activities should be definitely transparent to the user. However, as accountable developers, we should take care of the backup in terms of application recovery. In addition, while dealing with large-scale applications, it is very important to think about the most efficient strategies to protect our solution from accidental data loss and to provide the entire system a fast and robust way to recover to a consistent state.

I would personally divide the problem into two areas: offline backup and online backup. Offline backup means that in case of a failure, we have the backup of the last running instance somewhere, more or less, *far* from the production environment. By *far* we mean logically far or long to restore, comparing the offline backup to the old school backup made on magnetic tapes.

Online backup means that in case of a failure, we have a running copy of the last running instance somewhere very *near* to the production environment. Compared to an offline backup, a *near* backup is very close (in terms of the time taken to restore it).

The Azure SQL Database offers, at the time of writing this book, a good offline backup solution, pushing a BACPAC (a self-contained DB unit with schema and data) into the Blob Storage service. This service, called Automated Export, is efficient, inexpensive, and completely managed and available through the Azure portal. Users could connect to the Azure Portal, configure a storage account and the backup schedule, and let Azure do the rest.

Restoring a backup from a BACPAC in the storage account is a simple but long operation. A BACPAC for a 10-GB database could take up to 30 minutes or 1 hour to be online again, and in fact, there is no predictable time to get back online.

Another good (but expensive) solution is to provide online backup by performing an online database copy through a simple SQL Database copy statement, as we will see in the *There's more...* section. This leads to a duplicate database, with relevant costs connected.

With the introduction of the new service tiers (Basic/Standard/Premium), many availability-related features have been introduced:

> ▶ **Point-in-time restore**: A user can restore a previous version of a SQL Database of a given date and time

> ▶ **Geo-restore**: A user can restore the latest full backup of a SQL Database to a different Azure Region

- ▶ **Geo-copy**: A user can copy a database from one server to another, even if the target is located in another Region
- ▶ **Active/Passive Geo-replication**: A user can set up some secondary active (readable) or passive (offline) replicas of the primary database across all the Azure Regions

 The latest option (Geo-replication) is more suited for disaster recovery than application backup, as from the application's perspective, a malicious operation on the DB (a mistake while writing, such as a table drop) would be replicated to the distributed replicas as well.

In this recipe, we will see how to restore a SQL Database and how to set up a secondary replica for a given database.

Getting ready

This recipe uses a SQL Database created at least 1 day (24 hours) in advance. This requirement is due to the point-in-time restore to have sufficient backup history to work.

In addition, this recipe uses the new service tiers (Basic/Standard/Premium) that, at the time of writing this book, could be in preview. In such a case, subscribe to the proper preview feature at `http://azure.microsoft.com/en-us/services/preview/`.

Create a new database with the Standard Edition service tier. We will see how to do this in the *Creating a SQL Database server and database* recipe.

How to do it...

We are going to restore a SQL Database to a previous version of the last 24 hours. Then, we create a disconnected database copy on a different Region of Azure, and we set up a connected but offline (passive) Geo-replica. We will do this using the following steps:

1. In the Azure Portal, select **SQL DATABASES** from the left menu and locate the SQL Database created for the purpose of the recipe.
2. Select it without navigating into its details; a bottom menu will appear.
3. Click on the **RESTORE** button; a **Restore [db]** window will appear.
4. Select **ON** as the **POINT IN TIME** option.
5. Change or leave the default value in the **DATABASE NAME** field.
6. Choose a destination server (even the same as the source).
7. Slide appropriately the **RESTORE POINT** slider to decide which version of database would be restored, and confirm.

Cross-region database copy

8. In the **SERVERS** tab of the **SQL DATABASES** section of the Azure Portal, add a new server, as mentioned in the first recipe of this chapter. The server must be located at a different Region than the one that hosts the database of the recipe.

9. In the Azure Portal, select **SQL DATABASES** from the left menu and locate the SQL Database created for the purpose of the recipe.

10. Select it without navigating into its details; a menu will appear at the bottom of the screen.

11. Click on the **COPY** button; a **COPY SQL DATABASE** window will appear.

12. Choose the **NAME** of the destination database, as well as the **TARGET SERVER** (the one in a different Region), and confirm.

Setup a passive Geo-Replication

13. Select the source SQL Database and go to the **GEO-REPLICATION** tab.

14. In the bottom menu, click on **ADD SECONDARY**; a **New secondary for geo replication** window will appear.

15. Select the **TARGET SERVER** where Azure will maintain the replica, and confirm.

How it works...

In steps 1 and 2, we located the SQL Database created for the purpose of this recipe. In step 3, we initiated the restore process, specifying that we want a point-in-time restore in step 4 to choose the specific date and time of the backup we set in step 7. In steps 5 and 6, we chose the target database **Name** and the **Target** server that could be different from the source one but located in the same Region.

If we choose OFF as the **POINT IN TIME** option, we ask Azure for the latest backup of the current database. This time, the **Target** server could also be located in a different Region.

In step 8, we created a new server in a different Region of the previously created Database. This is to demonstrate the ability to create cross-Region copies of a given SQL Database. From steps 9 to 12, we located the database and initiated the copy process to the **Target** server.

In step 13, we initiated the Geo-replication setup process. As we deal with a SQL Database of Standard Edition, we can only create a passive (synchronized but offline) replica of the source database. With Premium, we can create an active (synchronized and online, but read only) replica. At the time of writing this book, a user can create up to four active replicas of a Premium database.

 Be aware that the costs connected to usage of Standard and Premium database are much higher than the *old* Web and Business Editions. The updated pricing page can be found at `http://azure.microsoft.com/en-us/pricing/details/sql-database/#basic-standard-and-premium`

Each copy/restore/add-replica operation could take several minutes or hours, depending on the size and usage of the source database. Remember to delete/deallocate the unused database resources after the completion of the recipe.

There's more...

We can use the `COPY DATABASE` command to create a transactionally consistent copy of a SQL Database by connecting to the master database and invoking the following Transact SQL command:

```
CREATE DATABASE NEW_DATABASE_NAME

AS COPY OF DATABASE_NAME
```

The copy is performed asynchronously. The `sys.dm_database_copies` system view can be queried to check on its status as follows:

```
select * from sys.dm_database_copies
```

Deleted databases

For each SQL Database of the Basic/Standard/Premium Editions that has been deleted, a user can restore a copy with the point-in-time selection for a limited timeframe (depending on the service tier).

Automated Exports

As mentioned in the introduction of the recipe, a cheap way to backup a SQL Database is by performing periodical exports via BACPACs. This could be leveraged in the Azure Portal as follows:

1. Go to the **CONFIGURE** tab of a given database

2. In the **Automated Export** section, select **Automatic**

3. Select a storage account where Azure should save the BACPACs

4. Select a schedule for the automatic export as well as a retention period for old backups.

5. Specify the credentials, which can connect to the SQL Database to perform the export, and click on **Save**.

To restore a previously created BACPAC, a user can click on the **NEW DATABASE** button on the same page.

See also

Have a look at the following MSDN links to get additional information:

▸ The Azure SQL Database business continuity at `http://msdn.microsoft.com/en-us/library/azure/hh852669.aspx`

▸ Active Geo-Replication for the Azure SQL Database at `http://msdn.microsoft.com/en-us/library/azure/dn741339.aspx`

Monitoring SQL Database with the dynamic management views

A SQL Database resides on a physical server shared with many other SQL Databases. This sharing leads to resource constraints on the maximum size and operational throughput of a SQL Database. No data can be written to a SQL Database that has reached its maximum size. Connections are terminated when operational throughput limits are breached. It is therefore important that SQL Database usage is measured to avoid the consequences of hitting resource constraints. SQL Database exposes various dynamic management views that can be queried to measure resource usage.

The SQL Database allocates one partition for a table and one partition for each nonclustered index in a database. As the SQL Database manages the physical allocation of a database, it does not provide operations that support partition management. However, the `sys.dm_db_partition_stats` dynamic management view contains one row for each partition allocated in the database. Consequently, the view can be queried to find the current size of the database as well as the objects in it. These queries are useful in ensuring that the database is not approaching its maximum size and in identifying which objects are consuming the most space.

The `sys.dm_exec_sessions` dynamic management view contains information about all connections on the SQL Database server. It can be used to observe current usage of the server. The `sys.dm_exec_query_stats` dynamic management view contains information on the performance of cached queries. It can be used to identify those queries that consume the most resources with regard to CPU time as well as logical and physical data access.

In this recipe, we will see how to measure the usage of the SQL Database.

Getting ready

This recipe uses an existing SQL Database. We have seen how to create this in the *Creating a SQL Database server and database* recipe.

How to do it...

We are going to invoke various queries against dynamic management views of a SQL Database to collect information that helps us manage our use of the database. We will do this using the following steps:

1. Connect to the SQL Database.

2. We invoke the following query to calculate the total size of the current database in MB:

```
SELECT
   DB_NAME() AS [Database],
   SUM(reserved_page_count) * 8.0 / 1024 AS [Size in MB]
FROM
   sys.dm_db_partition_stats;
```

3. We invoke the following query to calculate the total size in MB of each object in the current database:

```
SELECT
      o.name AS [table_name],
      sum(p.reserved_page_count) * 8.0 / 1024 / 1024 AS [size_in_
gb],
      p.row_count AS [records]
FROM
      sys.dm_db_partition_stats AS p,
      sys.objects AS o
WHERE
      p.object_id = o.object_id
      AND o.is_ms_shipped = 0
GROUP BY o.name , p.row_count
ORDER BY o.name
```

4. We invoke the following query to calculate the total size of each partition in the current database in MB:

```
SELECT
   OBJECT_NAME(object_id) AS [Name],
   index_id AS [Index Id],
   row_count AS [Row Count],
   used_page_count * 8.0 / 1024 AS [Used in MB],
   reserved_page_count * 8.0 / 1024 as [Reserved in MB]
FROM
   sys.dm_db_partition_stats
```

5. We invoke the following query to view CPU usage of active connections to the current database:

```
SELECT
   ec.connection_id AS [Connection ID],
   es.session_id AS [Session ID],
   es.cpu_time AS [CPU in ms] ,
   es.last_request_end_time AS [Last Used]
FROM
   sys.dm_exec_sessions AS [es]
INNER JOIN
   sys.dm_exec_connections AS [ec]
ON
   es.session_id = ec.session_id
```

6. We invoke the following query to view the top five queries, by average worker time, in the current database:

```
SELECT TOP 5
   query_stats.query_hash AS [Query Hash],
   SUM(query_stats.total_worker_time) /
      (1000000.0 * SUM(query_stats.execution_count))
        AS [Avg CPU Time (s)],
   SUM(query_stats.total_logical_reads) /
        (1000000.0 * SUM(query_stats.execution_count))
          AS [Avg Logical Reads (s)],
   SUM(query_stats.total_logical_writes) /
        (1000000.0 * SUM(query_stats.execution_count))
          AS [Avg Logical Writes (s)],
   MIN(query_stats.statement_text) AS [Statement Text]
FROM
   (SELECT
     qs.*,
     SUBSTRING(st.text, (qs.statement_start_offset/2) + 1,
     ((CASE statement_end_offset
     WHEN -1 THEN DATALENGTH(st.text)
      ELSE qs.statement_end_offset END
     - qs.statement_start_offset)/2) + 1) AS [statement_text]
   FROM
     sys.dm_exec_query_stats AS [qs]
   CROSS APPLY
     sys.dm_exec_sql_text(qs.sql_handle) AS [st])
        AS [query_stats]
   GROUP BY
   query_stats.query_hash
```

How it works...

In step 1, we connected to the desired SQL Database. Note that the queries do not work against the master database.

In step 2, we invoked a query to retrieve the total size of the current SQL Database. We can use this query to check how close we are to hitting the size limit for the database.

In step 3, we invoked a query to retrieve the total size of each object in the current SQL Database. We can use this query to find out which objects are taking up most space in the database. With the `is_ms_shipped` toggle set to `zero` (0), we can only check the user-defined objects; otherwise every table, including the ones provided by default, is counted in.

In step 4, we invoked a query to retrieve the total size of each partition used by each object in the current SQL Database. We can use this query to identify when it might be useful to rebuild nonclustered indexes in particular, as each of these is in its own partition. A large difference between the used and reserved page count indicates that an index rebuild might help free up space.

In step 5, we invoked a query to retrieve the total CPU time used by current connections to the database as well as the last time each of them was used. We can use this information to find out the current usage of our SQL Database.

In step 6, we invoked a query to retrieve five queries with the highest average CPU time. We can use this information to focus our attention on optimizing these queries. This query also returns the average logical reads and writes for these queries. The query uses a standard technique, using `sys.dm_exec_sql_text()`, to generate the query text from the query handle.

There's more...

Users can enable the SQL Database Auditing feature to audit operations against a given SQL Database. At the time of writing this book, the feature is in preview (and it needs a specific activation), and it is available only through the new management portal at `https://portal.azure.com`.

To audit a SQL Database, follow these steps:

1. Create a storage account where Azure could save Audit Logs.
2. Go to the management portal, select the SQL Database, and under **Auditing**, configure the storage account to collect data.
3. Replace, in the desired applications, each connection string in the `[server].database.windows.net` form with `[server].database.secure.windows.net`.

Azure will automatically catch each request from the applications that go to the SQL Database, logging them into the proper storage account. After that, a complete Excel workbook is available for download to navigate to the details of the audited data.

See also

Have a look at these MSDN links to get additional information:

- ▸ SQL Database dynamic management views at `http://msdn.microsoft.com/en-us/library/ff394114.aspx`

- ▸ Getting started with SQL Database Auditing at `http://azure.microsoft.com/en-us/documentation/articles/sql-database-auditing-get-started/`

Handling connection failures to a SQL Database

The Azure SQL Database is a distributed system in which each server hosts many databases. This sharing of resources leads to capacity constraints on operational throughput. The SQL Database handles these capacity constraints by throttling operations and closing connections that are using too many resources. SQL Database also closes connections when it alleviates operational hot spots by switching from a primary SQL Database to one of its two backup copies. Furthermore, connectivity to a SQL Database is likely to be less reliable than connectivity to a Microsoft SQL Server database on a corporate LAN. It is imperative, therefore, that applications using the SQL Database must be designed to withstand connection failures that are far more likely to occur than with Microsoft SQL Server.

One of the mantras of cloud development is design for failure. It is important that applications that use the SQL Database be designed to handle failures appropriately. There are two kinds of errors: permanent errors, which indicate a general failure of part of the system, and transient errors, which exist only for a brief time. Permanent errors, perhaps, indicate a logical problem with the application and handling them might require code changes. However, an application should handle transient errors gracefully by retrying the operation that led to the error in the hope that it does not recur. A dropped connection should be regarded as transient, and an application should respond to a dropped connection by opening a new connection and retrying the operation.

There remains the problem of distinguishing permanent errors from transient ones. This can be done by comparing the error returned from a failed operation with a known list of transient errors. An application can, therefore, include a retry mechanism that checks the status of operations and retries any operations that experienced a transient error.

Microsoft has made available on NuGet the assemblies for the **Transient Fault Handling Application Block**. This comprises a set of classes that can be used to detect transient failures and retry SQL operations. It contains an extensible way to identify transient failures, with various examples that include the one that compares an error with a list of known transient failures. The Transient Fault Handling Framework provides various built-in retry backoff techniques that specify how often and frequently an operation should be retried following a transient failure. These include both a fixed interval and an exponential delay between retries. The classes in the Transient Fault Handling Application Block include various extension methods that simplify the use of the framework, thereby minimizing the work required to add the handling of dropped connections and other transient failures to an application using Azure.

In this recipe, we will learn how to use the Transient Fault Handling Application Block to handle dropped connections and other transient failures when using WASD.

Getting ready

This recipe uses an existing SQL Database. We have seen how to create this in the *Creating a SQL Database server and database* recipe.

How to do it...

We are going to connect to the SQL Database using ADO.NET and perform a simple operation with a retry policy to handle transient errors. We will do this using the following steps:

1. Add the following assembly references to the project:

   ```
   EnterpriseLibrary.TransientFaultHandling
   System.Configuration
   ```

2. Add a new class named `RetryConnectionExample` to the project.

3. Add the following `using` statements to the top of the class file:

   ```
   using Microsoft.Practices.EnterpriseLibrary.
   TransientFaultHandling;
   using Microsoft.Practices.EnterpriseLibrary.WindowsAzure.
   TransientFaultHandling.SqlAzure;
   using System.Data;
   using System.Data.SqlClient;
   using System.Configuration;
   ```

4. Add the following `private` members to the class:

   ```
   String connectionString;
   ```

5. Add the following constructor to the class:

```
public RetryConnectionExample()
{
    connectionString = ConfigurationManager
        .ConnectionStrings["MyTestDBConnectionString"]
.ConnectionString;
}
```

6. Add the following method, to perform a simple operation, to the class:

```
public String GetSessionTracingId<T>()
    where T: ITransientErrorDetectionStrategy, new()
{
    String commandText =
        "SELECT CONVERT(NVARCHAR(36), CONTEXT_INFO())";
    String sessionTracingId;
    var retryPolicy = new RetryPolicy<T>(3,
        TimeSpan.FromSeconds(3));
    retryPolicy.Retrying+=retryPolicy_Retrying;
    using (SqlConnection connection =
        new SqlConnection(connectionString))
    {
        connection.OpenWithRetry(retryPolicy);
        using (SqlCommand sqlCommand =
        connection.CreateCommand())
        {
            sqlCommand.CommandText = commandText;
            sessionTracingId =
            sqlCommand.ExecuteScalarWithRetry(retryPolicy)
                as String;
        }
    }
    return sessionTracingId;
}
```

7. Add the following callback method to the class:

```
void retryPolicy_Retrying(object sender, RetryingEventArgs e)
{
    Exception ex = e.LastException;
TimeSpan delay = e.Delay;
Int32 retryCount = e.CurrentRetryCount;
}
```

Add the following class to the project:

```
public class CustomSQLRetryStrategy
    : ITransientErrorDetectionStrategy
{
    public bool IsTransient(Exception ex)
    {
        return true;
    }
}
```

8. Add the following method, using the method added earlier, to the class:

```
public static void UseRetryConnectionExample()
{
    RetryConnectionExample example =
        new RetryConnectionExample();
    example.GetSessionTracingId
        <SqlDatabaseTransientErrorDetectionStrategy>();
    example.GetSessionTracingId
        <CustomSQLRetryStrategy>();
}
```

9. Add the following section to the `App.config` file:

```
<connectionStrings>
    <add name="MyTestDBConnectionString" connectionString="data
source=
        tcp:[serverName].database.windows.net;
        Database=myTest;Uid=[user]@[serverName];
        Pwd=[password];Encrypt=yes;"/>
</connectionStrings>
```

How it works...

In step 1, we added references to the Transient Fault Handling Application Block and the configuration assemblies. In steps 2 and 3, we set up the class and added the `using` clauses.

In step 4, we added a member to hold the connection string that we obtained from the configuration, in the constructor added in step 5.

In step 6, we implemented a method that performed a very simple operation, just to get the SessionID from Azure. We instantiated a retry logic based on the strategy passed as the generic parameter-less argument, T. A strategy is an implementation of ITransientErrorDetectionStrategy that has a single bool method that determines if an exception is the result of a transient error or just an error. Using the strategy passed as a parameter, the method uses the default FixedInterval method to retry, based on a retry count value (3 in the example) and an interval between consecutive retries (3 seconds in the example). In step 7, we added a callback for the Retrying event of the RetryPolicy class, and finally, we used the ADO.NET classes as usual, with the slight difference of the OpenWithRetry and ExecuteScalarWithRetry methods. These two methods are extension methods provided by the library and accept a retry policy as a parameter.

 The retryPolicy_Retrying callback is given a RetryingEventArgs argument, with some details about the transient error that occurred. First, the LastException property indicates the exception that caused the retry conditions to occur. The Delay property indicates how long the current thread will be suspended before the next iteration is invoked. The CurrentRetryCount property finally indicates the retry count of the operation.

In step 8, we added a class that represented a custom strategy to determine if an exception is due to a transient error or not. In this trivial implementation, we assumed that every exception was the result of a transient error.

In step 9, we added a method that invoked the method added earlier. If we intentionally made a mistake in the connection string (for example, wrong password), the first call with the *official* retry policy would result in an application exception, never passing from the callback. Instead, the second call, using the custom retry strategy, would deal with the exception as a transient error, invoking the Retrying callback added in step 7. In step 10, we added a connection string in the App.config file. We needed to replace the [serverName], [user], and [password] fields with the actual values.

There's more...

The Transient Fault Handling Application Block can also be used to retry operations against the Azure Storage service and the Azure Service Bus.

With Entity Framework 6, Microsoft shipped a bundled support to manage Windows Azure SQL Database's transient errors. In the *Connecting to a SQL Database with Entity Framework* recipe, we connected to an SQL Database using EF without dealing with any retry logic at all. However, introducing this logic has a minimal impact in EF6 because we only need to add a class (with minimal implementation) that inherits from the `DbConfiguration` class, to the project as follows:

```
public class SQLDatabaseConfiguration:DbConfiguration
{
    public SQLDatabaseConfiguration()
    {
        SetExecutionStrategy("System.Data.SqlClient",
            () => new SqlAzureExecutionStrategy
                (1, TimeSpan.FromSeconds(30)));
    }
}
```

The following `using` clauses are needed too:

```
using System.Data.Entity;
using System.Data.Entity.SqlServer;
```

This class is instantiated every time a `DbContext` class is created, so we do not need to modify the existing code to create an aware EF code.

See also

Have a look at the following MSDN links to get additional information:

- Transient Fault Handling Application Block at `http://msdn.microsoft.com/en-us/library/hh680934(v=pandp.50).aspx`
- More about using the Transient Fault Handling Framework at `http://msdn.microsoft.com/en-us/library/dn440719(v=pandp.60).aspx`

5
Going NoSQL with Azure Tables

In this chapter, we will cover the following topics:

- ▸ Creating a table
- ▸ Inserting, updating, deleting, and querying data against the Table service
- ▸ Using entity group transactions
- ▸ Using continuation tokens and server-side paging
- ▸ Going inside continuation tokens and segmented queries
- ▸ Handling entity serialization events
- ▸ Facilitating NoSQL with client-side projection

Introduction

The **Microsoft Azure Table Service** is the Storage service feature that provides cost-effective scalable storage of entities.

During the last 3 decades, relational databases have become the dominant data storage systems. Relational databases are transaction oriented and implement **ACID** semantics in which database transactions are **atomic**, **consistent**, **isolated**, and **durable**. These are important considerations for a data system where data fidelity is of absolute importance, such as those used in a financial system. However, large-scale data systems that implement ACID semantics are extremely expensive, as they require huge infrastructures behind them.

In the last decade, there has been a growing interest in creating cost-effective, large-scale data systems. This interest is driven primarily by those in need of data collection, such as the data-mining needs of social websites that generate enormous amounts of click-stream data or scientific datasets. Much of this data is read only, so there is less emphasis on support for transactions. Furthermore, these data systems typically do not provide support for SQL, so they are referred to as **NoSQL** systems with **No** being an acronym for not only.

Some NoSQL data systems implement BASE semantics that are basically available in the soft state; they are eventually consistent rather than ACID semantics. The idea is that a change to stored data does not have to be immediately consistent across the data system as long as it is eventually consistent.

The **Table** service is the NoSQL data system provided by the Azure Platform. It provides large-scale storage at a cost significantly lower than that provided by the Azure SQL Database, the relational database provided in the Azure Platform.

The Table service uses storage accounts to provide an authentication boundary. Unlike a relational database, these tables have no fixed schema, and each entity stored in the table defines its own schema. We see how to create a table in the *Creating a table* recipe.

An entity is a collection of properties and their associated values. The primary key for a table is the combination of two properties, `PartitionKey` and `RowKey`, that must be present in each entity stored in the table. The Table service uses `PartitionKey` to provide scalability (partitioning data) and `RowKey` to ensure uniqueness within a given partition. The entities in a table with the same `PartitionKey` property comprise a partition.

The Azure Storage Service REST API provides the definitive interface to the Table service. The Azure Storage library is a high-level, managed .NET API for the Table service that hides the underlying Storage Service REST interface. The Storage Client library, at the time of writing this book, supports two methods to operate against the Table service: a former one and a newer one. The former extends the WCF Data Services stack, while the latter introduces a new Table service layer (also based on OData) with major performance optimization and new features. It is likely that the former method will be eventually deprecated, but as it is used by many existing applications and is still effective, we decided to implement both in this book.

 In the recipes of this chapter, we will see how to achieve results in both the patterns/methods mentioned earlier; we call these patterns/methods **Method1** (the WCF Data Service pattern) and **Method2** (the new Table service layer).

The Storage library provides developers with a functionality specific to the Table service, such as authentication, server-side paging, and automated retry logic. All the recipes in this chapter use the Storage library.

In the WCF Data Services paradigm, we associate table entities with a model class. To some extent, this imposes a schema on the table, although many model classes could be associated with a single table. It uses a context to track instances of the model class; these instances represent the entities to be inserted in the table or retrieved from the table. We will go further into this in the *Inserting, updating, deleting, and querying data against the Table service* recipe.

The Table service provides limited support for ACID semantics. Up to 100 storage operations against the same partition might be batched into a single entity group transaction and performed as a single transaction in which either all operations succeed or all operations are rejected (with a maximum total payload size of 4 MB). We will consider these in the *Using entity group transactions* recipe. Note that the Table service does not implement BASE semantics, as it uses hard state, with all data changes being strongly consistent.

Optimistic concurrency is a technique used in NoSQL data systems to avoid the scalability problems caused by data being locked to prevent simultaneous updates by different clients. The Table service implements optimistic concurrency by providing an entity tag (`ETag`) with each entity it returns to a client. A subsequent update succeeds only if the current `ETag` tag is provided. This provides a lightweight and scalable way to manage concurrent updates to an entity. We will look at optimistic concurrency in the *Using entity group transactions* recipe.

The Table service supports the concept of server-side paging in which no more than 1,000 entities are returned in response to a query, in no more than 5 seconds. When this throttling occurs, the Table service also returns continuation tokens that the client can use to reissue the query for the next page of data. We will show this in the *Using continuation tokens and server-side paging* and Going *inside continuation tokens and segmented queries* recipes.

The Azure Storage library takes care of the serialization/deserialization of entities against the REST API, but we can customize this behavior, thanks to some extension endpoints in the library. In the *Handling entity serialization events* recipe, we will see how to control the serialization process.

NoSQL data stores are generally classified by how they organize their aggregates, the single and minimal unit of storage. In RDBMS, we can say that the row is the minimal unit of storage, while in NoSQL, it can vary. The Azure Table service organizes its data in entities; an entity is defined by the `PartitionKey` and `RowKey` properties, but it can contain several key-value pairs. We can also say that an entity is a key-value pair collection. Under these circumstances, it could not be easy to define a single entity model (in a programming language) that could map the result of a given query against the service. Instead, a more generic result for a given entity should be a collection of key-value pairs. In the *Facilitating NoSQL with client-side projection* recipe, we will see how to deal with this.

Creating a table

The Azure Table service supports a simple two-level hierarchy. There is a single level of tables, each of which contains zero or more entities. An entity can have up to 255 properties, including three system-defined properties, and there is no requirement that different entities in the same table have the same properties. This feature makes the Table service schemaless. The only requirement of entities in a table is that the combination of `PartitionKey` and `RowKey` properties is distinct for each entity in a table. Consequently, when a table is created, the only required information is its name.

The Azure Storage library contains a `CloudTableClient` class that provides a set of synchronous and asynchronous methods that support the creation and deletion of tables. It also supports the listing of the tables associated within an Azure Storage service's storage account.

In this recipe, we will learn how to use the synchronous methods to create and delete tables as well as list them.

Getting ready

This recipe assumes that the following lines of code are in the application's configuration file:

```
<appSettings>
  <add key="DataConnectionString"
value="DefaultEndpointsProtocol=https;AccountName={ACCOUNT_
NAME};AccountKey={ACCOUNT_KEY}"/>
</appSettings>
```

We must replace `{ACCOUNT_NAME}` and `{ACCOUNT_KEY}` with appropriate values for the account name and access key, respectively.

How to do it...

We are going to create two tables, list the tables, and then delete a table. We will do this using the following steps:

1. Add a new class named `TablesExample` to the project.

2. Install the `WindowsAzure.Storage NuGet` package and add the following assembly references to the project:

   `System.Configuration`

3. Add the following `using` statements to the top of the class file:

```
using Microsoft.WindowsAzure.Storage;
using Microsoft.WindowsAzure.Storage.Table;
using System.Configuration;
```

4. Add the following member to the class:

```
private CloudTableClient cloudTableClient;
```

5. Add the following constructor to the class:

```
TablesExample()
{
    CloudStorageAccount cloudStorageAccount =
        CloudStorageAccount.Parse(
        ConfigurationManager.AppSettings[
        "DataConnectionString"]);
    cloudTableClient =
        cloudStorageAccount.CreateCloudTableClient();
}
```

6. Add the following method, creating a table, to the class:

```
public void CreateTable(String tableName,
    Boolean checkExistence = false)
{
    CloudTable table=cloudTableClient
        .GetTableReference(tableName);
    if (checkExistence)
    {
        table.CreateIfNotExists();
    }
    else
    {
        table.Create();
    }
}
```

7. Add the following method, deleting a table, to the class:

```
public bool DeleteTable(String tableName)
{
    CloudTable table = cloudTableClient
        .GetTableReference(tableName);
    table.DeleteIfExists();
    return !table.Exists();
}
```

8. Add the following method, listing the tables, to the class:

```
protected void ListTables(String tableNamePrefix)
{
  IEnumerable<CloudTable> listTablesPrefix =
      cloudTableClient.ListTables(tableNamePrefix);
  Int32 countListTablesPrefix =
      listTablesPrefix.Count();

   IEnumerable<CloudTable> listTables =
      cloudTableClient.ListTables();
  Int32 countListTables = listTables.Count();
}
```

9. Add the following method to the class:

```
public static void UseTablesExample()
{
  TablesExample example = new TablesExample();
  example.CreateTable("Stars");
  example.CreateTable("Planets", true);
  example.ListTables("P");
  example.DeleteTable("Planets");
}
```

How it works...

In steps 1 through 3, we set up the class. In step 4, we added a `private` member to store the `CloudTableClient` instance used to connect to the Table service. We initialized this in the constructor we added in step 5.

In step 6, we added a method that shows two ways to create a table, starting from an instance of `CloudTable`. The first invoked `CreateIfNotExists()`, which created the table only if it did not already exist. The second invoked `Create()`, which throws an exception if the table already existed (HTTP error code 409, which means **Conflict**). In step 7, we added a method that deleted a table. This method is safe due to the `DeleteIfExists()` method.

In step 8, we added a method to list all the tables in the storage account. It did so in two different ways: with and without using a prefix. In step 9, we added a simple method to use the methods we added earlier. We created a couple of tables, listed all the tables in the storage account, and then deleted one of the tables.

There's more...

The Azure Table service is cloud based. In the Azure SDK, Microsoft provides a Storage Emulator, which runs in the development environment and can be used for local development and testing. This emulator uses LocalDB, but it can also be configured to the use Microsoft SQL Server.

There are some circumstances in which the Storage Emulator and the Table service behave differently. Consequently, when problems are identified while developing with the Storage Emulator, it is often useful to check whether the problem exists when using the Table service.

The Azure Storage Service REST API is the definitive way to interact with the Table service. The Azure Storage library is a high-level .NET library that sits on top of the Storage Service REST API.

A utility such as Fiddler, which allows us to inspect HTTP traffic, can be helpful in identifying problems when developing against either the Table service or the Storage Emulator. Fiddler makes it easy to verify that the correct REST operations are invoked and to check the request, response headers, and payloads. These can be compared with the MSDN documentation in the Azure Storage Service REST API. Fiddler also provides direct access to any error message returned by the Storage Service REST API.

No special configuration is required to use Fiddler with the Table service. Fiddler merely needs to be running to capture all the network traffic to and from the Azure Table service. However, a special connection string must be provided when using Fiddler with the Storage Emulator. In this case, the data connection string must be set to the following:

```
UseDevelopmentStorage=true;DevelopmentStorageProxyUri=http://ipv4.
fiddler
```

Although Fiddler is useful in identifying problems, it can introduce problems when used with the Storage Emulator, while it always behaves correctly when used with the real cloud environment.

See also

Have a look at these MSDN links to get additional information:

▶ Differences between the Storage Emulator and Azure Storage at `http://msdn.microsoft.com/en-us/library/azure/gg433135.aspx`

▶ Using the Table storage from Node.js at `http://azure.microsoft.com/en-us/documentation/articles/storage-nodejs-how-to-use-table-storage/`

Inserting, updating, deleting, and querying data against the Table service

The Azure Storage library uses both WCF Data Services and OData to invoke table operations in the Azure Storage Services REST API. The library has methods that provide functionality specific to the Azure Table service, such as the retry functionality that allows methods to be retried automatically in the event of failure and continuation token functionality that supports server-side paging.

In the Storage library, instances of a model class represent entities of a table. When saving an instance to a table, the Storage library creates a property in the entity for each public property of the instance. The model class must contain the primary key properties for the entity: `PartitionKey` and `RowKey`. An entity can have no more than 252 user-defined properties (due to the primary key properties plus the `Timestamp` properties). Furthermore, if it is used to store query results, the model class must have a default constructor that takes no parameters. The Storage library provides a convenient base class from which to derive model classes for both Method1 and Method2. They are the `TableServiceEntity` and the `TableEntity` classes, respectively.

The Storage Client library supports only the following datatypes for entities:

- `Byte[]`
- `Boolean`
- `DateTime`
- `Double`
- `Guid`
- `Int32`
- `Int64`
- `String`

Both `Byte[]` and `String` are limited to no more than 64 KB. Note that the Storage Client library automatically converts `DateTime` values to the local time zone when retrieving entities. Each entity has a maximum size of 1 MB.

Method1 uses `DataServiceContext` to expose storage operations and queries, as well as to track entities used in these storage operations and queries. Entities are tracked by adding them as new entities using `DataServiceContext.AddObject()` or attaching them to the context with the `DataServiceContext.AttachTo()` method that provides additional functionality to update entities. Entities returned by queries are also tracked. Any changes to tracked entities are submitted as individual storage operations when the `SaveChanges()` method is invoked on the context.

The Storage library contains a `TableServiceContext` class, derived from `DataServiceContext`, which adds the retry functionality to the synchronous and asynchronous `SaveChanges()` methods through the provision of the `SaveChangesWithRetries()` methods. It can be convenient to create a model-dependent class derived from `TableServiceContext`. This can be generalized by creating a generic class parameterized by the type of the model class. Doing so simplifies the text of queries and provides type-safe methods to manage entities.

The following two code fragments demonstrate this simplification:

```
from c in tableServiceContext.CreateQuery<Country>("Country")
from c in countryContext.GenericEntities
```

The first example explicitly uses `TableServiceContext` to create a query, while the second uses a generic context class that exposes a `GenericEntities` property, which encapsulates the `CreateQuery<Country>()` method.

Contexts should not be reused, that is, unrelated storage operations should use different contexts.

 When we have asynchronous operations being performed against the Table Storage service, the operations might take longer than expected and leave the context in an unpredictable state. Hence, it is recommended that the context be recreated even to retry the same operation, to isolate the retry attempts completely.

Method2 uses a `CloudTable` reference to execute commands against the Table service, with the `Execute` and `ExecuteQuery` methods. The first method takes an instance of `TableOperation` as a parameter; it identifies a CRUD action against the datastore. The second one takes a `TableQuery` instance that can be constructed by string-based queries as follows:

```
new TableQuery().Where("PartitionKey eq 'Italy'")
```

To help developers while writing this challenging syntax, `TableQuery` provides a static method to generate the necessary strings for the query operators needed by the `Where` clause. To further help developers who work on a familiar set of classes and with LINQ, there is also a LINQ provider to query data against a table, using the `CreateQuery<T>` method on the `CloudTable` instance.

In this recipe, we'll learn how to create a model class and use the two methods to perform various storage operations and queries.

Getting ready

This recipe assumes that the following lines of code are in the application's configuration file:

```
<appSettings>
  <add key="DataConnectionString"
value="DefaultEndpointsProtocol=https;AccountName={ACCOUNT_
NAME};AccountKey={ACCOUNT_KEY}"/>
</appSettings>
```

We must replace {ACCOUNT_NAME} and {ACCOUNT_KEY} with the appropriate values for the account name and access key, respectively.

How to do it...

We are going to perform an insert, update, and delete operation on the Table service for a query to retrieve data. We will do this using the following steps:

1. Add a new class named ModelContextExample to the project.

2. Install the WindowsAzure.Storage NuGet package and add the following assembly references to the project:

   ```
   System.Configuration
   ```

3. Add the following using statements to the top of the class file:

   ```
   using Microsoft.WindowsAzure.Storage;
   using Microsoft.WindowsAzure.Storage.Table;
   using Microsoft.WindowsAzure.Storage.Table.DataServices;
   using System.Configuration;
   ```

4. Add the following member to the class:

   ```
   private CloudTableClient cloudTableClient;
   ```

5. Add the following constructor to the class:

   ```
   private ModelContextExample(String tableName)
   {
       CloudStorageAccount cloudStorageAccount =
           CloudStorageAccount.Parse(
           ConfigurationManager.AppSettings[
           "DataConnectionString"]);
       cloudTableClient =
           cloudStorageAccount.CreateCloudTableClient();
       var table=cloudTableClient.GetTableReference(tableName);
       table.CreateIfNotExists();
   }
   ```

Now, let's proceed with Method1.

6. Add the following class in the project:

```
public class CountryDS : TableServiceEntity
{
    private readonly String partitionKey = "country";

    public String CapitalCity { get; set; }
    public Int64 Population { get; set; }

    public CountryDS() { }

    public CountryDS(String name, String capitalCity,
        Int64 population)
    {
        PartitionKey = partitionKey;
        RowKey = name;
        CapitalCity = capitalCity;
        Population = population;
    }
}
```

7. Add the following method to the `ModelContextExample` class:

```
private void InsertQueryAndUpdateMethod1()
{
    TableServiceContext tableServiceContext =
        cloudTableClient.GetTableServiceContext();

    tableServiceContext.AddObject("Country",
        new CountryDS("Australia", "Canberra", 22558947));
    tableServiceContext.AddObject("Country",
        new CountryDS("India", "New Delhi", 1189914000));
    tableServiceContext.SaveChangesWithRetries();

    var query = tableServiceContext.CreateQuery<CountryDS>("Count
ry")
        .Where(p => p.PartitionKey == "country" && p.RowKey ==
"Australia");

    CountryDS country = query.FirstOrDefault<CountryDS>();

    country.Population += 100000;
    tableServiceContext.UpdateObject(country);
    tableServiceContext.SaveChangesWithRetries();
}
```

8. Add the following method to the `ModelContextExample` class:

```
private void DeleteAllMethod1()
{
    TableServiceContext tableServiceContext =
        cloudTableClient.GetTableServiceContext();
    var items = tableServiceContext.CreateQuery<CountryDS>("Count
ry");
    foreach (var item in items)
    {
        tableServiceContext.DeleteObject(item);
    }
    tableServiceContext.SaveChangesWithRetries();
}
```

 Now, let's proceed with Method2.

9. Add the following class to the project:

```
public class Country : TableEntity
{
    private readonly String partitionKey = "country";

    public String CapitalCity { get; set; }
    public Int64 Population { get; set; }

    public Country() { }

    public Country(String name, String capitalCity,
        Int64 population)
    {
        PartitionKey = partitionKey;
        RowKey = name;
        CapitalCity = capitalCity;
        Population = population;
    }
}
```

10. Add the following method to the `ModelContextExample` class:

```
private void InsertQueryAndUpdateMethod2()
{
    var table = cloudTableClient.GetTableReference("Country");

    var c1= new Country("Australia", "Canberra", 22558947);
```

```
    var c2 = new Country("India", "New Delhi", 1189914000);
    var op1=TableOperation.Insert(c1);
    var op2=TableOperation.Insert(c2);

    table.Execute(op1);
    table.Execute(op2);

    var query=table.CreateQuery<Country>()
        .Where(p => p.PartitionKey == "country" &&
            p.RowKey == "Australia");

    Country country = query.FirstOrDefault();

    country.Population += 100000;
    table.Execute(TableOperation.Merge(country));


}
```

11. Add the following method to the ModelContextExample class:

```
private void DeleteAllMethod2()
{
    var table = cloudTableClient.GetTableReference("Country");
    var items = table.CreateQuery<Country>();
    foreach (var item in items)
    {
        table.Execute(TableOperation.Delete(item));
    }
}
```

[📝 In both cases, follow this final step.]

12. Add the following method to the ModelContextExample class:

```
public static void UseModelContextExample()
{
    String tableName = "Country";
    ModelContextExample example =
        new ModelContextExample(tableName);
    example.InsertQueryAndUpdateMethod1();
    example.DeleteAllMethod1();
    example.InsertQueryAndUpdateMethod2();
    example.DeleteAllMethod2();
}
```

How it works...

In steps 1 through 4, we set up the `ModelContextExample` class, and in step 5, we created a constructor that initializes the `CloudTableClient` instance to create a table that was specified as argument.

We then split the recipe into two branches: the first for the Method1 and second for the Method2.

In step 6, we added a model class named `CountryDS`, which inherits from `TableServiceEntity`, to represent entities that describe various properties of countries. The `PartitionKey` property is always set to the country for entities created using this class. The `RowKey` property is set to the name of the country. The `Timestamp` property, even if it is not directly visible (due to its belonging to the base class), is one of the three system properties present in each entity. In practice, it is not really needed in the model class. There are two constructors: one being the required parameterless constructor and the other fully initializing an instance of the model class.

In step 7, we added a method that uses `TableServiceContext` to add several entities to the `Country` table. It then queried the table to retrieve a single entity and updated this entity to the table. We used the `SaveChangesWithRetries()` method, which performs automatic retries, in case of transient failures on the service side.

While writing distributed applications (not only for Azure), a common approach to follow is to design software that is failure proof or, better, designed for failures. The Azure Storage service is a great service, but it can throttle a request or can be temporarily out of service. In some cases, a denial of service is due to a transient failure, and the corresponding action to recover it is just the *retry*.

In step 8, we added a method to delete each object of the `Country` table. As shown in the code, it is required to first fetch the entities and then delete them one by one.

In step 9, since we followed Method2, we created another model class, inheriting now the `TableEntity` base class. This new model class is used by the Table service layer to perform operations against the table, even if it is actually identical to its peer created in step 6.

In step 10, we added a method that uses the `Execute` method of a `CloudTable` instance to add several entities to the `Country` table. Since the `Execute` method is operation aware, we needed to build the operation in advance with the helpers provided by the static methods of the `TableOperation` class. It then queried the table to retrieve a single entity and updated that entity to the table, using the same pattern by invoking the `Execute` method.

In step 11, we added a method to delete each object of the Country table. As shown in the code, it is still required to first fetch the entities and then delete them one by one. However, it is possible to optimize this behavior using the DynamicTableEntity pattern, as shown in the *Facilitating NoSQL with client-side projection* recipe.

In step 12, we added a method that uses the methods we added in the previous steps.

There's more...

Now, we see how to work with a custom context and how to choose partition and row keys appropriately.

Dealing with a custom context

With Method1, instead of using the TableServiceContext class to operate against the Table service, we can also create our custom context to wrap the strongly typed entities to simplify the further query needs (or to use the Repository pattern instead of using context methods) as follows:

1. Add the following class to the project:

```
public class CustomContext<T> : TableServiceContext
{
    public String TableName { get; set; }

    public CustomContext(
      CloudTableClient client)
        : base(client)
    {
        Type type = typeof(T);
        TableName = type.Name;
    }
    public void AddEntity(T entity)
    {
        AddObject(TableName, entity);
    }
}
```

```
        public void DeleteEntity(T entity)
        {
            DeleteObject(entity);
        }
        public IQueryable<T> GenericEntities
        {
            get { return CreateQuery<T>(TableName); }
        }
    }
```

2. Add the following method to the `ModelContextExample` class:

```
private void InsertQueryAndUpdateMethod1bis()
{
    CustomContext<Country> countryContext =
        new CustomContext<Country>(cloudTableClient);
    countryContext.AddEntity(
      new Country("France", "Paris", 63900000));
    countryContext.AddEntity(
      new Country("Italy", "Rome", 59600000));
    countryContext.SaveChangesWithRetries();

    var query = countryContext.GenericEntities
        .Where(p => p.PartitionKey == "country"
            && p.RowKey == "France");

    Country country = query.FirstOrDefault();

    country.Population += 100000;
    countryContext.UpdateObject(country);
    countryContext.SaveChangesWithRetries();
}
```

In step 1, we added a generic-context class, `GenericContext<T>`, derived from `TableServiceContext`. We inferred the table name from the name of the type. The constructor for this class simply invoked the base class constructor. We added a type-safe method to add objects to the context. Finally, we added a `GenericEntities` property that returned an `IQueryable<T>` class, which we used to simplify the syntax for queries.

In step 2, we added a method that used `GenericContext<Country>` to add several entities to the `Country` table. It then queried the table to retrieve a single entity and updated this entity in the table.

Choosing a good combination of PartitionKey and RowKey

The primary key for a table in the Azure Table service is the combination of `PartitionKey` and `RowKey`. These properties are not symmetric, in that `PartitionKey` and `RowKey` serve different purposes. The `PartitionKey` property provides scalability for a table, while the `RowKey` property ensures uniqueness for a given value of `PartitionKey`.

A set of entities with the same `PartitionKey` property in a table is referred to as a partition. The Table service has a scalability target for a partition that is lower than that for the storage account. Consequently, performance can be improved by ensuring that data access is distributed across partitions. It is important for `PartitionKey` to be designed so that performance is optimized for the actual workload of a service while minimizing unnecessary partitioning or interrelated data.

When a query is executed against a table, the resulting entities are ordered by `PartitionKey` and then by `RowKey`. The Table service does not support any other index. Consequently, if entities must be retrieved in a particular order, the `RowKey` property must be constructed to facilitate this order. An interesting case is where entities must be retrieved in reverse chronological order. Each `DateTime` has an associated `Ticks` property that specifies the number of ticks since the earliest `DateTime` property. A chronological order for `RowKey` can be achieved using the `Ticks` count for a `DateTime` property of `RowKey`. A reverse chronological ordering can be achieved by subtracting the number of ticks from the `Ticks` count for the maximum value of `DateTime`. For example, the following code calculates the number of ticks remaining from now until the maximum number of ticks:

```
DateTime.MaxValue.Ticks - DateTime.UtcNow.Ticks
```

When converted to a string, as required for the `RowKey` property, this requires 19 characters to ensure that all the possible values can be represented. The `Ticks` count can be converted as follows:

```
String.Format("{0:D19}",
    DateTime.MaxValue.Ticks - DateTime.UtcNow.Ticks);
```

This creates a 19-character string that, when used for the `RowKey` property, creates a reverse chronological ordering.

See also

Have a look at the following MSDN links to get additional information:

▸ More about the Table service data model at `http://msdn.microsoft.com/en-us/library/azure/dd179338.aspx`

▸ The WCF Data Service documentation center at `http://msdn.microsoft.com/en-us/data/odata.aspx`

Using entity group transactions

The Azure Table service supports entity group transactions in which a group of storage operations on entities with the same `PartitionKey` property are handled automatically. That is, if any operation in the group fails, then all the operations are rolled back. Unlike transactions in a traditional SQL database, entity group transactions cannot span tables or even partitions.

A single entity group transaction is limited to no more than 100 entities and a total size of 4 MB. An individual entity can be used only once in an entity group transaction. Any combination of the create, update, and delete operations can be contained in an entity group transaction. Alternatively, it can contain only query operations. However, an entity group transaction might not combine queries with the create, update, and delete operations.

Handling batch operations differs much between Method1 and Method2. With WCF Data Services, we control the save operation with the `SaveChanges()` method. The default behavior when a `SaveChanges()` or `SaveChangesWithRetries()` method is invoked on a context is that any changes to entities tracked by the context are submitted to the Table service, one storage operation at a time. Specifying a `SaveChangesOptions.Batch` parameter for these methods causes all the changes to be submitted as a single entity group transaction.

With the new Table service layer, we have a new explicit `ExecuteBatch()` method on the `CloudTable` instance. This method takes a `TableBatchOperation` class as a parameter; this class is a sort of container for multiple operations.

Regardless of how many individual storage operations a single entity group transaction contains, it is billed as a single storage operation. This will considerably save costs over performing the storage operations individually.

In this recipe, we will learn how to use entity group transactions.

Getting ready

This recipe uses model classes named `Country` and `CountryDS` that are declared in the *Inserting, updating, deleting, and querying data against the Table service* recipe. This recipe also assumes that the following lines of code are in the application's configuration file:

```
<appSettings>
  <add key="DataConnectionString"
value="DefaultEndpointsProtocol=https;AccountName={ACCOUNT_
NAME};AccountKey={ACCOUNT_KEY}"/>
</appSettings>
```

We must replace `{ACCOUNT_NAME}` and `{ACCOUNT_KEY}` with appropriate values for the account name and access key, respectively.

How to do it...

We are going to show one entity group transaction that inserts two entities in a table and another entity group transaction that updates one entity and deletes another from the same table. We will do this using the following steps:

1. Add a new class named `EntityGroupTransactionsExample` to the project.

2. Install the `WindowsAzure.Storage` NuGet package and add the following assembly references to the project:

   `System.Configuration`

3. Add the following `using` statements to the top of the class file:

   ```
   using Microsoft.WindowsAzure.Storage;
   using Microsoft.WindowsAzure.Storage.Table;
   using Microsoft.WindowsAzure.Storage.Table.DataServices;
   using System.Configuration;
   ```

4. Add the following `private` members to the class:

   ```
   private CloudTableClient cloudTableClient;
   private String tableName = "Country";
   ```

5. Add the following constructor to the class:

   ```
   public EntityGroupTransactionsExample()
   {
       CloudStorageAccount cloudStorageAccount =
           CloudStorageAccount.Parse(
               ConfigurationManager.AppSettings[
               "DataConnectionString"]);
       cloudTableClient =
           cloudStorageAccount.CreateCloudTableClient();
       cloudTableClient.GetTableReference(tableName)
           .CreateIfNotExists();
   }
   ```

 Now, let's proceed with Method1.

6. Add the following method, showing an insert-only entity group transaction, to the class:

   ```
   public void BatchInsertMethod1()
   {
       TableServiceContext tableServiceContext =
           cloudTableClient.GetTableServiceContext();
       CountryDS pakistan = new CountryDS(
           "Pakistan", "Islamabad", 171365000);
   ```

```
tableServiceContext.AddObject(tableName, pakistan);
CountryDS bangladesh = new CountryDS(
    "Bangladesh", "Dhaka", 149715000);
tableServiceContext.AddObject(tableName, bangladesh);
tableServiceContext.SaveChangesWithRetries(
    SaveChangesOptions.Batch);
}
```

7. Add the following method, showing a mixed-operation entity group transaction, to the class:

```
public void MixedBatchMethod1()
{
    TableServiceContext tableServiceContext =
        cloudTableClient.GetTableServiceContext();
    CountryDS turkey = new CountryDS(
        "Turkey", "Istanbul", 72561312);
    tableServiceContext.AddObject(tableName, turkey);
    CountryDS pakistan = new CountryDS(
        "Pakistan", "Islamabad", 171000000);
    tableServiceContext.AttachTo(tableName, pakistan, "*");
    tableServiceContext.UpdateObject(pakistan);
    CountryDS bangladesh = new CountryDS()
    {
        PartitionKey = "country",
        RowKey = "Bangladesh"
    };
    tableServiceContext.AttachTo(tableName, bangladesh, "*");
    tableServiceContext.DeleteObject(bangladesh);
    tableServiceContext.SaveChangesWithRetries(
        SaveChangesOptions.Batch);
}
```

 Now, let's proceed with Method2.

8. Add the following method, showing an insert-only entity group transaction, to the class:

```
public void BatchInsertMethod2()
{
    var table = cloudTableClient
        .GetTableReference(tableName);
    var batch = new TableBatchOperation();
    Country italy = new Country(
```

```
            "Italy", "Rome", 60000000);
        batch.Insert(italy);
        Country uk = new Country(
            "UK", "London", 63000000);
        batch.Insert(uk);
        table.ExecuteBatch(batch);
    }
```

9. Add the following method, showing a mixed-operation entity group transaction, to the class:

```
public void MixedBatchMethod2()
{
    var table = cloudTableClient
        .GetTableReference(tableName);
    var batch = new TableBatchOperation();
    Country germany = new Country(
        "Germany", "Berlin", 81000000);
    batch.Insert(germany);
    Country italy = new Country(
        "Italy", "Rome", 61000000) { ETag = "*" };
    batch.Replace(italy);
    Country uk = new Country(
        "UK", "London", 0) { ETag = "*" };
    batch.Delete(uk);
    table.ExecuteBatch(batch);
}
```

 In both cases, follow this final step.

10. Add the following method, invoking the other methods, to the class:

```
public static void UseEntityGroupTransactionsExample()
{
    EntityGroupTransactionsExample example =
        new EntityGroupTransactionsExample();
    example.BatchInsertMethod1();
    example.BatchInsertMethod2();
    example.MixedBatchMethod1();
    example.MixedBatchMethod2();
}
```

How it works...

In steps 1 through 4, we set up the `EntityGroupTransactionsExample` class, and in step 5, we created a constructor that initializes the `CloudTableClient` instance to create a table specified as an argument.

We then split the recipe into two branches: the first for Method1 the and second for Method2.

In step 6, we added a `BatchInsertMethod1()` method. In it, we created a new context. Then, we created two entities and added them to the context with `AddObject()`, before invoking `SaveChangesWithRetries(SaveChangesOptions.Batch)` to send the appropriate insert operations to the Table service as a single entity group transaction.

In step 7, we added a `MixedBatchMethod1()` method. In it, we created a new context and used it to update one entity and delete another. As we are performing storage operations on existing entities, we need to take into account the optimistic concurrency provided by the Table service. We do this using `AttachTo()` with an ETag of * to have the context track the entities.

 This special ETag value allows us to override the optimistic concurrency used by the Table service and make it update or delete this entity in the table. A valid ETag must be provided when updating or deleting objects. A valid value is the one returned that is with the entity as the result of a query or the special value of * as in this example.

After attaching the entities, we use `UpdateObject()` with one entity and `DeleteObject()` with the other to indicate which storage operation should be used. Finally, we invoked `SaveChangesWithRetries(SaveChangesOptions.Batch)` to send the appropriate update and delete operations to the Table service as a single entity group transaction.

In step 8, we added a `BatchInsertMethod2()` method. We used a `TableBatchOperation` instance to add, with the `Insert()` method, two entities into it. We called the `ExecuteBatch()` method on the `CloudTable` instance to send the appropriate insert operations to the Table service as a single entity group transaction.

In step 9, we added a `MixedBatchMethod2()` method. We now used two other methods (`Replace()` and `Delete()`) of the `TableBatchOperation` class, finally committing the entire operation onto the table. The same considerations of the ETag value * apply to the second method.

In step 10, we added a method that uses the methods we added in the previous steps.

There's more...

While dealing with entity group transactions, remember the following rules:

▶ All entities in a transaction group must have the same `PartitionKey` value

▶ Multiple `PartitionKey` values in the same group transaction would throw error

▶ One entity can appear only once and with only one operation as part of the entity group transactions

See also

Have a look at these MSDN links to get additional information:

▶ Designing a scalable partitioning strategy for the Azure Table storage at `http://msdn.microsoft.com/en-us/library/azure/hh508997.aspx`

▶ Implementing retries via the enterprise library at `http://msdn.microsoft.com/en-us/library/hh680934(v=pandp.50).aspx`

Using continuation tokens and server-side paging

The Azure Table service uses **partition servers** to manage the entities stored in a table. One partition server manages all the entities with the same `PartitionKey` value in the table. However, different partition servers might manage entities with different values of `PartitionKey`. This distribution of entities among partition servers is, in general, transparent to clients of the Table service. This partitioning scheme is central to the scalability of the Table service.

When processing a query, the Table service submits the query to the first partition server (ordered by `PartitionKey`) that manages entities that satisfy any filter on `PartitionKey`. It then returns the first page of up to 1,000 entities retrieved by the partition server. The Table service inserts two headers, `x-ms-continuation-NextPartitionKey` and `x-ms-continuation-NextRowKey`(possibly null), into the response if there are additional results. These headers comprise the continuation tokens for the query.

Any remaining results can be retrieved one page at a time by adding the continuation tokens as request headers to the query. The Table service uses these continuation tokens to start the query processing at the correct page. This might be on the current partition server or the next partition server if the previous query had returned all the entities it managed that matched the query. The client can reuse the continuation tokens if a previously requested page of data is needed. This paging functionality is referred to as server-side paging.

Note that it is possible that a query execution returns no entities but does return a continuation token, which indicates that there are additional results. This can happen if a query spans multiple partition servers, but the current partition server has found no entities that match the query.

Handling of continuation tokens is completely transparent to the user in both Method1 and Method2. However, Method1 supports automated handling of continuation tokens with the `TableServiceQuery<T>` class, a subtype of `DataServiceQuery<T>`. If a large number of entities satisfy a query invoked using a synchronous method of the `TableServiceQuery<T>` class, the method might not return for a considerable time. The `AsTableServiceQuery<T>()` method in the `TableServiceExtensions` class can be used to convert `DataServiceQuery<T>` into `TableServiceQuery<T>`.

The `TableServiceQuery<T>` class supports retries. It also provides synchronous execution of queries through the `Execute()` method and asynchronous execution through the `BeginExecuteSegmented()` and `EndExecuteSegmented()` methods.

Method2 supports automatic continuation token handling though the `TableQuery` class, and, we should explicitly make a segmented query to avoid this. We go under the hood about segmented queries in the *Going inside continuation tokens and segmented queries* recipe.

In this recipe, we will learn how to handle server-side paging.

Getting ready

This recipe uses model classes named `Country` and `CountryDS` that are declared in the *Inserting, updating, deleting, and querying data against the Table service* recipe. This recipe also assumes that the following lines of code are in the application's configuration file:

```
<appSettings>
  <add key="DataConnectionString"
value="DefaultEndpointsProtocol=https;AccountName={ACCOUNT_
NAME};AccountKey={ACCOUNT_KEY}"/>
</appSettings>
```

We must replace `{ACCOUNT_NAME}` and `{ACCOUNT_KEY}` with appropriate values for the account name and access key, respectively.

How to do it...

We are going to invoke a query in two different ways, for both Method1 and Method2. In one, we do not handle the automatic server-side pagination support, while in the other, we do. We will proceed as follows:

1. Add a class named `ContinuationTokensExample` to the project.

2. Install the `WindowsAzure.Storage` NuGet package and add the following assembly references to the project:

   `System.Configuration`

3. Add the following `using` statements to the top of the class file:

   ```
   using Microsoft.WindowsAzure.Storage;
   using Microsoft.WindowsAzure.Storage.Table;
   using Microsoft.WindowsAzure.Storage.Table.DataServices;
   using System.Configuration;
   ```

4. Add the following `private` members to the class:

   ```
   private CloudTableClient cloudTableClient;
   private String tableName = "Country";
   ```

5. Add the following constructor to the class:

   ```
   public ContinuationTokensExample()
   {
       CloudStorageAccount cloudStorageAccount =
           CloudStorageAccount.Parse(
               ConfigurationManager.AppSettings[
               "DataConnectionString"]);
       cloudTableClient =
           cloudStorageAccount.CreateCloudTableClient();
       cloudTableClient.GetTableReference(tableName)
           .CreateIfNotExists();
   }
   ```

6. Add the following method, uploading 10,000 entities, to the class:

   ```
   private void Insert10000Rows()
   {
       var table = cloudTableClient.GetTableReference(tableName);
       int counter = 1;
       for (int i = 0; i < 100; i++)
       {
   ```

```
        var batch = new TableBatchOperation();
        for (int j = 0; j <100; j++,counter++)
        {
            batch.Insert(new Country("Country" + counter,
                "Capital", 0));
        }
        table.ExecuteBatch(batch);
    }
}
```

 Now, let's proceed with Method1.

7. Add the following method, using `DataServiceQuery`, to the class:

```
private void GetEntitiesNoContinuationMethod1()
{
    var ctx=cloudTableClient.GetTableServiceContext();
    var res=ctx.CreateQuery<CountryDS>(tableName)
        .ToArray();
}
```

Add the following method, using `TableServiceQuery`, to the class:

```
private void GetEntitiesWithContinuationMethod1()
{
    var ctx = cloudTableClient.GetTableServiceContext();
    var res = ctx.CreateQuery<CountryDS>(tableName)
        .AsTableServiceQuery(ctx)
        .ToArray();
}
```

 Now, let's proceed with Method2.

8. Add the following method, forcing the segmentation of the query, to the class:

```
private void GetEntitiesNoContinuationMethod2()
{
    var table = cloudTableClient.GetTableReference(tableName);
    var res = table.ExecuteQuerySegmented<Country>(
        table.CreateQuery<Country>(),null)
        .ToArray();
}
```

9. Add the following method, handling continuation support, to the class:

```
private void GetEntitiesWithContinuationMethod2()
{
    var table = cloudTableClient.GetTableReference(tableName);
    var res = table.CreateQuery<Country>()
        .ToArray();
}
```

 In both cases, follow this final step.

10. Add the following method, invoking the other methods, to the class:

```
public static void UseContinuationTokensExample()
{
    ContinuationTokensExample example =
        new ContinuationTokensExample();
    example.Insert10000Rows();
    example.GetEntitiesNoContinuationMethod1();
    example.GetEntitiesNoContinuationMethod2();
    example.GetEntitiesWithContinuationMethod1();
    example.GetEntitiesWithContinuationMethod2();
}
```

How it works...

In steps 1 through 3, we set up the `ContinuationTokensExample` class. In step 4, we added some `private` members to the class: one that specifies the name of the `Country` table and the other that contains `CloudTableClient` which we initialize in the constructor we added in step 5. In step 6, we added 10,000 entities to the `Country` table. We used Method2 with 100 batch inserts of 100 entities each (due to the limitation explained in the *Using entity group transactions* recipe, as it is the best way to accomplish the task from a performance perspective.

In step 7, we added a method that uses `DataServiceQuery`, which does not handle the continuation tokens returned by the Windows Azure Table service. In step 8, instead, we obtained the query object through `AsTableServiceQuery<T>()` to convert it to `TableServiceQuery<T>`. We then executed the query asking materialization of entities.

 Note that `AsTableServiceQuery<T>()` is a method in the `TableServiceExtensions` class of the Storage library. To let Visual Studio IntelliSense suggest it, the `Microsoft.WindowsAzure.Storage.Table.DataServices` namespace should be added to the code file.

In step 9, we replayed the behavior with Method2, using the new pattern based on the `TableQuery<T>` object. As the new pattern natively supports server-side pagination or, better, it does not have a `general-purpose` object to deal without it, we need to explicitly ask for a segmented query to ask for the first and only chunk of results.

In step 10, we used the same method that, without specifying anything, handles the server-side pagination that performs several queries on the data store.

 To see the behavior of the Storage library, open Fiddler while executing the methods that handle the pagination to see that 10 consecutive queries are performed against the Table service, hidden from the user.

In step 11, we added a method that uses the methods we added in the previous steps.

See also

Have a look at the following MSDN link to get additional information:

▶ Reference to the REST implementation of timeout and pagination at `http://msdn.microsoft.com/en-us/library/azure/dd135718.aspx`

Going inside continuation tokens and segmented queries

As we saw in the *Using continuation tokens and server-side paging* recipe, the Azure Storage library offers the capability to automatically handle the server-side pagination for queries that go over some boundaries (more than 1,000 entities, cross partition, and so on). Also, the library offers, through the concept of **segmented queries**, the capability to control the query process deeply, one iteration at a time.

Both Method1 and the Method2 have this capability through the `ExecuteSegmented` method of the `TableServiceQuery<T>` and `TableQuery<T>` classes, respectively. In addition, as the Azure Storage library uses the **Common Language Runtime** (**CLR**), this method is also provided with the Asynchronous Programming Model, to provide asynchronous versions in addition to that method, to nearly all the methods that access the Azure Storage service. The asynchronous methods that download lists, such as entities, tables, and so on, typically come in a matched pair named `BeginExecuteSegmented ()` and `EndExecuteSegmented()`, where the segmented suffix indicates that the results are returned as a result segment, which might not contain the complete result set. Essentially, these methods page through the data, one result segment at a time.

The `TableServiceQuery<T>` and `TableQuery<T>` classes expose the `BeginExecuteSegmented()` and `EndExecuteSegmented()` methods to implement the query execute functionality. The `BeginExecuteSegmented()` method takes a parameter that specifies the current `ContinuationToken` header along with the callback method in which `EndExecuteSegmented()` must be called to clean up resources used in the asynchronous call. The code can be simplified using a lambda expression in place of the callback method.

The `EndExecuteSegmented()` method returns a `TableQuerySegment<T>` class, which contains the current page of results (the `Results` property) as well as any continuation tokens returned by the Table service. Subsequent synchronous or asynchronous calls to the same methods should provide them with the `ContinuationToken` header returned by the Table service to obtain subsequent pages of data.

In this recipe, we will learn how to manually control the server-side pagination in conjunction with the use of the APM pattern.

Getting ready

This recipe uses the model classes named `Country` and `CountryDS` that are declared in the *Inserting, updating, deleting, and querying data against the Table service* recipe and performs queries on the 10,000-entity dataset uploaded in the *Using continuation tokens and server-side paging* recipe. This recipe also assumes that the following lines of code are in the application's configuration file:

```
<appSettings>
  <add key="DataConnectionString"
value="DefaultEndpointsProtocol=https;AccountName={ACCOUNT_
NAME};AccountKey={ACCOUNT_KEY}"/>
</appSettings>
```

We must replace {`ACCOUNT_NAME`} and {`ACCOUNT_KEY`} with appropriate values for the account name and access key, respectively.

How to do it...

We are going to execute segmented queries using the asynchronous `BeginExecuteSegmented()` and `EndExecuteSegmented()` methods. We will do this using the following steps:

1. Add a class named `AdvancedContinuationTokensExample` to the project.

2. Install the `WindowsAzure.Storage` NuGet package and add the following assembly references to the project:

   ```
   System.Configuration
   ```

3. Add the following `using` statements to the top of the class file:

```
using Microsoft.WindowsAzure.Storage;
using Microsoft.WindowsAzure.Storage.Table;
using Microsoft.WindowsAzure.Storage.Table.DataServices;
using System.Configuration;
using System.Threading;
```

4. Add the following `private` members to the class:

```
private CloudTableClient cloudTableClient;
private String tableName = "Country";
```

5. Add the following constructor to the class:

```
public AdvancedContinuationTokensExample()
{
    CloudStorageAccount cloudStorageAccount =
        CloudStorageAccount.Parse(
            ConfigurationManager.AppSettings[
            "DataConnectionString"]);
    cloudTableClient =
        cloudStorageAccount.CreateCloudTableClient();
    cloudTableClient.GetTableReference(tableName)
        .CreateIfNotExists();
}
```

 Now, let's proceed with Method1.

6. Add the following private members to the class:

```
private List<CountryDS> resultsDS = new List<CountryDS>();
private AutoResetEvent loadedDS = new AutoResetEvent(false);
```

7. Add the following method, demonstrating asynchronous server-side paging, to the class:

```
private void ManualContinuationMethod1()
{
    var ctx = cloudTableClient.GetTableServiceContext();
    TableServiceQuery<CountryDS> query =
        ctx.CreateQuery<CountryDS>(tableName)
        .AsTableServiceQuery(ctx);
    query.BeginExecuteSegmented(null, SegmentedStepMethod1,
query);
    loadedDS.WaitOne();
}
```

8. Add the callback method needed by the previous asynchronous call:

```
private void SegmentedStepMethod1(IAsyncResult obj)
{
    var query = obj.AsyncState as TableServiceQuery<CountryDS>;
    TableQuerySegment<CountryDS> segmented
        = query.EndExecuteSegmented(obj);
    resultsDS.AddRange(segmented.Results);
    if (segmented.ContinuationToken != null)
    {
        query.BeginExecuteSegmented(segmented.ContinuationToken
            , SegmentedStepMethod1, query);
    }
    else
    {
        loadedDS.Set();
    }
}
```

 Now, let's proceed with Method2.

9. Add the following `private` members to the class:

```
private List<Country> results = new List<Country>();
private AutoResetEvent loaded = new AutoResetEvent(false);
```

10. Add the following method, demonstrating asynchronous server-side paging, to the class:

```
private void ManualContinuationMethod2()
{
    var table = cloudTableClient.GetTableReference(tableName);
    TableQuery<Country> query = table.CreateQuery<Country>();
    query.BeginExecuteSegmented(null, SegmentedStepMethod2,
query);
    loaded.WaitOne();
}
```

11. Add the callback method needed by the previous asynchronous call:

```
private void SegmentedStepMethod2(IAsyncResult obj)
{
    var query = obj.AsyncState as TableQuery<Country>;
    TableQuerySegment<Country> segmented
        = query.EndExecuteSegmented(obj);
    results.AddRange(segmented.Results);
    if (segmented.ContinuationToken != null)
    {
```

```
        query.BeginExecuteSegmented(segmented.ContinuationToken
            , SegmentedStepMethod2, query);
    }
    else
    {
        loaded.Set();
    }
}
```

 In both cases, follow this final step.

12. Add the following method using the methods we added earlier:

```
public static void UseAdvancedContinuationTokensExample()
{
    AdvancedContinuationTokensExample example =
        new AdvancedContinuationTokensExample();

    example.ManualContinuationMethod1();
    example.ManualContinuationMethod2();
}
```

How it works...

In steps 1 through 3, we set up the `ContinuationTokensExample` class. In step 4, we added some `private` members to the class, one that specifies the name of the `Country` table and the other that contains the `CloudTableClient` table which we initialized in the constructor we added in step 5. In step 6, we proceeded with the `DataServices` pattern, adding two `private` members to the class: a list, to save the `CountryDS` instances returned by the queries, and an `AutoResetEvent` class, to block the execution of the asynchronous queries.

In step 7, we created a `TableServiceQuery` class using the `AsTableServiceQuery()` extension method, and we began to execute the asynchronous chain of operations. The `WaitOne()` method gets blocked to avoid program termination, and it is intended for demonstration purposes only.

In step 8, we added the callback method that ends the segmented query, adds the partial results to the list of items, and reiterates a new segmented query, calling the `BeginExecuteSegmented()` method again; this time, it passed a valid continuation token until it is null, meaning that there are no more entities to fetch from the table.

Steps 9 and 10 are basically the same as 7 and 8, with the exception that with Method2, some classes change. We used a `TableQuery` class instead of a `TableServiceQuery` class, but the callback method used a `TableServiceSegment` class for results, as it did for Method1.

In step 12, we added a method that uses the methods we added earlier.

There's more...

In the current recipe, we see how to perform segmented queries with the APM pattern. However, it is possible to perform these queries in a synchronous way as follows:

```
private void ManualContinuationMethod2Sync()
{
    var table = cloudTableClient.GetTableReference(tableName);
    TableQuery<Country> query = table.CreateQuery<Country>();
    TableContinuationToken token=null;
    var list=new List<Country>();
    do
    {
        var res = query.ExecuteSegmented(token);
        token = res.ContinuationToken;
        list.AddRange(res.Results);
    } while (token != null);
}
```

As shown in the code snippet, we cycle over a `ContinuationToken` condition to check if there is more data to fetch from the Table service.

See also

We will see how to use the Storage Client library to download blobs asynchronously in the *Downloading a blob asynchronously* recipe of *Chapter 3, Getting Storage with Blobs in Azure*.

Have a look at this MSDN link to get additional information:

▶ The Azure Table storage while implementing Cloud solutions at `http://msdn.microsoft.com/en-us/library/ff803362.aspx`

Handling entity serialization events

The Azure Table service exposes a RESTful interface in which an entity is represented in various formats. Initially, there was only the **Atom** format to support JSON in recent years. In saving an instance to a table, the Azure Storage library serializes the instance into the appropriate format before invoking the appropriate REST operation on the Table service. Similarly, when retrieving an entity from a table, the Storage Client library deserializes the entry into an instance of the model class.

The Table service supports a limited set of simple datatypes for the properties of entities. These datatypes are listed in the *Inserting, updating, deleting, and querying data against the Table Service* recipe. By default, the Storage Client library serializes an instance of a model class by converting each public property of one of the supported datatypes into an element in a result entry. Deserialization simply reverses this process.

Method1 and Method2 differ dramatically in how deserialization can be controlled or influenced. The first method, based on WCF Data Services, allows us to operate on the `TableServiceContext` configuration to intercept serialization events in the request pipeline. The second one passes the control of serialization events to the entity involved in the process.

In this recipe, we will learn how to influence the serialization events to modify the default serialization and deserialization behaviors when saving and retrieving data from a table.

Getting ready

This recipe assumes that the following lines of code are in the application's configuration file:

```
<appSettings>
  <add key="DataConnectionString"
value="DefaultEndpointsProtocol=https;AccountName={ACCOUNT_
NAME};AccountKey={ACCOUNT_KEY}"/>
</appSettings>
```

We must replace `{ACCOUNT_NAME}` and `{ACCOUNT_KEY}` with appropriate values for the account name and access key, respectively.

How to do it...

We are going to create model classes to represent cars, books, and customers. We want to save these entities in the same table while marking the items with their type, to perform a filtered retrieval subsequently. We will proceed with the two methods separately, as they differ a lot:

1. Add a class named `ReadingWritingEntityExample`.

2. Install the `WindowsAzure.Storage` NuGet package and add the following assembly references to the project:

   ```
   System.Configuration
   ```

3. Add the following `using` statements to the top of the class file:

   ```
   using Microsoft.Data.OData;
   using Microsoft.WindowsAzure.Storage;
   using Microsoft.WindowsAzure.Storage.Table;
   using Microsoft.WindowsAzure.Storage.Table.DataServices;
   using System.Configuration;
   using System.Collections.Generic;
   using System.Configuration;
   using System.Data.Services.Client;
   using System.Xml.Linq;
   ```

4. Add the following `private` members to the class:

   ```
   private CloudTableClient cloudTableClient;
   private String tableName = "Stuff";
   ```

5. Add the following constructor to the class:

   ```
   public ReadingWritingEntityExample()
   {
       CloudStorageAccount cloudStorageAccount =
           CloudStorageAccount.Parse(
               ConfigurationManager.AppSettings[
               "DataConnectionString"]);
       cloudTableClient =
           cloudStorageAccount.CreateCloudTableClient();
       cloudTableClient.GetTableReference(tableName)
           .CreateIfNotExists();
   }
   ```

[Now, let's proceed with Method1.]

6. Add the `BaseEntityDS` class to the code after the namespace declaration:

```
public class BaseEntityDS : TableServiceEntity
{
    public string Type { get; set; }
    public BaseEntityDS()
    {
        PartitionKey = "variousDS";
    }
}
```

7. Add the model classes after the preceding class declaration:

```
public class CarDS : BaseEntityDS
{
    public string Brand { get; set; }
}
public class BookDS : BaseEntityDS
{
    public string Author { get; set; }
}
public class CustomerDS : BaseEntityDS
{
    public string Name { get; set; }
}
```

8. Add this method, performing a 100-entity bulk insert, to the class:

```
private void AddSomeEntitiesMethod1()
{
    var ctx = cloudTableClient.GetTableServiceContext();
    ctx.Configurations.RequestPipeline.OnEntryEnding(a =>
    {
        var typeName = a.Entity.GetType().Name;
        var props = a.Entry.Properties.ToList();
        var type = props
            .FirstOrDefault(p => p.Name == "Type");
        if (type == null)
        {
            type = new ODataProperty() { Name = "Type" };
            props.Add(type);
            a.Entry.Properties = props;
        }
        type.Value = typeName;
    });
    int counter = 1;
    for (int i = 0; i < 100; i++)
```

```
    {
        BaseEntityDS entity = null;
        if (counter == 1) entity =
            new CarDS() { Brand = "BMW" + i,
                RowKey = i.ToString() };
        if (counter == 2) entity =
            new BookDS() { Author = "Whitman" + i,
                RowKey = i.ToString() };
        if (counter == 3) entity =
            new CustomerDS() { Name = "Steve" + i,
                RowKey = i.ToString() };
        counter = (counter == 3 ? 1 : counter + 1);
        ctx.AddObject("Stuff", entity);
    }
    ctx.SaveChangesWithRetries(SaveChangesOptions.Batch);
}
```

9. Add this method, reading only certain type of entities, to the class:

```
public void ReadingEntitiesMethod1()
{
    var ctx = cloudTableClient.GetTableServiceContext();
    var res = ctx.CreateQuery<CarDS>("Stuff")
        .Where(p => p.Type == "CarDS")
        .ToArray();
}
```

 Now, let's proceed with Method2.

10. Add the `BaseEntity` class to the code after the namespace declaration:

```
public class BaseEntity:TableEntity
{
    public string Type { get; set; }
    public BaseEntity()
    {
        PartitionKey = "various";
    }

    public override IDictionary<string, EntityProperty>
WriteEntity(OperationContext operationContext)
    {
        var dict= base.WriteEntity(operationContext);
        dict["Type"]= new EntityProperty(this.GetType().Name);
        return dict;
    }
}
```

11. Add the model classes after the preceding class declaration:

```
public class Car : BaseEntity
{
    public string Brand { get; set; }
}
public class Book : BaseEntity
{
    public string Author { get; set; }
}
public class Customer : BaseEntity
{
    public string Name { get; set; }
}
```

12. Add this method, performing a 100-entity bulk insert, to the
    `ReadingWritingEntityExample` class:

```
public void AddSomeEntitiesMethod2()
{
    var table = cloudTableClient
        .GetTableReference(tableName);
    int counter = 1;
    var batch = new TableBatchOperation();
    for (int i = 0; i < 100; i++)
    {
        BaseEntity entity = null;
        if (counter == 1) entity =
            new Car() { Brand = "BMW"+i,
                RowKey = i.ToString() };
        if (counter == 2) entity =
            new Book() { Author = "Whitman"+i,
                RowKey = i.ToString() };
        if (counter == 3) entity =
            new Customer() { Name= "Steve"+i,
                RowKey = i.ToString() };
        counter=(counter==3?1:counter+1);
        batch.Insert(entity);
    }
    table.ExecuteBatch(batch);
}
```

13. Add this method, reading only certain type of entities, to the class:

```
public void ReadingEntitiesMethod2()
{
    var table = cloudTableClient.GetTableReference(tableName);
    var res = table.CreateQuery<Car>().Where(p=>p.Type=="Car")
        .ToArray();
}
```

 In both cases, follow this final step.

14. Add the following method using the methods we added earlier:

```
public static void UseReadingWritingEntityExample()
{
    ReadingWritingEntityExample example =
        new ReadingWritingEntityExample();
    example.AddSomeEntitiesMethod1();
    example.ReadingEntitiesMethod1();
    example.AddSomeEntitiesMethod2();
    example.ReadingEntitiesMethod2();
}
```

How it works...

In steps 1 through 3, we set up the `ReadingWritingEntityExample` class. In step 4, we added some `private` members to the class: one that specifies the name of the `Stuff` table and the other that contains the `CloudTableClient` class which we initialize in the constructor we added in step 5.

In step 6, we proceeded with the `DataServices` pattern, creating a `BaseEntityDS` father type, writing its instances to the `variousDS` partition. In step 7, we added the `CarDS`, `BookDS`, and `CustomerDS` subtypes. As done with the `Country` data model (of the previous recipes), we wrote two separate models to deal independently from Method1 and Method2.

In step 8, we added 100 entities to the `Stuff` table, using an index technique to equally distribute them across subtypes. Before invoking the `SaveChangesWithRetries()` batch, we injected a custom serialization function in `RequestPipeline` to make it called each time the `TableServiceContext` class tried to serialize an entity before sending it to the cloud. Hence, we asked for the properties being serialized, and we injected the `Type` field to the entity type name. We needed to reassign the `Properties` property of the `Entry` instance due to the `(IEnumerable<ODataProperty>)` property type that is not editable.

In step 9, we made a simple query that performed a filter onto the `Type` property, to retrieve only the entities that are of the `CarDS` type.

In step 10, we proceeded with the new pattern, declaring a base entity type (writing to the `various` partition), which directly handled its serialization logic by overriding the `WriteEntity` method of the `TableEntity` type. The semantic of this method is to influence a dictionary of properties before returning it to the storage library. So, it is quite simple to add the interested property to the dictionary and return it.

As done for Method1, in step 11, we added the `car`, `book`, and `customer` subtypes to the code, and we added 100 entities of mixed types in step 12. The batch operation performed a single query with the whole dataset, as explained better in the *Using entity group transactions* recipe. Finally, in step 13, we used `CloudTable.CreateQuery<T>` to perform a query, filtered by the type we are interested in.

In step 14, we added a method that uses the methods we added earlier.

There's more...

As we can imagine, as we deal with the event during serialization, we can even handle the event during the deserialization process. With WCF Data Services, we can influence the entire `RequestPipeline` property to fit our needs of customization. In particular, we have to handle these events as follows:

```
public class DataServiceClientRequestPipelineConfiguration
{
    public Func<DataServiceClientRequestMessageArgs,
        DataServiceClientRequestMessage> OnMessageCreating { get; set;
}
    public DataServiceClientRequestPipelineConfiguration
        OnEntityReferenceLink(Action<WritingEntityReferenceLinkArgs>
action);
    public DataServiceClientRequestPipelineConfiguration
        OnEntryEnding(Action<WritingEntryArgs> action);
    public DataServiceClientRequestPipelineConfiguration
        OnEntryStarting(Action<WritingEntryArgs> action);
    public DataServiceClientRequestPipelineConfiguration
        OnMessageWriterSettingsCreated(Action<MessageWriterSettingsAr
gs> args);
    public DataServiceClientRequestPipelineConfiguration
        OnNavigationLinkEnding(Action<WritingNavigationLinkArgs>
action);
    public DataServiceClientRequestPipelineConfiguration
        OnNavigationLinkStarting(Action<WritingNavigationLinkArgs>
action);
}
```

During the response, when the entities are deserialized from the HTTP stream, we have these events too:

```
public class DataServiceClientResponsePipelineConfiguration
{
    public DataServiceClientResponsePipelineConfiguration
        OnEntityMaterialized(Action<MaterializedEntityArgs> action);
    public DataServiceClientResponsePipelineConfiguration
        OnEntryEnded(Action<ReadingEntryArgs> action);
    public DataServiceClientResponsePipelineConfiguration
        OnEntryStarted(Action<ReadingEntryArgs> action);
    public DataServiceClientResponsePipelineConfiguration
        OnFeedEnded(Action<ReadingFeedArgs> action);
    public DataServiceClientResponsePipelineConfiguration
        OnFeedStarted(Action<ReadingFeedArgs> action);
    public DataServiceClientResponsePipelineConfiguration
        OnMessageReaderSettingsCreated(Action<MessageReaderSettingsAr
gs> messageReaderSettingsAction);
    public DataServiceClientResponsePipelineConfiguration
        OnNavigationLinkEnded(Action<ReadingNavigationLinkArgs>
action);
    public DataServiceClientResponsePipelineConfiguration
        OnNavigationLinkStarted(Action<ReadingNavigationLinkArgs>
action);
}
```

With the new pattern, we can override the ReadingEntity method in each son of the TableEntity type. This lets us customize the deserialization process; this is very useful while dealing with third-party objects nested in our model classes.

Legacy approach to custom serialization with Atom feeds

The Storage Client library exposes extension points, the WritingEntity and ReadingEntity events, that can be used to modify the default behavior of serialization and deserialization, but only while using an XML Atom feed as the negotiating format. An argument of the ReadingWritingEntityEventArgs type is passed into the WritingEntity and ReadingEntity handlers. This argument provides access to both the instance properties, and the Atom entry allows them to be inspected and modified as desired.

The following is an excerpt of how to deal with that:

```
var ctx = cloudTableClient.GetTableServiceContext();
XNamespace ns = ctx.DataNamespace;
XNamespace meta = ctx.DataNamespace + "/metadata";
ctx.Format.UseAtom();
ctx.WritingEntity += (s, e) =>
{
    var entity = e.Entity as BaseEntityDS;
    entity.Type = entity.GetType().Name;
    XElement properties = e.Data.Descendants(
        meta + "properties").First();
    properties.Add(new XElement(ns + "Type", entity.Type));
};
```

As we can see, this kind of customization involves the specific format, and it is generally deprecated.

See also

We learned about the data model used by the Table service in the *Inserting, updating, deleting, and querying data against the Table service* recipe.

Have a look at the following MSDN links to get additional information:

- ▶ Performance considerations with Table storage, serialization, and JSON at `http://blogs.msdn.com/b/windowsazurestorage/archive/2013/12/05/windows-azure-tables-introducing-json.aspx`

- ▶ AtomPub specifications at `http://msdn.microsoft.com/en-us/library/dd541369.aspx`

Facilitating NoSQL with client-side projection

The Azure Table service is a powerful storage service that enables an application to save and query entities (potentially schemaless) with an unbelievable scalability target and, of course, minimal governance. As we can save several types of aggregates of different topologies into the same table, the Storage library helps us deal with this, performing client-side projection to provide the application with the strong-typed model, instead of a collection of key-value items for each entity.

In this chapter, we wrote about two different ways to accomplish tasks with the Table service. We called them Method1 (for the WCF Data Services way) and Method2 (for the *new* officially supported OData method). In this recipe, we will only show how to proceed with Method2, as there are no valid counterparts to Method1.

In this brief recipe, we will see how to notice the SDK to manipulate returning entities before giving them back to the application.

Getting ready

This recipe uses the `BaseEntity`, `Car`, `Book`, and `Customers` classes defined in the *Handling entity serialization events* recipe. Although a complete reading of the recipe is useful to proceed, only the class model is needed to proceed.

This recipe also assumes that the following lines of code are in the application's configuration file:

```
<appSettings>
  <add key="DataConnectionString"
value="DefaultEndpointsProtocol=https;AccountName={ACCOUNT_
NAME};AccountKey={ACCOUNT_KEY}"/>
</appSettings>
```

We must replace `{ACCOUNT_NAME}` and `{ACCOUNT_KEY}` with appropriate values for the account name and access key, respectively.

How to do it...

We are going to query the `DynamicStuff` table to obtain each entity, but as they are different in type and properties, we want a client-side resolver that wraps each entity into the correct class type. We will proceed as follows:

1. Add a class named `ClientSideProjectionExample`.

2. Install the `WindowsAzure.Storage` NuGet package and add the following assembly references to the project:

   ```
   System.Configuration
   ```

3. Add the following `using` statements to the top of the class file:

   ```
   using Microsoft.WindowsAzure.Storage;
   using Microsoft.WindowsAzure.Storage.Table;
   using System.Configuration;
   using System.Collections.Generic;
   using System.Configuration;
   ```

4. Add the following `private` members to the class:

```
private CloudTableClient cloudTableClient;
private String tableName = "DynamicStuff";
```

5. Add the following constructor to the class:

```
public ClientSideProjectionExample()
{
    CloudStorageAccount cloudStorageAccount =
        CloudStorageAccount.Parse(
            ConfigurationManager.AppSettings[
            "DataConnectionString"]);
    cloudTableClient =
        cloudStorageAccount.CreateCloudTableClient();
    cloudTableClient.GetTableReference(tableName)
        .CreateIfNotExists();
}
```

6. Add the following method, to wrap each entity into the correct type, to the class:

```
public IEnumerable<BaseEntity> GetAllItemsByType()
{
    var table = cloudTableClient.GetTableReference(tableName);

    EntityResolver<BaseEntity> resolver =
        (pk, rk, ts, props, etag) =>
    {
        BaseEntity resolvedEntity = null;
        string type = props["Type"].StringValue;

        if (type == "Car") { resolvedEntity = new Car(); }
        else if (type == "Book") { resolvedEntity = new Book(); }
        else if (type == "Customer") { resolvedEntity
            = new Customer(); }

        resolvedEntity.PartitionKey = pk;
        resolvedEntity.RowKey = rk;
        resolvedEntity.Timestamp = ts;
        resolvedEntity.ETag = etag;
        resolvedEntity.ReadEntity(props, null);
        return resolvedEntity;
    };
    return table.ExecuteQuery(table
        .CreateQuery<BaseEntity>(), resolver);
}
```

7. Add the following method using the method we added earlier to print only the brand values of the `Car` entities:

```
public static void UseReadingWritingEntityExample()
{
    ClientSideProjectionExample example =
        new ClientSideProjectionExample();
    var items = example.GetAllItemsByType();
    foreach (var item in items.OfType<Car>())
    {
        Console.WriteLine(item.Brand);
    }
}
```

How it works...

In steps 1 through 3, we set up the `ClientSideProjectionExample` class. In step 4, we added some `private` members to the class: one that specifies the name of the `Stuff` table and the other that contains the `CloudTableClient` class which we initialized in the constructor we added in step 5.

In step 6, we created an `EntityResolver<BaseEntity>` instance, specifying that for each entity retrieved from the data store, a lambda must be called to handle a custom resolving logic. In the code, we discriminated the `Type` field to create a specific instance of the correct type. Then, we called the underlying deserialization logic with the `TableEntity.ReadEntity` method.

In step 7, we got all the items of the data store, and then, we used LINQ to cycle only the `Car` instances.

There's more...

There is really no need to build our custom data model to fit the Azure Table service. Instead, we can just work with a top-level implementation of `TableEntity` that wraps the entire content of an entity into a set of key-value items.

The `DynamicTableEntity` class is returned by the Storage library when the query is not bound to an actual type, so the library can't deserialize the entity into a custom object. With the `DynamicTableEntity` class, we can deal with heterogeneous queries, as it extends the `TableEntity` base class with heterogeneous updates as well.

To perform a generic query for all the elements in a specific partition, proceed as follows:

```
public IEnumerable<DynamicTableEntity> GetHeterogeneousItems()
{
    var table = cloudTableClient.GetTableReference(tableName);
    return table.ExecuteQuery(new TableQuery()
        .Where(TableQuery.GenerateFilterCondition
            ("PartitionKey",QueryComparisons.Equal,"various")));
}
```

Please note that the `Where` clause of the nongeneric `TableQuery` class does not have the LINQ expressions' overloads to use lambda for filters. Instead, it has a simple string-based query language (the OData language) that could also be generated using the `TableQuery` static helper members and the `QueryComparisons` helper class.

Each item of the returned set has the base properties of each `TableEntity` class plus every other property stored in an `IDictionary<string,EntityProperty>` property, and it is accessible as follows:

```
var heterogenous = example.GetHeterogeneousItems();
foreach (var item in heterogenous)
{
    Console.WriteLine(item["Type"].StringValue);
}
```

Finally, to perform a batch update of the heterogeneous entities, we can use the following line of codes:

```
public void PerformHeterogeneousUpdate(IEnumerable<DynamicTableEntity> set)
{
    var table = cloudTableClient.GetTableReference(tableName);
    TableBatchOperation batch = new TableBatchOperation();
    foreach (var item in set)
    {
        item["NewField"] =new EntityProperty("Hi");
        batch.Merge(item);
    }
    table.ExecuteBatch(batch);
}
```

See also

Have a look at these MSDN links to get additional information:

▶ Comparison between the Azure Table storage and Azure SQL Database at `http://msdn.microsoft.com/en-us/library/jj553018.aspx`

▶ The NoSQL perspective around the Table storage at `http://msdn.microsoft.com/en-us/magazine/dn166928.aspx`

6

Messaging and Queues with the Storage and Service Bus

In this chapter, we will cover the following topics:

- ▶ Managing Azure Storage queues
- ▶ Managing Azure Service Bus queues
- ▶ Adding messages to a Storage queue
- ▶ Adding messages to a Service Bus queue
- ▶ Receiving messages with Storage queues
- ▶ Receiving messages with Service Bus queues
- ▶ Implementing publish/subscribe with Service Bus topics
- ▶ Implementing Relayed messaging with the Service Bus
- ▶ Communication between .NET and Java with the Service Bus and AMQP

Introduction

Queues provide a way to decouple the connection between two actors, interconnecting heterogeneous systems by message-driven contact points. The producing actor inserts a message containing the details of the request into the queue. The consuming actor polls the queue and upon getting the message, performs the associated task. If necessary, the consuming actor can insert a message in another queue indicating completion of the task.

A more general view is that a generic queue service provides a way to manage the processing of a task so that it is more robust against failure. Azure is a scalable system and it is possible that a component of the system could fail at any time, causing the loss of any work in progress. The extent of this loss can be minimized by breaking the task into individual steps. The loss of work-in-progress for an individual step is less significant than that of the overall task. A queue service supports this functionality by providing a coherent way to track the work status of a task through the insertion of a message in a queue to indicate the completion of a step and allow the next step to start.

While developing cloud services, a queue facilitates their scalability by allowing disconnected communication between roles in it, allowing the roles to scale independently of each other. Indeed, they do not even need to be active at the same time.

More generally, the queue service provides a coherent way to manage the processing of a task comprising several steps. For example, a long-lived task could be broken up into steps and the status of these steps managed using queues, enabling scalable systems and patterns like CQRS.

The **Azure Storage queues** is the Azure feature that manages queues and the messages in them at the same level as blobs and tables, while the Azure Service Bus is the Azure building clock comprising another version of queues, plus Topic (publish/subscribe queues) and Relay services.

Storage queues were introduced first, as part of the Azure Storage service. Later, Microsoft released the Service Bus platform with apparently overlapping features. In addition, Service Bus queues offer a more featured service, compared to the Azure Storage queues. It is recent debate when to use Storage queues and when to use the Service Bus platform; this is something we try to discuss later in this chapter.

The following table is taken from `http://msdn.microsoft.com/en-us/library/hh767287.aspx`

Comparison Criteria	Queues	Service Bus Queues
Ordering guarantee	No	Yes, **First-In-First-Out** (**FIFO**)
		(through the use of messaging sessions)
Delivery guarantee	At-Least-Once	At-Least-Once
		At-Most-Once
Transaction support	No	Yes
		(through the use of local transactions)

Comparison Criteria	Queues	Service Bus Queues
Receive behavior	Nonblocking (completes immediately if no new message is found)	Blocking with/without timeout (offers long polling or the Comet technique) Nonblocking (through the use of .NET managed API only)
Push-style API	No	Yes OnMessage and OnMessage sessions managed (.NET) API
Receive mode	Peek & Lease	Peek & Lock Receive & Delete
Exclusive access mode	Lease-based	Lock-based
Lease/Lock duration	30 seconds (default) 7 days (maximum) (you can renew or release a message lease using the UpdateMessage API)	60 seconds (default) (you can renew a message lock using the RenewLock API)
Lease/Lock granularity	Message level (each message can have a different timeout value, which you can then update as needed while processing the message by using the UpdateMessage API)	Queue level (each queue has a lock granularity applied to all of its messages, but you can renew the lock using the RenewLock API)
Batched receive	Yes (explicitly specifying message count when retrieving messages, up to a maximum of 32 messages)	Yes (implicitly enabling a pre-fetch property or explicitly through the use of transactions)
Batched send	No	Yes (through the use of transactions or client-side batching)

In the preceding table, there is a comparison of the two services by their features and how they implement them differently. Refer to the following points for more information:

- **Ordering guarantee**: Storage queues do not guarantee ordering, so a message sent at time T could be processed after a message sent at time T+1.

- **Delivery guarantee**: When messages arrive to the consumer, it retrieves, processes and deletes them. If something goes wrong during this process, the message is put again on the queue. This is often referred to as At-Least-Once processing, compared to the At-Most-Once (supported by the Service Bus) that guarantees that the message is only processed once.

- **Transaction support**: Service Bus supports transaction and it is for transaction that provides the At-Most-Once delivery.

- **Receive behavior**: With Storage queues, we must perform a manual polling to the service to discover new messages, while the Service Bus provides itself blocking calls if no messages are found in the queue.

- **Push-style API**: This means the Service Bus library supports notifications via .NET managed callbacks.

- **Receive mode**: In both services, a read message becomes invisible for a given timeout. After that, it becomes available again to clients for further processing. So, the client should delete it before the lease/lock expires. In Service Bus queues, we can perform a Receive & Delete call, avoiding the second-pass deletion.

.NET Applications can operate against queues by using the following two libraries, respectively:

- **Azure Storage Library**: This is used for the Storage queues, using the same foundation classes of the Storage blobs and tables

- **Azure Service Bus Library**: This is used for the Service Bus queues, using Topics and Relay services

In the *Managing Azure Storage queues* and *Managing Azure Service Bus queues* recipes, we will see how to allocate resources and start using the two platforms. In the *Adding messages to a Storage queue* and *Adding messages to a Service Bus queue* recipes, we will see message insertion with expiration and delayed delivery, while in the *Receiving messages with Storage queues* and *Receiving messages with Service Bus queues* recipes, we will get the `Get`, `Peek`, and `Bulk receive` messages from the queues.

In the *Implementing publish/subscribe with Service Bus topics* recipe, we will see the unique publish/subscribe feature of Azure, implemented by the Service Bus with Topics. Also, the relayed messaging feature, enabling WCF services to register themselves to a public-faced endpoint of Azure, is a unique feature of Service Bus. We will see this in the *Implementing Relayed messaging with the Service Bus* recipe.

Finally, since Azure Service Bus queues support the AMQP protocol, we see how to integrate non-.NET solutions with queues, as described in the *Communication between .NET and Java with the Service Bus and AMQP* recipe.

Managing Azure Storage queues

The Azure Storage Service partitions data to provide scalability and has a lower scalability target for data in a single partition than for a storage account. The queue service stores each queue in its own partition. At the time of writing, the scalability target for a single queue is 2,000 messages per second, while the scalability target for an entire storage account is up to 20,000 messages per second. Consequently, scalability may be improved by using multiple queues.

In the Azure Storage library, the `CloudQueue` class provides both synchronous and asynchronous methods to manage queues and the messages in them. These include methods to create, delete, and clear queues. Although queues may have metadata associated with them, only the queue name is needed to create a queue. The queue name may comprise only lowercase letters, numbers, and the dash character.

In this recipe, we'll learn how to manage queues.

Getting ready

This recipe assumes the following code is in the application configuration file:

```
<appSettings>
  <add key="DataConnectionString"
value="DefaultEndpointsProtocol=https;AccountName={ACCOUNT_
NAME};AccountKey={ACCOUNT_KEY}"/>
</appSettings>
```

We must replace {ACCOUNT_NAME} and {ACCOUNT_KEY} with appropriate values of the account name and access key.

How to do it...

We are going to create a queue, look at some of its attributes, and then delete the queue. We do this as follows:

1. Add a new class named `ManageStorageQueueExample` to the project.

2. Install the `WindowsAzure.Storage` NuGet package and add the following assembly references to the project:

    ```
    System.Configuration
    ```

3. Add the following `using` statements to the top of the class:

    ```
    using Microsoft.WindowsAzure.Storage;
    using Microsoft.WindowsAzure.Storage.Queue;
    using System.Configuration;
    ```

4. Add the following `private` member to the class:

    ```
    private CloudQueueClient cloudQueueClient;
    ```

5. Add the following constructor to the class:

    ```
    public ManageStorageQueueExample()
    {
        CloudStorageAccount cloudStorageAccount =
            CloudStorageAccount.Parse(
            ConfigurationManager.AppSettings[
            "DataConnectionString"]);
        cloudQueueClient =
            cloudStorageAccount.CreateCloudQueueClient();
    }
    ```

6. Add the following method, creating a queue, to the class:

    ```
    public void CreateQueue(String queueName)
    {
        CloudQueue cloudQueue =
            cloudQueueClient.GetQueueReference(queueName);
        cloudQueue.CreateIfNotExists();
    }
    ```

7. Add the following method, retrieving queue information, to the class:

    ```
    public void GetQueueInformation(String queueName)
    {
        CloudQueue cloudQueue =
            cloudQueueClient.GetQueueReference(queueName);
    ```

```
    int? approximateMessageCount =
        cloudQueue.ApproximateMessageCount;
    cloudQueue.FetchAttributes();
    approximateMessageCount = cloudQueue.ApproximateMessageCount;
    Uri uri = cloudQueue.Uri;
    foreach (String key in cloudQueue.Metadata.Keys)
    {
        String metadataValue = cloudQueue.Metadata[key];
    }
}
```

8. Add the following method, deleting the queue, to the class:

```
public void DeleteQueue(String queueName)
{
    CloudQueue cloudQueue =
        cloudQueueClient.GetQueueReference(queueName);
    cloudQueue.DeleteIfExists();
}
```

9. Add the following method, using the methods added earlier, to the class:

```
public static void UseCreateQueueExample()
{
    String queueName = "{QUEUE_NAME}";
    ManageStorageQueueExample example = new
ManageStorageQueueExample();

    example.CreateQueue(queueName);
    example.GetQueueInformation(queueName);
    example.DeleteQueue(queueName);
}
```

How it works...

In steps 1 through 3, we set up the class. In step 4, we added a private member to store the `CloudQueueClient` object used to connect to the queue service. We initialized this in the constructor we added in step 5.

In step 6, we added a method that initializes a `CloudQueue` object and uses it to create a queue. It is always preferable to use the `CreateIfNotExists()` method to avoid runtime exceptions while creating the remote resources.

In step 7, we added a method that initializes a `CloudQueue` object and uses it to retrieve the approximate message count of the queue. We asked for that property twice, since the first time the queue's attributes are not fetched from the remote service. The second time, after calling `FetchAttributes()`, we have the property actually populated.

> The `GetQueueReference()` method builds only a class instance pointing to the URI of the Storage queue passed as an argument. So, since there is no exchange between client and server, the `ApproximateMessageCount` property is null. This is why we ask the `FetchAttributes()` method on the server side to populate the property as long as the metadata of the queue.

We then retrieved and looked at the queue attributes, including the URI and any user-defined metadata associated with the queue.

In step 8, we added a method that initializes a `CloudQueue` object and uses it to delete a queue (also, it is preferable to use the safer `DeleteIfExists()` method).

In step 9, we added a method that invokes the methods we added earlier. We need to replace `{QUEUE_NAME}` with an appropriate name for a queue.

> The queue name should be in lower case with names no longer than 63 characters (with a minimum of three characters); the first and the last letters of the name should be alphanumeric and the dash (-) is the only nonalphanumeric character permitted.

There's more...

As for every Storage endpoint (tables and blobs), the queues also support the listing of the current queues of a storage account. To get that list, we can proceed as follows:

```
public IEnumerable<CloudQueue> GetQueues()
{
    return cloudQueueClient.ListQueues()
        .ToArray();
}
```

In the `ListQueues()` method, an optional string could be passed to filter the queues result by a prefix.

Nagle's algorithm

TCP operates with algorithms that help it to enhance transmission performance. One of them is Nagle's algorithm. Nagling is an optimization that merges requests (on the sender part) to avoid network congestion while sending small requests (of less than the default TCP packet size). Under certain conditions, for example, during many HTTP subsequent calls to the Azure Storage service, this behavior could be cumbersome and we can power up the wire using the following statement:

```
ServicePointManager.UseNagleAlgorithm = false;
```

See also

Have a look at the following links to get additional information:

- ▶ The Storage queue documentation at `http://azure.microsoft.com/en-en/documentation/articles/storage-dotnet-how-to-use-queues/`
- ▶ Learn more about Nagle's algorithm at `http://en.wikipedia.org/wiki/Nagle's_algorithm`

Managing Azure Service Bus queues

Service Bus is a comprehensive set of enterprise-ready connectivity tools to enable messaging between endpoints. It differs from the Storage service as mentioned in the introduction, and talking about queues, it offers many more features than that.

To provide our application with a Service Bus queue, a Service Bus endpoint should be created as explained in the following section. The Service Bus integrates the **Access Control Service** (**ACS**) to provide fine-grained security across its objects (such as queues, topics, and relays).

 Here and later in the chapter, we use ACS with default credentials (**owner** user) to operate against the Service Bus. It is a common approach, even if it is not recommended in production where a fine-grained security should be implemented. For testing and learning purposes, the following approach is effective as well.

At the time of writing, the average latency of the Azure Storage is said to be slightly less than the Service Bus: 100 ms for Service Bus and 10 ms for Storage Bus, under certain conditions.

In the previous recipe, we showed how to maximize the performance of multiple and consecutive small requests with the Storage service, disabling the TCP Nagle algorithm. Since Service Bus queues are also available through TCP over TLS, disabling Nagle is not necessary anymore.

In the Azure Service Bus, there is a central management connection string (the **owner** one) that lets us operate completely on the endpoint as for its objects. With that connection string, we use the `NamespaceManager` and the `MassagingFactory` classes to operate, respectively, on the Service Bus entirely and on the `Queues` and `Topic` objects.

In this recipe, we'll learn how to manage queues.

Getting ready

This and further recipes assume you have previously created a valid Service Bus namespace in the Azure Portal. The steps are as follows:

1. Go to `http://manage.windowsazure.com`.

2. Locate the **SERVICE BUS** section on the right, and click on it.

3. In the bottom menu, click on **CREATE** and provide information needed to create the queue, which comprises the following:

   ❑ **Namespace name**: This is the friendly name of the entire endpoint

   ❑ **Region**: This is the region of the datacenter where we place the endpoint

   ❑ **Subscription**: This is the subscription that is billed for the service

4. When the provisioning process is completed, click on the **Connection Information** icon on the bottom menu to obtain the connection string for the endpoint.

This recipe assumes that the following code is in the application configuration file:

```
<appSettings>
  <add key="ServiceBusConnectionString"
        value="Endpoint=sb://[your namespace].servicebus.windows.net;S
haredSecretIssuer=owner;SharedSecretValue=[your secret]" />
</appSettings>
```

We must replace `[your namespace]` and `[your secret]` with appropriate values of the namespace name and owner access key.

How to do it...

We are going to create a queue, look at some of its attributes, and then delete the queue. We do this as follows:

1. Add a new class named `ManageServiceBusQueueExample` to the project.

2. Install the `WindowsAzure.ServiceBus` NuGet package and add the following assembly references to the project:

   ```
   System.Configuration
   ```

3. Add the following `using` statements to the top of the class:

   ```
   using Microsoft.ServiceBus;
   using Microsoft.ServiceBus.Messaging;
   using System.Configuration;
   ```

4. Add the following private member to the class:

   ```
   private NamespaceManager manager;
   ```

5. Add the following constructor to the class:

   ```
   public ManageServiceBusQueueExample()
   {
       var conn = ConfigurationManager
           .AppSettings["ServiceBusConnectionString"];
       manager = NamespaceManager.CreateFromConnectionString(conn);
   }
   ```

6. Add the following method, creating a queue, to the class:

   ```
   public void CreateQueue(String queueName)
   {
       if (!manager.QueueExists(queueName))
       {
           var descr = new QueueDescription(queueName);
           descr.DefaultMessageTimeToLive
               = TimeSpan.FromDays(14);
           descr.EnableDeadLetteringOnMessageExpiration = true;
           descr.RequiresDuplicateDetection = true;
           descr.DuplicateDetectionHistoryTimeWindow
               = TimeSpan.FromMinutes(10);
           descr.LockDuration
               = TimeSpan.FromSeconds(30);
           descr.MaxDeliveryCount = 10;
           descr.Status = EntityStatus.Active;
           manager.CreateQueue(descr);
       }
   }
   ```

7. Add the following method, retrieving queue information, to the class:

```
public void GetQueueInformation(String queueName)
{
    QueueDescription queue =
        manager.GetQueue(queueName);

    long messageCount = queue.MessageCount;
    MessageCountDetails details = queue.MessageCountDetails;
    var detail1 = details.ActiveMessageCount;
    var detail2 = details.DeadLetterMessageCount;
    var detail3 = details.ScheduledMessageCount;
    var detail4 = details.TransferDeadLetterMessageCount;
    var detail5 = details.TransferMessageCount;

    string metadata = queue.UserMetadata;
    bool ordering = queue.SupportOrdering;
    long size = queue.SizeInBytes;
    bool session = queue.RequiresSession;
    bool anonymous = queue.IsAnonymousAccessible;
    string forward = queue.ForwardTo;
    bool available = queue.AvailabilityStatus
        == EntityAvailabilityStatus.Available;
}
```

8. Add the following method, deleting the queue, to the class:

```
public void DeleteQueue(String queueName)
{
    if (manager.QueueExists(queueName))
    {
        manager.DeleteQueue(queueName);
    }
}
```

9. Add the following method, using the methods added earlier, to the class:

```
public static void UseCreateQueueExample()
{
    String queueName = "{QUEUE_NAME}";
    ManageServiceBusQueueExample example
        = new ManageServiceBusQueueExample();
    example.CreateQueue(queueName);
    example.GetQueueInformation(queueName);
    example.DeleteQueue(queueName);
}
```

How it works...

In steps 1 through 3, we set up the class. In step 4, we added a `private` member to store the `NamespaceManager` object used to connect to the Service Bus. We initialized this in the constructor we added in step 5.

In step 6, we added a method that creates a `QueueDescription` object and uses it to create a queue. We first checked the queue existence through the `NamespaceManager` object and then customized the queue properties before creating it, as shown in step 6. Note the following points to customize the queue:

- We specify that after 14 days in the queue, a message should be marked as expired. We also tell the queue that expired messages should be placed into the `dead letter` queue.
- We specify that Service Bus should check for duplicates in the queue. The control of duplicate messages is performed by checking the `MessageId` of a given message against a history maintained by the Service Bus for a period specified in the `DuplicateDetectionHistoryTimeWindows` property.
- We specify that when picking a message from the queue, it should remain locked for a period of 30 seconds (default is 1 minute and maximum 5 minutes). After that, if the message has not been completed, it becomes available to the receivers again.
- We specify that after a message is delivered to a client 10 times, it is considered dead in order to prevent the poison message problem.

In step 7, we added a method that retrieves information about the queue into a `QueueDescription` instance and uses it to retrieve the message count of the queue. Thus, we dig into the various counting details about the queue. Finally, we checked the following:

- The `UserMetadata` info (`null` by default)
- Whether the queue supports ordering (`true` by default)
- The total current size of the queue in bytes
- Whether the queue supports sessions (`false` by default)
- Whether the queue supports anonymous access (`false` by default)
- The second queue to whom the current queue should forward the messages received (`null` by default)
- The availability status of the queue (it differs from `available` in the case of transient errors)

In step 8, we added a method that retrieves information about the queue into a `QueueDescription` instance and uses it to delete the queue.

In step 9, we added a method that invokes the methods we added earlier. We need to replace `{QUEUE_NAME}` with an appropriate name for a queue.

The queue names for Service Bus queue have less restrictive rules compared to the rules for naming Storage queues. They can contain up to 260 characters and some special characters too (periods, numbers, hyphens, and underscores).

There's more...

We can use `NamespaceManager` to list the current queues in the Service Bus endpoint. To get that list, we can proceed as follows:

```
public IEnumerable<QueueDescription> GetQueues()
{
    return manager.GetQueues().ToArray();
}
```

In the `GetQueues()` method, an optional string could be passed to filter the queues result by a prefix.

See also

Have a look at the following MSDN links to get additional information:

▶ Learn more about Azure Access Control Service at `http://azure.microsoft.com/en-us/documentation/articles/active-directory-dotnet-how-to-use-access-control/`

▶ Learn more about the best practices for using Service Bus messaging at `http://msdn.microsoft.com/en-us/library/hh545245.aspx`

Adding messages to a Storage queue

The `CloudQueue` class in the Azure Storage library provides both synchronous and asynchronous methods to add a message to a queue. A message comprises up to 64 KB bytes of data (48 KB if encoded in Base64). By default, the Storage library Base64 encodes message content to ensure that the request payload containing the message is valid XML. This encoding adds overhead that reduces the actual maximum size of a message.

A message for a queue should not be intended to transport a big payload, since the purpose of a queue is just messaging and not storing. If required, a user can store the payload in a blob and use a queue message to point to that, letting the receiver fetch the message along with the blob from its remote location.

Each message added to a queue has a time-to-live property, after which it is deleted automatically. The maximum and default time-to-live value is 7 days.

In this recipe, we'll learn how to add messages to a queue.

Getting ready

This recipe assumes the following code is in the application configuration file:

```
<appSettings>
  <add key="DataConnectionString"
value="DefaultEndpointsProtocol=https;AccountName={ACCOUNT_
NAME};AccountKey={ACCOUNT_KEY}"/>
</appSettings>
```

We must replace {ACCOUNT_NAME} and {ACCOUNT_KEY} with appropriate values of the account name and access key.

How to do it...

We are going to create a queue and add some messages to it. We do this as follows:

1. Add a new class named `AddMessagesOnStorageExample` to the project.

2. Install the `WindowsAzure.Storage` NuGet package and add the following assembly references to the project:

   ```
   System.Configuration
   ```

3. Add the following `using` statements to the top of the class file:

   ```
   using Microsoft.WindowsAzure.Storage;
   using Microsoft.WindowsAzure.Storage.Queue;
   using System.Configuration;
   ```

4. Add the following `private` member to the class:

   ```
   private CloudQueue cloudQueueClient;
   ```

5. Add the following constructor to the class:

   ```
   public AddMessagesOnStorageExample(String queueName)
   {
       CloudStorageAccount cloudStorageAccount =
           CloudStorageAccount.Parse(
           ConfigurationManager.AppSettings[
           "DataConnectionString"]);
       CloudQueueClient cloudQueueClient =
           cloudStorageAccount.CreateCloudQueueClient();
       cloudQueue = cloudQueueClient.GetQueueReference(queueName);
       cloudQueue.CreateIfNotExists();
   }
   ```

6. Add the following method to the class, adding two messages:

```
public void AddMessages()
{
    String content1 = "Do something";
    CloudQueueMessage message1 = new CloudQueueMessage(content1);
    cloudQueue.AddMessage(message1);

    String content2 = "Do something that expires in 1 day";
    CloudQueueMessage message2 = new CloudQueueMessage(content2);
    cloudQueue.AddMessage(message2, TimeSpan.FromDays(1.0));

    String content3 = "Do something that expires in 2 hours,"+
        " starting in 1 hour from now";
    CloudQueueMessage message3 = new CloudQueueMessage(content3);
    cloudQueue.AddMessage(message2,
        TimeSpan.FromHours(2),TimeSpan.FromHours(1));
}
```

7. Add the following method, that uses the `AddMessage()` method, to the class:

```
public static void UseAddMessagesExample()
{
    String queueName = "{QUEUE_NAME}";
    AddMessagesOnStorageExample example = new
AddMessagesOnStorageExample (queueName);
    example.AddMessages();
}
```

How it works...

In steps 1 through 3, we set up the class. In step 4, we added a private member to store the `CloudQueue` object used to interact with the Queue service. We initialized this in the constructor we added in step 5 where we also created the queue.

In step 6, we added a method that adds three messages to a queue. We created three `CloudQueueMessage` objects. We added the first message to the queue with the default time-to-live of seven days, the second is added specifying an expiration of 1 day, and the third will become visible after 1 hour since its entrance in the queue, with an absolute expiration of 2 hours.

Note that a client (library) exception is thrown if we specify a visibility delay higher than the absolute TTL of the message. This is naturally obvious and it is enforced at the client side, instead making a (failing) server call.

In step 7, we added a method that invokes the methods we added earlier. We need to replace {QUEUE_NAME} with an appropriate name for a queue.

There's more...

To clear the queue from the messages we added in this recipe, we can proceed by calling the Clear() method in the CloudQueue class as follows:

```
public void ClearQueue()
{
    cloudQueue.Clear();
}
```

See also

Have a look at the following MSDN links to get additional information:

- Best practices to maximize scalability using queues at http://msdn.microsoft. com/en-us/library/azure/hh697709.aspx
- Guidance for resilient cloud architectures at http://msdn.microsoft.com/en- us/library/azure/jj853352.aspx

Adding messages to a Service Bus queue

In the chapter introduction, there is a comprehensive comparison between Service Bus queues and Storage queues. However, from the producer's perspective (which is the purpose of this recipe), we must keep in mind the following constraints:

- The total message must be maximum 256 KB (quadruple of the Storage service)
- The total queue size is up to 5 GB (significantly smaller than the Storage service)
- In the case of TCP communication, there is a cap on the concurrent connections (currently the value is 100)

We are comparing the two platforms by pursuing the same goals; the Service Bus queue adds more advanced features that the Storage service does not implement.

In this recipe, we'll learn how to add messages to a Service Bus queue.

Getting ready

This recipe assumes the following code is in the application configuration file:

```
<appSettings>
  <add key="ServiceBusConnectionString"
       value="Endpoint=sb://[your namespace].servicebus.windows.net;S
haredSecretIssuer=owner;SharedSecretValue=[your secret]" />
</appSettings>
```

We must replace [your namespace] and [your secret] with appropriate values of the namespace name and owner access key.

How to do it...

We are going to attach to a queue, adding some messages. The steps are as follows:

1. Add a new class named AddMessagesOnServiceBusExample to the project.

2. Install the WindowsAzure.ServiceBus NuGet package and add the following assembly references to the project:

   ```
   System.Configuration
   System.Transactions
   ```

3. Add the following using statements to the top of the class:

   ```
   using Microsoft.ServiceBus;
   using Microsoft.ServiceBus.Messaging;
   using System.Configuration;
   using System.Transactions;
   ```

4. Add the following private members to the class:

   ```
   private NamespaceManager manager;
   private MessagingFactory factory;
   ```

5. Add the following constructor to the class:

   ```
   public AddMessagesOnServiceBusExample(string queueName)
   {
       var conn = ConfigurationManager
           .AppSettings["ServiceBusConnectionString"];
       manager = NamespaceManager.CreateFromConnectionString(conn);
       if (!manager.QueueExists(queueName))
       {
   ```

```
        var descr = new QueueDescription(queueName);
        descr.RequiresDuplicateDetection = true;
        manager.CreateQueue(descr);
    }
    factory = MessagingFactory.CreateFromConnectionString(conn);
}
```

6. Add the following method to the class to add messages to the queue:

```
public void AddMessages(string queueName)
{
    MessageSender sender = factory.CreateMessageSender(queueName);
    String content1 = "Do something";
    BrokeredMessage message1 =new BrokeredMessage(content1);
    sender.Send(message1);
    String content2 = "Do something that expires in 1 day";
    BrokeredMessage message2 = new BrokeredMessage(content2)
    {
        TimeToLive=TimeSpan.FromDays(1)
    };
    sender.Send(message2);
    String content3 = "Do something that expires in 2 hours," +
        " starting in 1 hour from now";
    BrokeredMessage message3 = new BrokeredMessage(content3)
    {
        TimeToLive = TimeSpan.FromHours(2),
        ScheduledEnqueueTimeUtc=DateTime.UtcNow.AddHours(1)
    };
    sender.Send(message3);
}
```

7. Add the following method, using the methods added earlier, to the class:

```
public static void UseAddMessagesExample()
{
    String queueName = "{QUEUE_NAME}";
    AddMessagesOnServiceBusExample example
        = new AddMessagesOnServiceBusExample(queueName);
    example.AddMessages(queueName);
}
```

How it works...

In steps 1 through 3, we set up the class. In step 4, we added two private members to the store, the `NamespaceManager` object used to connect to the Service Bus and the `MessagingFactory` object to create the `MessageSender` instance, respectively. We initialized this in the constructor that we added in step 5.

> The namespace points to `System.Transactions`, which is not used in these steps of the recipe. As for the `descr.RequiresDuplicateDetection = true;` statement, it will be useful when we discuss transaction and duplicate detection in the *There's more...* section for further details.

In step 6, we added some messages with different options. We started by creating a `MessageSender` instance, and then we instantiated three `BrokeredMessage` objects and send them to the queue. As we saw in the previous recipe, the three messages have the following different properties:

- **First**: This is instantly visible in the queue with infinite TTL
- **Second**: This is instantly visible in the queue with a TTL of 1 day
- **Third**: This is visible in the queue only after 1 hour, and expires in 2 hours

> Where do *expired messages* go? During the queue creation, we can provide the `descr.EnableDeadLetteringOnMessageExpiration = true;` flag that instructs the Service Bus to move expired messages into a special queue called the dead letter queue.

In step 7, we added a method that invokes the method we added earlier. We need to replace `{QUEUE_NAME}` with an appropriate name for a queue.

There's more...

Service Bus SDK integrates with the Transactions API to provide developers with a simple way to handle multiple Service Bus operations within the same transaction boundaries. A revised version of the `AddMessages()` method is provided here, using a `TransactionScope` method to write all or nothing. Refer to the following code:

```
public void AddMessagesWithTransaction(string queueName)
{
    MessageSender sender = factory.CreateMessageSender(queueName);
    using (var scope = new TransactionScope())
    {
```

```
       String content1 = "Do something";
       BrokeredMessage message1 = new BrokeredMessage(content1);
       sender.Send(message1);
       String content2 = "Do something else";
       BrokeredMessage message2 = new BrokeredMessage(content2);
       sender.Send(message2);
       scope.Complete();
    }
  }
```

We call `Complete()` to commit the two operations in a single transaction.

Detecting duplicates

A common problem in messaging solutions is to identify duplicated messages in order to avoid reprocessing of already-processed items. Actually, a good software solution should guarantee idempotency by design, but since it is not always actionable, any help provided by the technology is definitely not bad. To add some duplicate messages, proceed as follows:

```
public void AddDuplicateMessages(string queueName)
{
    MessageSender sender = factory.CreateMessageSender(queueName);
    String content1 = "Do something";
    BrokeredMessage message1 = new BrokeredMessage(content1)
    { MessageId = "MSG01" };
    sender.Send(message1);
    String content2 = "Do something else";
    BrokeredMessage message2 = new BrokeredMessage(content2)
    { MessageId = "MSG01" };
    sender.Send(message2);
}
```

Thanks to the creation flag of the queue (`descr.RequiresDuplicateDetection = true;`), it now automatically detects and deletes duplicates in the default timeframe (10 minutes) by looking at the `MessageId` property.

To troubleshoot and test more efficiently the Service Bus, we use the Service Bus Explorer. You can download it from `http://code.msdn.microsoft.com/windowsazure/Service-Bus-Explorer-f2abca5a`.

See also

Have a look at the following MSDN links to get additional information:

▶ Brokered messaging tutorial with Service Bus at `http://msdn.microsoft.com/en-us/library/hh367512.aspx`

▶ Learn more about the best practices for performance using the Service Bus at `http://msdn.microsoft.com/en-us/library/hh528527.aspx`

Receiving messages with Storage queues

The `CloudQueue` class in the Azure Storage library provides both synchronous and asynchronous methods to retrieve messages from a queue. The `GetMessage()` method retrieves a message from a queue while the `GetMessages()` method retrieves up to 32 messages at a time. The `GetMessages()` method reduces the number of storage operations used to access a queue and can improve scalability of an Azure cloud service.

Messages retrieved in this way have a visibility timeout during which they cannot be retrieved by additional calls to the Azure Queue service. The maximum visibility timeout for a message is 7 days and the default is 30 seconds. This visibility timeout enhances the durability of a hosted service. If a consumer fails while processing a message, the expiration of the visibility timeout causes the message to be visible once again on the queue from which another consumer can retrieve it.

One consequence of the visibility timeout is that if a consumer fails to process a message before the visibility timeout expires, another consumer may retrieve the message and start processing it. This can cause problems if message processing is not idempotent, that is, the same result arises whenever a message is processed.

The Queue service also uses optimistic concurrency to manage message deletion. When a message is retrieved, it includes a pop receipt that must be provided to delete the message from the queue. Even after the visibility timeout expires, the pop receipt remains valid until the message is next retrieved from the queue. In the Azure Storage Client library, the `CloudQueue.DeleteMessage()` method is used to delete messages.

The Queue service supports the concept of peeking at a message. This allows a consumer to retrieve a message while leaving it visible to other consumers of the queue. Consequently, a consumer can retrieve and delete a message that another consumer is peeking at. The Queue service does not generate a pop receipt when a message is peeked at, so the consumer peeking at the message is unable to delete it from the queue. The Storage Client library has the `PeekMessage()` and `PeekMessages()` methods in the `CloudQueue` class. These mimic the functionality of the equivalent `GetMessage()` and `GetMessages()` methods.

In this recipe, we'll learn how to retrieve messages from a queue.

Getting ready

This recipe assumes the following code is in the application configuration file:

```
<appSettings>
  <add key="DataConnectionString"
value="DefaultEndpointsProtocol=https;AccountName={ACCOUNT_
NAME};AccountKey={ACCOUNT_KEY}"/>
</appSettings>
```

We must replace {ACCOUNT_NAME} and {ACCOUNT_KEY} with appropriate values of the account name and access key.

How to do it...

We are going to add some messages to a queue. We do this as follows:

1. Add a new class named `GetMessagesFromStorageExample` to the project.

2. Install the `WindowsAzure.Storage` NuGet package and add the following assembly references to the project:

   ```
   System.Configuration
   ```

3. Add the following `using` statements to the top of the class file:

   ```
   using Microsoft.WindowsAzure.Storage;
   using Microsoft.WindowsAzure.Storage.Queue;
   using System.Configuration;
   ```

4. Add the following `private` member to the class:

   ```
   private CloudQueue cloudQueueClient;
   ```

5. Add the following constructor to the class:

   ```
   public GetMessagesFromStorageExample(String queueName)
   {
     CloudStorageAccount cloudStorageAccount =
         CloudStorageAccount.Parse(
         ConfigurationManager.AppSettings[
         "DataConnectionString"]);
     CloudQueueClient cloudQueueClient =
         cloudStorageAccount.CreateCloudQueueClient();
     cloudQueue = cloudQueueClient.GetQueueReference(queueName);
   }
   ```

6. Add the following method to the class to set up the recipe:

```
public void SetupRecipe()
{
  cloudQueue.CreateIfNotExists();
  for (Int32 i = 0; i < 100; i++)
  {
    String content = String.Format("Message_{0}", i);
CloudQueueMessage message = new CloudQueueMessage(content);
    cloudQueue.AddMessage(message);
  }
}
```

7. Add the following method, retrieving a message, to the class:

```
public void GetMessage()
{
  CloudQueueMessage cloudQueueMessage =
      cloudQueue.GetMessage();
  if (cloudQueueMessage != null)
  {
    String messageText = cloudQueueMessage.AsString;
    // use message
    cloudQueue.DeleteMessage(cloudQueueMessage);
  }
}
```

8. Add the following method to the class to peek at a message:

```
public void PeekMessage()
{
  CloudQueueMessage cloudQueueMessage =
      cloudQueue.PeekMessage();
}
```

9. Add the following method, retrieving 20 messages, to the class:

```
public void GetMessages()
{
  IEnumerable<CloudQueueMessage> cloudQueueMessages =
      cloudQueue.GetMessages(20);
  foreach (CloudQueueMessage message in cloudQueueMessages)
  {
    String messageText = message.AsString;
    // use message
    cloudQueue.DeleteMessage(message);
  }
}
```

10. Add the following method, using the methods added earlier, to the class:

```
public static void UseGetMessagesExample()
{
    String queueName = "{QUEUE_NAME}";
    GetMessagesFromStorageExample example =
        new GetMessagesFromStorageExample(queueName);
      example.SetupRecipe();
    example.GetMessage();
    example.PeekMessage();
    example.GetMessages();
}
```

How it works...

In steps 1 through 3, we set up the class. In step 4, we added a `private` member to store the `CloudQueue` object used to interact with the queue. We initialized this in the constructor we added in step 5. In step 6, we added a method to set up the recipe by creating a queue and adding 100 messages to it.

In step 7, we added a `GetMessage()` method that requests a message from the queue. If a message is retrieved, we get its content as a string, use the message, and finally delete it. In step 8, we added a method that peeks at a message. In this case, we can't delete the message because `PeekMessage()` does not retrieve the pop receipt for the message. In step 9, we added a method that retrieves up to 20 messages, processes them, and then deletes them.

In step 10, we added a method that uses the other methods in the class.

There's more...

When using an Azure Storage queue to drive processing, the simplest technique for a consumer is to poll the queue and initiate processing when it retrieves a message. This works well when the queue contains messages. However, when the queue is empty for an extended period, it can lead to unnecessary storage operations.

The Queue service, at the time of writing, has a scalability target of 2,000 messages per second, which corresponds to 7.2 million messages per hour. At the standard current billing rate for storage operations ($0.005/100 K operations), this amounts to $0.36 per hour which is (although minimal) useless. Consequently, when the queue is empty, it may be worth implementing a strategy to throttle the polling of the queue.

The basic idea is that once a consumer finds the queue to be empty, it should introduce a wait interval between successive polls of the queue. This reduces the polling frequency. If the queue remains empty, it could also further increase the wait interval. The consumer should not increase the wait interval to a level where there would be a significant delay when messages are added to the queue. The consumer can reset the wait interval when it retrieves a message from the queue as follows:

```
public void GetMessagesPerpetually()
{
    while (true)
    {
        var message = cloudQueue.GetMessage();
        if (message == null) Thread.Sleep(1000);
        else cloudQueue.DeleteMessage(message);
    }
}
```

In the preceding code, we perpetually check for new messages on the queue, waiting for a fixed time of 1 second if the queue doesn't contain any new message. As mentioned previously, an incremental waiting time could be considered as well. However, due to the really low costs of this solution (0.00018$/hour), it could be good for many scenarios.

Poison messages

The standard way to use an Azure Storage queue is to retrieve a message, perform some processing based on the message, and then delete the message from the queue. A problem arises if the content of the message causes an error during processing that prevents the consumer from deleting the message from the queue. When the message once again becomes visible on the queue, another consumer will retrieve it and the failure process begins again. Such a message is referred to as a poison message because it poisons the queue and prevents messages in it from being processed. When there is only a single consumer, a poison message can completely block processing of the queue.

A poison message has to be identified, removed from the queue, and logged for subsequent investigation. A convenient way to log the poison message is to insert it in a poison message queue where it is not processed in a way that causes problems. When a consumer requests a message, the Queue service provides a dequeue count that specifies the number of times the message has been dequeued. If this count exceeds some application-specific value, the message can be identified as a poison message and diverted into poison message handling. The Azure Storage library exposes the dequeue count as `CloudQueueMessage.DequeueCount` as follows:

```
if (message.DequeueCount > 10)
{
    //Handle Poison message
}
```

See also

Have a look at the following MSDN link to get additional information:

▶ The Queue Service REST API reference at `http://msdn.microsoft.com/en-us/library/azure/dd179363.aspx`

Receiving messages with Service Bus queues

Service Bus is the fully-featured service for companies that are looking for a robust and scalable solution of messaging and integrating disconnected and heterogeneous systems. In the *Managing Azure Service Bus queues* recipe, we saw how to create a queue in a specific namespace and we saw how to add messages into it in the *Adding Messages to a Service Bus queue* recipe.

The most important entity that represents a message travelling in the queue is the `BrokeredMessage` class. Each message on the queue is represented by this object model that wraps a large set of message-specific properties such as user-defined properties and, of course, content. The body content could be everything that is compatible with `DataContractSerializer`, while `Properties` is a key-value collection of user-defined properties; it is probably the most interesting feature of the entire Service Bus. In fact, a `BrokeredMessage` property could be used for the following purposes:

▶ To deliver the payload of the message, instead of using the body

▶ To define metadata that is useful for clients who want to conditionally process an incoming message

▶ To define filters that are useful to route messages at a subscription level (we see what a subscription is in the *Implementing publish/subscribe with Service Bus topics* recipe)

A `BrokeredMessage` instance also contains the methods to manage the lifecycle of the message itself. When the client completes processing the message, it should call the `Complete()` method to remove the message from the queue; if not, the message becomes available again to the queue for reprocessing after a lock period. If the client knows in advance that it cannot process the message correctly, it should call the `Abandon()` method to avoid the waiting time of the lock period.

There are several differences between a message handled by the Service Bus and ones handled by the Storage service, as mentioned in the chapter introduction. By the way, `MessageReceiver` is a useful class while dealing with receiving messages or while wrapping the `Receive()` method to receive a message or the `ReceiveBatch()` method to receive multiple messages.

Getting ready

This recipe assumes the following code is in the application configuration file:

```
<appSettings>
  <add key="ServiceBusConnectionString"
       value="Endpoint=sb://[your namespace].servicebus.windows.net;S
haredSecretIssuer=owner;SharedSecretValue=[your secret]" />
</appSettings>
```

We must replace [your namespace] and [your secret] with appropriate values of the namespace name and owner access key.

How to do it...

We are going to attach to a queue, adding some messages. The steps are as follows:

1. Add a new class named GetMessagesFromServiceBusExample to the project.

2. Install the WindowsAzure.ServiceBus NuGet package and add the following assembly references to the project:

    ```
    System.Configuration
    ```

3. Add the following using statements to the top of the class:

    ```
    using Microsoft.ServiceBus;
    using Microsoft.ServiceBus.Messaging;
    using System.Configuration;
    ```

4. Add the following private members to the class:

    ```
    private NamespaceManager manager;
    private MessagingFactory factory;
    ```

5. Add the following constructor to the class:

    ```
    public GetMessagesFromServiceBusExample(string queueName)
    {
        var conn = ConfigurationManager
            .AppSettings["ServiceBusConnectionString"];
        manager = NamespaceManager.CreateFromConnectionString(conn);
        if (!manager.QueueExists(queueName))
        {
            var descr = new QueueDescription(queueName);
            descr.RequiresDuplicateDetection = true;
            manager.CreateQueue(descr);
        }
        factory = MessagingFactory.CreateFromConnectionString(conn);
    }
    ```

6. Add the following method to the class to retrieve a message:

```
public void GetMessage(string queueName)
{
    MessageReceiver receiver =
        factory.CreateMessageReceiver(queueName);
    BrokeredMessage message = receiver.Receive();
    if (message!=null)
    {
        string messageText = message.GetBody<string>();
        message.Complete();
    }
    receiver.Close();
}
```

7. Add the following method to the class to peek at a message:

```
public void PeekMessage(string queueName)
{
    MessageReceiver receiver = factory.CreateMessageReceiver(queue
Name);
    BrokeredMessage message = receiver.Peek();
    receiver.Close();
}
```

8. Add the following method to the class to retrieve 20 messages:

```
public void GetMessages(string queueName)
{
    MessageReceiver receiver = factory.CreateMessageReceiver(queue
Name);
    IEnumerable<BrokeredMessage> messages = receiver.
ReceiveBatch(20);
    foreach (var message in messages)
    {
        string messageText = message.GetBody<string>();
        message.Complete();
    }
    receiver.Close();
}
```

9. Add the following method, using the methods added earlier, to the class:

```
public static void UseGetMessagesExample()
{
    String queueName = "{QUEUE_NAME}";
    GetMessagesFromServiceBusExample example =
        new GetMessagesFromServiceBusExample(queueName);
    example.GetMessage(queueName);
    example.PeekMessage(queueName);
    example.GetMessages(queueName);
}
```

How it works...

In steps 1 through 3, we set up the class. In step 4, we added two private members to the store, the `NamespaceManager` object used to connect to the Service Bus and the `MessagingFactory` object to create the `MessageReceiver` instance, respectively. We initialized this in the constructor we add in step 5.

In step 6, we added a method to retrieve a single message from the queue. Actually, the runtime stops at the `Receive()` method until a server timeout has reached. This is blocking the receive behavior, which is different from the Storage service that returns immediately even if no messages are found. After reading the body content of the message, we call `Complete()` to definitely remove it from the queue. Please note that the body of a message could be an arbitrary object, so the `GetBody<T>()` method could end up as an exception.

In step 7 we peeked into a message, that is, we are reading from the top element without locking it—usually for testing purposes only. In step 8, we asked the receiver to fetch up to 20 messages at a time and we eventually cycle over them.

In step 9, we added a method that invokes the method we added earlier. We need to replace `{QUEUE_NAME}` with an appropriate name for a queue.

There's more...

The Service Bus SDK provides a wide variety of features to better deal with queues and messages. One of them is the ability to create an event-based message receive, instead of using a polling pattern:

```
public void EventBasedReceiver(string queueName)
{
    QueueClient client=factory.CreateQueueClient(queueName);
    var options = new OnMessageOptions()
    {
      AutoComplete=true,
      MaxConcurrentCalls=1
    };
    options.ExceptionReceived += (sender, args) =>
    {
        var ex = args.Exception;
    };
    client.OnMessage(message =>
    {
        //Process message
    }, options);
    Thread.Sleep(10000);
    client.Close();
}
```

In the preceding lines, we used the `QueueClient` class instead of the `MessageReceiver` class. For the purpose of this example, the two classes are equal, exposing both the `OnMessage()` methods. However, the `QueueClient` class is a generic implementation for both receivers and senders, offering the union of the respective methods to read/write a queue. In the event-based example, we pass a lambda to the `OnMessage()` method with a `OnMessageOptions` instance, providing an exception handler and some delivery properties such as the maximum number of concurrent receiving threads as for the auto complete behavior for delivered messages. Finally, we forced the main thread to sleep, for testing purposes only (the `OnMessage` method is callback based), or it would end immediately.

Dead lettering

The dead letter queue is the hidden queue associated to a plain queue, intended for those messages that have related issues. For instance, a poison message should go out from a main queue and could probably go into the dead letter one (in the *Receiving messages with Storage queues* recipe, we explained the concept of poison messages better). Also, an expired message could go into the dead letter queue. This is done automatically if we specify the flag on queue creation as follows:

```
queueDescription.EnableDeadLetteringOnMessageExpiration = true;
```

The process to move, automatically or not, a message into the dead letter queue is often known as **dead lettering**.

In the example below, we dead letter a message that has been processed more than 10 times (because probably it is a poison message) as follows:

```
public void GetMessagesUntilCancellation
    (string queueName,CancellationToken token)
{
    MessageReceiver receiver =
        factory.CreateMessageReceiver(queueName);
    while (!token.IsCancellationRequested)
    {
        var message = receiver.Receive();
        if (message.DeliveryCount > 10) message.DeadLetter();
        else
        {
            message.Complete();
        }
    }
    receiver.Close();
}
```

We also used the cancellation pattern to stop the receiver between a receive operation and the next one. Please note that the default timeout is 60 seconds, so this is the time a client could take to realize that it should cancel.

However, how can a client read from the dead letter queue? The answer is *exactly as it was done for a standard queue*, changing only the queue name/path as follows:

```
public void ReadFromDeadLetter(string queueName)
{
    var receiver=factory.CreateMessageReceiver(
        QueueClient.FormatDeadLetterPath(queueName));
    BrokeredMessage message=null;
    while ((message = receiver.Receive(TimeSpan.FromSeconds(1)))
        !=null)
    {
        message.Complete();
    }
}
```

The static `QueueClient.FormatDeadLetterPath()` method simply appends the conventional name of the dead letter queue to the standard queue. The remaining code is equal to the examples in the recipe.

See also

Have a look at the following MSDN link to get additional information:

▸ Service Bus samples at `http://msdn.microsoft.com/en-us/library/azure/dn194201.aspx`

Implementing publish/subscribe with Service Bus topics

Messaging systems are implemented in hundreds of different technologies, but often they implement mainly two patterns: queue-based and publish/subscribe. The first, which is the main character of this chapter, stands on the concept of a single queue in which someone (one or many) sends a message and someone (and only one) receives the message to process and delete it.

Queue-based messaging is often implemented with a **FIFO** (**First-In-First-Out**) pattern and sometimes ordering is guaranteed (for example, in the Service Bus). On the other hand, there is the publish/subscribe messaging pattern that is the key component in many interconnected enterprise systems, known in the Service Bus as the Topic service.

In this pattern, a topic is created (like a queue) to make the messages go through, differently from a queue; along with the topic one or many subscriptions must be created. As Subscription tells which messages are of interest for it, based on some filtering rules that are applied declaratively on subscription creation. These rules are built upon the message metadata (`BrokeredMessage.Properties`), which the sender could customize to let the message be routed correctly.

The `SubscriptionDescription` instance defines the subscription name and the topic, along with a filter implementation, which checks against the actual message properties during reception. A SqlFilter is one implementation of the `Filter` base class, that provides developers with a familiar SQL92-like syntax to filter messages (for example, *Property > 10*).

In this recipe, we will see how to implement the publish/subscribe pattern with Service Bus topics and how to create filtered subscriptions.

Getting ready

This recipe assumes the following code is in the application's configuration file:

```
<appSettings>
  <add key="ServiceBusConnectionString"
        value="Endpoint=sb://[your namespace].servicebus.windows.net;S
haredSecretIssuer=owner;SharedSecretValue=[your secret]" />
</appSettings>
```

We must replace [your namespace] and [your secret] with appropriate values of the namespace name and owner access key.

How to do it...

We are going to create a new topic, a producer, and two different consumers. The first consumer will catch all messages of the topic and the second will catch only the flagged messages. We do this as follows:

1. Add a new class named `PublishAndSubscribeExample` to the project.

2. Install the `WindowsAzure.ServiceBus` NuGet package and add the following assembly references to the project:

    ```
    System.Configuration
    ```

3. Add the following `using` statements to the top of the class:

    ```
    using Microsoft.ServiceBus;
    using Microsoft.ServiceBus.Messaging;
    using System.Configuration;
    using System.Threading;
    using System.Threading.Tasks;
    ```

4. Add the following `private` members to the class:

    ```
    private NamespaceManager manager;
    private MessagingFactory factory;
    ```

5. Add the following constructor to the class:

```
public PublishAndSubscribeExample(string topicName)
{
    var conn = ConfigurationManager
        .AppSettings["ServiceBusConnectionString"];
    manager = NamespaceManager.CreateFromConnectionString(conn);
    if (!manager.TopicExists(topicName))
    {
        var descr = new TopicDescription(topicName);
        manager.CreateTopic(descr);
        var sub1 = new SubscriptionDescription(topicName, "all");
        manager.CreateSubscription(sub1);
        var sub2 = new SubscriptionDescription(
            topicName, "flagged");
        manager.CreateSubscription(sub2,
            new SqlFilter("flagged=true"));
    }
    factory = MessagingFactory.CreateFromConnectionString(conn);
}
```

6. Add the following method that produces messages to the class:

```
public void ProduceOnTopic(string topicName)
{
    TopicClient producer = factory.CreateTopicClient(topicName);
    for (int i = 0; i < 10; i++)
    {
        bool flag = i % 2 == 0;
        BrokeredMessage msg = new BrokeredMessage();
        msg.Properties.Add("flagged", flag);
        producer.Send(msg);
    }
}
```

7. Add the following method to the class in order to consume (perpetually) messages of a given topic and on a given subscription:

```
public void ListenForNotifications(
    string topicName,string name)
{
    SubscriptionClient listener = factory.
CreateSubscriptionClient(
        topicName, name, ReceiveMode.ReceiveAndDelete);
    while (true)
    {
        var message = listener.Receive();
    }
}
```

8. Add this method, calling the methods created before, to the class:

```
public static void UseGetMessagesExample()
{
    String topicName = "{TOPIC_NAME}";
    PublishAndSubscribeExample example =
        new PublishAndSubscribeExample(topicName);
    var consumer1 = Task.Factory.StartNew(() =>
    {
        example.ListenForNotifications(topicName, "all");
    });
    var consumer2 = Task.Factory.StartNew(() =>
    {
        example.ListenForNotifications(topicName, "flagged");
    });

    var producer = Task.Factory.StartNew(() =>
    {
        example.ProduceOnTopic(topicName);
    });
    consumer2.Wait();
}
```

How it works...

In steps 1 through 3, we set up the class. In step 4, we added two `private` members to store—the `NamespaceManager` object is used to connect to the Service Bus and the `MessagingFactory` object is used to create the `MessageReceiver` instance. We initialized this in the constructor we added in step 5. In step 5, together with the creation of the `Topic` instance itself, we also created two different subscriptions: one for all messages, with no filter rules applied, and one for the *flagged* messages (the messages with a property `flagged` set to `true`, as stated in the `SqlFilter` instance).

In step 6, we added a method to produce messages on a given topic, putting 10 messages—5 of them `flagged` and 5 of them `unflagged`. In step 7, we defined a generic method that could listen on a particular topic and subscription, retrieving the message to perform some action. The `ReceiveMode.ReceiveAndDelete` object tells the SDK to perform an automatic `Complete` after receiving the message (an explicit call to the `Complete()` method raises an `Exception`). This is opposed to the standard `PeekAndLock` method.

In step 8, we added a method that invokes the method we added earlier. We used tasks to start three parallel jobs, one to produce messages and two to consume (or better, to listen to) them. The latter (`consumer2`) will be notified only by the `flagged` messages. We need to replace `{TOPIC_NAME}` with an appropriate name for a queue.

See also

Have a look at these MSDN links to get additional information:

▸ The Service Bus topics documentation at `http://azure.microsoft.com/en-en/documentation/articles/service-bus-dotnet-how-to-use-topics-subscriptions/`

▸ Comparison of queues and topics at `http://msdn.microsoft.com/en-us/library/hh367516.aspx`

Implementing relayed messaging with the Service Bus

When talking about Service Bus, or **Enterprise Service Bus** (**ESB**), we are often talking about integrating heterogeneous systems and decoupling them through a middleware. Azure Service Bus not only offers messaging services such as queues and topics, but also offers a **Relay** service that provides a bridge between non-Azure services and the Azure infrastructure. The Relay service is sometimes referred as the service to integrate on premises solutions with the cloud but it is suitable for integrating different clouds too.

A Relay service consists of a public endpoint, available in the URI form `[name].servicebus.windows.net` bound to a private endpoint and hosted somewhere. Since it is really hard to expose a private endpoint in the public Internet, the Relay service provides a bridge between those clients who are Internet faced to the hosted private services, for example, inside the private LAN of a company's datacenter.

To do that, the company's service should register itself onto the Service Bus Relay service, using WCF bindings; then, for each call to the public endpoint, Service Bus forwards the request to the bounded service. Since the latter initiated the communication first, there is no need to traverse the company firewall or NAT or to know the network topology.

WCF is a huge platform and going deep in it is completely out of the scope of this book. In this recipe, we see how to minimally implement a Relay service using a WCF endpoint that is hosted locally on a developer machine and is available globally through its public endpoint as well.

On the service side, `ServiceHost` is the class responsible for the self-hosting of WCF services, the `NetTcpBinding` class is responsible for the WCF binding listening of TCP, and the `NetTcpRelayBinding` class is the binding specific to the endpoints being forwarded.

From the consumer perspective, `ChannelFactory` is the proxy to the remote service, strongly-typed against the service interface. This simplifies the development phase, providing a transparent proxy to the remote methods exposed by the service.

In this recipe, we are going to create a service, bind it to the Service Bus, and call it from a consumer.

Getting ready

Since we configure WCF in the code, there is no need to set up the configuration file in the application.

How to do it...

We are going to create a new service interface along with its implementation. We bind it to the cloud and consume it locally. We do this as follows:

1. Add this interface to the project, defining the contract of the service:

```
[ServiceContract(Namespace = "urn:ts")]
interface ITimeService
{
    [OperationContract]
    DateTime UtcTime();
}
```

2. Add this interface to the project, defining the service channel for the proxy:

```
interface ITimeServiceChannel : ITimeService, IClientChannel { }
```

3. Add this service implementation to the project:

```
public class TimeService : ITimeService
{
    public DateTime UtcTime()
    {
        return DateTime.UtcNow;
    }
}
```

4. Add a new class named `RelayExample` to the project.

5. Install the `WindowsAzure.ServiceBus` NuGet package to the project.

6. Add the following `using` statements to the top of the class file:

```
using Microsoft.ServiceBus;
using System.Threading.Tasks;
```

7. Add this method to the class to start and bind the service to the Service Bus :

```
public void StartServiceHost(string ns,string key
    ,Action onChannelReady)
{
    ServiceHost sh = new ServiceHost(typeof(TimeService));
```

```
    sh.AddServiceEndpoint(
    typeof(ITimeService), new NetTcpBinding(),
    "net.tcp://localhost:9999/time");

    sh.AddServiceEndpoint(
    typeof(ITimeService), new NetTcpRelayBinding(),
    ServiceBusEnvironment.CreateServiceUri("sb", ns, "time"))
        .Behaviors.Add(new TransportClientEndpointBehavior
        {
            TokenProvider = TokenProvider.
CreateSharedSecretTokenProvider
            ("owner", key)
        });

    sh.Open();
    Console.WriteLine("Press ENTER to close");
    onChannelReady();
    Console.ReadLine();
    sh.Close();
}
```

8. Add this method to the class to connect and consume the service through its remote endpoint:

```
public void CallRelayService(string ns,string key)
{
    var cf = new ChannelFactory<ITimeServiceChannel>(
        new NetTcpRelayBinding(),
        new EndpointAddress(ServiceBusEnvironment.CreateServiceUri
            ("sb", ns, "time")));

    cf.Endpoint.Behaviors.Add(new TransportClientEndpointBehavior
        { TokenProvider = TokenProvider.
CreateSharedSecretTokenProvider
        ("owner", key)});

    using (var ch = cf.CreateChannel())
    {
        var res = ch.UtcTime();
    }
}
```

9. Add the following method, using the methods above, to the class:

```
public static void UseRelayExample()
{
    string ns="{NAMESPACE}";
    string ownerKey = "{KEY}";
    RelayExample example = new RelayExample();
    var serverAndClient = Task.Factory.StartNew(() =>
    {
        example.StartServiceHost(ns, ownerKey,
            ()=>example.CallRelayService(ns,ownerKey));
    });
    serverAndClient.Wait();
}
```

How it works...

In step 1, we prepared the service, writing its interface and decorating it with the `ServiceModel` attributes. In WCF, the `ServiceContract` attribute defines the contract for a service, while the `OperationContract` attribute defines that a method should be exposed through the service endpoint. In step 2, we prepared the service channel used by the client/consumer to invoke the service through a transparent proxy. In step 3, we finished preparing the service and implementing its interface with a simple method to get the current UTC time.

In step 4, we added the class containing our logic methods. In steps 5 and 6, we added the Service Bus reference from NuGet along with its `using` statements. Note that the previous code about WCF services is bundled in the .NET Framework and it does not depend on the Service Bus SDK. In step 7, we started the service host by binding the service implementation to a local endpoint and then to the public endpoint of the Service Bus, using the `TokenProvider` class to authenticate against it.

 This method uses a callback action `onChannelReady` to invoke a custom method after the binding completes. It is for demonstration purposes only.

In step 8, we added the consumer code, instantiating a channel based on the `ITimeService` interface and providing a transparent proxy to the client. After being authenticated by the Service Bus through its public endpoint, we called the `UtcTime()` method.

In step 9, we used the methods added before, using tasks to perform parallel operations. Note that the program is never exited (and replace the `{NAMESPACE}` and `{KEY}` strings with the appropriate values).

See also

Have a look at these MSDN links to get additional information:

- ▶ The Service Bus relayed messaging tutorial at `http://msdn.microsoft.com/en-us/library/ee706736.aspx`

- ▶ The Service Bus relayed messaging documentation at `http://msdn.microsoft.com/en-us/library/jj860549.aspx`

- ▶ Learn more about WCF bindings for Service Bus at `http://msdn.microsoft.com/en-us/library/hh410102.aspx`

Communication between .NET and Java with the Service Bus and AMQP

By default, the Service Bus SDK uses a .NET-friendly protocol to exchange messages, which is primarily supported by the Service Bus service. In the real world, however, enterprise systems are often built in different technologies, and it is not unusual that a receiver system could be developed in a completely different language/platform than the sender system.

This is why the market (and recently the OASIS organization) went to a common definition of a standard for messaging protocol, **Advanced Message Queuing Protocol** (**AMQP**). This protocol provides many benefits, from the absence of lock-in to full interoperability between heterogeneous systems.

Azure Service Bus implements the AMQP protocol. From the .NET perspective, using one or another is a configuration detail. It is only necessary to append this parameter to the existing connection string as follows:

```
TransportType=Amqp
```

It is irrelevant which protocol is used because the Service Bus will operate seamlessly in every case. However, from a Java application's point of view, it is easier to use the AMQP endpoint due to the large library support in the Java ecosystem.

Java Message Service (**JMS**) is the official Java API specification to operate against queues. In this recipe, we use the Apache AMQP Qpid library through the JMS contract to connect to the Service Bus and read messages.

Getting ready

This recipe uses Eclipse as Java Development IDE. The following steps fit Eclipse but they are very similar in other environments. To use Eclipse, download and install the latest version from `https://www.eclipse.org/downloads/`.

To run the example, it is strongly recommended to follow the *Adding Messages to a Service Bus queue* recipe to read the existing messages added with .NET, from the Java client.

How to do it...

We will connect to an existing queue to read messages with the AMQP protocol. The steps are as follows:

1. In Eclipse, go to **File | New | Other** then select **Maven Project**.

2. In the **New Maven Project** window, perform the following steps:

    1. Check the **Create a simple project** checkbox.

    2. Specify SBTests as **Group id**.

    3. Specify AMQPExample as **Artifact id**.

3. In the `root` folder of the project, add a text file named `servicebus.properties` and populate it as follows:

    ```
    connectionfactory.ServiceBus = amqps://owner:[key]@[ns].
    servicebus.windows.net
    queue.Name = [queue_name]
    ```

4. In the `pom.xml` file, add the following XML to declare the project dependencies:

    ```xml
    <dependencies>
      <dependency>
        <groupId>javax.jms</groupId>
        <artifactId>javax.jms-api</artifactId>
        <version>2.0</version>
      </dependency>
      <dependency>
        <groupId>org.apache.qpid</groupId>
        <artifactId>qpid-amqp-1-0-client-jms</artifactId>
        <version>0.26</version>
      </dependency>
    </dependencies>
    ```

5. In the `src/main/java` file, add a class named `AMQPExample.java`.

6. Add the following `imports` statements to the class:

```
import java.util.Hashtable;
import javax.jms.Connection;
import javax.jms.ConnectionFactory;
import javax.jms.Destination;
import javax.jms.JMSException;
import javax.jms.Message;
import javax.jms.MessageConsumer;
import javax.jms.MessageListener;
import javax.jms.Session;
import javax.naming.Context;
import javax.naming.InitialContext;
```

7. Add the following `main` method, to perform the entire sample:

```
public static void main(String[] args) throws Exception{
  Hashtable<String, String> env
  = new Hashtable<String, String>();
    env.put(Context.INITIAL_CONTEXT_FACTORY,
            "org.apache.qpid.amqp_1_0.jms"+
    ".jndi.PropertiesFileInitialContextFactory");
    env.put(Context.PROVIDER_URL, "servicebus.properties");
    Context context = new InitialContext(env);
    ConnectionFactory cf =
        (ConnectionFactory) context.lookup("ServiceBus");
    Destination queue = (Destination) context.lookup("Name");

    Connection connection = cf.createConnection();

    Session receiveSession = connection
        .createSession(false, Session.CLIENT_ACKNOWLEDGE);
    MessageConsumer receiver = receiveSession.
createConsumer(queue);
    receiver.setMessageListener(new MessageListener() {
    public void onMessage(Message arg0) {
      try {
```

```
        System.out.println(arg0.getJMSMessageID());
      } catch (JMSException e) {
        // TODO Auto-generated catch block
        e.printStackTrace();
      }
    }
  });
    connection.start();
    System.in.read();
    }
}
```

How it works...

In step 1 and 2, we set up the project and configure Maven (an open infrastructure to manage project lifecycle and dependencies). In step 3, we defined a custom properties files where the information about the Service Bus endpoint is located. We must replace the `[key]`, `[ns]`, and `[queue_name]` fields with the appropriate values. In step 4, we declared the dependencies in the Maven `pom.xml` file: the first is the specification, while the second is the implementation (they will be automatically downloaded during the build).

In step 6, we declared the classes that we are going to use in step 7, where we added the `main` method. In the `main` method, we initialized the JNDI/JMS context that looks into the `servicebus.properties` file. After creating the receiver through the `MessageConsumer` class, we registered a listener to handle incoming messages in the anonymous inner class pattern. In the `onMessage()` method, eventually, the MessageID is printed on the console.

See also

Have a look at these links to get additional information:

▸ AMQP on Wikipedia at `http://en.wikipedia.org/wiki/Advanced_Message_Queuing_Protocol`

▸ Apache implementation for AMQP at `http://activemq.apache.org/amqp.html`

▸ Official OASIS site for AMQP at `http://www.amqp.org/`

7

Managing Azure Resources with the Azure Management Libraries

In this chapter, we will cover the following topics:

- ▶ Setting up the management client
- ▶ Managing the Storage service
- ▶ Deploying Cloud Services
- ▶ Inspecting and managing Cloud Services
- ▶ Managing and using the Azure Scheduler
- ▶ Monitoring and automating infrastructure operations
- ▶ Automating the SQL Database operations
- ▶ Using Azure PowerShell

Introduction

The Microsoft Azure Portal provides a convenient and easy-to-use way of managing all the available services of an Azure subscription, as well as many configuration settings for each of these services. Microsoft also provides a REST API to access Azure resources in order to allow developers to build custom management clients or automation solutions.

The **Service Management API** provides almost complete control over the resources contained in a Microsoft Azure subscription. All operations using this API must be authenticated using an **X509** management certificate, which is generated on the client side and trusted by Azure by uploading its public key onto the Azure Portal.

We will see how to create this trust in the *Setting up the management client* recipe. Once the trust is created, a programmatic client can transmit messages through a secure, encrypted connection, calling HTTP methods in a typical REST convention.

In the first half of 2014, Microsoft released a new set of libraries for the public to remotely manage Azure (using the Service Management REST API) using .NET. These libraries are available for developers through NuGet and allow building .NET clients to create powerful automation solutions with managed code.

Microsoft will update these libraries to reflect platform changes over time, as they expose RPC-like interfaces and strong-typed models, according to the current/latest version of services. While the libraries are built to elegantly support the natural underlying platform's evolution, it is expected that they will change.

As we stated earlier, in the *Setting up the management client* recipe, we will set up the trust between us and Azure by creating a valid X509 certificate, using it to connect to the Management API with the .NET libraries. This is the starting point to perform other management operations such as managing the storage service. In the *Managing the Storage service* recipe, we will see how to list existing Storage accounts to create new ones using a different programming pattern. At the end of the chapter, in the *Monitoring and automating infrastructure operations* recipe, we will see how to perform advanced operations on the subscription and on the library itself, to intercept request/response flow events.

One by one, we will continue with Cloud Services management, a particularly hot topic for companies that wish to automate their monitoring processes or build a custom continuous-integration solution. It is common to see similar solutions currently implemented with the Powershell cmdlets that are provided, as we will see in the *Using Azure PowerShell* recipe. Despite being a valid method and actually used by many automation solutions, it requires specific skills on Powershell that developers often do not have. We will understand how to use the Service API to monitor and manage Cloud Services in the *Deploying Cloud Services* recipe, while we go deep into deployment details in the *Inspecting and managing Cloud Services* recipe.

To enable advanced scenarios where automation is strongly needed, the Azure Scheduler is the right service for those who need a service that is completely managed, performing periodical actions against a cloud infrastructure (hosted on Azure or not). With the introduction of the Management Libraries, it is possible to configure Scheduler items from managed code, making this a good point of interest for .NET developers, as we will see in the *Managing and using the Azure Scheduler* recipe.

Setting up the management client

Microsoft Azure implements a Management API via HTTP, the same one that is used by the Portal itself to execute commands against the platform. While in the Portal, the authentication is enforced by a Microsoft account (or an Azure Active Directory account) from a remote client that we are supposed to identify ourselves using a certificate.

After the trust is established, we can call the HTTP API through a managed proxy with strongly-typed models for requests and responses. Almost every response inherits from the `OperationResponse` class of `OperationStatusResponse` in order to show the status of the REST operation to the client.

 The `OperationResponse` class is a base class that provides a RequestId and `HttpStatusCode` parameter to the client's request, while `OperationStatusResponse` is its derived class, which provides additional domain-specific information such as error information and the status of operation.

For each specific management library, there is a base namespace for the proxy classes and a subnamespace (called Models) for the models involved in communication. It is common to find a response-model that implements `IEnumerable<T>`, making it iterable and queryable by LINQ. For example, the `LocationsListResponse` class implements `IEnumerable<LocationsListResponse.Location>`, an inner **POCO** class that contains the model of the single location item.

Getting ready

This recipe assumes that we have a valid X509 certificate on the local machine, with its public key already uploaded to the Azure Portal. To set up the management client, proceed as follows:

1. Open a developer command prompt and go to a local folder where the certificate's public key is stored.

2. Run the following command, replacing `CertificateName` with the real values:

   ```
   makecert -sky exchange -r -n "CN=<CertificateName>" -pe -a sha1
   -len 2048 -ss My "<CertificateName>.cer"
   ```

3. After that:

   1. In the current folder, a `.cer` file is created.

   2. Then, in the local user store, a complete certificate is saved.

4. To make the entire certificate (including its private key) portable, press *Windows + R* (the **Run** command) and run `mmc`.

5. Then, navigate to **File | Add/Remove Snap-in** and select **Certificates** (my user account).

6. In the **Personal | Certificates** folder, find the certificate created earlier (it will be shown as `CertificateName` according to the one specified earlier).

7. Right-click on the certificate. Then, navigate to **All Tasks | Export** and follow the wizard to export a PFX file wherever convenient (select **Yes, export the private key** and specify a good password).

8. To create the trust between Azure and our certificate, upload the public key to the Portal. Then go to the Azure Portal and locate the **Management Certificates** tab in the **Settings** section.

9. Then, in the bottom menu, click on **Upload** and upload the `.cer` file created earlier.

Before closing the browser instance, write down the subscription ID where the certificate was uploaded. We will use it along with the PFX created here in every recipe of the chapter.

How to do it...

We are going to obtain and list some platform-wide information such as the following:

- ▸ Available Regions with their available services
- ▸ Affinity groups of the subscriptions
- ▸ Virtual machines available in the platform

We will do this using the following steps:

1. Add a new class named `SetupManagementClientExample` to the project.

2. Install the `Microsoft.WindowsAzure.Management` NuGet package.

3. Add the following `using` statements to the top of the class file:
   ```
   using Microsoft.WindowsAzure;
   using Microsoft.WindowsAzure.Management;
   using Microsoft.WindowsAzure.Management.Models;
   using System.Security.Cryptography.X509Certificates;
   using System.IO;
   ```

4. Add the following `private` member to the class:
   ```
   ManagementClient client = null;
   ```

5. Add the following constructor to the class:

```
public SetupManagementClientExample(string subId,
    byte[] certificate,string password=null)
{
    client = new ManagementClient(
        new CertificateCloudCredentials(subId,
            new X509Certificate2(certificate, password)));
}
```

6. Add the following method, listing location and services, to the class:

```
public void ListLocationAndServices()
{
    LocationsListResponse list = client.Locations.List();
    foreach (LocationsListResponse.Location item in list)
    {
        Console.WriteLine(
            string.Format("Region: {0} with services: {1}",
            item.Name, string.Join(", ", item.
AvailableServices)));
    }
}
```

7. Add the following method, listing the affinity groups of the subscription, to the class:

```
private void ListAffinityGroups()
{
    var list = client.AffinityGroups.List();
    foreach (AffinityGroupListResponse.AffinityGroup item in list)
    {
        Console.WriteLine(string.Format("{0} in {1}"
            ,item.Name,item.Location));
    }
}
```

8. Add the following method, listing the available **virtual machine (VM)** sizes, to the class:

```
private void ListVMSizes()
{
    var list = client.RoleSizes.List();
    foreach (RoleSizeListResponse.RoleSize item in list)
    {
        Console.WriteLine(item.Label);
        if (item.SupportedByVirtualMachines)
```

```
                    Console.WriteLine("Available for VMs");
            if (item.SupportedByWebWorkerRoles)
                    Console.WriteLine("Available for Cloud Services");
            Console.WriteLine("-----");
        }
    }
```

9. Add the following method, using the methods added earlier, to the class:

```
public static void RunExample()
{
    string subId = "{SUB_ID}";
    string certPath = @"{PFX_PATH}";
    string certPwd = "{PFX_PASSWORD}";

    SetupManagementClientExample example =
        new SetupManagementClientExample(subId,
            File.ReadAllBytes(certPath), certPwd);
    example.ListLocationAndServices();
    example.ListAffinityGroups();
    example.ListVMSizes();
}
```

How it works...

In steps 1 through 3, we set up the class.

> The Azure Management Libraries are a composable set of libraries
> under a common top-level namespace. By adding the NuGet reference to
> `Microsoft.WindowsAzure.Management`, we also add every specific
> library currently available, such as `Compute`, `Scheduler`, `Storage`,
> `WebSites`, and more. To work only with a specific library, it is preferable to
> add it directly; we can avoid downloading and referencing the entire set.

In step 4, we added a `private` member to store the `ManagementClient` object used to
connect to the Management service. We initialized this in the constructor we add in step 5.

In step 6, we asked the client for a list of the currently available Regions in Azure
(also known as Data Centers). Almost each method of the class that inherits the base
`ManagementClient` object implements a `Request/Response-object` pattern that
wraps the actual result of the query operation in a general purpose object; this object
contains references and additional information about the request generated. In step 6,
`LocationListResponse` is inherited from the base `OperationResponse` class, which
contains the following:

▶ `RequestId`: This is a string with a unique trace identifier of the request issued. It is very useful for troubleshooting requests.

▶ `StatusCode`: This is an HTTP status code, which represents the low-level status code of the operation.

In REST, there are conventions about the semantic association between HTTP status codes and application status. However, it is not always intuitive to expect a **Created (201)** status in the case of a successful `creating` operation (perhaps, a **OK (200)** status should be expected by someone). Often, in the Management Libraries, we also see a high-level status code, which is provided through the `OperationStatusResponse` object (a subclass of `OperationResponse`) in the **property** status. This status is a domain-specific status that could be **InProgress**, **Succeeded**, or **Failed**.

In step 7, we listed the affinity groups created in our subscription, if any, and we showed the name and location (Region) for each one. In step 8, we asked Azure to list the VM size that is currently available to use in our services. Note that shipped in the `RoleSize` object, there are two flags (`SupportedByVirtualMachines` and `SupportedByWebWorkerRoles`) that tell us if the VM could be used by the Virtual Machine service (IaaS), the Cloud Services (PaaS or the web and worker roles), or both. It is common, in fact, to have a VM size (that we should call **Instance** instead of VM) that is available to specific services.

In step 9, we called the methods added earlier, specifying the Subscription ID where we need to operate, with respect to the physical path of the PFX certificate and its password. Replace the `{SUB_ID}`, `{PFX_PATH}`, and `{PFX_PASSWORD}` parts with the actual values.

There's more...

While debugging the REST services, an HTTP proxy could be our best friend, inspecting all the request/response flows, and helping us detect errors and better understand object types and properties returned by remote services. While the Management Libraries provide a comprehensive set of method/classes, sometimes, a plain, old HTTP debugger is appreciated. So, consider using Fiddler while developing with REST.

See also

Have a look at these MSDN links to get additional information:

▶ Management Libraries reference at `msdn.microsoft.com/library/azure/dn602775(v=azure.11).aspx`

Managing the Storage service

The Azure Management Libraries are a composable set of libraries under a common top-level namespace. Along with this, Microsoft shipped a single sublibrary for each of the services of the entire Azure surface, enforcing separation of concerns, in order to maintain them independently.

We will see for the first time that the `CloudContext` factory is instantiating the management clients. This factory is smartly created with extension methods lying in each satellite library. At the time of writing this book, this makes visible for the Management clients only those factory methods that are physically referenced by the project.

From the beginning of Azure, a storage account is a container of three services: Blob, Tables, and Queues. Recently, Azure Files have been introduced, so we can inspect these endpoints with the `StorageAccount.Properties.Endpoints` collection, expecting three (or four) public URIs as results. Since, in the last years, Microsoft introduced new options for storage, we can check if the `GeoReplicationEnabled` flag is set to `true` or `false`, and in the case it is positive, we can check which Region is designated to host the secondary replica. In the case of a Geo-replicated storage account, the secondary replica could also be accessed to scale our applications. Prior to the activation of the right option (**RA-GRS**, **Read Access**, and **Geo-Redundant Storage**), the public URI that represents the replica will reply to the clients' requests.

A storage account also has two access keys, used to authenticate the service from a remote client. As these keys could be lost or stolen, Azure lets the user regenerate them through the Portal or via the Management API.

Finally, the Management Libraries send textual information encoded in Base64 strings. This is generally made by the library itself, but sometimes, a manual conversion is required. To see it in action, inspect a client request issued by the library with Fiddler and see how it converts our strings.

In this recipe, we will use the Storage Management Library, which is useful for automating operations on storage accounts.

Getting ready

This recipe assumes that we created a valid certificate, and we exported it to a CER file and a PFX file. The first file should be uploaded to the Azure Portal, and the second (with its password) has to be used in the code. We also need the Subscription ID of the subscription on which we operate against. To complete these steps, please read the *Setting up the management client* recipe.

How to do it...

We are going to list the storage accounts of the subscription with their main properties. Then, we will create a new storage account and change its properties as well. We will do using the following steps:

1. Add a new class named `ManagingStorageExample` to the project.

2. Install the `Microsoft.WindowsAzure.Management` NuGet package.

3. Add the following `using` statements to the top of the class file:

    ```
    using Microsoft.WindowsAzure;
    using Microsoft.WindowsAzure.Management.Storage;
    using Microsoft.WindowsAzure.Management.Storage.Models;
    using System.Security.Cryptography.X509Certificates;
    using System.IO;
    ```

4. Add the following `private` member to the class:

    ```
    StorageManagementClient client = null;
    ```

5. Add the following constructor to the class:

    ```
    public ManagingStorageExample(string subId,
        byte[] certificate, string password=null)
    {
        client = CloudContext.Clients.CreateStorageManagementClient(
            new CertificateCloudCredentials(subId,
                new X509Certificate2(certificate, password)));
    }
    ```

6. Add the following method, listing storage accounts, to the class:

    ```
    public void ListStorageAccount()
    {
        StorageAccountListResponse list = client.StorageAccounts.
    List();
        foreach (StorageAccount item in list)
        {
            Console.WriteLine(string.Format("Account: {0}",item.
    Name));
            foreach (var ep in item.Properties.Endpoints)
            {
                Console.WriteLine(ep.ToString());
            }
            Console.WriteLine(string.Format("Geo-replication: {0}",
                item.Properties.GeoReplicationEnabled?"Enabled in "
                +item.Properties.GeoSecondaryRegion:"Disabled"));
        }
    }
    ```

7. Add the following method, creating a new storage account, to the class:

```
public bool CreateStorageAccount(string name)
{
    var r1 = client.StorageAccounts.CheckNameAvailability(name);
    if (r1.IsAvailable)
    {
        var bytes = Encoding.UTF8.GetBytes(name);
        var base64Name= Convert.ToBase64String(bytes);
        OperationStatusResponse r2= client.StorageAccounts
            .Create(new StorageAccountCreateParameters()
            {
                GeoReplicationEnabled=true,
                Location="North Europe",
                Name=name,
                Label=base64Name
            });
        if (r2.Status == OperationStatus.Succeeded)
        {
            return true;
        }
    }
    return false;
}
```

8. Add the following method, regenerating keys, to the class:

```
public void RegenerateKeys(string name)
{
    StorageAccountRegenerateKeysResponse r1= client
        .StorageAccounts.RegenerateKeys(
        new StorageAccountRegenerateKeysParameters()
    {
        KeyType=StorageKeyType.Primary,
        Name=name
    });
    Console.WriteLine(string
        .Format("New key: {0}",r1.PrimaryKey));
}
```

9. Add the following method, disabling geo-replication, to the class:

```
public void DisableGeoReplication(string name)
{
    client.StorageAccounts.Update(name,
        new StorageAccountUpdateParameters()
    {
        GeoReplicationEnabled=false
    });
}
```

10. Add the following method, using the methods added earlier, to the class:

```
public static void RunExample()
{
    string subId = "{SUB_ID}";
    string certPath = @"{PFX_PATH}";
    string certPwd = "{PFX_PASSWORD}";
    string storageAccount = "{NEW_ACCOUNT}";

    ManagingStorageExample example =
        new ManagingStorageExample(subId,
            File.ReadAllBytes(certPath), certPwd);
    example.ListStorageAccount();
    if (example.CreateStorageAccount(storageAccount))
    {
        example.RegenerateKeys(storageAccount);
        example.DisableGeoReplication(storageAccount);
    }
}
```

How it works...

In steps 1 through 3, we set up the class. In step 4, we added a `private` member to store the `StorageManagementClient` object used to connect to the Management service. We initialized this in the constructor we add in step 5.

> In the first recipe, we used the constructor of the `ManagementClient` class to create an instance. However, the `CloudContext` class exposes a static `Clients` property on which some extension methods provide factories to the actual clients. This method, alternative to the previous method, is easy to use to determine which clients are available and which ones are not.

In step 6, we listed the storage accounts of the subscription, and for each account found, we showed its public HTTP endpoints. We expect three (or four) endpoints for each account: one for the Blob service, one for the Table service, and one for the Queue service.

Storage accounts created after TechEd NA 2014 (mid-May 2014) might have four endpoints, including the `File` endpoint, while the preview period depends on whether the appropriate preview has been opted for.

Finally, we showed the secondary Region of replica, in case Geo replication is enabled for the account.

In step 7, we created a storage account by name. Assuming that the name is compliant with the platform requirements, we checked its availability before creating it. We then called a `create` operation on the `StorageAccounts` property, passing a wrapper object that contains some settings: Geo replication status, location, name, and label.

To retrieve the list of the currently available locations/regions, please see the *Setting up the management client* recipe. Moreover, note that we encode the label's value in Base64. This is generally implemented by the libraries themselves in other clients; for the storage one, we have to do this manually.

The `Create` operation, under the hood, acts as follows:

1. It submits an initial request to the platform, which replies immediately with an accepted/not-accepted response, including a RequestId.

2. However, as the create operation could take up to a few minutes, the libraries periodically check the status of the request by asking it to the platform, using the RequestId obtained earlier.

   It does this step in a loop until the status of the operation, in the **In-Progress** status, changes.

3. When, finally, the status of the operation changes to **Failed** or **Succeeded**, the `Create` method returns, and the control is passed back to the custom code.

In step 8, we called the API to regenerate access keys of a given storage account. There are two access keys (primary and secondary), and we can regenerate them one by one. Except for some transient error in communication, it is uncommon that this operation could fail, so we don't check the `StatusCode` object of the response, as we are quite sure it was a success.

In step 9, we disabled Geo replication, updating the settings of a given existing storage account.

In step 10, we called the methods added earlier, specifying the Subscription ID on which we need to operate , with respect to the physical path of the PFX certificate, its password, and the storage account to create. Replace the {SUB_ID}, {PFX_PATH}, {PFX_PASSWORD}, and {NEW_ACCOUNT} parts with actual values.

There's more...

For each long-running operation (as is the case of the Create method on StorageAccounts), there is a version that returns immediately and allows the user to check the status subsequently, polling the service manually.

We implement this pattern as follows:

```
public bool CreateStorageAccountBeginAndPolling(string name)
{
    var r1 = client.StorageAccounts.CheckNameAvailability(name);
    if (r1.IsAvailable)
    {
        var bytes = Encoding.UTF8.GetBytes(name);
        var base64Name = Convert.ToBase64String(bytes);
        OperationResponse r2 = client.StorageAccounts
            .BeginCreating(new StorageAccountCreateParameters()
            {
                GeoReplicationEnabled = false,
                Location = "North Europe",
                Name = name,
                Label = base64Name
            });
        if (r2.StatusCode == System.Net.HttpStatusCode.Accepted)
        {
            OperationStatusResponse r3 = null;
            while ((r3=client.GetOperationStatus(r2.RequestId))
                .Status == OperationStatus.InProgress) Thread.
Sleep(1000);
            return r3.Status == OperationStatus.Succeeded;
        }
    }
    return false;
}
```

We used BeginCreating to submit the request to the platform, which immediately returns a RequestId associated to the operation. Then, in a while/sleep loop (not too elegant, but effective), we periodically checked the status of the operation, and when it completes, we returned. This is exactly how the Management Library works under the hood when we call the blocking methods such as the Create() method we used in the recipe.

See also

Have a look at the following MSDN links to get additional information:

- ▶ How to manage storage accounts at `http://azure.microsoft.com/en-us/documentation/articles/storage-manage-storage-account/`

- ▶ Operations on storage accounts at `http://msdn.microsoft.com/en-us/library/azure/ee460790.aspx`

Deploying Cloud Services

Azure services have similar self-provisioning models. The user reserves a name/namespace for the **deployment unit**, and then, they deploy its service using the specific technology of the actual service. For storage, the deployment unit is the storage account itself. For compute, it is represented by the concept of Cloud Services, a robust and fully featured container of web applications (web roles) and generic processes (worker roles).

The `ComputeManagementClient` object is the specific client to work with Cloud Services and VMs. In this book, however, VMs are not covered. A Cloud Service-hosting web or worker role is represented by a service name with two (staging and production) deployment slots. A user can deploy the same solution to both the slots that have two independent environments, which are swappable at runtime in a few seconds, thanks to the VIP swap functionality.

VIP swap is a user-initiated process that swaps the load-balancer pointer to the deployment slot opposite to the one at which it is currently pointed. So, if the **Virtual IP** (**VIP**) points to the staging slot before a swap, after that, it will point to the production slots, with no downtime.

A sample development/deployment process flow, following best practices, could be as follows:

1. The developer initially deploys their solution to a production slot.
2. The public start to use the service, with no stops, 24/7.
3. The developer builds a second version, deploying it to the staging slot.

    The QA team tests if everything is good to go live.

4. The developer swaps the two environments, performing the following action:
    - ❑ Making that change transparent for the user
    - ❑ Taking offline the *old* production slot, which now becomes the current staging

In this recipe, we will automate a deployment operation, swapping slots and changing the service configuration programmatically.

Getting ready

This recipe assumes that we created a valid certificate, and we exported it to a CER file and a PFX file. The first should be uploaded to the Azure Portal, and the second (with its password) has to be used in the code. We also need the Subscription ID of the subscription on which we operate. To complete these steps, please read the *Setting up the management client* recipe.

This recipe also assumes that we have a CSPKG package (which contains a valid Cloud Service) uploaded into the blob storage of an account in the same subscription as the one currently managed, in a public blob, or in a private blob accessible with **Shared Access Signature (SAS)**.

How to do it...

We are going to create a Cloud Service in North Europe, deploying an existing cloud package into its staging slot. After that, we will swap the deployment slots and update the service configuration. We will do this using the following steps:

1. Add a new class named `DeployingCloudServicesExample` to the project.

2. Install the `Microsoft.WindowsAzure.Management` NuGet package.

3. Add the following `using` statements to the top of the class file:

```
using Microsoft.WindowsAzure;
using Microsoft.WindowsAzure.Management.Compute;
using Microsoft.WindowsAzure.Management.Compute.Models;
using System.Threading.Tasks;
using System.Security.Cryptography.X509Certificates;;
using System.IO;
```

4. Add the following `private` member to the class:

```
ComputeManagementClient client = null;
```

5. Add the following constructor to the class:

```
public DeployingCloudServicesExample(string subId,
    byte[] certificate,string password=null)
{
    client = new ComputeManagementClient(
        new CertificateCloudCredentials(subId,
            new X509Certificate2 (certificate, password)));
}
```

6. Add the following method, creating and deploying the Cloud Service into the staging slot, to the class:

```
public async Task<bool> CreateServiceSlotAndDeploy
    (string sn,string pack,string conf)
{
    HostedServiceCheckNameAvailabilityResponse res
        = await client.HostedServices.
CheckNameAvailabilityAsync(sn);
    if (res.IsAvailable)
    {
        OperationResponse r1= await client.HostedServices
            .CreateAsync(new HostedServiceCreateParameters()
        {
            Label=sn,
            ServiceName=sn,
            Location="North Europe"
        });
        if (r1.StatusCode == System.Net.HttpStatusCode.Created)
        {
            OperationStatusResponse r2= client.Deployments
                .Create(sn, DeploymentSlot.Staging,
                new DeploymentCreateParameters()
                {
                    Configuration=File.ReadAllText(conf),
                    Label=sn,
                    Name="V1",
                    PackageUri=new Uri(pack),
                    StartDeployment=true,
                    TreatWarningsAsError=false
                });
            return r2.Status == OperationStatus.Succeeded;
        }
    }
    return false;
}
```

7. Add the following method, swapping deployment slots, to the class:

```
public void SwapDeploymentSlots(string sn)
{
    OperationStatusResponse resp = client.Deployments.Swap(sn
        , new DeploymentSwapParameters() { SourceDeployment = "V1"
    });
```

```
        if (resp.Status != OperationStatus.Succeeded)
        {
            //Check why
        }
    }
```

8. Add the following method, changing the service configuration, to the class:

```
public void ChangeConfiguration(string sn, string newConf)
{
    //We intentionally lose the OperationResponse returned
    client.Deployments.ChangeConfigurationBySlot(sn,
        DeploymentSlot.Production
        , new DeploymentChangeConfigurationParameters()
        {
            Mode=DeploymentChangeConfigurationMode.Auto,
            Configuration=File.ReadAllText(newConf)
        });
}
```

9. Add the following method, using the methods added earlier, to the class:

```
public static void RunExample()
{
    string subId = "{SUB_ID}";
    string certPath = @"{PFX_PATH}";
    string certPwd = "{PFX_PASSWORD}";
    string packagePath = "{CSPKG_URI}";
    string configPath = @"{CSCFG_PATH}";
    string serviceName = "{SERVICE_NAME}";

    DeployingCloudServicesExample example =
        new DeployingCloudServicesExample(subId,
            File.ReadAllBytes(certPath), certPwd);
    example.CreateServiceSlotAndDeploy(serviceName,
        packagePath, configPath)
        .ConfigureAwait(continueOnCapturedContext: false)
        .GetAwaiter().GetResult();
    example.SwapDeploymentSlots(serviceName);
    example.ChangeConfiguration(serviceName, configPath);
}
```

How it works...

In steps 1 through 3, we set up the class. In step 4, we added a `private` member to store the `ComputeManagementClient` object used to connect to the Management service. We initialized this in the constructor we added in step 5.

 Management Libraries recommend the use of the Async/Await pattern, if used in applications where responsiveness of the UI is important or where we need to execute operations asynchronously. For almost each method of the Management libraries, there is an Async/Await version.

In step 6, we created an Async-aware method to create a Cloud Service and deployed a Cloud Package into its staging slot. We first check the availability of the service name we choose. If it is available, we create the service in the North Europe region. In the `DeploymentCreateParameters` object, we passed `PackageUri` for the configuration XML. The configuration XML is passed as a plain string to the method, which is converted in Base64 by the library. We also specified to immediately start the deployment; once the deployment completes, we can proceed with the operation, even in the case of warnings.

We must remember that a stopped deployment continues to consume resources, and consequently, we incur charges. Finally, there are some settings that cause warnings in the deployment process, such as the number of instances (should be two or more). If the `TreatWarningsAsError` property is set to `true`, the deployment stops in the case of similar warnings.

In step 7, we swapped the deployment slots, while in step 8, we changed the configuration of an existing service by passing a new one. This will cause the roles involved in the change to be upgraded, according to the current upgrade domains.

In step 9, we called the methods added earlier, specifying the Subscription ID on which to operate, its password for the physical path of the PFX certificate, the new package with its configuration, and the Cloud Service to update. Replace the `{SUB_ID}`, `{PFX_PATH}`, `{PFX_PASSWORD}`, `{CSPKG_URI}`, `{CSCFG_PATH}`, and `{SERVICE_NAME}` parts with the actual values.

There's more...

Changing the configuration of a running Cloud Service could result in topology changes or cause the running instance to reboot. The way Azure manages these updates relies on the concept of **Upgrade Domain**. An Upgrade Domain is a logical grouping between the instances of a Cloud Service, made to let Azure upgrade one domain at time, without causing service interruption. If the service has only two instances, we have two Upgrade Domains. If there are more, Azure divides the instances into 5 logical groups of Upgrade Domains by default; these will be updated one by one in case of an in-place update.

With the Management API, we can control this behavior, *walking* the upgrade process manually, and updating the domains of the running service one by one. This is done using the following code:

```
public void ChangeConfigurationAndUpgradeManually(string sn, string
newConf)
{
    DeploymentGetResponse dep = client.Deployments
        .GetBySlot(sn, DeploymentSlot.Production);
    var operation= client.Deployments.ChangeConfigurationBySlot(sn,
        DeploymentSlot.Production
        , new DeploymentChangeConfigurationParameters()
        {
            Mode = DeploymentChangeConfigurationMode.Manual,
            Configuration = File.ReadAllText(newConf)
        });
    if (operation.Status == OperationStatus.Succeeded)
    {
        for (int i = 0; i < dep.UpgradeDomainCount; i++)
        {
            var singleDomainResult = new OperationStatusResponse()
            {
                Status=OperationStatus.Failed
            };
            while (singleDomainResult.Status != OperationStatus.
Succeeded)
            {
                singleDomainResult= client.Deployments
                    .WalkUpgradeDomainByDeploymentSlot(sn,
DeploymentSlot.Production,
                        new DeploymentWalkUpgradeDomainParameters()
                        {
                            UpgradeDomain = i
                        });
            }
        }
    }
}
```

We initially called the GetBySlot() method of the Deployments property to obtain information about the current deployment in the production slot. We then called ChangeConfigurationBySlot to start the upgrade process, specifying the following:

```
Mode = DeploymentChangeConfigurationMode.Manual
```

The preceding code instructs Azure to allow us to decide when to upgrade the instances. If the operation succeeded, we set up a loop on the total count of Upgrade Domains of the `Deployment` property. For each one, we simply called `WalkUpgradeDomainByDeploymentSlot` to start the upgrade of that specific logical group of instances.

See also

Have a look at the following MSDN links to get additional information:

- API reference about Cloud Service Management at `http://msdn.microsoft.com/en-us/library/azure/ee460812.aspx`

- Updating an Azure service at `http://msdn.microsoft.com/en-us/library/azure/hh472157.aspx`

Inspecting and managing Cloud Services

As we saw in the *Deploying Cloud Services* recipe, we can automate the deployment operations of Cloud Services to build rich automation solutions. When a Cloud Service has at least one deployment with any role, under the hood, there are virtual machines (also known as Instances) that hold the code of the web application or the worker process.

These VMs run a specific Windows Server OS, also called Azure Guest OS. Each Azure Guest OS is a modified version of Windows Server based on 2008 (now deprecated), 2008 R2, 2012, and so on.

We use the `OperatingSystems` property of the `ComputeManagementClient` object to obtain the currently available Azure operating system's versions. In this collection, OSes are grouped per family, which is a logical group based on the major version of Guest OS (that is, 2008, 2012, and so on).

In the *Deploying Cloud Services* recipe, we saw how to deploy and update a running role. In this recipe, we will see how to inspect it, walking over some properties of the active deployment. We use `BeginRebootingRoleInstanceByDeploymentSlot` to reboot a physical instance of a given role and `BeginReimagingRoleInstanceByDeploymentSlot` to reimage it.

Getting ready

This recipe assumes that we created a valid certificate, and we exported it to a CER file and a PFX file. The first file should be uploaded to Azure Portal, and the second (with its password) has to be used in the code. We also need the Subscription ID of the subscription on which we operate. To complete these steps, please read the *Setting up the management client* recipe.

This recipe also assumes that we have an up-and-running Cloud Service to inspect. To have such a Cloud Service, deploy a sample worker role to Azure and take note of the service name.

How to do it...

We are going to list the supported operating systems for our deployments, understanding which ones are available for Cloud Services, virtual machines, or both. We then inspect all the existing Cloud Services in the subscription, having at least an active deployment. Finally, we refresh an existing deployment. We will do this using the following steps:

1. Add a new class named `InspectingManagingCloudServicesExample` to the project.

2. Install the `Microsoft.WindowsAzure.Management` NuGet package.

3. Add the following `using` statements to the top of the class file:

```
using Microsoft.WindowsAzure;
using Microsoft.WindowsAzure.Management.Compute;
using Microsoft.WindowsAzure.Management.Compute.Models;
using System.Security.Cryptography.X509Certificates;
using System.IO;
```

4. Add the following `private` member to the class:

```
ComputeManagementClient client = null;
```

5. Add the following constructor to the class:

```
public InspectingManagingCloudServicesExample(string subId,
    byte[] certificate,string password=null)
{
    client = new ComputeManagementClient(
        new CertificateCloudCredentials(subId,
            new X509Certificate2(certificate, password)));
}
```

6. Add the following method, obtaining the default platform OS, to the class:

```
public void GetDefaultOSs()
{
    OperatingSystemListFamiliesResponse familiesWithOss
        = client.OperatingSystems.ListFamilies();
    OperatingSystemListFamiliesResponse.OperatingSystem def
        =familiesWithOss.SelectMany(p=>p.OperatingSystems)
        .FirstOrDefault(p=>p.IsDefault);
    Console.WriteLine(def.Label);
    Console.WriteLine(def.Version);
}
```

7. Add the following method, inspecting a Cloud Service, to the class:

```
public void InspectCloudService()
{
    HostedServiceGetDetailedResponse serviceWithActiveDeployments
        = client.HostedServices.List()          .Select(p=>client.
HostedServices.GetDetailed(p.ServiceName))
        .FirstOrDefault(p=>p.Deployments
            .Any(q=>!string.IsNullOrWhiteSpace(q.SdkVersion)));
    if (serviceWithActiveDeployments != null)
    {
        Console.WriteLine(serviceWithActiveDeployments.
ServiceName);
        HostedServiceProperties props =
serviceWithActiveDeployments.Properties;
        Console.WriteLine(string.Format("Service {0} created on
{1} in {2}",
            props.Label,props.DateCreated,props.Location));
        foreach (HostedServiceGetDetailedResponse.Deployment item
            in serviceWithActiveDeployments.Deployments)
        {
            var roles=item.RoleInstances.GroupBy(p=>p.RoleName)
                .Select(p=>new {Role=p.Key,Instances=p.Count()});
            Console.WriteLine(string.Format("Deployment {0} in
{1}: {2}"
                ,item.Name,item.DeploymentSlot,item.Status));
            Console.WriteLine(string.Format("Public url:
{0}",item.Uri));
            Console.WriteLine(string.Format("Public IP: {0}",
                item.VirtualIPAddresses.First().Address));
            Console.WriteLine(string.Format("Packaged with SDK:
{0}",
                item.SdkVersion));
            Console.WriteLine(string.Format("{0} roles with
average of {1} instances"
                ,roles.Count(),roles.Average(p=>p.Instances)));
        }
    }
}
```

8. Add the following method, refreshing an existing role instance, to the class:

```
public void Refresh1stRoleInstance(string sn,bool
rebootOnly=false)
{
    var service=client.HostedServices.GetDetailed(sn);
    if (service.Deployments.Any())
    {
        var dep=service.Deployments
            .FirstOrDefault(p=>p.DeploymentSlot
                ==DeploymentSlot.Staging && p.RoleInstances.
Any());
        if (dep!=null){
            var instance=dep.RoleInstances.First();
            Console.WriteLine(string.Format(
                "Refreshing: {0} instance {1}",
                instance.RoleName,instance.InstanceName));
            OperationResponse resp= rebootOnly?
                client.Deployments
                .BeginRebootingRoleInstanceByDeploymentSlot(sn,
                dep.DeploymentSlot, instance.InstanceName):
                client.Deployments
                .BeginReimagingRoleInstanceByDeploymentSlot(sn,
                dep.DeploymentSlot, instance.InstanceName);
        }
    }
}
```

9. Add the following method, using the methods added earlier, to the class:

```
public static void RunExample()
{
    string subId = "{SUB_ID}";
    string certPath = @"{PFX_PATH}";
    string certPwd = "{PFX_PASSWORD}";
    string serviceName = "{SERVICE_NAME}";

    InspectingManagingCloudServicesExample example =
        new InspectingManagingCloudServicesExample(subId,
            File.ReadAllBytes(certPath), certPwd);
    example.GetDefaultOSs();
    example.InspectCloudService();
    example.Refresh1stRoleInstance(serviceName, true);
}
```

How it works...

In steps 1 through 3, we set up the class. In step 4, we added a `private` member to store the `ComputeManagementClient` object used to connect to the Management service. We initialized this in the constructor we added in step 5.

In step 6, we asked Azure to list all the currently available operating system families of the platform. We filtered the results to get the default operating system (usually the latest) used to build new services.

In step 7, we used LINQ to get the first Cloud Service, which has at least one active deployment. We listed the following properties of this Cloud Service:

- ▸ The running status of the deployment
- ▸ The public URL and IP of the Cloud Service
- ▸ The SDK version used to package the deployment
- ▸ The average instances per role

 We also asked for the `!string.IsNullOrWhiteSpace(q.SdkVersion)` condition to make sure it is a user-uploaded service (web or worker role).

In step 8, with a given up-and-running Cloud Service, we got its staging deployment, and tried to reboot or reimage the first instance we find. Rebooting is simple to understand, while reimaging is the process that destroys the existing machine that builds another one, starting from the Service Package (CSPKG) used to build the original machine image.

 In the case of a reboot, the local storage of the instance is preserved, while in the case that the role instance is reimaged, there is no guarantee that the local storage is preserved, even if Azure tries to do it. So, do not rely on the local storage of role instance, preferring to persist data into the appropriate places.

In step 9, we call the methods added earlier, specifying the Subscription ID on which to operate, with respect to the physical path of the PFX certificate, its password, and the Cloud Service to refresh. Replace the `{SUB_ID}`, `{PFX_PATH}`, `{PFX_PASSWORD}`, and `{SERVICE_NAME}` parts with the actual values.

There's more...

While building a Cloud Service wrapper project for a web role or a worker role, we have a service definition and service configuration. Among settings, endpoints, and storage configurations, we could also set up some additional processes that run in the role instances when they have been deployed to Azure. These processes, such as the Remote Desktop module, the Diagnostics module, the Active Directory integration, the Monitoring Agent, and the Antimalware, are called **Extensions**. To know which extensions are currently supported (and available) on a role instance, we use the following method:

```
public void ListExtensions()
{
    IEnumerable<string> exts
        = client.HostedServices.ListAvailableExtensions()
        .Select(p => p.Description);
    foreach (string item in exts)
    {
        Console.WriteLine(item);
    }
}
```

See also

Have a look at the following MSDN links to get additional information:

- Azure Guest OS releases at `http://msdn.microsoft.com/en-us/library/azure/ee924680.aspx`

- Extensions for virtual machines at `http://msdn.microsoft.com/en-us/library/azure/dn606311.aspx`

Managing and using the Azure Scheduler

The Azure Scheduler lets us create scheduled actions against an HTTP or HTTPS endpoint for a storage queue. By implementing complex infrastructures, we often need to schedule some actions with specific recurrence. Also, the Windows Task Scheduler helps us run custom processes in a scheduled fashion. However, having a Task Scheduler that runs on a user-managed VM involves maintenance and skills, although that is not to say that it is not a highly available solution, as the underlying VM represents a single point of failure.

The Azure Scheduler, via the Azure Portal or the Management API, lets us submit jobs of the following two types:

- ▸ HTTP endpoint call
- ▸ Message in queue

In the former case, we can customize the request by appending custom headers and choosing the appropriate method (GET, POST, and so on). In the latter, we can put a message on a storage queue, supposing there is someone on the other side ready to process it, before or later.

The Azure Scheduler does not run custom code in either .NET or other runtimes. Triggered by Azure itself and following the recurrence rules, its purpose is to start a user process. In this recipe, we will see how to manage the Scheduler service and how to use it to submit new jobs.

Getting ready

This recipe assumes that we created a valid certificate, and we exported it to a CER file and a PFX file. The first file should be uploaded to Azure Portal, and the second (with its password) has to be used in the code. We also need the Subscription ID of the subscription on which we operate. To complete these steps, read the *Setting up the management client* recipe.

How to do it...

We are going to create a **Job Collection**, putting a Job into it, waiting for the first execution, and checking the status of the action that is executed. We will do this using the following steps:

1. Add a new class named ManagingUsingSchedulerExample to the project.

2. Install the Microsoft.WindowsAzure.Management NuGet package.

3. Add the following using statements to the top of the class file:

   ```
   using Microsoft.WindowsAzure;
   using Microsoft.WindowsAzure.Management.Scheduler;
   using Microsoft.WindowsAzure.Management.Scheduler.Models;
   using Microsoft.WindowsAzure.Scheduler;
   using Microsoft.WindowsAzure.Scheduler.Models;
   using System.Security.Cryptography.X509Certificates;
   using System.Threading;
   using System.IO;
   using System.Collections.Generic;
   ```

4. Add the following private member to the class:

   ```
   SchedulerManagementClient client = null;
   ```

5. Add the following constructor to the class:

```
public ManagingUsingSchedulerExample(string subId,
    byte[] certificate, string password = null)
{
    client = new SchedulerManagementClient(
        new CertificateCloudCredentials(subId,
            new X509Certificate2(certificate, password)));
}
```

6. Add the following method, enabling the resource provider for the Scheduler service, to the class:

```
public void CheckIfEnableAndPrintProperties()
{
    try { client.RegisterResourceProvider(); }
    catch { }

    IDictionary<string, string> props =
        client.GetResourceProviderProperties().Properties;
    foreach (var keyValue in props)
    {
        Console.WriteLine(string.Format("{0}: {1}",
            keyValue.Key, keyValue.Value));
    }
}
```

7. Add the following method, a new resource holder (formally, Cloud Service), to the class:

```
public void CreateNewResourceHolder(string name)
{
    CloudServiceManagementClient csClient =
        CloudContext.Clients
        .CreateCloudServiceManagementClient(client.Credentials);

    var list = csClient.CloudServices.List();
    foreach (CloudServiceListResponse.CloudService item in list
        .Where(p => p.Resources.Any()))
    {
        Console.WriteLine(string.Format("{0} in {1} with: ",
            item.Name, item.GeoRegion));
        foreach (var resource in item.Resources)
        {
            Console.WriteLine(string.Format("{0}: {1}",
                resource.Name, resource.Type));
```

```
            }
        }
        if (!list.Any(p => p.Name.Equals(name,
            StringComparison.InvariantCultureIgnoreCase)))
        {
            csClient.CloudServices.Create(name,
                new CloudServiceCreateParameters()
            {
                Description = name,
                Label = name,
                GeoRegion = "North Europe"
            });
        }
    }
```

8. Add the following method, creating a Job collection, to the class:

```
public void CreateJobCollection(string cs, string jobCollection)
{
    client.JobCollections.Create(cs, jobCollection,
        new JobCollectionCreateParameters()
    {
        Label = "My Job collection",
        IntrinsicSettings = new JobCollectionIntrinsicSettings()
        {
            Plan = JobCollectionPlan.Standard
        }
    });
}
```

9. Add the following method, creating a monitoring Job, to the class:

```
public string CreateMonitoringJob(string cs, string jobCollection)
{
    SchedulerClient jobClient = CloudContext.Clients
            .CreateSchedulerClient(client.Credentials, cs,
jobCollection);
    var job = jobClient.Jobs.Create(new JobCreateParameters()
    {
        StartTime=DateTime.UtcNow.AddMinutes(1),
        Recurrence = new JobRecurrence()
        {
            Frequency=JobRecurrenceFrequency.Hour,
            Count=10
        },
        Action = new JobAction()
```

```
        {
            Type=JobActionType.Http,
            RetryPolicy = new RetryPolicy()
            {
                RetryCount=5,
                RetryInterval=TimeSpan.FromMinutes(5),
                RetryType=RetryType.Fixed
            },
            Request = new JobHttpRequest()
            {
                Uri=new Uri("http://www.microsoft.com"),
                Method="GET"
            },
            ErrorAction = new JobErrorAction()
            {
                Type=JobActionType.Http,
                Request = new JobHttpRequest()
                {
                    Uri=new Uri("http://myService/
log?error?ID=001"),
                    Method="GET",
                    Headers = new Dictionary<string, string>()
                    { {"Auth","Key"}}
                }
            }
        }
    });
    if (job.StatusCode == System.Net.HttpStatusCode.Created)
    {
        return job.Job.Id;
    }
    else return null;
}
```

10. Add the following method, checking the status of the Job, to the class:

```
public void CheckExecutionStatus(string cs,
    string jobCollection,string jobId)
{
    SchedulerClient jobClient = CloudContext
        .Clients.CreateSchedulerClient(client.Credentials,
        cs, jobCollection);
    JobGetHistoryResponse list= jobClient.Jobs
        .GetHistory(jobId, new JobGetHistoryParameters()
        {
```

```
            Top=10,
            Skip=0
        });
        foreach (JobGetHistoryResponse.JobHistoryEntry item in list)
        {
            Console.WriteLine(string.Format("Execution of: {0} - {1}",
                item.EndTime, item.Status));
        }
    }
```

11. Add the following method, using the methods added earlier, to the class:

```
public static void RunExample()
{
    string subId = "{SUB_ID}";
    string certPath = @"{PFX_PATH}";
    string certPwd = "{PFX_PASSWORD}";
    string resourceHolder = "{CLOUD_SERVICE}";
    string jobCollection = "{JOB_COLL_NAME}";

    ManagingUsingSchedulerExample example =
        new ManagingUsingSchedulerExample(subId,
            File.ReadAllBytes(certPath), certPwd);
    example.CreateNewResourceHolder(resourceHolder);
    example.CreateJobCollection(resourceHolder, jobCollection);
    string id = example.CreateMonitoringJob(
        resourceHolder, jobCollection);
    if (id != null)
    {
        //Wait a minute
        Thread.Sleep(60000);
        example.CheckExecutionStatus(resourceHolder,
            jobCollection, id);
    }
}
```

How it works...

In steps 1 through 3, we set up the class. In step 4, we added a `private` member to store the `SchedulerManagementClient` object used to connect to the Management service. We initialized this in the constructor we added in step 5.

In step 6, we registered the resource provider. The Scheduler service, as for many other new services in the Azure Platform, comes like an optional add-on for an existing subscription. In fact, people can choose to entitle the subscription to its usage, so it is necessary to explicitly add it into the subscription, using the `RegisterResourceProvider()` method.

In step 7, we again dealt with the concept of Cloud Service, this time, differently from the previous times in the book. Cloud Services could be endpoints for our web or worker roles, VM, and now, even for resource providers.

 Note that the name of a Cloud Service for resource providers does not match the name of a publicly faced Cloud Service (for web/worker roles or VMs). This could be confusing.

Therefore, we created a Cloud Service (in the recipe, we also call it a resource holder), and in step 8, we created a Job Collection into it, specifying the Standard (paid) mode in the `Plan` property.

In step 9, we submitted a new Job definition. This job should call an HTTP URL (Microsoft's home page) 10 times every hour, starting in 1 minute. We state that if something goes wrong, the Job should retry the operation up to five times, every 5 minutes. Finally, if the job fails for some reason, it must call a custom web endpoint, passing a custom HTTP header (`Auth`).

In step 10, we used the previously created job reference to check its execution status, printing the occurrences. In the case of failure, we will see many executions according to the `RetryPolicy` class.

In step 11, we called the methods added earlier, specifying the Subscription ID on which to operate with respect to the physical path of the PFX certificate, its password, the Cloud Service, and the Job Collection to create. Replace the `{SUB_ID}`, `{PFX_PATH}`, `{PFX_PASSWORD}`, `{CLOUD_SERVICE}`, and `{JOB_COLL_NAME}` parts with the actual values.

There's more...

As the Scheduler actually accepts two kinds of job types, we will see how to put a message in a storage queue, instead of calling an HTTP service as follows:

```
public string CreateJobWithMessageQueue(
    string cs, string jobCollection, string storage,
    string queue, string sasToken)
{
    SchedulerClient jobClient = CloudContext.Clients
        .CreateSchedulerClient(client.Credentials, cs, jobCollection);
    var job = jobClient.Jobs.Create(new JobCreateParameters()
    {
```

```
        StartTime = DateTime.UtcNow.AddMinutes(1),
        Action = new JobAction()
        {
            Type = JobActionType.StorageQueue,
            QueueMessage=new JobQueueMessage(){
                StorageAccountName=storage,
                QueueName=queue,
                Message="Message from Scheduler",
                SasToken=sasToken
            }
        }
    });
    if (job.StatusCode == System.Net.HttpStatusCode.Created)
    {
        return job.Job.Id;
    }
    else return null;
}
```

We just need a storage account with a queue that is accessible through an SAS token, and the Scheduler will put a message into it. HTTP endpoints are exposed to the public, and even if we can authenticate the request with headers over HTTPS, the Queue mechanism is generally more secure or, at least, more private.

See also

Have a look at these MSDN links to get additional information:

- The Azure Scheduler documentation center at `http://azure.microsoft.com/en-us/documentation/services/scheduler/`
- Using Scheduler from the Management Portal at `http://msdn.microsoft.com/en-us/library/azure/dn495651.aspx`

Monitoring and automating infrastructure operations

When a user initiates an operation on the Azure Portal, it is given with a RequestId to keep track of its status, in case it's needed. In the *Managing the Storage service* recipe, we saw how to use that RequestId to check the status of a request, but we might need to ask Azure for a list of every operation in a specific timeframe.

Going back to the `ManagementClient` class, which manages infrastructure services, we can use the `ListOperations()` method to obtain a complete list of the operation history against the platform; this is initiated by us or someone else who has the rights to the subscription.

For each operation, we can track:

- ▶ The operation name
- ▶ Who made it (the e-mail address) and from where (the IP address)
- ▶ The current status of the operation and when it occurred

As the purpose of the Management Libraries is to mirror the functionalities of the Azure Portal, we can also use them to install new client certificates, automating the management process itself.

Finally, through the `SubscriptionGetResponse` class, we can get useful information about the current subscription, knowing if we reached the quota for any service we used. In this recipe, we dig into the operation log, the capability of uploading new certificates, and the quotas for services.

Getting ready

This recipe assumes that we created a valid certificate, and we exported it to a CER file and a PFX file. The first file should be uploaded to the Azure Portal, and the second one (with its password) has to be used in the code. We also need the Subscription ID of the subscription on which we operate. To complete these steps, please read the *Setting up the management client* recipe.

This recipe also assumes that we have a new X509 certificate, different from the one used to connect to the Management service, ready to be uploaded by the code.

How to do it...

We are going to do some basic monitoring to the subscription, verifying the usage limits. We also list management certificates, uploading a new one, eventually exporting a list of management operations that took place in the last hour. We will do this using the following steps:

1. Add a new class named `MonitoringAutomatingExample` to the project.

2. Install the `Microsoft.WindowsAzure.Management` NuGet package.

3. Add the following `using` statements to the top of the class file:

```
using Microsoft.WindowsAzure;
using Microsoft.WindowsAzure.Management;
using Microsoft.WindowsAzure.Management.Models;
using System.Threading;
using System.Threading.Tasks;
using System.Net;
using System.Net.Http;
using System.Security.Cryptography.X509Certificates;
using System.IO;
```

4. Add the following `private` member to the class:

```
ManagementClient client = null;
```

5. Add the following constructor to the class:

```
public MonitoringAutomatingExample(string subId,
    byte[] certificate,string password=null)
{
    client = new ManagementClient(
        new CertificateCloudCredentials(subId,
            new X509Certificate2(certificate, password)));
}
```

6. Add the following method, checking subscription limits, to the class:

```
private void SubscriptionCountersCheck()
{
    Action<string,int, int> checkAndPrint = (name,current, max) =>
    {
        string message = string.Format("{0}: {1} of {2} "
            , name, current, max);
        if (current>(max*0.75)) message+=" - Attention";
        else message +=" - OK";
        Console.WriteLine(message);
    };
```

```
SubscriptionGetResponse status = client.Subscriptions.Get();
Console.WriteLine(string.Format(
    "Subscription: {0} ({1}) with admin: {2}",
    status.SubscriptionName, status.SubscriptionStatus,
    status.AccountAdminLiveEmailId));
checkAndPrint("Cores used",status.CurrentCoreCount,
    status.MaximumCoreCount);
checkAndPrint("DNS servers used", status.CurrentDnsServers,
    status.MaximumDnsServers);
checkAndPrint("Cloud Services used", status.
CurrentHostedServices,
    status.MaximumHostedServices);
checkAndPrint("Network sites used", status.
CurrentLocalNetworkSites,
    status.MaximumLocalNetworkSites);
checkAndPrint("Storage accounts used", status.
CurrentStorageAccounts,
    status.MaximumStorageAccounts);
checkAndPrint("Virtual network sites used", status.
CurrentVirtualNetworkSites,
    status.MaximumVirtualNetworkSites);
}
```

7. Add the following method, listing current certificates, to the class:

```
private void ListCertificates()
{
    var list = client.ManagementCertificates.List();
    foreach (ManagementCertificateListResponse
        .SubscriptionCertificate item in list)
    {
        Console.WriteLine(string.Format("{0} certificate found",
            item.Thumbprint));
    }
}
```

8. Add the following method, uploading a new management certificate, to the class:

```
public void UploadManagementCertificate(byte[] certificate)
{
    X509Certificate2 X509 = new X509Certificate2();
    X509.Import(certificate);
    try
    {
        OperationResponse resp = client.ManagementCertificates.
Create(
```

```
            new ManagementCertificateCreateParameters()
            {
                PublicKey = certificate,
                Thumbprint = X509.Thumbprint
            });
            if (resp.StatusCode == HttpStatusCode.Created)
            {
                Console.WriteLine("Operation submitted with id: {0}",
                    resp.RequestId);
            }
        }
        catch (CloudException ex)
        {
            //Details
        }
    }
```

9. Add the following method, listing the last hour's operations, to the class:

```
private void ListManagementOperations()
{
    var list= client.Subscriptions.ListOperations(
        new SubscriptionListOperationsParameters()
        {
            StartTime=DateTime.UtcNow.AddDays(-1),
            EndTime=DateTime.UtcNow,
            OperationStatus=OperationStatus.Succeeded
        });
    foreach (SubscriptionListOperationsResponse.
SubscriptionOperation
        item in list.SubscriptionOperations)
        {
        Console.WriteLine(string.Format("Operation: {0}",
            item.OperationName));
        Console.WriteLine(string.Format("By user: {0} from {1}",
            item.OperationCaller.UserEmailAddress,
            item.OperationCaller.ClientIPAddress));
        Console.WriteLine(string.Format("Status: {0}",
            item.OperationStatus));
        Console.WriteLine(string.Format("Started: {0} - Ended:
{1}",
            item.OperationStartedTime
        ,item.OperationCompletedTime));
    }
}
```

10. Add the following method, using the methods added earlier, to the class:

```
public static void RunExample()
{
    string subId = "{SUB_ID}";
    string certPath = @"{PFX_PATH}";
    string certPwd = "{PFX_PASSWORD}";
    string newCertPath = @"{NEW_CERT_PATH}";

    MonitoringAutomatingExample example =
        new MonitoringAutomatingExample(subId,
            File.ReadAllBytes(certPath), certPwd);
    example.SubscriptionCountersCheck();
    example.ListCertificates();
    example.UploadManagementCertificate(File
        .ReadAllBytes(newCertPath));
    example.ListManagementOperations();
}
```

How it works...

In steps 1 through 3, we set up the class. In step 4, we added a `private` member to store the `ManagementClient` object used to connect to the Management service. We initialized this in the constructor we added in step 5.

In step 6, we built a lambda that takes two numbers (current and max) and prints a result by the following rules:

▶ If the current number is 75 percent more than the max number, the lambda shows **Attention**

▶ If the current number is less than or equal to 75 percent of the max number, the lambda shows **OK**

After printing the subscription name and the administrator's e-mail, we then ask Azure for every current counter of our subscription, printing its status of saturation using the lambda defined earlier.

 For each subscription, Azure defines some limits for its resources. We must take these limits into planning considerations, when we design an infrastructure, not by a numerical perspective (many of them could be increased by calling Microsoft Support) but knowing that they exist and designing our software to react to saturation, properly.

In step 7, we listed the current management certificates. You can expect to see many results if you used Visual Studio to connect to Azure from different devices.

In step 8, we uploaded a new `.CER` certificate to the management portal. If we hold the private key of the new certificate; we could also use it instead of the old one. Remember that the new certificate must be different from any of the previously uploaded ones, or an error would occur. In step 9, we used the `ListOperations()` method to obtain the operation log for the last hour.

In step 10, we called the methods added earlier, specifying the Subscription ID on which we need to operate with respect to the physical path of the PFX certificate, its password, and the path of the new certificate to upload. Replace the `{SUB_ID}`, `{PFX_PATH}`, `{PFX_PASSWORD}`, and `{NEW_CERT_PATH }` parts with the actual values.

There's more...

Under the hood, the `ManagementClient` class and its subclasses implement HTTP operations using the new Async-ready .NET stack, with the `HttpClient` library. According to its model, `ManagementClient` could be extended to intercept HTTP operations through the concept of `DelegatingHandler`. A `DelegatingHandler` class is a handler that is called during the request/response pipeline, where the user can add custom code to perform workflow operations.

In the following example, we create a `DelegatingHandler` class that tries to get a custom header from the HTTP response, launching a custom action behind the scenes:

```
public class TraceRequestDelegatingHandler : DelegatingHandler
{
    ManagementClient client = null;
    public TraceRequestDelegatingHandler(ManagementClient client)
    {
        this.client = client;
    }
    protected override async Task<HttpResponseMessage> SendAsync
        (HttpRequestMessage request, CancellationToken
cancellationToken)
    {
        return await base.SendAsync(request, cancellationToken)
            .ContinueWith<HttpResponseMessage>(task=>{
                HttpResponseMessage response = task.Result;

                if (response.IsSuccessStatusCode)
                {
                    var requestId = response.Headers
                        .GetValues("x-ms-request-id").
FirstOrDefault();
```

```
                    if (requestId!=null)
                    {
                        OperationStatusResponse status
                            = client.
GetOperationStatus(requestId);
                        if (status.Status == OperationStatus.
Failed)
                        {
                            //do something
                        }
                    }

                }
                return response;
            },TaskContinuationOptions.OnlyOnRanToCompletion);
        }
    }
```

When we override the `SendAsync` method, we tell the base handler to process the request, and in the case of success, we tell it to execute a custom script, extracting from the headers a specific one (the RequestId of the last request). To integrate this handler into the `ManagementClient` pipeline, the following code is required:

```
private void InterceptResponseFlow()
{
    client = client.WithHandler(
        new TraceRequestDelegatingHandler(client));
    //Do something
}
```

Every subsequent operation of the `WithHandler()` registration will pass through the custom handler.

See also

Have a look at these MSDN links to get additional information:

- Azure subscription and service limits, quotas, and constraints at `http://azure.microsoft.com/en-us/documentation/articles/azure-subscription-service-limits/`

- How to increase limits at `http://azure.microsoft.com/blog/2014/06/04/azure-limits-quotas-increase-requests/`

- HTTP message handlers at `http://www.asp.net/web-api/overview/working-with-http/http-message-handlers`

Automating SQL Database operations

The Azure SQL Database is the fully managed PaaS version of a SQLServer-like database engine in the cloud.

When dealing with big multitenant infrastructures, where we pool group of tenants into the same database, automation solutions on database management are necessary.

Let's assume that we need to automate the creation process of a new database. As far as we know, we can proceed as follows:

1. Use the Azure T-SQL (**create database**).
2. Use the Management API (even through the managed libraries).

If then we need to create new servers, only the second option remains available. It is easy to understand that if we want to scale out automatically, an automated management solution has to be implemented on the Management API side.

In this recipe, we will see some basics of SQL Database management through the APIs.

Getting ready

This recipe assumes that we created a valid certificate, and we exported it to a CER file and a PFX file. The first file should be uploaded to the Azure Portal, and the second one (with its password) has to be used in the code. We also need the Subscription ID of the subscription on which we operate. To complete these steps, read the *Setting up the management client* recipe.

How to do it...

We are going to list the current SQL Database servers and databases, looking at some properties. We will then create a new server and database. We will do this using the following steps:

1. Add a new class named `AutomatingSQLDatabaseExample` to the project.
2. Install the `Microsoft.WindowsAzure.Management` NuGet package.
3. Add the following `using` statements to the top of the class file:

```
using Microsoft.WindowsAzure;
using Microsoft.WindowsAzure.Management.Sql;
using Microsoft.WindowsAzure.Management.Sql.Models;
using System.Security.Cryptography.X509Certificates;
using System.IO;
```

4. Add the following `private` member to the class:

```
SqlManagementClient client = null;
```

5. Add the following constructor to the class:

```
public AutomatingSQLDatabaseExample(string subId,
    byte[] certificate, string password = null)
{
    client = new SqlManagementClient(
        new CertificateCloudCredentials(subId,
            new X509Certificate2(certificate, password)));
}
```

6. Add the following method, listing servers and databases, to the class:

```
public void ListServersAndDatabases()
{
    ServerListResponse servers = client.Servers.List();
    foreach (Server server in servers)
    {
        Console.WriteLine(string.Format("Server: {0} - Admin: {1}",
            server.Name, server.AdministratorUserName));
        Console.WriteLine(string.Format("Version: {0} - Location: {1}",
            server.Version, server.Location));
        DatabaseListResponse databases =
            client.Databases.List(server.Name);
        foreach (Database db in databases)
        {
            Console.WriteLine(string.Format(
                "DB: {0} - Edition: {1} - Size: {2} - MaxSize: {3}",
                db.Name, db.Edition, db.SizeMB, db.
MaximumDatabaseSizeInGB));
        }
    }
}
```

7. Add the following method, creating a new database, to the class:

```
public void CreateNewServerAndDatabase(string admin,
    string password, string databaseName)
{
    ServerCreateResponse resp= client.Servers
        .Create(new ServerCreateParameters()
        {
```

```
            AdministratorUserName=admin,
            AdministratorPassword=password,
            Version="2.0",
            Location="West Europe"
    });
    if (resp.StatusCode == System.Net.HttpStatusCode.Created)
    {
        var db=client.Databases.Create(resp.ServerName,
            new DatabaseCreateParameters()
        {
            Edition="BASIC",
            MaximumDatabaseSizeInGB=1,
            Name=databaseName
        });
        if (db.StatusCode == System.Net.HttpStatusCode.Created)
        {
            Database database = db.Database;
        }
    }
}
```

8. Add the following method, using the methods added earlier, to the class:

```
public static void RunExample()
{
    string subId = "{SUB_ID}";
    string certPath = @"{PFX_PATH}";
    string certPwd = "{PFX_PASSWORD}";
    string adminName = "{S_ADMIN}";
    string adminPassword = "{S_PASSWORD}";
    string dbName = "{DB_NAME}";

    AutomatingSQLDatabaseExample example =
        new AutomatingSQLDatabaseExample(subId,
            File.ReadAllBytes(certPath), certPwd);
    example.ListServersAndDatabases();
    example.CreateNewServerAndDatabase(
        adminName, adminPassword, dbName);
}
```

How it works...

In steps 1 through 3, we set up the class. In step 4, we added a `private` member to store the `SqlManagementClient` object used to connect to the Management service. We initialized this in the constructor we added in step 5.

In step 6, we listed the current servers of the subscription, looking, among other properties, at the server version. Version 1.0, to be discontinued in 2015, is the one supporting the Web and BusinessDB editions, while Version 2.0 is the one supporting the Basic, Standard, and Premium DB performance levels.

Therefore, in step 7, we created a Version 2.0 server with a basic database in it.

In step 8, we called the methods added earlier, specifying the Subscription ID on which to operate with respect to the physical path of the PFX certificate, its password, the new database name, and the credentials of the server to use. Replace the `{SUB_ID}`, `{PFX_PATH}`, `{PFX_PASSWORD}`, `{DB_NAME}`, `{S_ADMIN}`, and `{S_PASSWORD}` parts with the actual values.

There's more...

The SQL Database offers an **Import/Export** feature that lets customers export the entire database (schema and data) into a self-contained unit called BACPAC. This feature could be scheduled to run automatically and periodically, but we can also use the Management API to perform manual imports and exports.

The following code show how to create a new database by importing an existing BACPAC, which is located in a storage account:

```
public void ImportBACPAC(string serverName,string admin,
    string password,string database, Uri storageUri,string
storageKey)
{
    DacImportExportResponse res = client.Dac
        .Import(serverName, new DacImportParameters()
    {
        AzureEdition = "Business",
        BlobCredentials = new DacImportParameters
            .BlobCredentialsParameter()
        {
            Uri = storageUri,
            StorageAccessKey = storageKey
        },
```

```
            ConnectionInfo = new DacImportParameters
                .ConnectionInfoParameter()
            {
                DatabaseName = database,
                ServerName = serverName,
                UserName = admin,
                Password = password
            },
            DatabaseSizeInGB = 150
    });
    if (res.StatusCode == System.Net.HttpStatusCode.OK)
    {
        //Check async import status
    }
}
```

Note that the destination server version must be 1.0 in order to permit the Business edition to be created correctly.

See also

Have a look at the following MSDN links to get additional information:

▶ Using a DAC BACPAC to migrate a database at `http://msdn.microsoft.com/en-us/library/jj156148.aspx`

▶ Azure SQL Database service tiers at `http://msdn.microsoft.com/en-us/library/dn741336.aspx`

Using Azure PowerShell

Azure PowerShell uses the Azure Service Management REST API to expose service management operations as PowerShell cmdlets. The cmdlets provide a convenient way to manage many aspects of an Azure subscription.

In this recipe, we will learn how to use Azure PowerShell cmdlets to invoke various service operations in the Azure Service Management REST API, and we will create a sample Azure cache endpoint.

Getting ready

If necessary, we can download Azure PowerShell from **Web Platform Installer**.

How to do it...

We are going to use the Azure PowerShell to retrieve various properties of an Azure subscription, as follows:

1. Open the **Azure PowerShell** console.

 The first time we use the Azure PowerShell console, we might be required to authorize the execution of various pieces of software. We can select **R** (run once) or **A** (always run) for each module to be loaded.

2. Type `Add-AzureAccount` and press *Enter*. A pop-up window might appear. Type your credentials that are connected to a valid Azure subscription and continue.

3. Type `Get-AzureWebsite` to retrieve the list of current websites.

4. Type `Get-AzureSqlDatabaseServer` to retrieve the list of current SQL Database servers.

5. Type `Get-AzureLocation` to retrieve the currently available Regions.

6. Type `Get-AzureManagedCache` to retrieve the currently available caches.

7. Type the following command to create a new cache endpoint:

    ```
    New-AzureManagedCache -Name myCache -Location "West Europe" -Sku
    Standard -Memory 1GB
    ```

8. Type `Get-AzureService` to retrieve the current Cloud Services.

9. Type the following command to create a new Cloud Service:

    ```
    New-AzureService -ServiceName myService -Location "North Europe"
    ```

How it works...

In step 1, we open **Azure PowerShell**, authorizing it to execute its scripts. In step 2, we linked our Azure subscriptions to PowerShell. The process is automatic, as PowerShell asks for a valid management credential. If we have multiple subscriptions, everything is now linked to PowerShell.

In step 3, we listed all the current websites; for step 4, we listed the SQL Database servers; and in step 5, we listed the Regions. In steps 6 and 7, we listed the existing cache endpoints and create a new one.

In steps 7 and 8, we finally listed the available Cloud Services and created a new one, specifying the service name for the Region where we need to place it.

There's more...

An incredible set of cmdlets are available in Azure PowerShell, performing almost every operation available in the platform. To get a complete list of commands, type the following command:

```
help azure
```

To refine the search on a single area (for example, the SQL Database), type the following command:

```
help sqldatabase
```

PowerShell will filter the search result in the help libraries according to the selection.

See also

Have a look at the following MSDN links to get additional information:

- ▶ Getting started with Azure Powershell at `http://azure.microsoft.com/en-us/documentation/articles/install-configure-powershell/`
- ▶ Getting started with the Azure Cross-Platform Command-Line Interface at `http://azure.microsoft.com/en-us/documentation/articles/xplat-cli/`

8

Going In-memory with Azure Cache

In this chapter, we will cover the following topics:

- ▶ Building a simple cache for applications
- ▶ Using local cache and notifications
- ▶ Diagnosing cache and optimizing performance
- ▶ Using advanced caching features
- ▶ Using Redis Cache in Azure

Introduction

Today's software applications often need to be designed to be resilient under varying degrees of load that originates from web or mobile clients. Either we are dealing with a web service tier (or web API) or just frontend web applications. Scaling to thousands or millions of users is something that is not only up to the infrastructure, but, mainly, it is a software aspect. Best practices while writing software could avoid bottlenecks and performance issues. We can save some CPU cycles (and potentially, save money on Azure by allocating less instances) by optimizing the most used functions, and we can rely on common sense to protect our core resources from the external attacks (database, for example).

At the end of what we can optimize in terms of software, we have the ubiquitous, big issue of data access. Scalable persistence stores have been a very important problem to solve in recent years, especially for the correlation between **persisting something** and **slow performance**. We write something on the disk either using the OS filesystem API or through a database engine. This is a slow operation as compared to the in-memory operations and CPU cycles. The world of software tried to mix disk and memory to gain some points in the benchmarks, making hybrid scenarios of storage system, which support quick in-memory reads/writes that are eventually consistent.

> For many years, disks have been considered the slowest alternative in terms of memory. Nowadays, with the advent of **Solid State Drives** (**SSDs**), disks are faster mostly due to decreased latency. The conjunction between faster disks and in-memory strategies could lead to a great gain of performance in most software applications.

NoSQL momentum also focuses on this dogma, telling us that if we want scalability, redundancy, and high availability, we must sacrifice the synchrony of systems. In fact, **eventually consistent** suggests that there is something to persist on the data storage here. Do this as soon as possible; in the meantime, data will not be consistent.

Potentially, in the future, the performance of disk operations will be compared to the in-memory counterparts. However, now, the difference is very high (even with SSDs), and we must consider hybrid scenarios to implement fast applications.

Azure Managed Cache is the managed, in-memory, and fast cache service to read/write frequently used data. On almost each tier of a complex application, there is some kind of caching system. The foundation of cache is: The first time we access the real data storage (slower), we save the results in the cache. From then on, we access the cache (faster) until someone or the cache itself removes the cached item due to its expiration. Cached data that is inconsistent with the real data storage (because it is deprecated) is called **stale data**.

Azure Cache is a standalone service that we can access remotely (from everywhere) and, of course, from every Azure compute service such as Websites, Cloud Services, and Virtual Machines. This makes the Cache service also a place to store shared objects between different applications and sources. As it is managed, we are not involved in scalability consideration, and there is no throttling or quotas, except for the reserved size of the cache that we declare at the time of configuration. Azure Cache is completely integrated with the .NET platform through a library (also available on NuGet); for other platforms, there is a shim (an adapter) that provides a Memcache abstraction layer to non-.NET clients, translating calls to the Azure Cache service.

Anyway, the best cache solution for non-.NET clients could be the new **Azure Redis Cache**, which is based on Redis and is compatible with every Redis client developed by the community. Redis Cache is also a NoSQL key-value store, and it is supported in .NET applications as well, through a variety of libraries.

In the *Building a simple cache for applications* recipe, we set up a cache endpoint and perform some simple operations to explore the basic APIs. Azure Cache is secured by the transport (that could be over SSL), and access is guaranteed by a shared key. There are some interesting features of Cache, such as notifications, depending on the version we choose in the Azure Portal. In the *Using local cache and notifications* recipe, we show how to be informed about changes made by other clients on the cache itself. Local cache speeds up the application performance by establishing an additional layer of cache on the client side, avoiding useless TCP calls to the distributed cache service. Even if Azure Cache is a fast, in-memory, and managed service, local cache helps gain another small percentage on the overall performance counters.

This chapter is about Cache, but it is really about performance. Caching is made to gain performance, and we need to move in that direction for every choice we make while using it. In the *Diagnosing cache and optimizing performance* recipe, we will see how to evaluate the performance indicators of the Cache service and how to control the connections and the serialization process. Despite the Cache service being a powerful service from the client's perspective; it is quite a simple service in terms of functionalities, as compared to the growing Azure Redis Cache service.

> To be complete, today, there are three ways to implement an in-memory cache in Azure. In addition to the Azure Managed Cache and the new Redis Cache (both discussed in the chapter), users can use their own worker roles in Cloud Services to host an arbitrary amount of memory dedicated to cache. This is often referred to as In-Role Caching, and more information about it can be found at http://azure.microsoft.com/en-en/documentation/articles/cache-dotnet-how-to-use-in-role/.

In the *Using advanced caching features* recipe, we will see how to use user-defined regions together with the tagging capability, to search for semantically stored items. We will also see a brief excursus on optimistic and pessimistic concurrency with multiple clients. Finally, in the *Using Redis Cache in Azure* recipe, we will cover a short introduction to the Redis Cache, using the well-known, popular, and fast `StackExchange.Redis` library.

Building a simple cache for applications

Azure Cache is a managed service with (at the time of writing this book) the following three offerings:

- **Basic**: This service has a unit size of 128 MB, up to 1 GB with one named cache (the default one)
- **Standard**: This service has a unit size of 1 GB, up to 10 GB with 10 named caches and support for notifications
- **Premium**: This service has a unit size of 5 GB, up to 150 GB with ten named caches, support for notifications, and high availability

Different offerings have different unit prices, and remember that when changing from one offering to another, all the cache data is lost. In all offerings, users can define the items' expiration.

The Cache service listens to a specific TCP port. Accessing it from a .NET application is quite simple, with the Microsoft ApplicationServer Caching library available on NuGet. In the `Microsoft.ApplicationServer.Caching` namespace, the following are all the classes that are needed to operate:

- ▸ **DataCacheFactory**: This class is responsible for instantiating the Cache proxies to interpret the configuration settings.

- ▸ **DataCache**: This class is responsible for the read/write operation against the cache endpoint.

- ▸ **DataCacheFactoryConfiguration**: This is the model class of the configuration settings of a cache factory. Its usage is optional as cache can be configured in the `App/Web.config` file in a specific configuration section.

Azure Cache is a key-value cache. We can insert and even get complex objects with arbitrary tree depth using string keys to locate them. The importance of the key is critical, as in a single named cache, only one object can exist for a given key. The architects and developers should have the proper strategy in place to deal with unique (and hierarchical) names.

Getting ready

This recipe assumes that we have a valid Azure Cache endpoint of the standard type. We need the standard type because we use multiple named caches, and in later recipes, we use notifications.

We can create a standard cache endpoint of 1 GB via PowerShell, as mentioned in the *Using Azure PowerShell* recipe of *Chapter 7, Managing Azure Resources with the Azure Management Libraries*.

Perform the following steps to create the standard cache endpoint :

1. Open the Azure PowerShell and type `Add-AzureAccount`. A popup window might appear. Type your credentials connected to a valid Azure subscription and continue.

   ❑ Optionally, select the proper **Subscription**, if not the default one.

2. Type this command to create a new cache endpoint, replacing `myCache` with the proper unique name:

   ```
   New-AzureManagedCache -Name myCache -Location "West Europe" -Sku
   Standard -Memory 1GB
   ```

3. After waiting for some minutes until the endpoint is ready, go to the Azure Portal and look for the **Manage Keys** section to get one of the two Access Keys of the cache endpoint.

4. In the **Configure** section of the cache endpoint, a cache named `default`is created by default. In addition, create two named caches with the following parameters:

   ❑ Expiry Policy: **Absolute**

   ❑ Time: **10**

   ❑ Notifications: **Enabled**

> Expiry Policy could be Absolute (the default expiration time or the one set by the user is absolute, regardless of how many times the item has been accessed), Sliding (each time the item has been accessed, the expiration timer resets), or Never (items do not expire).

This Azure Cache endpoint is now available in the Management Portal, and it will be used in the entire chapter.

How to do it...

We are going to create a DataCache instance through a code-based configuration. We will perform simple operations with Add, Get, Put, and Append/Prepend, using a secondary-named cache to transfer all the contents of the primary one.

We will do this by performing the following steps:

1. Add a new class named `BuildingSimpleCacheExample` to the project.

2. Install the `Microsoft.WindowsAzure.Caching` NuGet package.

3. Add the following `using` statement to the top of the class file:

   ```
   using Microsoft.ApplicationServer.Caching;
   ```

4. Add the following `private` members to the class:

   ```
   private DataCacheFactory factory = null;
   private DataCache cache = null;
   ```

5. Add the following constructor to the class:

   ```
   public BuildingSimpleCacheExample(string ep,
       string token,string cacheName)
   {
   ```

```
            DataCacheFactoryConfiguration config
                = new DataCacheFactoryConfiguration();
            config.AutoDiscoverProperty
                = new DataCacheAutoDiscoverProperty(true, ep);
            config.SecurityProperties
                = new DataCacheSecurity(token, true);

            factory = new DataCacheFactory(config);
            cache = factory.GetCache(cacheName);
    }
```

6. Add the following method, creating a palindrome string into the cache:

```
public void CreatePalindromeInCache()
{
    var objKey = "StringArray";
    cache.Put(objKey, "");
    char letter = 'A';
    for (int i = 0; i < 10; i++)
    {
        cache.Append(objKey,
            char.ConvertFromUtf32((letter+i)));
        cache.Prepend(objKey,
            char.ConvertFromUtf32((letter + i)));
    }
    Console.WriteLine(cache.Get(objKey));
}
```

7. Add the following method, adding an item into the cache to analyze its subsequent retrievals:

```
public void AddAndAnalyze()
{
    var randomKey = DateTime.Now.Ticks.ToString();
    var value="Cached string";
    cache.Add(randomKey, value);
    DataCacheItem cacheItem = cache.GetCacheItem(randomKey);
    Console.WriteLine(string.Format(
        "Item stored in {0} region with {1} expiration",
        cacheItem.RegionName,cacheItem.Timeout));
    cache.Put(randomKey, value, TimeSpan.FromSeconds(60));
    cacheItem = cache.GetCacheItem(randomKey);
    Console.WriteLine(string.Format(
        "Item stored in {0} region with {1} expiration",
        cacheItem.RegionName, cacheItem.Timeout));
```

```
    var version = cacheItem.Version;
    var obj = cache.GetIfNewer(randomKey, ref version);
    if (obj == null)
    {
        //No updates
    }
}
```

8. Add the following method, transferring the contents of the cache named initially into a second one:

```
public void BackupToDestination(string destCacheName)
{
    var destCache = factory.GetCache(destCacheName);
    var dump = cache.GetSystemRegions()
        .SelectMany(p => cache.GetObjectsInRegion(p))
        .ToDictionary(p=>p.Key,p=>p.Value);
    foreach (var item in dump)
    {
        destCache.Put(item.Key, item.Value);
    }
}
```

9. Add the following method to clear the cache named first:

```
public void ClearCache()
{
    cache.Clear();
}
```

10. Add the following method, using the methods added earlier, to the class:

```
public static void RunExample()
{
    var cacheName = "[named cache 1]";
    var backupCache = "[named cache 2]";
    string endpoint = "[cache endpoint]";
    string token = "[cache token/key]";

    BuildingSimpleCacheExample example
        = new BuildingSimpleCacheExample(endpoint,
            token, cacheName);
    example.CreatePalindromeInCache();
    example.AddAndAnalyze();
    example.BackupToDestination(backupCache);
    example.ClearCache();
}
```

How it works...

From steps 1 to 3, we set up the class. In step 4, we added `private` members to store the `DataCacheFactory` object used to create the `DataCache` object to access the Cache service. In the constructor that we added in step 5, we initialized the `DataCacheFactory` object using a configuration model class (`DataCacheFactoryConfiguration`). This strategy is for code-based initialization whenever settings cannot stay in the `App.config`/`Web.config` file.

In step 6, we used the `Put()` method to write an empty string into the `StringArray` bucket. We then used the `Append()` and `Prepend()` methods, designed to concatenate strings to existing strings, to build a palindrome string in the memory cache.

This sample does not make any sense in real-world scenarios, and we must pay attention to some of the following issues:

- ▸ Writing an empty string into the cache is somehow useless.
- ▸ Each `Append()` or `Prepend()` operation travels on TCP to the cache and goes back. Though it is very simple, it requires resources, and we should always try to consolidate calls.

In step 7, we used the `Add()` method to add a string to the cache. The difference between the `Add()` and `Put()` methods is that the first method throws an exception if the item already exists, while the second one always overwrites the existing value (or writes it for the first time). `GetCacheItem()` returns a `DataCacheItem` object, which wraps the value together with other metadata properties, such as the following:

- ▸ **CacheName**: This is the named cache where the object is stored.
- ▸ **Key**: This is the key of the associated bucket.
- ▸ **RegionName** (user defined or system defined): This is the region of the cache where the object is stored. More about regions can be found in the *Using advanced caching features* recipe.
- ▸ **Size**: This is the size of the object stored.
- ▸ **Tags**: These are the optional tags of the object, if it is located in a user-defined region.
- ▸ **Timeout**: This is the current timeout before the object would expire.
- ▸ **Version**: This is the version of the object. This is a `DataCacheItemVersion` object whose properties are not accessible due to their modifier. However, it is not important to access this property, as the `Version` object is used as a token against the Cache service to implement the optimistic concurrency. As for the timestamp value, its semantic can stay hidden from developers.

The first `Add()` method does not specify a timeout for the object, leaving the default global expiration timeout, while the next `Put()` method does, as we can check in the next `Get()` method. We finally asked the cache about the object with the `GetIfNewer()` method, passing the latest version token we have. This conditional `Get` method returns null if the object we own is already the latest one.

In step 8, we listed all the keys of the first named cache, using the `GetSystemRegions()` method (to first list the system-defined regions), and for each region, we asked for their objects, copying them into the second named cache. In step 9, we cleared all the contents of the first cache.

In step 10, we called the methods added earlier, specifying the cache endpoint to connect to and the token/password, along with the two named caches in use. Replace `[named cache 1]`, `[named cache 2]`, `[cache endpoint]`, and `[cache token/key]` with actual values.

There's more...

Code-based configuration is useful when the settings stay in a different place as compared to the default config files for .NET. It is not a best practice to hardcode them, so this is the standard way to declare them in the `App.config` file:

```
<configSections>
  <section name="dataCacheClients" type="Microsoft.ApplicationServer.
Caching.DataCacheClientsSection, Microsoft.ApplicationServer.Caching.
Core" allowLocation="true" allowDefinition="Everywhere" />
</configSections>
```

The XML mentioned earlier declares a custom section, which should be as follows:

```
<dataCacheClients>
  <dataCacheClient name="[name of cache]">
    <autoDiscover isEnabled="true" identifier="[domain of cache]" />
    <securityProperties mode="Message" sslEnabled="true">
      <messageSecurity authorizationInfo="[token of endpoint]" />
    </securityProperties>
  </dataCacheClient>
</dataCacheClients>
```

In the upcoming recipes, we will use this convention to set up the `DataCache` objects.

ASP.NET Support

With almost no effort, the Azure Cache can be used as Output Cache in ASP.NET to save the session state. To enable this, in addition to the configuration mentioned earlier, we need to include those declarations in the `<system.web>` section as follows:

```
<sessionState mode="Custom" customProvider="AFCacheSessionStateProvid
er">
  <providers>
    <add name="AFCacheSessionStateProvider" type="Microsoft.
Web.DistributedCache.DistributedCacheSessionStateStoreProvider,
Microsoft.Web.DistributedCache" cacheName="[named cache]"
dataCacheClientName="[name of cache]" applicationName="AFCacheSession
State"/>
  </providers>
</sessionState>
<caching>
  <outputCache defaultProvider="AFCacheOutputCacheProvider">
    <providers>
      <add name="AFCacheOutputCacheProvider" type="Microsoft.Web.
DistributedCache.DistributedCacheOutputCacheProvider, Microsoft.Web.
DistributedCache" cacheName="[named cache]" dataCacheClientName="[name
of cache]" applicationName="AFCacheOutputCache" />
    </providers>
  </outputCache>
</caching>
```

The difference between [name of cache] and [named cache] is as follows:

- ▸ The [name of cache] part is a friendly name of the cache client declared above an alias.
- ▸ The [named cache] part is the named cache created in the Azure Cache service.

See also

Have a look at the following MSDN links to get additional information:

- ▸ Azure Managed Cache documentation at `http://msdn.microsoft.com/en-us/library/azure/dn386094.aspx`
- ▸ More about Output Cache at `http://msdn.microsoft.com/en-us/library/vstudio/sfw2210t(v=vs.100).aspx`

Using local cache and notifications

Distributed cache solves a series of critical issues when we develop distributed systems. In these systems, often made by many servers working in a pool, the state should be persisted somewhere out of process. In fact, in case of a scalable web application made by *N* identical stateless servers in parallel, no one can safely own the state of something either because it might fail or because the other servers cannot access the web application and they can't even know that something is stored into a peer's state.

So, distributed cache solves this big problem by keeping the state out of process, out of server, and sometimes out of datacenter. However, this comes at a price. First is the latency of networks due to the physical distance between the client (stateless application) and server (caching endpoint). Second, the network bandwidth is not infinite, and it is certainly slower than in-process memory operations. Therefore, we must reduce the number of cache calls for frequently accessed data, especially if those data are not updated. We can call it just a local cache. The local cache is the fastest, in-process cache that runs in the same memory area for the application that uses it. It is only a client abstraction as it does not require any configuration on the endpoint side; in fact, the cache endpoint can never know anything about it.

Local cache can be configured via code or configuration file, providing some settings that tell the Azure Cache library how to behave and refresh it during the time. The `DataCacheLocalCacheProperties` class defines the following properties:

- **ObjectCount**: This defines how many objects to keep in the local cache.
- **InvalidationPolicy**: This defines how to determine if an object is stale. Refer to the following points:
  - **TimeoutBased**: using the `DefaultTimeout` property, we specify how much time the local cache must wait to remove an object
  - **NotificationBased**: using the notification feature, the local cache is notified as soon as the real item (on the cache side) is expired or changed

Notification features allow the `DataCache` object to be notified about the changes that happened in the real cache tier. Actually, the Azure Cache does not actively notify the remote clients; instead, it collects a list of occurred events that a client can read (by polling) and makes the appropriate decisions. Notifications, in conjunction with the local cache, let their objects be removed gracefully in a very short time after the server event occurs.

On the client side, we can control the notification with the following methods:

- `AddCacheLevelCallback`: This is called whenever a specified operation occurs on the entire cache
- `AddItemLevelCallback`: This is called when a specified operation occurs on a single item

In this recipe, we demonstrate the local cache features for the notification mechanism.

Getting ready

This recipe assumes that we created a valid cache endpoint. This section should be included in the application configuration file:

```
<configSections>
  <section name="dataCacheClients" type="Microsoft.ApplicationServer.
Caching.DataCacheClientsSection, Microsoft.ApplicationServer.Caching.
Core" allowLocation="true" allowDefinition="Everywhere" />
</configSections>
```

The XML mentioned earlier declares a custom section, which should be as follows:

```
<dataCacheClients>
  <dataCacheClient name="[name of cache]">
    <autoDiscover isEnabled="true" identifier="[domain of cache]" />
    <securityProperties mode="Message" sslEnabled="true">
      <messageSecurity authorizationInfo="[token of endpoint]" />
    </securityProperties>
  </dataCacheClient>
</dataCacheClients>
```

Replace [name of cache] with an alias (in the recipe, we use the default named cache), replace [domain of cache] with the endpoint's fully qualified domain name, and replace [token of endpoint] with the token/password obtained by the Azure Portal.

How to do it...

We are going to create three independent DataCache instances to operate on the same Azure Cache endpoint, showing how the local cache works and how to be notified of changes. We will do this by performing the following steps:

1. Add a new class named LocalCacheNotificationExample to the project.

2. Install the Microsoft.WindowsAzure.Caching NuGet package.

3. Add the following using statements to the top of the class file:

```
using Microsoft.ApplicationServer.Caching;
using System.Threading;
using System.Threading.Tasks;
```

4. Add the following private members to the class:

```
private DataCache firstCachePointer = null;
private DataCache secondCachePointer = null;
private DataCache thirdCachePointer = null;
private string objectKey = "LocalCacheNotificationExample";
```

5. Add the following constructor to the class:

```
public LocalCacheNotificationExample(string cacheName)
{
    var firstCacheConfig = new DataCacheFactoryConfiguration("defa
ult");
    var localConfig = new DataCacheLocalCacheProperties(
        objectCount: 1000,
        defaultTimeout: TimeSpan.FromSeconds(5),
        invalidationPolicy: DataCacheLocalCacheInvalidationPolicy.
TimeoutBased);
    firstCacheConfig.LocalCacheProperties = localConfig;
    firstCachePointer = new DataCacheFactory(firstCacheConfig).
GetCache(cacheName);

    secondCachePointer = new DataCacheFactory().
GetCache(cacheName);

    var thirdCacheConfig = new DataCacheFactoryConfiguration("defa
ult");
    var notificationConfig = new DataCacheNotificationProperties(
        maxQueueLength: 1000,
        pollInterval: TimeSpan.FromSeconds(1));
    thirdCacheConfig.NotificationProperties = notificationConfig;
    thirdCachePointer = new DataCacheFactory(thirdCacheConfig).
GetCache(cacheName);
}
```

6. Add the following method, using notifications, to the class:

```
public void MonitorRemoteCacheChanges()
{
    thirdCachePointer.AddCacheLevelCallback(
        DataCacheOperations.AddItem |
        DataCacheOperations.RemoveItem |
        DataCacheOperations.ReplaceItem,
        (cName, cRegion, oKey, oVersion, opId, nDescriptor) =>
        {
            var version = oVersion.GetType()
                .GetProperty("InternalVersion",
                System.Reflection.BindingFlags.NonPublic
                | System.Reflection.BindingFlags.Instance)
                .GetValue(oVersion).ToString();
            Console.WriteLine(string.Format(
                "{0} occurred in {1} for item {2} with version
{3}",
                opId,cName,oKey,version));
        });
}
```

375

7. Add the following method, replacing the item after a delay, to the class:

```
public void WaitAndReplaceItem()
{
    Task.Delay(2000).ContinueWith(t =>
    { secondCachePointer.Put(objectKey,
        "Summer is Coming!"); });
}
```

8. Add the following method, continuously replacing the item, to the class:

```
public void PutAndGet10Times()
{
    DataCacheItemVersion current= firstCachePointer
        .Put(objectKey, "Winter is Coming!");
    firstCachePointer.AddItemLevelCallback(
        objectKey, DataCacheOperations.ReplaceItem,
        (cName, cRegion, oKey, oVersion, opId, nDescriptor) =>
        {
            Console.WriteLine(
                "The item " +objectKey+" has been replaced");
        });
    for (int i = 0; i < 10; i++)
    {
        var obj = firstCachePointer.Get(objectKey);
        Console.WriteLine(string.Format(
            "Element {0}:{1} retrieved"
            ,i,obj));
        Thread.Sleep(1000);
    }
}
```

9. Add the following method, using the methods added earlier, to the class:

```
public static void RunExample()
{
    var cacheName = "[named cache]";
    LocalCacheNotificationExample example
        = new LocalCacheNotificationExample(cacheName);
    example.MonitorRemoteCacheChanges();
    example.WaitAndReplaceItem();
    example.PutAndGet10Times();
}
```

How it works...

From steps 1 to 3, we set up the class. In step 4, we added `private` members to store the three `DataCache` objects used to access the Cache service and a string key that represents the cache item that we are working on.

In step 5, we added a complex constructor that acts as follows:

- For the first cache pointer, it instantiates a `DataCacheFactoryConfiguration` object based on the configuration it reads from the `App.config` file. Then, it adds the local cache feature by specifying a timeout of 5 seconds and a maximum of 1000 objects.
- The second cache pointer is instantiated using the default configuration.
- For the third cache pointer, it instantiates a `DataCacheFactoryConfiguration` object that is customized with the notifications feature. It specifies a polling interval of 1 second, and 1000 notification elements are read each time.

> Please note that a notification polling interval of 1 second is not recommended. We should design the application to overcome some delays.

In step 6, we added a cache-level callback for some remote events (`Add`, `Remove`, and `Replace`). We used the third `DataCache` object to be sure that we are not working locally with the local cache.

> There are other events related to user-defined regions that we are not interested in for this example (`CreateRegion`, `RemoveRegion`, and `ClearRegion`).

The callback signature is quite complex, and even if we can guess it from the code, it adheres to this delegate:

```
public delegate void DataCacheNotificationCallback(string cacheName,
string regionName, string key, DataCacheItemVersion version,
DataCacheOperations cacheOperation, DataCacheNotificationDescriptor
nd);
```

Code inside the callback is for demonstration purposes only. In fact, as mentioned earlier in the chapter, the `DataCacheItemVersion` type does not expose public properties as it is used as a token from the library itself. However, we used reflection to look into the object to show how it manages the version identifiers.

In step 7, we launched a parallel task to overwrite the object into the cache after 2 seconds of delay. We used the second `DataCache` object to avoid the local cache to be updated, so the first `DataCache` object cannot know about these changes until it checks the Cache service.

In step 8, we put the initial value for the cache object, and subsequently, we got this 10 times to show how the various notifications behave from different `DataCache` objects. We expected to see an immediate notification from the `MonitorRemoteCacheChanges()` method, while no item-level notification will appear for the `AddItemLevelCallback` method added here. This is because we did not enable the notification feature for the first `DataCache` pointer. Finally, as we used a timeout-based local cache, we saw the updated item in the `Get` loop after 5 seconds.

In step 9, we called the methods added earlier, specifying the named cache used. Then, we replaced `[named cache]` with the actual value.

There's more...

Notifications can work via the following standalone callbacks:

- `AddCacheLevelBulkCallback`: This is a catch-all callback for cache operations on all regions and items
- `AddCacheLevelCallback`: This is a customizable callback for the entire cache and only the specified operations occurred
- `AddFailureNotificationCallback`: This is a callback for missed notifications
- `AddItemLevelCallback`: This is the item-level callback for cache operations on a specific object and for specific operations
- `AddRegionLevelCallback`: This is the region-level callback for cache operations in a specific region for specific operations

However, notifications can also be used in conjunction with the local cache mechanism, to avoid waiting for the local expiration to timeout. To enable the first `DataCache` pointer to receive notifications on the local cache, we can change the constructor as follows:

```
var firstCacheConfig = new DataCacheFactoryConfiguration("default");
var localConfig = new DataCacheLocalCacheProperties(
    objectCount: 1000,
    defaultTimeout: TimeSpan.FromSeconds(50),
    invalidationPolicy: DataCacheLocalCacheInvalidationPolicy.
NotificationBased);
var notificationConfig = new DataCacheNotificationProperties(
    maxQueueLength: 1000,
    pollInterval: TimeSpan.FromSeconds(1));
```

```
firstCacheConfig.NotificationProperties = notificationConfig;
firstCacheConfig.LocalCacheProperties = localConfig;
firstCachePointer = new DataCacheFactory(firstCacheConfig).
GetCache(cacheName);
```

We can now run the example and see that the local cache is immediately notified when items are changed on the cache side.

See also

Have a look at the following MSDN links to get additional information:

▶ Azure Managed Cache and local cache reference at `http://msdn.microsoft.com/en-us/library/azure/dn386096.aspx`

▶ Azure Managed Cache and notifications reference at `http://msdn.microsoft.com/en-us/library/azure/dn386095.aspx`

Diagnosing cache and optimizing performance

Azure Cache is a managed cache service provided as a service for Cloud and non-Cloud applications (as we saw in the previous recipes, we can even use it from a local environment).

Azure Portal provides developers with a simple chart-based dashboard to quickly understand cache metrics, which will help them while troubleshooting. We can explore the monitoring options of the Cache service by going on the Azure Portal in the **Monitor** section of a specific cache. Here, we see some metrics added by default:

▶ **Bandwidth used**: This refers to the percentage of committed bandwidth used by applications. The larger the objects in the cache, the higher will be this value.

▶ **Compute used**: This refers to the percentage of committed CPUs in the read/write operations. If this value is high, there will be an increase in the latency that might occur.

▶ **Memory used**: This refers to the percentage of total memory used by applications. Do not expect the exact byte-count value because there are some factors that influence this indicator (regions, tags, and notifications).

▶ **Cache miss**: This refers to the percentage of calls that do not find any values for the given key. A higher cache-miss value is generally bad due to some mistakes in the application logic.

▶ **Read/Write requests/sec**: This refers to the rate of requests in a given time frame.

Along with these metrics added by default, we have other options to explore, by clicking on the **Add Metrics** button in the bottom menu. Some of these are object count, bytes received/sent, expired objects, evicted objects, and so on.

 What is an **Evicted object**? Eviction is a process of removal of old resources, based on an **last recently used** (**LRU**) algorithm. Eviction is useful to prevent the cache memory from being saturated, removing the last-accessed objects first in order to free up some space.

Avoiding bottlenecks on the cache is very important to build scalable applications. In the *Using local cache and notifications* recipe, we saw how to increase throughput by maintaining a local in-process cache on the client side, which results in a good compromise between accuracy of data and performance. We must also avoid storing large objects in a single cache item. Despite being faster than DB or disk, an application should be designed to work against cache at a fine-grained level, caching many small objects instead of few large ones.

In this recipe, we will see how to implement a custom serialization to speed up the performance.

Getting ready

This recipe assumes that we created a valid cache endpoint. This section should be included in the application configuration file:

```
<configSections>
  <section name="dataCacheClients" type="Microsoft.ApplicationServer.
Caching.DataCacheClientsSection, Microsoft.ApplicationServer.Caching.
Core" allowLocation="true" allowDefinition="Everywhere" />
</configSections>
```

The XML mentioned earlier declares a custom section, which should be as follows:

```
<dataCacheClients>
  <dataCacheClient name="[name of cache]">
    <autoDiscover isEnabled="true" identifier="[domain of cache]" />
    <securityProperties mode="Message" sslEnabled="true">
      <messageSecurity authorizationInfo="[token of endpoint]" />
    </securityProperties>
  </dataCacheClient>
</dataCacheClients>
```

Replace [name of cache] with an alias (in the recipe, we use the default named cache), replace [domain of cache] with the endpoint's fully qualified domain name, and replace [token of endpoint] with the token/password obtained by the Azure Portal.

How to do it...

We are going to save a list of 100 items in the cache, using a custom serializer based on Json. NET. We will do this by performing the following steps:

1. Add a new class named `DiagnosingAndOptimizingExample` to the project.

2. Install the `Microsoft.WindowsAzure.Caching` and `Newtonsoft.Json` NuGet packages.

3. Add the following `using` statements to the top of the class file:

    ```
    using Microsoft.ApplicationServer.Caching;
    using Newtonsoft.Json;
    using System.Collections.Generic;
    using System.IO;
    using System.Linq;
    using System.Runtime.Serialization;
    ```

4. Add the following `private` members to the class:

    ```
    private DataCacheFactory factory = null;
    private DataCache cache = null;
    private string objectKey = "ListOf100Items";
    private DateTime operationStarted;
    private List<TimeSpan> elaspedValues = new List<TimeSpan>();
    ```

5. Add the following constructor to the class:

    ```
    public DiagnosingAndOptimizingExample(string cacheName)
    {
        var cacheConfig = new DataCacheFactoryConfiguration("defau
    lt");
        cacheConfig.IsCompressionEnabled = true;
        cacheConfig.MaxConnectionsToServer = 10;
        cacheConfig.RequestTimeout = TimeSpan.FromSeconds(1);
        cacheConfig.SerializationProperties =
            new DataCacheSerializationProperties(
                DataCacheObjectSerializerType.CustomSerializer,
                new JsonSerializer());
        factory = new DataCacheFactory(cacheConfig);
        cache=factory.GetCache(cacheName);
    }
    ```

6. Add the following class to the project:

```
public class JsonSerializer : IDataCacheObjectSerializer
{
    public object Deserialize(System.IO.Stream stream)
    {
        using (var reader = new StreamReader(stream))
        {
            return JsonConvert
                .DeserializeObject(reader.ReadToEnd());
        }
    }
    public void Serialize(System.IO.Stream stream, object value)
    {
        using (var output = new StreamWriter(stream))
        {
            output.Write(JsonConvert
                .SerializeObject(value));
        }
    }
}
```

7. Add the following class to the project:

```
public class Item
{
    public Guid ID { get; set; }
    public string Description { get; set; }
    public DateTime? Occurred { get; set; }
    public string Data { get; set; }

    public Item()
    {
        Data = "".PadRight(8388608);
    }
}
```

8. Add the following method, generating random items, to the `DiagnosingAndOptimizingExample` class:

```
public IEnumerable<Item> GenerateSomeItems()
{
    var list = new List<Item>();
    for (int i = 0; i < 10; i++)
    {
        list.Add(new Item()
        {
```

```
                    ID = Guid.NewGuid(),
                    Description = "Random string: " + Guid.NewGuid(),
                    Occurred = DateTime.UtcNow
            });
        }
        return list;
    }
```

9. Add the following callback methods to the `DiagnosingAndOptimizingExample` class:

```csharp
void cache_CacheOperationStarted(object sender,
    CacheOperationStartedEventArgs e)
{
    operationStarted = DateTime.Now;
}
void cache_CacheOperationCompleted(object sender,
    CacheOperationCompletedEventArgs e)
{
    if (e.HasSucceeded)
    {
        var elapsed = DateTime.Now.Subtract(operationStarted);
        elaspedValues.Add(elapsed);
        Console.WriteLine(string.Format(
            "Operation {0} ended in {1}",
            e.OperationType, elapsed));
    }
}
```

10. Add the following method, saving an object into the cache, to the `DiagnosingAndOptimizingExample` class:

```csharp
public void PutListMeasurePerformance()
{
    var list = GenerateSomeItems();
    cache.Put(objectKey, list);

    cache.CacheOperationStarted +=
        cache_CacheOperationStarted;
    cache.CacheOperationCompleted +=
        cache_CacheOperationCompleted;
    var localStarted = DateTime.Now;
    for (int i = 0; i < 100; i++)
    {
        try
        {
```

```
            cache.Put(objectKey, list);
        }
        catch (DataCacheException ex)
        {
            if (ex.ErrorCode == DataCacheErrorCode.RetryLater)
            {
                //Transient failure
            }
        }
    }
    Console.WriteLine("Average milliseconds: "
        + elaspedValues.Average(p=>p.Milliseconds));
    Console.WriteLine("Total: "
        + DateTime.Now.Subtract(localStarted).ToString());
}
```

11. Add the following method, using the methods added earlier, to the
    DiagnosingAndOptimizingExample class:

```
public static void RunExample()
{
    var cacheName = "[named cache]";
    DiagnosingAndOptimizingExample example
        = new DiagnosingAndOptimizingExample(cacheName);
    example.PutListMeasurePerformance();
}
```

How it works...

From steps 1 to 3, we set up the class. In step 4, we added private members to store
the objects we use later in the class. In step 5, we initialized the DataCache object using
a DataCacheFactoryConfiguration object based on the configuration file. We added
some customization to improve the application's performance and reliability as follows:

- ▶ IsCompressionEnabled: This saves bandwidth

- ▶ MaxConnectionsToServer: This scales out locally

- ▶ RequestTimeout: This sets a client SLA; operations slower than 1 second should
  be dropped by the application code

- ▶ SerializationProperties: This instructs the DataCache client to use our
  custom serializer instead of the default one (NetDataContractSerializer)

In step 6, we created a custom serializer using the Json.NET implementation. In step 7, we declared a custom `Item` class with a big string inside each instance, and in step 8, we generated a list of these items. Step 9 defined the two callbacks used to measure the cache operation times (please avoid using these callbacks in production, as they are declared by Microsoft for internal use only).

In step 10, we registered the callback methods and subsequently put the same collection into the cache. The `DataCacheException` method is thrown whenever something happens at the cache-client level. A `DataCacheErrorCode.RetryLater` error occurs for transient failures, for example, if the cache is not currently available. A developer should manage this situation by performing the retry operation, using the preferred retry strategy.

In step 11, we called the methods added earlier, specifying the named cache used. Replace `[named cache]` with the actual value.

There's more...

Azure Cache library supports the following three modes to serialize an object into the cache:

- ▶ `NetDataContractSerializer`: This is the default mode and is widely used in the .NET ecosystem
- ▶ `CustomSerializer`: This is a user-provided serializer that implements `IDataCacheObjectSerializer`
- ▶ `BinaryFormatter`: This is the old-school serializer that requires the `[Serializable]` attribute

Most serializers use reflection to get object properties, and it could be very slow under some circumstances, for example, when there are many object properties. We can always implement the serialization logic ourselves by implementing the `ISerializable` interface as follows:

- ▶ The `GetObjectData()` method to serialize values
- ▶ The `Serialization` special constructor to deserialize values back into an object

We can edit the `Item` class as follows to enable manual serialization logic:

```
[Serializable]
public class Item:ISerializable
{
    public Guid ID { get; set; }
    public string Description { get; set; }
    public DateTime? Occurred { get; set; }
    public string Data { get; set; }
```

```
        public Item()
        {
            Data = "".PadRight(8388608);
        }
        public Item(SerializationInfo info,
            StreamingContext context)
        {
            ID = (Guid)info.GetValue("ID", typeof(Guid));
            Description = info.GetString("Description");
            Occurred = info.GetDateTime("Occurred");
            Data = info.GetString("Data");
        }
        public void GetObjectData(SerializationInfo info,
            StreamingContext context)
        {
            info.AddValue("ID", ID);
            info.AddValue("Description", Description);
            info.AddValue("Occurred", Occurred);
            info.AddValue("Data", Data);
        }
    }
```

In small objects, this method can also be slower than reflection, but when you increase the object complexity, it should represent a good choice to save some CPU time.

Using advanced caching features

Azure Cache Service has simple functionalities to enable in-memory distributed cache for applications. As it is a data storage service (even though it is not persistent), some sort of search is required. As search in the whole cache surface could be slow, the Cache service is designed to support searches for only those objects that are located in user-defined regions. A user-defined region of cache is a logical group of key-value pairs located in the same portion of memory. We do not need to know how the Cache service behaves; however, think of regions like partitions for the Table Storage service.

In *Chapter 5, Going NoSQL with Azure Tables*, we saw how to use the Table Storage service, a scalable NoSQL-like key-value storage service. Table Storage organizes data into partitions that are logical groups of items located together.

The `DataCache` class exposes methods to manage user-defined regions such as `CreateRegion`, `ClearRegion`, `RemoveRegion`, and so on. Objects put in user-defined regions can be tagged with specific keywords to enable further lookup based on these keys. There is an overload of most of the methods to support the regions; for example, `Put()`, `Add()`, `Get()`, and so on have proper overloads.

Azure Cache library also provides classes and methods to work with concurrency. We can use the library for both optimistic and pessimistic concurrency models, which are described as follows:

- In **optimistic concurrency**, we use a version token as a timestamp against the storage service. The drawback is the probability of failing an update due to a meantime update from different sources.

- In **pessimistic concurrency**, the person who wants to get an object locks it for a while, until he releases the lock or a timeout occurs (to prevent deadlocks). This is safe and guarantees consistency; however, it is slower and can cause race conditions.

In this recipe, we will see how to tag an object in user-defined regions and how to implement optimistic and pessimistic concurrencies.

Getting ready

This recipe assumes that we created a valid cache endpoint. This section should be included in the application's configuration file:

```
<configSections>
    <section name="dataCacheClients" type="Microsoft.ApplicationServer.
Caching.DataCacheClientsSection, Microsoft.ApplicationServer.Caching.
Core" allowLocation="true" allowDefinition="Everywhere" />
</configSections>
```

The XML mentioned earlier declares a custom section, which should be as follows:

```
<dataCacheClients>
    <dataCacheClient name="[name of cache]">
        <autoDiscover isEnabled="true" identifier="[domain of cache]" />
        <securityProperties mode="Message" sslEnabled="true">
            <messageSecurity authorizationInfo="[token of endpoint]" />
        </securityProperties>
    </dataCacheClient>
</dataCacheClients>
```

Replace [name of cache] with an alias (in the recipe, we use the `default` named cache), replace [domain of cache] with the endpoint's fully qualified domain name, and replace [token of endpoint] with the token/password obtained by the Azure Portal.

How to do it...

We are going to create a user-defined region, placing some blog posts along with their keywords/tags. We use the `DataCache` methods to look up posts using these tags. After that, we simulate two processes that increment a remote counter: first, using an optimistic approach and finally, using a pessimistic one. We will do this by performing the following steps:

1. Add a new class named `AdvancedCachingExample` to the project.

2. Install the `Microsoft.WindowsAzure.Caching` NuGet package.

3. Add the following `using` statements to the top of the class file:

   ```
   using Microsoft.ApplicationServer.Caching;
   using System.Threading;
   using System.Threading.Tasks;
   ```

4. Add the following `private` members to the class:

   ```
   private DataCacheFactory factory = null;
   private DataCache firstCache = null;
   private DataCache secondCache = null;
   private string counterItemKey = "ProcessingCounter";
   ```

5. Add the following constructor to the class:

   ```
   public AdvancedCachingExample(string cacheName)
   {
       factory = new DataCacheFactory();
       firstCache = factory.GetCache(cacheName);
       secondCache = new DataCacheFactory().GetCache(cacheName);
   }
   ```

 Regions and Tagging.

6. Add the following method, caching blog posts, to the class:

   ```
   public void CacheRegionWithTaggedItems()
   {
       var myRegion = "BlogPosts";
       firstCache.CreateRegion(myRegion);
       firstCache.ClearRegion(myRegion);
   ```

```
    firstCache.Put(Guid.NewGuid().ToString(), "My first blog
post",
        new DataCacheTag[] { new DataCacheTag("fun"),
            new DataCacheTag("sport") }, myRegion);
    firstCache.Put(Guid.NewGuid().ToString(), "My second blog
post",
        new DataCacheTag[] { new DataCacheTag("food"),
            new DataCacheTag("drinks") }, myRegion);
    firstCache.Put(Guid.NewGuid().ToString(), "My third blog
post",
        new DataCacheTag[] { new DataCacheTag("food"),
            new DataCacheTag("fun") }, myRegion);
    firstCache.Put(Guid.NewGuid().ToString(), "My fourth blog
post",
        new DataCacheTag[] { new DataCacheTag("animals"),
            new DataCacheTag("sport") }, myRegion);
    firstCache.Put(Guid.NewGuid().ToString(), "My fifth post",
        new DataCacheTag[] { new DataCacheTag("drinks"),
            new DataCacheTag("life") }, myRegion);
    firstCache.Put(Guid.NewGuid().ToString(), "My sixth post",
        new DataCacheTag[] { new DataCacheTag("night"),
            new DataCacheTag("life") }, myRegion);

    var exactSearch = firstCache.GetObjectsByTag(
        new DataCacheTag("fun"), myRegion)
        .Select(p => p.Value).ToArray();
    var orSearch = firstCache.GetObjectsByAnyTag(
        new DataCacheTag[] { new DataCacheTag("sport"),
            new DataCacheTag("food") }, myRegion)
            .Select(p => p.Value).ToArray();
    var andSearch = firstCache.GetObjectsByAllTags(
        new DataCacheTag[] { new DataCacheTag("life"),
            new DataCacheTag("drinks") }, myRegion)
            .Select(p => p.Value).ToArray();
}
```

 Optimistic concurrency.

7. Add the following method, simulating temporized increments, to the class:

```csharp
private void OptimisticIncrement100Times(DataCache cache)
{
    var random = new Random(DateTime.Now.Millisecond);
    for (int i = 0; i < 100; i++)
    {
        var cacheItem = cache.GetCacheItem(counterItemKey);
        int counter = (int)cacheItem.Value;
        int newValue = counter + 1;
        //Simulate operation time
        Thread.Sleep(random.Next(500));
        try
        {
            cache.Put(cacheItem.Key, newValue, cacheItem.Version);
            var threadId = "Thread-" +
                Thread.CurrentThread.ManagedThreadId;
            Console.WriteLine(threadId + " updated counter from "
                + counter + " to " + newValue);
        }
        catch (DataCacheException ex)
        {
            if (ex.ErrorCode == DataCacheErrorCode
                .CacheItemVersionMismatch) continue;
            else throw;
        }
    }
}
```

8. Add the following method, creating two increment clients, to the class:

```csharp
public void OptimisticParallelProcess()
{
    firstCache.Put(counterItemKey, 0);
    var t1 = Task.Factory.StartNew(() =>
        OptimisticIncrement100Times(firstCache));
    var t2 = Task.Factory.StartNew(() =>
        OptimisticIncrement100Times(secondCache));
    Task.WaitAll(t1, t2);
}
```

 Pessimistic concurrency.

9. Add the following method, simulating temporized increments, to the class:

```
private void PessimisticIncrement100Times(DataCache cache)
{
    var random = new Random(DateTime.Now.Millisecond);
    for (int i = 0; i < 100; i++)
    {
        DataCacheLockHandle handle;
        while (true)
        {
            try
            {
                var counter = (int)cache.GetAndLock(
                    counterItemKey, TimeSpan.FromSeconds(1), out
handle);
                int newValue = counter + 1;
                //Simulate operation time
                Thread.Sleep(random.Next(500));

                cache.PutAndUnlock(counterItemKey,
                    newValue, handle);
                var threadId = "Thread-" +
                    Thread.CurrentThread.ManagedThreadId;
                Console.WriteLine(threadId + " updated counter
from "
                    + counter + " to " + newValue);
                break;
            }
            catch (DataCacheException ex)
            {
                if (ex.ErrorCode == DataCacheErrorCode
                    .ObjectLocked) Thread.Sleep(random.Next(100));
                else throw;
            }
        }
    }
}
```

10. Add the following method, creating two increment clients, to the class:

```
public void PessimisticParallelProcess()
{
    firstCache.Put(counterItemKey, 0);
    var t1 = Task.Factory.StartNew(() =>
```

```
        PessimisticIncrement100Times(firstCache));
    var t2 = Task.Factory.StartNew(() =>
        PessimisticIncrement100Times(secondCache));
    Task.WaitAll(t1, t2);
}
```

11. Add the following method, using the methods added earlier, to the class:

```
public static void RunExample()
{
    var cacheName = "[named cache]";
    AdvancedCachingExample example
        = new AdvancedCachingExample(cacheName);
    example.CacheRegionWithTaggedItems();
    example.OptimisticParallelProcess();
    example.PessimisticParallelProcess();
}
```

How it works...

From steps 1 to 3, we set up the class. In step 4, we added `private` members to store the two `DataCache` objects used to connect to the Cache service. We initialized this in the constructor we add in step 5.

In step 6, we demonstrated the usage of the tagging feature. First, we created a region, clear it (because the `CreateRegion` method works even if the region already exists), and put some blog posts (strings) using the overload that carries the region name and tag list (tags must be `IEnumerable` of `DataCacheItem`). We performed the following three searches:

- ▸ `GetObjectsByTag()`: This searches everything that is tied to the specified tag passed

- ▸ `GetObjectsByAnyTag()`: This searches everything that is tied to at least one of the tags passed (it is an OR search)

- ▸ `GetObjectsByAllTags()`: This searches everything that is tied to every tag passed (it is an AND search)

All the three methods mentioned earlier need the user-defined region where the search is to be performed.

In step 7, we defined a method that gets a specific item (integer counter), increments it, simulates a sort of processing time, and puts it back into the cache, using the `Put()` overload with the item's version. This overload accepts the item only if the passed version matches the server version. In case a concurrency is detected, a `DataCacheException` class with a `CacheItemVersionMismatch` error code is thrown. In step 8, we initialized the counter value and spawned two threads that simulate concurrency. Only a few of the 100 `put` operations per thread will succeed.

In step 9, we followed the same logic as the previous steps, except for the locking behavior of the `GetAndLock()` method, which prevents other clients from locking the cache element. This time, the client that loses the acquisition must catch a `DataCacheException` class with the `ObjectLocked` error code and perform its retry strategy. In step 10, we initialized the counter value and spawn two threads that simulate concurrency. Every 100 `put` operations will succeed.

In step 9, we called the methods added earlier, specifying the named cache used. Then, we replaced `[named cache]` with the actual value.

There's more...

The previous example tries to explain how concurrency models work. However, to perform safe increment/decrement operations, Azure Cache provides two methods specially designed for this purpose. We can proceed as follows:

```
private void Increment100Times(DataCache cache)
{
    var key = "IncrementCounter";
    for (int i = 0; i < 100; i++)
    {
        var value = cache.Increment(key, 1, 0);
        var threadId = "Thread-" +
            Thread.CurrentThread.ManagedThreadId;
        Console.WriteLine(threadId + " updated counter from "
            + (value - 1) + " to " + value);
    }
}
```

The preceding code uses the `Increment()` method to increase the value of the counter. The method returns the new value after increment.

See also

Have a look at the following MSDN links to get additional information:

- ▶ Azure Managed Cache, regions, and tagging reference at `http://msdn.microsoft.com/en-us/library/azure/dn386102.aspx`
- ▶ More about pessimistic concurrency at `http://blogs.msdn.com/b/cie/archive/2013/05/19/windows-azure-cache-pessimistic-concurrency-model.aspx`

Using Redis Cache in Azure

Redis is an open source, high-performance data store written in ANSI C. As its name stands for Remote Dictionary Server, it is a key-value data store with optional durability. Since its wide adoption in 2010, it became one of the most popular in-memory cache and also NoSQL data store. Today, there are Redis clients for almost every popular language used by developers around the world (an updated list is available at `http://redis.io/clients`), making it a good choice for heterogeneous systems as well.

Microsoft decided to add support for the Redis software through Azure, offering a fully managed Redis service of the same flavor as every other Azure building block. At the beginning of 2014, a new Azure Portal rose at `https://portal.azure.com`. Here, there is the support for this new emerging cache endpoint.

Redis service is a complex software with many features and explaining them is out of the scope of the book. In this recipe, however, we use a .NET, community-driven library to operate against it by performing simple operations.

Getting ready

This recipe assumes that we have a valid Redis Cache endpoint. We can obtain one by performing the following steps:

1. Go to `https://portal.azure.com`
2. Follow the instructions to create a new Redis Cache:
    1. Specify the smallest pricing tier (that is **Basic**)
    2. Choose the location (that is **North Europe**)
    3. Give it a name (in the **[name].redis.cache.windows.net** form)

After a few minutes, click on the Redis Cache created earlier and take note of one of the two authentication keys.

How to do it...

We are going to list the existing items in the Redis Cache and store some strings. We will do this by performing the following steps:

1. Add a new class named `UsingRedisExample` to the project.
2. Install the `StackExchange.Redis` NuGet package.
3. Add the following `using` statements to the top of the class file:

```
using StackExchange.Redis;
```

4. Add the following `private` members to the class:

```
private IDatabase cache = null;
private ConnectionMultiplexer connection=null;
```

5. Add the following constructor to the class:

```
public UsingRedisExample(string ep,string token,int db)
{
    var config = new ConfigurationOptions()
    {
        EndPoints = { {ep }},
        Password=token,
        SyncTimeout=10000,
        Ssl=true,
        AllowAdmin=true
    };
    connection= ConnectionMultiplexer.Connect(config);
    cache = connection.GetDatabase(db);
}
```

6. Add the following method, listing and removing the existing values, to the class:

```
public void KeyListAndFlush(int db)
{
    var servers = connection.GetEndPoints()
        .Select(p=>connection.GetServer(p));
    var keys=servers.SelectMany(p=>p.Keys(db)).ToArray();
    foreach (var key in keys)
    {
        Console.WriteLine("Key: "+key);
    }
    foreach (var server in servers)
    {
        Console.WriteLine("Flushing: "+server.EndPoint);
        server.FlushDatabase(db);
    }
}
```

7. Add the following method, storing big strings, to the class:

```
public void StoreOfBigStrings()
{
    for (int i = 0; i < 10; i++)
    {
        var key=Guid.NewGuid().ToString();
```

```
            if (cache.StringSet(key, "".PadRight(1048576, '$')))
            {
                Console.WriteLine("Added: "+key);
            }
        }
    }
}
```

8. Add the following method, using the methods added earlier, to the class:

```
public static void RunExample()
{
    int db = 1; //choose a DB number
    string endpoint = "[redis endpoint]";
    string token = "[redis password]";
    UsingRedisExample example
        = new UsingRedisExample(endpoint, token, db);
    example.KeyListAndFlush(db);
    example.StoreOfBigStrings();
}
```

How it works...

From steps 1 to 3, we set up the class. In step 4, we added a `private` member to store the `ConnectionMultiplexer` object used to create the `IDatabase` object used to connect to the Redis service.

> The `StackExchange.Redis` library is one of the most performant client libraries for Redis for .NET applications. We use this as this is also recommended by Microsoft.

In step 5, the constructor used the settings provided to create a connection to Redis, using the `ConfigurationOptions` model class, specifying a 10-second timeout for operations that are SSL enabled and in the Admin mode.

> We specify a high timeout due to the long-running operations we need to perform, while the Admin mode is set to `true` to permit the flushing of the database.

In step 6, we used the `GetServer()` API to obtain a list of keys currently stored on the specific DB passed. Redis can spawn over many servers, so there is no method to list every key over the entire multiserver area, because it would be probably too slow to be good enough.

> In Redis, a DB is a collection of key-value pairs that are analogous to the named cache concept we found in the Azure Managed Cache.

In step 7, we saved 10 big strings to the Redis store, and in step 8, we ran the example. Remember to replace the DB number with the one needed and the endpoint/password with actual values.

There's more...

As mentioned earlier, Redis is quite complex and has a lot of features. In the previous example, in step 7, we have to wait several seconds for the operation to complete due to the limited bandwidth between us and Azure and for the overall size of the big strings loaded. Redis also has the capability to save an item with the Fire-and-Forget pattern, without taking care of the result of the operation, and return immediately to the client. We will do this as follows:

```
public void FastestStoreOfBigStrings()
{
    for (int i = 0; i < 10; i++)
    {
        cache.StringSet(Guid.NewGuid()
            .ToString(), "".PadRight(1048576, '$')
            ,null,When.NotExists,CommandFlags.FireAndForget);
    }
}
```

The overload of the `StringSet` method allows us to pass an optional expiration (that we do not pass), a conditional set (only if it does not already exist), and the behavior of the command (Fire-and-Forget).

See also

Have a look at the following links to get additional information:

- MSDN reference to Azure Redis Cache at `http://azure.microsoft.com/en-en/documentation/articles/cache-dotnet-how-to-use-azure-redis-cache/`
- Redis clients at `http://redis.io/clients`

Index

local storage
  using, in instance 41-43
LocalStorage element 41
Login 183

M

makecert command
  used, for creating test certificate 40
management client
  setting up 319-323
metadata and properties, for blob
  setting 127-130
metadata properties, DataCacheItem object
  CacheName 370
  Key 370
  RegionName 370
  Size 370
  Tags 370
  Timeout 370
  Version 370
methods, for notification control
  AddCacheLevelCallback 373
  AddItemLevelCallback 373
methods, for search
  GetObjectsByAllTags() 392
  GetObjectsByAnyTag() 392
  GetObjectsByTag() 392
Microsoft Azure Cloud Service
  about 8-10
  changes, managing 59-61
  configuration changes, handling 52-57
  custom domain name, providing 35-37
  debugging, with Emulator or Emulator
      Express 14-17
  diagnostics, configuring 62-66
  publishing with options, from
      Visual Studio 18-23
  remote debugging, with Visual Studio 23-25
  roles 8
  service model, configuring 26-35
  solutions and projects, setting up 10-14
  topology changes, handling 52-57
  upgrades, managing 59-61
Microsoft Azure role
  startup tasks, using 48-51

Microsoft Azure Table Service. *See* **Table**
      Service
Microsoft Azure Web Sites 9
Microsoft Management Console (MMC) 146
MSDN reference, Azure Redis Cache
  URL 397
multiple websites
  hosting, in web role 44-48

N

Nagle's algorithm 281
Network Address Translation (NAT) 183
Network Share
  creating, Files used 153
NoSQL
  facilitating, with client-side
      projection 266-270
Not Found (404) error 113
notifications
  reference 379
  using 373-378
notifications working, with standalone
      callbacks
  AddCacheLevelBulkCallback 378
  AddCacheLevelCallback 378
  AddFailureNotificationCallback 378
  AddItemLevelCallback 378
  AddRegionLevelCallback 378

O

OnStop() method 53
Open Database Connectivity (ODBC) 198
optimistic concurrency 387
Output Cache
  URL 372

P

page blob
  about 141
  VHD, uploading 146-153
PartitionKey property 241
partition servers 247
performance
  optimizing 379-385

Thank you for buying
Microsoft Azure Development Cookbook
Second Edition

About Packt Publishing

Packt, pronounced 'packed', published its first book "*Mastering phpMyAdmin for Effective MySQL Management*" in April 2004 and subsequently continued to specialize in publishing highly focused books on specific technologies and solutions.

Our books and publications share the experiences of your fellow IT professionals in adapting and customizing today's systems, applications, and frameworks. Our solution-based books give you the knowledge and power to customize the software and technologies you're using to get the job done. Packt books are more specific and less general than the IT books you have seen in the past. Our unique business model allows us to bring you more focused information, giving you more of what you need to know, and less of what you don't.

Packt is a modern, yet unique publishing company, which focuses on producing quality, cutting-edge books for communities of developers, administrators, and newbies alike. For more information, please visit our website: www.PacktPub.com.

About Packt Enterprise

In 2010, Packt launched two new brands, Packt Enterprise and Packt Open Source, in order to continue its focus on specialization. This book is part of the Packt Enterprise brand, home to books published on enterprise software – software created by major vendors, including (but not limited to) IBM, Microsoft and Oracle, often for use in other corporations. Its titles will offer information relevant to a range of users of this software, including administrators, developers, architects, and end users.

Writing for Packt

We welcome all inquiries from people who are interested in authoring. Book proposals should be sent to author@packtpub.com. If your book idea is still at an early stage and you would like to discuss it first before writing a formal book proposal, contact us; one of our commissioning editors will get in touch with you.

We're not just looking for published authors; if you have strong technical skills but no writing experience, our experienced editors can help you develop a writing career, or simply get some additional reward for your expertise.

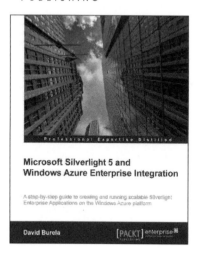

Microsoft Silverlight 5 and
Windows Azure Enterprise Integration

A step-by-step guide to creating and running scalable Silverlight
Enterprise Applications on the Windows Azure platform

David Burela

Microsoft Silverlight 5 and Windows Azure Enterprise Integration

ISBN: 978-1-84968-312-8   Paperback: 304 pages

A step-by-step guide to creating and running scalable
Silverlight Enterprise Applications on the Windows
Azure platform

1. This book and e-book details how enterprise
   Silverlight applications can be written to take
   advantage of the key features of Windows Azure
   to create scalable applications.

2. Provides an overview of the Windows Azure
   platform and how the different technologies can
   be integrated within your enterprise application.

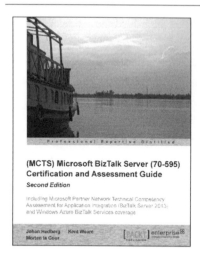

(MCTS) Microsoft BizTalk Server (70-595)
Certification and Assessment Guide
Second Edition

Including Microsoft Partner Network Technical Competency
Assessment for Application Integration (BizTalk Server 2013)
and Windows Azure BizTalk Services coverage

Johan Hedberg   Kent Weare
Morten la Cour

(MCTS) Microsoft BizTalk Server (70-595) Certification and Assessment Guide

Second Edition

ISBN: 978-1-78217-210-9   Paperback: 570 pages

Including Microsoft Partner Network Technical
Competency Assessment for Application Integration
(BizTalk Server 2013) and Windows Azure BizTalk
Services coverage

1. Features a comprehensive set of test questions
   and answers that will prepare you for the
   actual tests.

2. This second edition of the book is updated
   to target both BizTalk Server 2010 and
   BizTalk Server.

Please check **www.PacktPub.com** for information on our titles

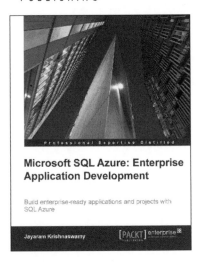
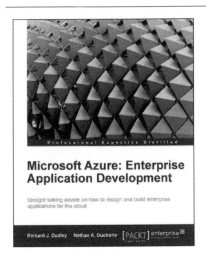

9156199R00233

Printed in Great Britain
by Amazon.co.uk, Ltd.,
Marston Gate.